Colorado's Continental Divide Trail

THE OFFICIAL GUIDE

TEXT BY
TOM LORANG JONES

FOREWORD AND
PHOTOGRAPHY BY
JOHN FIELDER

WESTCLIFFE PUBLISHERS

For Dad,
who introduced me
to the wilderness and
taught me, by quiet
example, respect and
appreciation;

and Mom,
whose unconditional
love and support have
made the difference.

—Tom Jones

Foreword   by John Fielder

For those of us who love the alpine and subalpine ecosystems, there can
be no greater joy than hiking America's Continental Divide National Scenic
Trail (CDNST). And the 759 miles that course the tops of Colorado's
mountain ranges may very well be the most magnificent of the roughly
3,000 total miles from Mexico to Canada.

From the remote South San Juan, Weminuche, and La Garita
wildernesses of southern Colorado to Mount Zirkel Wilderness near the
Wyoming border, including many other mountain ranges in between, the
CDNST is an elevated one. During the 80-mile hike in the Weminuche,
I can only remember being below treeline an hour or less. This makes
for lofty and lengthy views! Remember, trees quit growing this high.

Nestled in the alpine tundra are countless dwarf plants with names
like phlox, moss campion, and forget-me-not. Though small and delicate,
they burst with color disproportionate to their size. Lower down, their larger
cousins (paintbrush, columbine, and senecio) only dream of such garish
displays. Amongst all the color scurry marmot, pika, weasel, and marten,
with an occasional visit from coyote, bear, lynx, and lion.

Yet the CDNST is not just a haven for those who have no fear out
in the open (lightning is not something to ignore). The Colorado portion
descends into old growth forests of fir and spruce, aspen, lodgepole and
ponderosa pine. It is during these woodland respites that one can hide from
rain and snow (yes, it snows 12 months a year at 12,000 feet), or savor the
pungent aroma of coniferous denizens. And the trail skirts many a meadow.
I have fond memories of campsites on the edge of the forest with views
across creek and beaver pond-fed valleys of willow and grass.

Forest and tundra is spaced so felicitously that, in fact, one can set
up camp in either place without having to hike too far or too little on any
given day. Personally, I prefer the views, storms, outrageous atmospheric
lighting, and wind of the alpine zone for camping. I borrow my water from
fresh snow melt (and rarely purify as a result), cook ramen noodles under
the stars, and sip hooch at night after an evening of photography, soon to
dream about photographic expectations for morning.

Tarn, Collegiate Peaks Wilderness

Though the Colorado Trail (CT) is contiguous with the CDNST for about 200 of its 759 miles through Colorado, there is so much more. Like the CT, it is hikeable in a summer, as well as over a lifetime in increments. There are countless trailheads and side trails to visit and enjoy.

Tom Jones has done a thorough job of learning what, in large part, is a new trail. Though he hiked it once completely, he revisited many places in order to check facts, mileage, and route changes made while compiling this book. Armed with pedometer, tape recorder, and incomplete maps, Tom has redefined accurately all that you need to know in order to have a safe, enjoyable journey. Nevertheless, part of the fun of being in wilderness is not being completely secure. That is what wilderness is supposed to be: challenging, dangerous, invigorating, awe inspiring. I like getting a "little"

lost, for it is then that I see and photograph things I might never have experienced. Therefore, you can use this book in one of two ways: merely to prepare you for your excursion by allowing you to plan daily goals, or to guide you in the field along your way. Whichever method you choose, Mother Nature is certain to surprise you with her mysteries.

Have fun!

JOHN FIELDER is a nationally renowned nature photographer, and the author of 24 books of photography, including 19 about his adopted state of Colorado. He is a past recipient of the Sierra Club's Ansel Adams Award for Conservation Photography. Fielder photographed the CDNST through Colorado to illustrate this guide as well as his large format book *Along Colorado's Continental Divide Trail*. M. John Fayhee was the third member of the publishing team to hike the trail (each hiked it separately). His trail stories complement Fielder's photographs in *Along Colorado's Continental Divide Trail*.

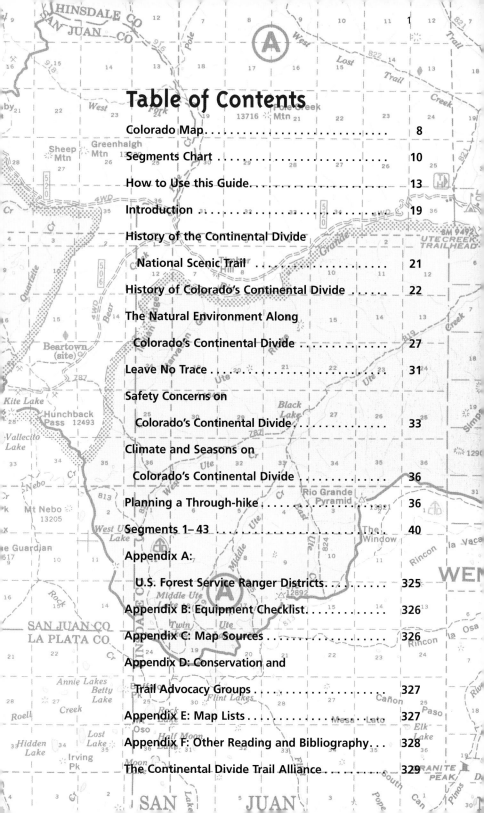

Table of Contents

For more information about other fine books and calendars from Westcliffe Publishers, please contact your local bookstore or write, call (303) 935-0900, or fax (303) 935-0903 for our free catalogue.

PLEASE NOTE:
Risk is always a factor in backcountry and high-mountain travel. Many of the activities described in this book can be dangerous, especially when weather is adverse or unpredictable, and when unforeseen events or conditions create a hazardous situation. The author has done his best to provide the reader with accurate information about backcountry travel, as well as to point out some of its potential hazards. It is the responsibility of the users of this guide to learn the necessary skills for safe backcountry travel, and to exercise caution in potentially hazardous areas, especially on glaciers and avalanche-prone terrain. The author and publisher disclaim any liability for injury or other damage caused by backcountry traveling, mountain biking, or performing any other activity described in this book.

COVER CAPTION:
Dave Sanders surveys the Front Range, Indian Peaks Wilderness

INTERNATIONAL STANDARD BOOK NUMBER:
1-56579-226-2

PHOTOGRAPHY COPYRIGHT:
John Fielder. All rights reserved.
Jon Osborne, page 91. All rights reserved.
Tom Jones, page 198. All rights reserved.
Tom Jones, Sr., page 296. All rights reserved.
Loretta McGrath, page 336. All rights reserved.

TEXT COPYRIGHT:
Tom Lorang Jones. All rights reserved
Mark Pearson, pages 27–30; reprinted with permission.

PRODUCTION MANAGER:
Harlene Finn, Westcliffe Publishers

EDITORS:
Pat Shea, Bonnie Beach

DESIGN AND PRODUCTION:
Rebecca Finkel, F + P Graphic Design; Boulder, CO

PUBLISHED BY:
Westcliffe Publishers, Inc.
2650 South Zuni Street
Englewood, Colorado 80110

Printed in Singapore by
CS Graphics Pte. Ltd.

Publisher's Cataloging in Publication

Jones, Tom Lorang.
    Colorado's Continental Divide Trail : the official guide /
text by Tom Lorang Jones ; foreword and photography by
John Fielder.
    p.cm.
    Includes index.
    ISBN: 1-56579-226-2

    1. Hiking—Colorado—Guidebooks. 2. Hiking—
Continental Divide Trail—Guidebooks. 3. Colorado—
Guidebooks. 4. Continental Divide Trail—Guidebooks.
I. Title

GV199.42.C6J66 1997   917.8804'33
                                       QBI97-40097

Preface   **by Tom Jones**

Elsewhere in this book, I make the analogy between preparing for a long hike and preparing for a marriage. Over the course of my hike, I certainly developed a relationship with this trail. In a very short time, I came to love it, resent it, laugh, listen, and compromise with it, lose it, return to it, and, eventually, say good-bye to it. Mostly, I just enjoyed its company, and looked forward every day for 88 days to what it would present next.

I've spent most of my life backpacking, either with my dad, who got me hooked in the first place, or with friends, or, more recently, by myself. As I grew older, I realized more and more that I would set out from whatever trailhead with the expectation of "finding something." In the absence of much spiritual stimulation back in day-to-day life, I always thought if I spent enough time in the wilderness, I would eventually have some sort of epiphany—a cosmic flash where the ghosts of Thoreau, Edward Abbey, and John Muir would simultaneously appear on the top of a remote peak and say: "The answer is…"

Of course, that never happened. I might occasionally experience subtle shifts or vague insights, but never a major revelation. Still, I never lost that sense, at the trailhead, that I was embarking on some unfulfilled search.

So it was when I set out on the Continental Divide Trail on June 20, 1996: wonder, awe, apprehension, fear, excitement, and a vague sense of anticipation and discovery. Within one week I had seen more elk than perhaps I had seen in all my prior experience—and that's a lot of elk. I endured rain and snow at 12,000 feet, watched foxes career across the tundra, slept in the shadow of primeval volcanic peaks, spent a lot of time talking to myself, and, at the end of 16 days, set a personal record for time alone in the wilderness. I did not notice it at the time, but I had grown, over those first 120 miles, to be pretty content.

Many more miles unfolded before me, and the wonders and fascination multiplied. Then, one day, I awoke as I had for so many weeks before: face buried in soft nylon and LiteLoft insulation, a fleece jacket wadded under my head, wet socks hanging from the tent ceiling. I emerged into the sublime, pale light of a clear Colorado dawn and ate granola with instant milk. I looked around and saw a stream; a vibrant, wildflower-speckled meadow; and imposing mountains—just as one would expect. I was perfectly content to just sit there. I didn't feel any pressure to get to the next destination for the day. Then it hit me: For some time—a few days, maybe a couple of weeks—I no longer had that sense of waiting.

For perhaps the first time in my life, I was content with everything around me, happily oblivious to the immediate future, or the recent past, or a year down the road. I realized I was no longer looking for something. And in that realization, I like to think, I had finally found what I was looking for.

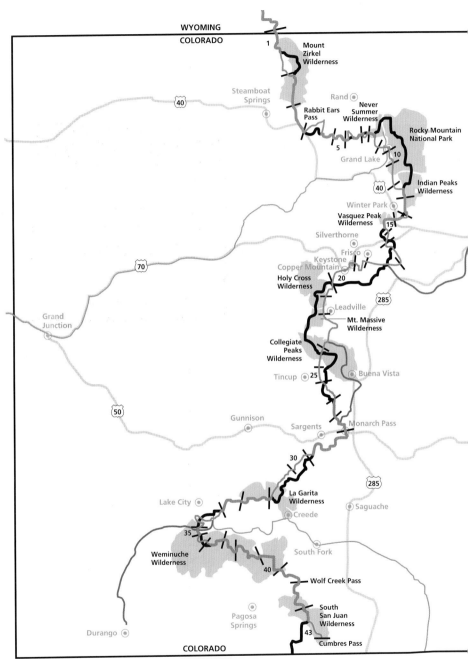

WYOMING
COLORADO

1

Mount
Zirkel
Wilderness

Steamboat
Springs

40

Rand

Never
Summer
Wilderness

Rabbit Ears
Pass

Rocky Mountain
National Park

5

Grand Lake

10

40

Indian Peaks
Wilderness

Winter Park

Vasquez Peak
Wilderness

15

Silverthorne

Frisco

Keystone

70

Copper Mountain

Holy Cross
Wilderness

20

Leadville

285

Mt. Massive
Wilderness

Grand
Junction

Collegiate
Peaks
Wilderness

Tincup

25

Buena Vista

50

Gunnison

Sargents

Monarch Pass

30

285

La Garita
Wilderness

Lake City

Saguache

Creede

35

Weminuche
Wilderness

South Fork

40

Wolf Creek Pass

South
San Juan
Wilderness

Pagosa
Springs

Durango

43

Cumbres Pass

COLORADO
NEW MEXICO

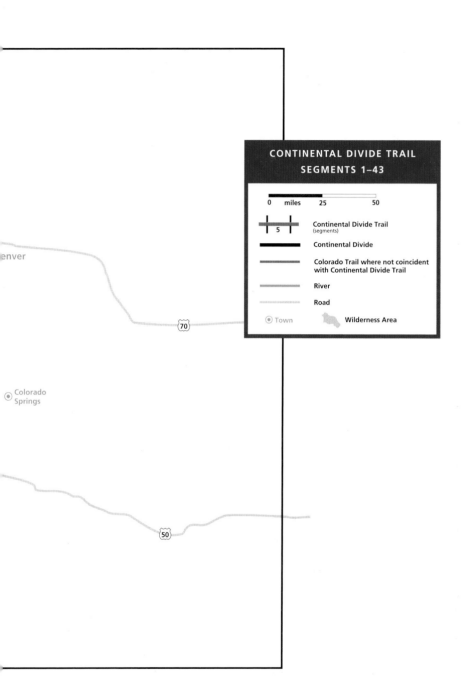

CONTINENTAL DIVIDE TRAIL
SEGMENTS 1–43

0   miles   25   50

Continental Divide Trail
(segments)

Continental Divide

Colorado Trail where not coincident
with Continental Divide Trail

River

Road

Town   Wilderness Area

enver

70

Colorado
Springs

50

SEGMENT	STARTING POINT	ENDING POINT	SEGMENT DIFFICULTY
1	Wyoming Trailhead	North Lake Trailhead	moderate
2	North Lake Trailhead	Buffalo Pass	strenuous
3	Buffalo Pass	US-40	easy
4	US-40	Forest Route 104	easy
5	Forest Route 104	Troublesome Pass	moderate
6	Troublesome Pass	Willow Creek Pass	strenuous
7	Willow Creek Pass	Illinois Creek Trailhead	moderate
8	Illinois Creek Trailhead	North Supply Trailhead	strenuous
9	North Supply Trailhead	Grand Lake	easy
10	Grand Lake	Monarch Lake Trailhead	easy
11	Monarch Lake Trailhead	Devils Thumb Park	moderate
12	Devils Thumb Park	Rollins Pass	strenuous
13	Rollins Pass	Rainbow Road	strenuous
14	Rainbow Road	Berthoud Pass	strenuous
15	Berthoud Pass	Herman Gulch Trailhead	strenuous
16	Herman Gulch Trailhead	Argentine Pass Trailhead	strenuous
17	Argentine Pass Trailhead	Gibson Lake Trailhead	strenuous
18	Gibson Lake Trailhead	Gold Hill Trailhead	moderate
19	Gold Hill Trailhead	Copper Mountain	moderate
20	Copper Mountain	Tennessee Pass	moderate
21	Tennessee Pass	Timberline Lake Trailhead	moderate
22	Timberline Lake Trailhead	Mt. Massive/Mt. Elbert TH	moderate
23	Mt. Massive/Mt. Elbert TH	Winfield/S. Clear Creek TH	strenuous
24	Winfield/S. Clear Creek TH	Cottonwood Pass Road	strenuous
25	Cottonwood Pass Road	Mirror Lake	moderate
26	Mirror Lake	Hancock	strenuous
27	Hancock	Monarch Pass	strenuous
28	Monarch Pass	Marshall Pass	easy
29	Marshall Pass	Colorado Highway 114	moderate
30	Colorado Highway 114	Saguache Park Road	easy
31	Saguache Park Road	San Luis Pass	strenuous
32	San Luis Pass	Spring Creek Pass	strenuous
33	Spring Creek Pass	Carson Saddle	strenuous
34	Carson Saddle	Stony Pass	strenuous
35	Stony Pass	Beartown Road	moderate
36	Beartown Road	Twin Lakes	strenuous
37	Twin Lakes	Weminuche Pass	strenuous
38	Weminuche Pass	Squaw Pass	strenuous
39	Squaw Pass	South River Peak	strenuous
40	South River Peak	Wolf Creek Pass	moderate
41	Wolf Creek Pass	Elwood Pass	moderate
42	Elwood Pass	Blue Lake	strenuous
43	Blue Lake	Cumbres Pass	moderate

MILEAGE	TOTAL ELEV. GAIN (FEET)	TRAILHEAD ACCESS	MTN. BIKE DIFFICULTY	PAGE	SEGMENT
24.0	2,543	graded or paved road	technical	41	1
21.6	4,460	bumpy road	prohibited	48	2
17.4	1,015	graded or paved road	easy	58	3
30.0	3,459	graded or paved road	technical	64	4
10.0	2,077	bumpy, 4WD road	technical	70	5
15.6	2,672	bumpy road	not rideable	74	6
9.9	1,375	graded or paved road	technical	82	7
10.7	2,790	bumpy road	prohibited	86	8
10.0	140	graded or paved road	prohibited	94	9
13.7	1,000	graded or paved road	prohibited	98	10
13.0	2,580	graded or paved road	prohibited	104	11
6.6	2,370	bumpy road, hike	prohibited	112	12
13.0	2,040	bumpy road	not rideable	116	13
12.4	3,592	4WD road	not rideable	124	14
19.4	3,436	graded or paved road	prohibited	128	15
19.5	5,534	graded or paved road	not rideable	138	16
21.5	3,671	bumpy road, hike	not rideable	144	17
29.2	4,708	bumpy, 4WD road	not rideable	152	18
13.1	3,625	graded or paved road	technical	158	19
24.3	3,876	graded or paved road	technical	164	20
13.3	1,905	graded or paved road	prohibited	170	21
12.9	2,120	graded or paved road	prohibited	176	22
27.1	5,200	bumpy road	not rideable	182	23
17.9	3,590	bumpy road	prohibited	190	24
11.4	2,125	graded or paved road	technical	198	25
13.5	2,644	bumpy road	not rideable	202	26
19.3	4,421	bumpy road	not rideable	210	27
11.5	883	graded or paved road	easy	216	28
35.4	5,813	graded or paved road	easy	222	29
13.3	1,258	graded or paved road	easy	230	30
25.7	4,515	graded or paved road	prohibited	234	31
14.5	2,914	4WD road, hike	prohibited	242	32
19.2	3,949	graded or paved road	technical	250	33
18.0	3,860	4WD road	not rideable	256	34
8.9	980	bumpy, 4WD road	prohibited	264	35
11.9	2,323	bumpy, 4WD road	prohibited	270	36
11.4	1,267	graded or paved road	prohibited	276	37
14.8	3,040	hike	prohibited	280	38
26.5	5,469	hike	prohibited	286	39
21.1	3,210	hike	prohibited	292	40
19.1	3,340	graded or paved road	not rideable	298	41
27.1	4,185	4WD road	prohibited	304	42
30.1	2,137	bumpy road, hike	prohibited	314	43

How to Use this Guide

NOTE: *Taking a few minutes to read this section will enhance your enjoyment of the book and help you to use it more efficiently.*

This book is equally useful for the day hiker, overnight camper, through-hiker, or mountain biker who wants to experience the wonders of the Continental Divide National Scenic Trail. (This is the trail's official name. It is generally called the Continental Divide Trail. In this book, I often abbreviate it further to "CDT.") The heart of this book is divided into 43 chapters that correspond to the 43 segments of the CDT in Colorado. Each segment represents a distinct section of the trail, with starting and ending points on or near highways, dirt roads, and, in a few cases, foot trails.

The segments chart on pages 10–11 lists segments by difficulty, mileage, total elevation gain, trailhead access, and mountain bike difficulty. By consulting this list, you can quickly choose a suitable segment or portion of a segment to hike. You'll also find a map of the entire trail on pages 8–9.

Because the segments are in geographical order from north to south, and because the trail description flows easily from one segment to the next, a through-hiker can use the book start to finish. I chose the north-to-south orientation for several reasons. First, the segments nearer New Mexico traverse the rugged San Juan Mountains, whose steep climbs and above-timberline forays are more frequent and sustained than are those near Wyoming. Assuming a through-hiker will be in better shape toward the end of the journey, it makes sense to tackle the more challenging segments last.

Second, the southern reaches of Colorado's CDT are quite remote. Over one stretch of 132 miles, the trail crosses no paved roads and the nearest towns are very far away. The northern segments certainly won't have you marching down Main Street of every nearby town, but, should you experience difficulties while working out the kinks during the first few weeks of a through-hike, help won't be quite as far away as it is down south.

Finally, there is the more aesthetic consideration of "saving the best for last." Although the incredible scenery starts with the first step from the Wyoming border, there is something about the San Juan Mountains and the surrounding wilderness areas that puts them in a class by themselves. You will be awestruck by northern and central Colorado, and virtually overwhelmed by the majesty and solitude of the southern part of the state.

Having said that, there is no reason you can't hike south to north. Northbound hikers will find important information throughout, marked with this symbol: **N**

SEGMENT INTRODUCTIONS

Each segment is a chapter in this book. Introductory information at the beginning of each chapter summarizes the important aspects of the segment. The first items you will see are the segment's distance in miles and difficulty rating. Difficulty ratings are easy, moderate, and strenuous. The background color of each segment's introductory page also corresponds to difficulty: green for easy, blue for moderate, and red for strenuous. Note that these ratings are highly subjective, and what is easy for the seasoned Colorado hiker may be quite strenuous for someone else.

Cinquefoil along Cochetopa Creek, La Garita Wilderness

You will see a graphic elevation profile at the bottom of each segment's introductory page. This illustrates elevation gain and loss and also notes the total elevation gain over the entire segment. The profile box indicates the trail mileage from Wyoming and New Mexico. These figures are based on the segment's starting point.

Information about other trail uses can be found next to each profile box, ranging from foot-traffic-only to automobiles.

INTRODUCTORY INFORMATION

After the elevation profile, several paragraphs describe the segment. This is where you will find information about water, camping, highlights and pitfalls, and some local history. The last paragraph, titled "Mountain Bike Notes," tells you if you may ride—or encounter—bikes on the trail. The following symbols accompany that paragraph and provide a quick visual reference:

 Most of the terrain is non-technical, but there may be some elevation gain. Check the segment's elevation profile.

 You will find steep or technical riding on most of the segment, and you may have to carry your bike in spots. These segments are not recommended for novice cyclists.

 Some or all of the terrain on the segment is not rideable due to rocks, steepness, lack of a trail, environmental sensitivity, etc.

 The segment passes through a designated wilderness area, national park, or some other area where bikes are prohibited by law.

The last item you will find here are the names of the ranger districts through which the trail passes. For management purposes, the U.S. Forest Service divides forests into distinct jurisdictions. If you have questions about the trail, you should contact the appropriate districts. You will find their addresses and phone numbers in Appendix A on page 325.

MAPS

The next piece of information in each chapter is a list of the maps that cover the segment. There are three kinds of maps: Trails Illustrated, United States Geological Survey (USGS) quadrangles, and U.S. Forest Service.

This section also tells you where in the book to find a reproduction of the U.S. Forest Service map for the segment. These maps give a good overview of a segment's location, surroundings, and accessibility, but they do not lend themselves to precise navigation. The best maps for that purpose are the topographical quadrangles put out by the USGS. The scale for USGS maps is 1:24,000, and the detail is excellent for navigation if you know how to use a map and compass. However, there are almost 100 of these maps for the entire CDT, and they cost $4 apiece.

The maps put out by Trails Illustrated (TI) are the best value. They are water-proof, tear-proof, and more up-to-date than the others. Each one (with a few exceptions) is a reproduction of eight USGS maps and sells for around $8 or $9. Some TI maps cover even more territory, such as the one for the Weminuche Wilderness, which includes all 13 USGS maps required for that area. TI maps use a smaller scale than the USGS maps and it is a little more difficult to obtain precise readings from them, but they are generally sufficient for hiking the CDT.

See Appendix C, on page 326, for a list of map sources, and Appendix E, on page 327, for lists of the maps required for the entire trail.

ACCESS TO TRAILHEADS

After the map information, you will find detailed directions for driving to the segment's trailheads.

The segments are divided logically so you can reach their beginning and ending points as easily as possible on good roads. Because the Continental Divide is in the middle of some of the most remote land in Colorado, there are many segments where you may have to take dirt roads or four-wheel-drive roads to reach the trailheads. To give you a quick visual reference of what kind of terrain to expect, the following symbols precede each set of driving directions:

 The trailhead is accessible with a normal passenger car. The road is either paved or well-graded dirt.

 A normal passenger car can get to the trailhead, but the road is not paved and may be quite rough. Adverse weather conditions may make these routes impassable.

 You will need a high-clearance, four-wheel-drive vehicle.

 A hike is required to reach the Continental Divide Trail.

The symbols may be used in combination, and mileage is given for each one. In the following example, you would drive 3.4 miles over bumpy or rough roads and hike an additional 0.7 mile to reach the CDT:

Distance from graded road		
	3.4 miles	0.7 miles

TRAIL MARKERS

These markers are regular features on the trail, and the book refers to them frequently:

 Continental Divide Trail marker

 Colorado Trail marker

tree blaze
(a cut in the tree that is shaped like a crude, lower-case i)

rock cairn

SUPPLIES, SERVICES, AND ACCOMMODATIONS

Through-hikers as well as segment hikers will find the information in this section useful for planning an itinerary. It gives the names of towns near the trail as well as the names, addresses, and phone numbers of important businesses, such as grocery stores, outdoor-gear shops, motels, and the post office. If you plan to send boxes of supplies ahead to post offices along the route before you depart, it is a good idea to give them a call first to check on business hours and to make sure they can accommodate general delivery.

OTHER HIKES AND RIDES

After the detailed segment description, which makes up the bulk of each chapter, you will find information on hikes and mountain bike rides near or on the trail segment. These range from short day hikes in the vicinity of the Divide to multi-day adventures that cross the Divide several times. You will find the distance and a difficulty rating at the beginning of each hike or ride, followed by a brief description. These descriptions are not as detailed as the regular segment descriptions, so you should supplement this information with a good map.

DIRECTIONS AND THE COMPASS

I believe people understand directions in one of two ways: one, using the cardinal directions (east, south) and compass bearings (145°); and two, using directions like up, down, left, and right, and cues such as landmarks, trail markers, and terrain variations. To make it as clear as possible for everyone, I employ both methods in this book.

There are times when the former method is the only way to be sufficiently accurate, so a compass and a basic understanding of how it works are invaluable. When you shop for a compass, look for a rotating dial with the degrees ticked off around it. For very precise or serious orienteering, an attached mirror is useful.

Particularly confusing or obscure areas in the trail description are marked with this symbol:

A FEW COMPASS FACTS

The circular compass dial is divided into 360 equal units called degrees, which are numbered starting with 0 at due north and increasing in a clockwise direction. Due east is at 90°, south is at 180°, and west is at 270°.

The needle always points toward magnetic north, but maps are based on "true north." The difference between the two, which varies with location, is listed in degrees at the bottom of the map. If magnetic north is 15° east of true north, then any direction you wish to find will lie 15° to the left, or counter-clockwise, of the direction indicated by using the compass needle.

Phrases such as "slightly east of south" appear frequently in the text. For "slightly east of south," you would take a bearing 5 or 10° toward the east from due south, or 170–175° on the compass dial. "Southeast," on the other hand, is a bearing precisely between due south and due east, or 135° on the compass dial. And "south-southeast" is a bearing precisely between southeast and due south, or 157.5°. (Degrees are divided into 60 equal units called minutes, for which the symbol is a single superscript hash mark ('), so this would be written 157° 30'.) Minutes are calculated to two decimal places.

Bearings provided in this book are based on true north and have a margin of error of ±10°.

GPS COORDINATES

GPS (Global Positioning System) coordinates, or waypoints, are provided occasionally in the trail description. **NOTE: WAYPOINTS PROVIDED DO NOT CONSTITUTE A ROUTE; THAT IS, THEY ARE NOT INTENDED TO GUIDE YOU AROUND OBSTACLES AND DANGERS SUCH AS CLIFFS, WATER, BUILDINGS, ETC.** Waypoint coordinates are intended to help verify your position on the trail and serve as a tool for finding trail-heads or the trail itself should you stray from it. Coordinates are based on readings from a Garmin GPS 38, which lists a margin of error of ±15 meters (50 feet), and are given in degrees, minutes, and fractions of a minute in decimal form. For instance, "38 degrees, 15 minutes, and 30 seconds" is written thus: 38° 15.5'.

A note on distance: Mileage in this book may not match U.S. Forest Service signs, which are frequently wrong.

Note that the trail is changing constantly, so parts of this book may be inaccurate after only one year. Call the U.S. Forest Service ranger districts for the segments you plan to hike to see if there are any significant changes.

If you have comments about the trail or its placement, please direct them to the appropriate Forest Service ranger district (see Appendix A, page 325). If you have comments about the way this guide describes the trail, please address them to Westcliffe Publishers.

Introduction

The Continental Divide splits North America into two gigantic watersheds in a continuous, 8,000-mile line from Wales, Alaska, to the Panama Canal. The Continental Divide National Scenic Trail follows the 3,100 miles of the Divide that pass through the United States from the Canadian border to the Mexican border.

This trail is unique among others in that its course is determined by a natural feature of the land, rather than by the whims and wanderings of humans. The trail allows us to trace this natural feature with our own feet, to touch it and experience it on its own terms. We will be on the very crest of America's rooftop, looking out with our mind's eye at two great oceans from this legendary line that determines the fate of every raindrop or snowflake that falls on the land.

We are privileged to be embarking on the most stunningly beautiful section of this trail: the 759 miles that pass through Colorado. Colorado's Rocky Mountain environment is so rugged and primitive that it provides some of the most remarkable scenery in the world, yet it is hospitable enough that life exists in colorful abundance. We see the gravity-defying spires evident in many of the world's other high mountain chains, but not the alien desolation which often accompanies them. There is just enough water to carpet the upper reaches of these slopes with a vibrant living ecosystem, but not so much rain that we find ourselves forced to hack through the overgrown tangle of a jungle, or spend weeks wondering when we will see the sun again. Colorado offers a perfect blend of beauty and danger, forbidding rock and fertile soil, glistening snow and cascading streams.

It is here, atop Colorado's Grays Peak, that the Divide reaches its highest point in the United States at 14,270 feet. Ours is the only state where the trail climbs above 12,000 feet, and, in the magnificent San Juan Mountains, stays at that altitude for most of 120 miles, meandering across the tundra of alpine ridges. And here in Colorado the trail passes through 11 of this country's most beautiful and pristine wilderness areas, from deep forests of pine, spruce and fir, to the higher reaches where verdant slopes fall away like emerald robes, jeweled with wildflowers, hung from the regal shoulders of awesome unnamed peaks.

Sunset over the South San Juan Wilderness

The stretch of trail described in this book offers a rich variety of things to see, ecosystems to explore, and natural wonders to take in. I have divided the trail into 43 logical sections, most of which are accessible by good roads. You can choose to wander along treeless alpine ridges with hundred-mile views, enjoy the cozy woodlands of the rolling Cochetopa Hills, or have the sense of actually gazing down on 14,000-foot peaks from the upper reaches of the Weminuche Wilderness. In the words and pictures that follow, we will show you how to explore all of these places—whether on a family day hike, a multi-night backpack trip, or a summer's through-hike of the entire trail.

It is not without some reservation that I offer this guide to the general public. Like John Fielder, I have fallen in love with Colorado and the places described in this book, and it would be tragic to discover we had somehow contributed to their degradation. For this reason, I urge you to read carefully the section in this book on the philosophy of Leave No Trace.

But much greater than these fears is our confidence that this book can help further the causes of conservation and protection. Now more than ever our public lands are in need of public support. I couldn't imagine a better way to develop a base of citizen advocacy than to help people experience, first-hand, the wonder of their natural surroundings. I am certain that anyone who travels these trails with open heart and mind will come to revere these lands as I do.

So pack your knapsack and load your camera, and come along with us to the top of the continent. On the great flanks of this Divide we will find some of the wildest places left in this country, where few humans have passed before, and the evidence of that passing is nonexistent. This is where nature remains the only force of change, and things are as they have been for centuries. As you set out for the high country, I leave you with this final thought: May your effect on this trail be minimal, but its effect on you be great; may you touch the trail only slightly, but be deeply touched by it. ●

History of the Continental Divide National Scenic Trail

The Continental Divide National Scenic Trail (CDNST) began in 1966 as the dream of Benton Makaye, an 87-year-old man who had already devoted much of his life to seeing the Appalachian Trail come to fruition. Makaye's idea was to create a trail that would connect a series of wilderness areas along the Divide from Montana's border with Canada to New Mexico's border with Mexico.

Makaye (rhymes with "deny") proposed his idea to Congress, which soon authorized a study of the trail under the National Trails Act of 1968. At around the same time, a Baltimore attorney by the name of Jim Wolf was hiking the 2,000-mile-long Appalachian Trail, which he completed in 1971. Inspired to seek out a new hiking challenge further afield, Wolf walked the Divide Trail from the Canadian border to Rogers Pass, Montana, in 1973. He soon published a guidebook to that section of the trail and devoted much of his time to advocating its official designation. After a 1976 study by the Bureau of Outdoor Recreation found the scenic quality of the trail to surpass anything available anywhere else in the country, the Congressional Oversight Committee of the National Trail System held hearings on the trail in 1978, at which Wolf testified. The CDNST received official recognition from Congress later that year under the National Parks and Recreation Act.

In that same year, Wolf founded the Continental Divide Trail Society (CDTS) to garner publicity for the trail and involve the public in work surrounding its construction, particularly route selection. Wolf continued to hike portions of the trail each summer, and by the mid-80s he had completed all of its 3,100 miles. The CDTS has grown to a membership of 200.

The United States Forest Service is responsible for managing most of the land through which the trail passes. In the 1980s, its work on the trail progressed at different rates in different areas, but it suffered in general from a lack of public involvement. In 1994, two trail advocates began working under the auspices of a group called the Fausel Foundation to raise funds and build support for the trail. By 1995, their efforts evolved into the Continental Divide Trail Alliance (CDTA), a non-profit organization devoted to fundraising, publicity, education about the trail, and grassroots volunteer coordination. Those people were Bruce Ward, formerly the president of the American Hiking Society, and his wife, Paula, a landscape architect. The CDTA is based in Pine, Colorado.

In its first year, the CDTA grew to include 425 individuals or families and 20 corporate sponsors, and had a budget of $400,000. Estimates suggest the Alliance coordinated volunteer work worth $70,000 in that first year. However, trail advocates are quick to point out that there is much work yet to be done. Only 70 percent of the trail is complete across the nation as a whole, and it is about 90 percent complete in Colorado. The estimated cost to finish the entire trail is $10.7 million. And, of course, the completed sections will require funding and volunteer coordination for maintenance well into the 21st century.

For information about joining the CDTA see page 329.

History of Colorado's Continental Divide

The history of civilization along the Continental Divide in the United States originates in Mexico and Asia. The first humans to inhabit the North American continent crossed the Bering Land Bridge into what is now Alaska from northeast Asia 20,000 to 40,000 years ago. For 10,000 years after their arrival, these people prospered and spread across the continent, developing individual cultures, languages, and civilizations.

Although the first Coloradans may have arrived here as early as 15,000 years ago, the earliest definitive evidence are some sharpened flint points found in northeastern Colorado that archaeologists have traced to 9200 B.C. They believe small bands of hunters used these spear points. A nomadic hunter-gatherer culture survived in southern Colorado beginning around 5000 B.C. and evolved into a civilization we now call the Anasazi. From 100 A.D. to 1300 A.D., the Anasazi flourished and developed sophisticated skills in farming, hunting, pottery, and weaving. You can see evidence of their building skills in elaborate cliff dwellings in places such as Mesa Verde National Park in southwestern Colorado.

Around 1300, the Anasazi left Colorado. The reasons are unclear, but they may include climatic changes, drought, and deforestation. At about the same time, the Ute Indians moved into Colorado from Nevada and Utah. Although less advanced than the Anasazi, the Utes thrived all along Colorado's Continental Divide, hunting deer and elk and foraging for nuts and berries.

Meanwhile, other immigrants from the Bering Land Bridge had continued south into what is now Mexico. Several notable civilizations evolved, but none as advanced or powerful as the Aztec Empire, which controlled land from Central Mexico to El Salvador and Guatemala until Spanish explorer Hernando Cortés led his armies against the Aztec nation and destroyed it in 1521. As the Spanish consolidated their control of Mexico, they looked to the north. By the early 1600s, settlement of the colony of "Nuevo Mexico" was well under way.

In 1777, King Charles III of Spain appointed the founder of San Francisco, Juan Bautista de Anza, governor of New Mexico. De Anza's first task in his new position was to quiet the rampaging Comanche Indians who were terrorizing Spanish colonists from Santa Fe to Taos. In August, 1779, de Anza assembled a force of about 600 to find and subdue a group of Comanches in the San Luis Valley of what is now Colorado. As de Anza worked his way north up the Rio Grande River, he was astonished to discover its sudden bend to the west, which contradicted the accepted belief that the river originated far to the north, perhaps as far as the North Pole. The Ute guides told de Anza of the great bend of mountains where the river's headwaters sprang from the earth and of a high, barren pass to the uncharted land beyond. Today, we know that landmark as Stony Pass (CDT Segment 35). Thus did the first European lay eyes on Colorado's mighty Continental Divide.

De Anza continued north to Saguache Creek, which flowed from a great gap in the high ridges to the west. The Utes identified this as Cochetopa—The Pass of the Buffalo—their easy route west to the Gunnison Valley (CDT Segment 30). De Anza continued north along the eastern slopes of the Divide to Monarch Pass (CDT Segment 28) before he turned east, toward Pikes Peak. Near this famous mountain he achieved his goal. In a brief skirmish, his men devastated a settlement of 1,000 Comanches by killing 18 warriors and 34 women and children and taking most of their horses and supplies.

In 1805, Meriwether Lewis and William Clark became the first whites to complete a meaningful traverse of the Continental Divide in the Rocky Mountains. As with de Anza, their party relied on the guidance of friendly Indians, including the legendary Snake Indian woman, Sacajawea, to reach their goal of the mouth of the Columbia River on the Pacific Ocean.

Lewis and Clark proved that the continent was not too large, nor the rocky spine that divided it too high, to stymie the expansion of a restless young nation. But they crossed the Divide far to the north.

What of Colorado? Its difficult, high passes pushed the nation's first east-west routes to the north and south. But important explorations were under way. Zebulon Pike (for whom Pikes Peak was named after he tried—and failed—to climb it) pushed deep into the Arkansas River Valley of Colorado during the fierce winter of 1806-07. On that expedition, Pike became the first white man to gaze on the fantastic peaks of the Sawatch Range, which carry the Divide through the heart of Colorado (CDT Segments 23 through 27). He also saw the mountain gaps that later became important passes with names like Boreas, Hoosier, Fremont, Tennessee, and Independence.

By the spring of 1807, many pioneers had begun the long journey to the West, lured by the promise of free land and unlimited opportunity.

In 1812, a young explorer named Robert Stuart discovered a flat and "welcoming" route across the Divide in today's southern Wyoming. This easy connection between the Great Plains and the West Coast would go unnoticed for a dozen years. Then a young trapper named Jedediah S. Smith rediscovered the pass and pioneered a route over it to California by way of Wyoming's Great Divide Basin. The Basin is a unique spot: The Divide splits there to encompass a vast area where water flows neither west nor east to the oceans, but remains trapped to evaporate or find its way to stagnant lakes.

Smith's discovery, dubbed South Pass, played a major role in the settlement of the western United States. The first major Continental Divide crossing used en masse by American travelers, South Pass was an important gateway on the 2,000-mile-long Oregon Trail. It guided thousands of 1840s pioneers from Independence, Missouri, to the rich farmland of Oregon.

Many French, British, and American trappers roamed the mountains along the Continental Divide in the 1820s and 1830s in search of fur-bearing animals— particularly beaver—whose pelts were valuable on the European market. In the course of their fur trade, these men established many new routes over the Divide. Among them was a St. Louis man named Antoine Robidoux who picked up in Colorado where Zebulon Pike had left off. He explored the mountains of Central Colorado and may have been the first American to cross Cochetopa Pass when he established a fur-trading route over it from Taos, New Mexico, to eastern Utah in 1825. Europeans had finally punctured the great barrier of Colorado's Continental Divide after decades of being forced around to easier crossings.

In 1843 and 1844, U.S. Army Lieutenant John Charles Fremont led an expedition of 39 men from St. Louis to search for passes through Colorado for military and migrant use. Fremont's path led north into Wyoming and then south into Colorado's

North Park. Over the next two months his party paralleled the path of the Continental Divide to the south, crossed the Divide into Middle Park at Muddy Pass (CDT Segment 4), fled up the Blue River near present-day Dillon Reservoir to escape Arapaho Indians (CDT Segment 18), and traversed the Divide again at Hoosier Pass. From there the party descended into South Park, southeast of the Divide, and returned east over the Great Plains.

During the early 1850s, the California Gold Rush enticed hundreds of thousands of fortune-seekers to brave the arduous traverse of the continent. But even then the Divide forced travelers north of Colorado. In fact, geographers had noted only four passes over Colorado's Rocky Mountain rooftop: Cochetopa, Muddy, Hoosier, and Tennessee, which Fremont had discovered on a return trip in 1845 (CDT Segment 21). But the isolation of Colorado's interior ceased abruptly in May, 1859, when a man from Georgia discovered gold near Denver. The region would never be the same.

Within a year, eager prospectors swarmed into every gulch, valley, and draw they could find. They worked up Clear Creek into South Park via Guanella and Kenosha Passes, up the Arkansas River to Tennessee Pass, and over Boreas Pass to found Breckenridge. From Silverton to the Front Range west of Denver, mining activity spread all along the Divide. For it was here that the tumult of the mountains' formation and subsequent erosion had exposed the precious ores.

As mining camps popped up in isolated pockets of the mountains, enterprising men built toll roads to service them. Ore flowed out, supplies flowed in, and camps grew into towns. The old pack trails over passes such as Cochetopa, Georgia, and Hoosier changed almost overnight into high-use roads.

Entrepreneurial pass-builders tackled the Divide's highest reaches with a fervor motivated more by ego than by profit. Some, with names like Loveland, Berthoud, and Rollins, succeeded. Others were less fortunate. Stephen Decatur sought to tap the growing need for transportation in Montezuma, in today's Summit County. He raised $10,000 to build a road across the Continental Divide between Georgetown and Montezuma at a lonely place called Argentine Pass. At 13,200 feet above sea level, it was the highest road on the Divide, but that impressive statistic became its greatest shortcoming. At that altitude, snow covered the road into July, leaving a window of less than two months for travel. In the rare snowless months, rock slides frequently rendered the road impassable. And the interminable wind! Some stories told of donkeys being blown off the ridge. The costs of upkeep prevented Decatur or subsequent owners from ever making the road pay, and it soon dwindled back to the status of a pack-train trail. (The CDT follows part of the Argentine Pass Trail on Segment 17.)

Toll-roads boomed only briefly because a faster, more efficient method of transport was steaming over the horizon. The first railroad line to cross the Divide, the Union Pacific, did so in southern Wyoming in 1868. Its Divide crossing lay halfway between the Colorado border and the Oregon Trail's South Pass in the unremarkable flats of the Great Divide Basin.

Trains reached Denver in 1870. Over the next decade, several rail companies would vie for the growing transportation market serving Colorado's booming mining industry. The Denver & Rio Grande line won a top prize when it pulled into the silver boomtown of Leadville in 1880. At that same time, the Denver, South Park, & Pacific worked its way to the upper reaches of the Divide, just north of present-day Monarch Pass, with the goal of tapping the growing Gunnison Basin market on the other side. But the D. S. P. & P. ran into difficulties while constructing the Alpine Tunnel under the Divide (CDT Segment 26), and the Denver & Rio Grande in 1881 became the first rail line to lay tracks over Colorado's Continental Divide. From this crossing at Marshall Pass (CDT Segment 29), the D. & R. G. raced to Gunnison and beat out the D. S. P. & P. by more than a year.

Rail lines spread quickly throughout the state, connecting the myriad small communities with larger towns, and shrinking the gap between Colorado's eastern and western slopes. In the promising light of wealth and opportunity, Colorado's population more than doubled during the 1880s.

The automobile was the next transportation innovation to shrink the vast distances of the American West. The first cars appeared in Denver in 1902, but they had difficulty climbing the mountain passes, and Coloradans did not immediately embrace them. According to historian Carl Abbott, a 1915 travel expert advised Colorado motorists always to carry a crowbar, hatchet, shovel, pulleys, rope, and extra oil, gas, and water. With the advent of more reliable vehicles, the Colorado mountains saw 2 million visitors by the late 1920s.

Like the railroads, the first transcontinental highway avoided the thicket of Colorado's rocky peaks and crossed the Divide in southern Wyoming. In its 3,100-mile traverse from New York to San Francisco, the Lincoln Highway, as it was called, followed roughly the route of today's Interstate 80. A second east-west roadway passed south of Colorado. Finally, highway officials paved a route from Colorado Springs to Utah, crossing the Divide between Leadville and Minturn at Tennessee Pass. The route, the present US-24, followed the Colorado River out of the state to the west. No transcontinental highway achievement surpasses Interstate 70, which avoids the winding mountain passes by crossing the Divide under 1,400 feet of solid rock via Eisenhower Tunnel (CDT Segment 17). The tunnel, which is almost 2 miles long, was completed in 1973.

Even as modern transportation carries millions of people over it, the Divide serves as a barrier in other ways. A relatively liberal social and political climate prevails in the cosmopolitan urban centers of Denver and Boulder on the eastern side. By contrast, the Western Slope nurtures the libertarian individualism of the early settlers. The western side tends to vote conservatively and espouses traditional values that often clash with the progressive attitudes of the Front Range.

One issue that exemplifies the effect of the Continental Divide on Colorado society is water policy. As early as 1934, interests on the drier Front Range side banded together to lobby for a massive diversion project to carry water from the Western Slope under the Divide and into the South Platte River drainage around Greeley. Conservationists and citizens of the Western Slope, represented by Congressman Edward Taylor, opposed the idea, but the Front Range prevailed and Congress approved the Colorado-Big Thompson Project in 1937. If you hike the section of the CDT south of Grand Lake (Segment 10), you can see the results of the project in Shadow Mountain Lake and

Granby Reservoir, artificial lakes whose waters flow east through a tunnel under the Continental Divide in Rocky Mountain National Park.

Other great water diversion efforts in Colorado include the Fryingpan–Arkansas Project, which supplies the cities of Colorado Springs and Pueblo; and Dillon Reservoir, which you can see from the CDT for many miles (Segments 18 and 19). When residents of the old town of Dillon could not make their tax payments during the Depression, the Denver Water Board shrewdly acquired property for much less than it was worth. By 1956, the Water Board owned enough of Dillon to make a startling announcement: They planned to dam the Blue River, and residents had five years to flee the coming flood.

Dillon fell into despair, unable to fight the powerful Denver Water Board. The daunting prospect of moving an entire town brought hardship and token resistance, but, in the end, the river was dammed, the waters rose, and the old town disappeared. Denver constructed the 23-mile Harold D. Roberts Tunnel 4,000 feet beneath the Continental Divide. Today it carries Denver's water supply from Dillon to an unceremonious confluence with the South Platte River near the tiny burg of Grant on US-285. New Dillon, with its handful of salvaged buildings, sits on a quiet hill overlooking beautiful Lake Dillon, which has become the centerpiece of a popular recreation destination.

Even today, the battle across the Divide flares. Dillon and surrounding communities fear the Denver Water Board will sell its lakeside property to the highest bidder, including developers who would build on the pristine land. And the Board announced in 1996 that it would not stop short of draining Dillon Reservoir should a sustained drought strike Colorado's Front Range. This was just one more reminder for the tourism-based mountain community of the formidable force on the other side of the Continental Divide.

The Natural Environment Along Colorado's Continental Divide

Ecologists generally use vegetation to categorize Colorado's ecosystems. Geology and topography strongly dictate vegetative communities because of their influence over climate and soils. Many wildlife species require specific habitats, thus vegetation defines the range of native animals. The following sections serve as a brief review of ecozones, geology, and fauna found along the CDT in Colorado.

ROCKY MOUNTAIN LIFE ZONES

Ecologists group the various habitats of the Rocky Mountains into life zones. At low elevations, for example, dry forests predominate; in higher, wetter locations aspen forests are the norm; and alpine tundra covers the highest reaches of our mountains.

Life zones are defined by the dominant species that grow there and are named for the geographic regions they represent. The lowest and driest zones are Lower Sonoran and Upper Sonoran in reference to the Arizona deserts. Moving higher, the Transition Zone bridges the gap between the Sonoran zones and the higher elevation Canadian and Hudsonian zones. The highest life zone is the Arctic-Alpine Zone. This figure illustrates the relationship of the life zones to one another and to elevation. What follows is a brief description of the indicator species of each community.

ROCKY MOUNTAIN ECOSYSTEMS

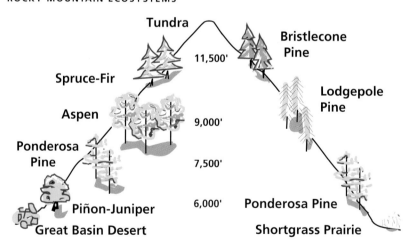

Tundra

Bristlecone Pine

11,500'

Spruce-Fir

Lodgepole Pine

Aspen

9,000'

Ponderosa Pine

7,500'

Piñon-Juniper

6,000'

Ponderosa Pine

Great Basin Desert

Shortgrass Prairie

PIÑON-JUNIPER FOREST

Forests of piñon pine and juniper represent the Upper Sonoran Zone. Gambel oak, sagebrush, and mountain mahogany fill in the forest's understory amidst abundant flowering species, such as Indian paintbrush, scarlet globemallow, and lupines.

Rowdy flocks of piñon jays, the trademark bird of this forest, rise in raucous twittering clouds when disturbed. Piñon jays and piñon pines depend symbiotically upon one another: The jays feed on the easily digestible pine nuts while the trees rely on jays to distribute seeds by burying them for winter storage. Other bird species that frequent this habitat include the ubiquitous mourning doves with their haunting "where-are-you" chant, bushtits, and canyon towhees. Mule deer and coyotes frequent this habitat as well.

PONDEROSA PINE FOREST

Ponderosa pine forests comprise the Transition Zone in the Rocky Mountains. The corky bark of mature ponderosas resists fire, and frequent, low-intensity ground fires preserve the characteristic open park-like settings of this forest. With modern fire suppression policies, however, ponderosa forests face severe challenges.

Quaking aspen and lodgepole pine often intermingle with ponderosa pines, with antelopebrush and mountain mahogany populating the understory. Western bluebirds, tanagers, and Steller's jays dart about the forest canopy. The tassel-eared squirrel, also called the Abert squirrel, is a common indicator species, along with the golden-mantled squirrel, porcupine, and mule deer. Ponderosa pines give off a fragrant vanilla scent if you press your nose close to the bark.

ASPEN GROVE

Quaking aspen explode in vivid color along many parts of the CDT in autumn, such as Van Tassel Gulch on Segment 31. Occurring from 7,500 to 10,000 feet in the Transition and Canadian Zones, aspen quickly repopulate open areas after disturbances such as fire and avalanches. Aspen reproduce primarily by sending up shoots through their root system, and large stands may consist of one genetically identical unit. They are often found intermixed with lodgepole pine or harboring silent invaders, such as Engelmann spruce and subalpine fir, that can easily overtake the aspen and shade them out. Common shrubs in aspen forests include chokecherry and roundleaf snowberry. The showy blue Colorado columbine, our state flower, brightens a lush undergrowth that includes ferns, wild geranium, loco, and yarrow. Beavers and porcupines join elk, mule deer, black bear, and abundant bird species in giving life to this forest.

LODGEPOLE PINE FOREST

Occupying the upper Transition and Canadian Zones between 8,500 and 10,000 feet, lodgepole pines depend on fire for reproduction. Their cones are serotinous, meaning they remain closed until heated by fire. If fire does not occur, lodgepole pines are doomed to successional replacement by more shade-tolerant species such as spruce and fir trees. Dense thickets of lodgepole pine growing in poor, dry soils often result in relatively barren and uninviting understories. Kinnikinnick and snowbrush are common shrubs in this habitat. Birders may spot white-breasted nuthatches, western wood-pewees, or blue grouse. The nocturnal pine marten lives here along with more common species, including mule deer, bobcat, elk, and weasel.

SPRUCE-FIR FOREST

Throughout the Colorado Rockies, Engelmann spruce and subalpine fir dominate the Canadian and Hudsonian Zones between 9,000 and 11,000 feet, the lower limit of timberline, above which trees do not grow. The dark, shady spruce-fir forest supports fewer wildflowers than more open aspen forests, but its moist coolness provides a welcome change to hikers climbing from dry lodgepole forests below.

Spruce and fir are readily distinguished by their needles: Spruce needles have sharp points and tend to roll between your fingers while fir needles are flat and softer. Spruce and fir needles grow individually from the tree branches in contrast to the clumped needles of pines. Below the canopy, clusters of bright lavender flowers reveal the presence of Jacob's ladder or skypilot.

Most hikers recognize the ever-begging gray jay, or camp robber. Other birds of the spruce-fir forest include red-breasted nuthatches, golden-crowned kinglets, and yellow-rumped warblers. It is in the shadowy confines of spruce-fir forests that more solitary species such as lynx, wolverine, and possibly even grizzly bears exist.

BRISTLECONE PINE FOREST

On dry and windswept mountains of the Hudsonian Zone, the spruce-fir forest fares poorly and is replaced by high forests of Rocky Mountain bristlecone and limber pine. Bristlecone pines are easily the oldest living trees in the Rocky Mountains, with some specimens exceeding 2,000 years in age. In deference to the hostile conditions of the Hudsonian Zone, bristlecone pines often take on gnarled and twisted storybook shapes. Hikers will find the shrubby and very common juniper interspersed among the bristlecone and limber pines. The panhandling Clark's nutcracker pesters hikers here, and some alpine species such as ptarmigan and marmots frequent this zone as well.

TIMBERLINE-ALPINE TUNDRA

The Arctic-Alpine Zone takes hold above 11,000 feet, where wind and cold preclude upright trees. Only Engelmann spruce in the form of stunted, wind-twisted trees known as krummholz can live in this extreme climate. Wind defines much of the alpine landscape; some areas are completely desiccated due to wind exposure while protected low spots collect melting snow. Look close to the ground for hardy alpine wildflowers such as elephant head and buttercup, and cushion plants including moss campion, alpine phlox, and forget-me-not. Arctic willow grows in small flower-like clumps.

Several memorable wildlife species inhabit this unforgiving zone, among them yellow-bellied marmots, whose piercing whistles of warning are a common sound to hikers. The pika, a rabbit relative, emits bleating sounds from tumbled mounds of talus. The white-tailed ptarmigan adapts to the tundra by changing color with the seasons, from stark white in winter to mottled brown in summer. Fearless mountain goats spring effortlessly from ledge to ledge along many high cliff faces and steep talus slopes in the Arctic-Alpine Zone.

RIPARIAN FOREST

One habitat that weaves its way among many of the others is the riparian forest, which flourishes along rivers and streams. Other than aspen forests, it is the only broadleaf habitat in the Rocky Mountains. Ranging from prairie rivers to mountain streams, four cottonwood species—the plains, Fremont, narrowleaf, and black—dominate the riparian forest. These trees and their attendant undergrowth—chokecherry, gooseberry, thinleaf alder, boxelder, and willows—grow along Rocky Mountain rivers from high valleys to desert canyons. The riparian forest is home to numerous bird species, including common indicators such as the cordilleran flycatcher and MacGillivray's warbler. Muskrat, beaver, skunk, fox, and raccoon thrive in this habitat as well.

GEOLOGY

The geology of Colorado's Continental Divide has a long and complex history. Starting about 300 million years ago, two mountainous islands rose above the surrounding seas. These two islands, called Frontrangia and Uncompahgria, comprised the Ancestral Rockies. Over the next 200 million years, erosion wore down the mountains, depositing great layers of sediments in the shallow seas around them. The Maroon Bells formation near Aspen is a remnant of these Ancestral Rockies.

Sixty-five million years ago, the present-day Rockies began to take shape during a massive mid-continental uplift that geologists call the Laramide orogeny, or mountain building. Geologists believe that the earth's crust consists of huge plates slowly sliding across the globe's surface, grinding and buckling at infinitesimal rates. The North American continent sits on one such plate, and the plate's crust grows particularly weak in Colorado. As this plate crashed into the Pacific plate 65 million years ago, the crust weakened and buckled, and the Rockies pushed skyward. Erosion ate away at these mountains for 25 or 30 million years, reducing much of them to rubble and in places revealing the basement bedrock underlying the North American continent, some of it more than 1.5 billion years old.

Approximately 28 million years ago, uplifting commenced once more and a broad dome of the continent stretching from Nebraska to Utah raised up another 5,000 feet, pushing the Continental Divide to its current heights. At the same time, the stresses placed on the earth's crust by this new warping opened cracks and fissures through which magma from deep within the crust flowed to the surface and poured over the landscape. Finally, some 15,000 to 20,000 years ago during the last ice age, glaciers scoured the landscape, forming many of the prominent features seen today—grand U-shaped valleys, alpine lakes called tarns, hanging glacial cirques, and craggy peaks.

Geologists categorize rocks into three types: sedimentary, igneous, and metamorphic. Sedimentary rocks result from the compression of layers of eroded rock or sediment. Most geologic formations demonstrating layering are sedimentary in nature. Igneous rocks originate from molten rock. If the rock cools below the surface, as with granite, it is called intrusive igneous rock; where the molten rock spills over the surface as lava flows, it is termed extrusive igneous rock. Metamorphic rocks result from great pressures and temperatures that alter preexisting sedimentary or igneous rock. Marble, gneiss, and schist are examples of metamorphic rocks.

The mountains of Colorado were formed by several processes. Many of the state's mountains—the Front Range, Sawatch Range, and Elk Mountains among them—are faulted anticlines. These formed when the crust raised upward, bowing overlying sediments in sweeping anticlines as the underlying basement rocks broke and faulted upward. The sedimentary hogback formations of the Front Range attest to these stresses. Most of these faulted anticlines consist of igneous granite or metamorphosed schist and gneiss.

In several places, molten rock oozed across the surface of rising domes or burst forth in great cataclysmic explosions. The volcanic flows and layers of ash and breccia of the San Juan Mountains were later carved by ice and water.

—Generously contributed by Mark Pearson.
Originally printed in *Colorado's Wilderness Areas,* Westcliffe Publishers.

Leave No Trace

The lands through which the Continental Divide Trail passes belong to every American, and they are administered by the Federal Government through agencies such as the Forest Service. The growing popularity of these areas has begun to overtake the Forest Service's ability to counteract the detrimental effects of overuse, so we are faced with a situation in which the responsibility of stewardship falls to every individual who uses and enjoys these last vestiges of American wildness. When we set foot here, we should accept a simple creed—that we will respect these places in their natural state, and that we will strive to leave no trace of our passing. To this end, the Forest Service has developed the principle of Leave No Trace, which should govern the behavior of every visitor to the Colorado backcountry. Please learn and practice the following trail ethics and Leave No Trace concepts.

TRAILS

Most of the CDT through Colorado follows established trails that are well-marked. Hiking single-file and staying on the trail helps to avoid trampling fragile plants and soft ground, which can result in wider trails or new trails altogether. Never cut switchbacks. Follow the trail through muddy or snowy sections, instead of creating a new trail around such impediments.

In those places where there is no trail, or where it is necessary to leave the trail, choose the most durable surfaces to walk on, such as rocks, dry ground, or a carpet of pine needles. In the absence of a trail, groups should fan out to disperse their impact.

When meeting other trail users such as mountain bikers and horse packers, be courteous and give them room to pass. The current standard is that bikers and hikers yield to horses, and bikers yield to hikers, but the prudent hiker will make room for a mountain biker. When passing a horse party, calmly make your presence known and move off the trail on the lower side until everyone has passed. Do not make any sudden movements or loud noises that might spook the horses.

SELECTING A CAMPSITE CONCENTRATE IMPACTS IN HIGH-USE AREAS

In well-traveled areas, it is best to select an established campsite that has already seen a lot of use. This reflects the philosophy that certain spots are sacrificed to be used again and again without the intention of restoring them to a natural state. Choose hard, dry ground with the least amount of vegetation for a tent site. Make sure your camp is at least 200 feet from streams, lakes, and trails, and be aware of "visual pollution"—how visible your tent and camp are to other visitors seeking a remote backcountry experience.

While moving about camp, be aware that each step is potentially harmful. If you are in a heavily used area, use existing trails instead of tromping down new ones. If you are in an area that has seen less human impact, try *not* to use the same route each time you travel around camp so that no single area becomes worn. Additionally, you can minimize the number of trips required to retrieve water by using water bags or other large-capacity containers. The cooking area should be situated on a durable surface, such as a large, flat rock. Wear light shoes instead of heavy, hard-soled hiking boots once you arrive at camp.

USE FIRE RESPONSIBLY

Campfires have long been a source of warmth and comfort, providing a sense of security in the vast darkness of the natural world. But they are an unnatural impact on the environment, leaving scars, gobbling nutrients, and sterilizing the soil. I encourage the CDT hiker to consider the rewards of experiencing the darkness of the forest on its own terms, as nature intended it, without the glaring interruption of a fire. A small backpacking stove provides a quick and efficient way to cook. Your eyes will see things they would have missed when blinded by the flames, and you will hear sounds otherwise drowned out. More exciting, you may have the opportunity to see nocturnal animals that stay well away from the crackle of a blazing fire.

If you must build a fire, make sure you are well below timberline and far from water sources or wetlands, in an area where there is an abundant supply of dead and downed wood. Use an existing fire ring or build a "mound fire" — **NEVER BUILD A NEW FIRE RING.** A mound fire is built by finding a source of mineral soil, such as a streambed during low water or the hole left by a tree that has blown over. Use a stuff sack to carry a large amount of this soil to the fire site, lay down a ground cloth, and use the soil to build a flat-topped mound 6 to 8 inches thick on top of the cloth. Build the fire on the mound. When it is time to break camp, scatter the few ashes, and then use the ground cloth to return the soil to its source. This is the fire-building method prescribed by the National Outdoor Leadership School in their Leave No Trace literature.

GARBAGE AND FOOD   PACK IT IN, PACK IT OUT

Nothing should be left in the woods that wasn't there before our passing, with the exception of human waste. Everything else, including toilet paper, personal hygiene items, and uneaten food, should be packed out. Most trash, even paper, will not burn completely in a camp fire, so it remains in the environment for a long time. Leaving food for animals or giving it to them directly habituates them to humans, alters their diet, and makes them less self-sufficient. It also gives animals an appetite for human food, which can result in more aggressive animals (everything from squirrels to bears). Never feed a wild animal.

Long-distance hikers should not use food caches in their planning strategy. A food cache is a stash of food that is deposited somewhere along the trail before a hike begins. They are not allowed in many areas, and they are often dug up by animals or simply left behind when a hiker's plans change. Careful planning will eliminate the need to cache food.

HUMAN WASTE   PROPERLY DISPOSE OF WHAT YOU CAN'T PACK OUT

The best way to dispose of solid human waste is via the "cat hole" method, which entails digging a hole 6 to 8 inches deep and filling it in after use. Toilet paper should be packed out; a double plastic bag works well for this.

DOMESTIC ANIMALS

Pets are best left at home during a trip to the backcountry, but if you must have yours along, be sure to use a leash. Be aware that a dog can be loud and disturbing to other visitors who seek a tranquil wilderness experience, and most dogs chase any wildlife they see.

Horses are also an unnatural representative of the animal kingdom in our national forests, and, bound as they are to a party of humans, their impact can be very concentrated and destructive. At camp, horses should be hitched to a highline. Select access to water where they will cause the least amount of erosion to stream banks and lake shores. Avoid tethering horses in a small area, such as at the base of a tree, where the ground will be devastated and unable to sustain any vegetation in the future, even after just one instance of equine presence. Horse parties can also cause extensive damage to trails. Horse packers can get more information on responsible practices by calling the Leave No Trace number listed below, or by contacting the Colorado Horsemen's Council at (303) 279-4546.

MOUNTAIN BIKING

It appears that mountain bikes are permitted on all parts of the CDT except where it passes through designated wilderness areas, but bikers should consult with local Forest Service representatives before heading out for a ride. Also, some sections of the trail are not suitable for mountain biking for a variety of reasons. Mountain bikers are reminded that it is their responsibility to ride in control and yield to all other users, and to conscientiously minimize their impact on the land.

The Adventure Cycling Association in Missoula, Montana, is currently working to create a Great Divide Mountain Bike Route. They can be contacted at (406) 721-1776. Or contact the International Mountain Bike Association in Boulder, Colorado, at (303) 545-9011.

For a more in-depth discussion of the concept of Leave No Trace, call the LNT office at (800) 332-4100 for copies of their brochures on various ecosystems.

Safety Concerns on Colorado's Continental Divide Trail

The Forest Service intends to manage the Continental Divide Trail to provide a primitive backcountry experience for those who are up to the challenge of leaving the comforts of modern civilization behind. Hikers should keep this in mind as they prepare for a visit to the Divide. There are places where help will be a great distance away, so prudent preparation and education about potential hazards, as well as how to deal with them in the absence of outside help, will be essential for a safe and enjoyable experience. Self-reliance is the key, and anyone considering a hike along the Divide should carefully evaluate his or her ability to cope with potential dangers before setting out. The following list is not complete or comprehensive, but is intended to educate the hiker about the most common hazards.

LIGHTNING

This serious hazard kills several hikers in Colorado each year, and it is a particular concern on the high, exposed ridges of the Continental Divide. Although a strike can occur anywhere at anytime, there are certain rules of thumb that can help hikers avoid a shocking experience in the backcountry.

Lightning usually accompanies the shapeless, dark clouds that often form in the Colorado afternoons of July and August. These clouds can be swift-moving, and their presence on a distant horizon should be a warning to the wise hiker to consider escape routes from high ridges or passes.

Lightning tends to seek the shortest path from earth to sky, so you should avoid high points of land or lone trees when a storm comes in. Experts recommend seeking out a low, treeless point in the terrain and squatting there until the storm passes. For those who are as concerned about getting drenched as they are about a lightning strike, taking shelter in a low-elevation stand of trees of uniform height may be preferable. Hiding in caves is not recommended.

WATER

The low moisture content of the Colorado air combined with the greater respiration rate required for hiking at altitude may result in dehydration, which is a potentially dangerous condition. Hikers should carry enough water to last their entire visit to the Divide, or they should be prepared to filter or purify water. Introductions to the trail segments in this guidebook provide information on water availability.

The greatest peril concerning drinking water in the high country is a small parasite called *Giardia lamblia,* which is transmitted via the fecal matter of animals, survives in very cold water at high altitudes, and causes severe intestinal discomfort in humans. Three methods of water treatment are recommended: boiling for three to five minutes; treating with iodine tablets; or using a filter. Filters are lightweight and easy to use, and they provide water that is immediately drinkable. Check the manufacturer's guidelines to make sure a filter is suitable for removing giardia. Iodine tablets require time to work, can cause a mild aftertaste, and should be researched further before they are considered for long-term repeated use.

WEATHER

Colorado's weather can change at any time, and its effects are magnified at the high reaches of the Continental Divide. Hikers should carry the proper clothing for snow, rain, high winds, or a combination of these. While a thunderstorm portends the danger of lightning, remember that rain accompanied by wind can cause *hypothermia* (see below). And even the calm of the Colorado sunshine is not without its perils. The sun's radiation is more intense at high altitude, making sunscreen and lip protection essential gear.

HYPOTHERMIA

Hypothermia is the lowering of the body's core temperature to dangerous levels. This can occur through a variety of ways, but the most common is when wet skin and clothing are exposed to heat-depleting high winds. Symptoms include a loss of coordination, shivering, and exhaustion. Hypothermia victims need to be warmed and protected from the elements immediately. They should be sheltered in a tent and given many layers of dry clothes as well as hot liquids (but no alcohol!). Surrounding a victim with the warm bodies of stripped-down fellow hikers is also recommended. Victims will need plenty of water, high-energy food, and rest.

Prevention is the best medicine here, and being prepared with plenty of warm clothes and a waterproof outer layer will make for a safe and enjoyable visit to the outdoors.

WILD ANIMALS Most animals you may encounter in the backcountry will be more frightened of you than you are of them. There may, however, be those rare instances when a large animal exhibits protective or aggressive behavior, which may be dangerous. Animals, or their prey, may be attracted by the smell of food. Maintaining a clean camp and keeping food in one place (such as a stuff sack or "food bag") 100 yards from camp will help minimize the chance of confronting a hungry visitor. Consider hanging food high off the ground from a slender branch—particularly if you are some distance from civilization or food resupply. Hiking a long distance on an empty stomach is not a pleasant experience!

Mountain lions and bears live near parts of the Continental Divide Trail, but they are shy of humans, and the chances of being approached by a large, tooth-bearing beast are much smaller than those of being struck by lightning. In the unlikely event that you do have such an encounter, experts suggest standing tall, waving your arms, making noise, and slowly backing up. Throwing rocks or a walking stick at a persistent mountain lion may also be effective.

Children are more vulnerable than adults, so keep an eye on them. And avoid direct contact with any wild animal, regardless of its size. Never feed a wild animal!

ACUTE MOUNTAIN SICKNESS

This most common of high-altitude maladies can strike anyone at any time, but visitors from lower elevations are more susceptible. Prevention, in the form of a few days of rest on arrival at altitude, is the best medicine.

Symptoms of acute mountain sickness include headache, nausea, dizziness, shortness of breath, loss of appetite, and insomnia. The best treatment is to descend to a lower altitude, drink plenty of water, and rest.

Hikers should be aware of the more serious affliction of High Altitude Pulmonary Edema, which is the condition of fluid buildup in the lungs. HAPE is characterized by the symptoms identified for Acute Mountain Sickness, as well as dry cough, difficulty breathing, and gurgling sounds. This illness can be fatal, and the only treatments are rapid descent to a lower altitude, and/or immediate administration of oxygen to the victim.

SNAGS

Snags are dead trees that are still standing, but whose root structures may be decayed to the point that the tree is ready to topple over at any moment. Although the danger of being hit by a falling tree is slight, a few people have been killed in the recent past. Be aware of the proximity of such danger when choosing a campsite, and remember that live trees are also susceptible to blowing over in a strong storm.

Climate and Seasons on Colorado's Continental Divide

The summer season at the elevations of Colorado's Continental Divide is a short one, generally lasting from early July to late September. The trail's accessibility is mostly a function of the amount of snow that fell during the preceding winter. The best ways to plan a hike are to keep an eye on snowfall amounts, which are often measured as "percent of normal" (a very general rule for finding a starting date is to add 10 days to July 1 for every 10 percent of normal over 100, and to subtract 10 days for every 10 percent under 100), and to call the Forest Service ranger districts along the trail (see Appendix A, on page 325, for addresses and phone numbers). Using the elevation profiles in this book will also help; many lower-elevation sections may open sometime in June.

Colorado's summer climate is among the most pleasant anywhere in the world, with low humidity, clear skies, and warm temperatures the general rule. There are, however, important exceptions to this idyllic scenario. Along the Continental Divide, you should always be prepared for snow and freezing cold, even in the height of summer.

In July and August, you can almost set your clock by the thunderstorms—and accompanying lightning—that boil up over the mountain ranges in early afternoon. It is best to plan your hiking so you are well off the trail's many exposed ridges and high points by one or two o'clock. At the very least, study the map for escape routes that lead to lower elevations. (See the discussion on lightning, page 33.)

Nighttime temperatures during summer routinely dip into the low 30s, so make sure your sleeping bag can handle freezing conditions.

By late September, the first lasting snows will have fallen, and depths over one foot are not uncommon. From this time until May or June, most of the Continental Divide will be reserved for those hardy souls on snowshoes and backcountry skis. Winter presents a whole different set of dangers, and you should seek instruction on winter travel in the backcountry before setting off for the incomparable solitude offered by Colorado's long season of snow and ice.

Planning a Through-hike

Planning a long hike is a little like trying to plan the course of a marriage before the wedding, even before you know who your spouse will be. To illustrate the metaphor, all you know about your future mate (the Continental Divide Trail) is what you've seen in photos (maps), heard through the rumor mill (trail descriptions from various sources), and gathered about character flaws (hazards like lightning storms, snow, etc.). Not much to go on! Here are some tips to minimize the likelihood that your trip will end in a nasty divorce.

Take time to plan thoroughly. Early planning can eliminate problems on the trail. Allow plenty of time to make an itinerary and recruit people for food drops. Measure out precise quantities of food for each resupply.

Make a precise itinerary if people are meeting you for resupply, and stick to it. Be realistic about the amount of time it will take to hike between food drops and how much you can carry per stretch. Allow for unexpected delays like nasty weather.

Make a detailed checklist, and use it to make sure you haven't forgotten anything. Check off things to take as well as things to do, such as contacting people who will be handling resupply. See Appendix B on page 326, for a gear checklist.

Carry plenty of the right kinds of food, and plan food drops carefully. Your calorie requirements can more than double when you hike the CDT. For instance, according to *Backpacker* magazine, the average 200-pound man needs about 3,600 calories in day-to-day life. But he will require an additional 3,000 calories or more to hike a trail with a heavy pack at high altitude. The source of those calories is also important. Carbohydrates should account for 60 to 70 percent of calories, protein 10 to 15 percent, and fat 20 to 25 percent. To give you an idea of where some foods stand, here are a few examples of the percentage of fat: cheddar cheese, 75 percent; salami, 80 percent; bread, dried beans, and vegetables, less than 20 percent.

An example of a balanced diet for a day would include oatmeal with dried fruit for breakfast; bagels with a thin layer of peanut butter for lunch along with carrots, trail mix, granola, and more fruit; and pasta or rice for dinner, along with dehydrated vegetables, bread or rolls, and, of course, dessert. In addition to this regimen, it is good to eat a snack every 60 to 90 minutes and occasionally add a sports drink mix to your water. Consult a nutritionist or a book on this subject for professional advice.

When you prepare your food-shopping list, estimate how much of every specific food item you will need per day on the trail and use your itinerary to multiply these figures by the number of days between food drops. Factor in at least one extra day for emergency rations. Prepare an individual box or other container for each food drop. Include a list of the perishable items you'll need, and ask the person doing the food drop to purchase them for you.

You can mail boxes ahead to yourself. Just write "General Delivery" and your name above the post office address and include instructions to "Hold for Continental Divide Trail hiker." You can find post office addresses and phone numbers in the town information boxes in this book's trail segment descriptions.

Be realistic about how far you can hike in one day. It does not take long to become worn out carrying 50 pounds on your back, climbing a total of several thousand feet per day, and breathing oxygen-poor air at high elevation. You will enjoy the hike more if you don't kill yourself trying to set distance records. Naturally, it will be easier to hike longer distances later in the trip when you've had a chance to acclimate and get your "trail legs."

Plan days off. Even for people who are in great shape, it doesn't take long for a hike like this to wear you down. A day of rest is surprisingly rejuvenating after several days of hiking. One day off for every four to six days of hiking is not unrealistic.

Carry reading material and a notebook if you like to write or draw.

Keep your pack as light as possible. This involves mostly common sense, but here are some suggestions:
- If you have a cook set with several pots, leave all but one pot at home. Use the lid as a plate.

- Avoid heavy food. Fresh fruit is nice, but it weighs much more than its dried counterparts. For dinners, freeze-dried food is light, and its quality has improved in recent years!

- Get rid of packaging overkill. Don't take the box the granola bars came in. Don't carry any heavy containers like glass. Repackage food and condiments in plastic bottles or bags, if necessary.

- Avoid unnecessary luxuries like a chair, shower, cassette tape player, etc.

- Be sure to take plenty of clothes, but avoid duplicating items. Remember, no one you meet will have had a shower lately either.

- Take only as much of a bulk item as you need. For instance, squeeze a small amount of toothpaste into a lightweight container instead of carrying the entire tube. Same for mayonnaise—leave the jar at home.

- Use food drops for more than just food. Put fresh clothes in your resupply boxes instead of trying to carry enough clothing for more than one stretch between drops. If the same person will be meeting you at several resupply points, give them one box with refill items in it to take to each point, such as that tube of toothpaste, fresh batteries, stove fuel, etc.

- Don't overestimate how much reading you will do. Take one good paperback and drop a couple more in the resupply boxes. There's not as much time for reading as you might think.

Keep water requirements in mind when you plan your itinerary. Use a map, and make sure you can camp near water or carry enough (a last resort) between sources.

Test items such as your stove and water filter before you leave. Set up the tent. Make sure your cook set will sit securely on the stove. Check your pack for frayed straps, loose pins, broken zippers, etc.

Give yourself plenty of time before the hike to break in new boots. Don't take a chance on this. Blisters can be more painful and threaten your trip more than a turned ankle. In any event, carry lightweight shoes to wear around camp and to give your feet an occasional break.

Get in shape. Hiking Colorado's Continental Divide Trail is a strenuous undertaking. A small amount of regular exercise starting well before your trip can make a big difference in your comfort and performance on the trail. Stress aerobic activity and leg-strengthening exercises.

And, finally, prepare yourself for one of the best summers of your life!

Rainbow in Weminuche Wilderness

Segment 1
Wyoming Trailhead to North Lake Trailhead

Sunrise below Mount Zirkel

24.0 miles
Difficulty: Moderate

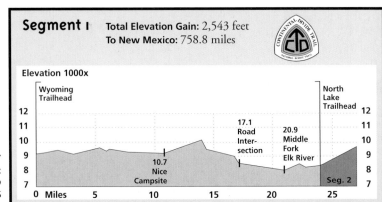

Segment 1 **Total Elevation Gain:** 2,543 feet
To New Mexico: 758.8 miles

CONTINENTAL DIVIDE TRAIL
CDT
NATIONAL SCENIC TRAIL

Elevation 1000x

Wyoming Trailhead

North Lake Trailhead

17.1 Road Inter-section

20.9 Middle Fork Elk River

10.7 Nice Campsite

Seg. 2

YOU MAY ENCOUNTER:
MOTORIZED VEHICLES

0 Miles   5   10   15   20   25

THE FIRST SEGMENT of Colorado's Continental Divide Trail is a study in contrasts. The first half follows the dry, quiet ridges of the Divide, but the second half strays off the Divide, featuring lush meadows, frequent bogs and stream crossings, and the roar of the Elk River's North Fork.

The trail hugs the boundary of the Mount Zirkel Wilderness for several miles, yet it is open to motorized vehicles for its entire length. And although you might feel isolated as you drive far from any Colorado town into these Wyoming backways, you might encounter a variety of outdoor enthusiasts at any time, including horse parties, motorcyclists, and drivers of all-terrain vehicles.

The trail is defined for its entire course by an old stock driveway, a rancher's "backcountry freeway" in which a wide, miles-long swath has been cut through the trees to allow the passage of large herds of stock. This driveway is marked irregularly by yellow signs tacked to the trees.

You won't encounter water for the first 10 miles of this segment, although it can be found at some distance off the trail, down the slopes of the Divide.

As of the summer of 1996, there were no CDT markers anywhere along this segment. Camping is permitted throughout. Don't count on hitchhiking here.

 NORTHBOUND HIKERS: Finishing here should arrange for a ride or be prepared for the extra mileage on foot.

 MOUNTAIN BIKE NOTES: The length of this segment is its most difficult aspect. It does have some challenging ascents and a few screaming downhills.

MAPS

TRAILS ILLUSTRATED: 116
USGS QUADRANGLES: Solomon Creek, WY; Dudley Creek, WY; West Fork Lake, Farwell Mtn., Mount Zirkel
USFS: Medicine Bow National Forest (WY), Routt National Forest, pages 46–47

BEGINNING ACCESS POINT

 WYOMING TRAILHEAD FROM STEAMBOAT SPRINGS: (This access will be preferable for segment hikers planning to finish near Seedhouse Campground at the end of this segment). Drive west on US-40 1.5 miles from downtown to a stoplight at County Road 129. Turn right (north) and continue 30 miles to Forest Route 550. Turn right toward Whiskey

The day

on which

one starts out

is not the time

to start one's

preparations.

—Nigerian Proverb

RANGER DISTRICTS:
Hayden (WY)
Hahns Peak

Park. Continue 16.3 miles to a limited parking area on Forest Route 550.2E, on the left next to mile marker 24 (N41° 0.90', W106° 54.39'). (Note that you will not see any mile markers for about the first 15 miles, and the first one will be #25.) At 0.1 mile past the intersection with Forest Route 550.2E, signs mark the trailhead on the right side of Forest Route 550. Tree blazes delineate the trail's passage east into the timber.

ALTERNATE ACCESS

 WYOMING TRAILHEAD FROM COLORADO HIGHWAY 125 (East side of the Divide): Starting at the intersection of Colorado Highways 14 and 125 with the odometer at 0.0, drive north on Highway 125 10.7 miles and turn left (west) onto County Road 6 in Cowdrey at a sign for Big Creek Lakes. Avoid the turnoff to Big Creek Lakes at mile 29.6, turn left onto County Road 6B at mile 31.2, and proceed to a fork at mile 35.3. Bear right toward Hog Park Reservoir and avoid the turnoff to Buffalo Ridge Trailhead at mile 39.4. Continue toward Hog Park Reservoir, passing the turnoff to Lakeview Campground at mile 51.6 and continuing to a left turn at mile 53.1 onto Forest Route 550, toward Steamboat Springs. (Note that the Forest Service and USGS maps mistakenly show the road passing along the south side of Hog Park Reservoir. The road actually goes around the lake on its north side.) At mile 61.0, signs on the left side of the road mark the trailhead, and tree blazes delineate the trail's passage east into the trees. There is limited parking on Forest Route 550.2E, 0.1 mile past the trailhead on the right.

ENDING ACCESS POINT

 NORTH LAKE TRAILHEAD: See the next segment.

TRAIL DESCRIPTION

There are no towns near this segment.

SUPPLIES, SERVICES, AND ACCOMMODATIONS

Follow tree blazes east through lodgepole pine trees 0.1 mile to a meadow. Keep an eye out for elk. Cross the meadow roughly due east, pass by a post, and follow tree blazes into the woods on the opposite side. The trail disappears into a clearcut at mile 0.3 (9,260); walk south of east until you reach a meadow on the far side. Look for the faint trail cutting through the meadow and exiting into trees near a post on the east side. Continue in the same direction to a second clearcut at mile 0.7, then onto a road leading uphill to the east-southeast. About 200 yards short of the top of the ridge (mile 1.0; 9,420), look to the right (south) for the opening in the trees (N41° 0.78', W106° 53.32') that marks the continuation of the trail along an old stock driveway and the Fireline Trail (not marked), trending away from the clearcut to the southeast.

Follow the faint trail along the left (east) side of the driveway for 0.3 mile to where the trees close in on both sides; the way is very faint now but marked by frequent Forest Service blazes on the trees. Note how the ambiguously rolling hills render the Divide as inconspicuous as the trail.

At mile 2.0, the trail begins to trend more to the east (left). Denuded ground on both sides of the trail is evidence of the millions of hooves that have been driven through this area. Welcome to Colorful Colorado at mile 3.0, where the CDT passes a large clearcut on the left (east) and a south-facing sign on the right announcing north-bound travelers' entry into Wyoming. At mile 3.4, cross Trail #1197, a clear single-track trail designated for motorcycles. At mile 3.5 (9,270), the trail enters an open area and bends to the east (left) as logging clearcuts on the opposing slopes come into view. The Forest Service blazes now disappear, but the trail is much clearer and easier to follow.

After a bend to the right (south) the trail descends for 0.2 mile, then climbs for 100 yards to its intersection with a road. Turn right and walk 25 yards around a switch-back; then turn onto a single-track trail on the right side that climbs sharply to the southeast. The trail soon widens back to the dimensions of the stock driveway and reaches the top of the climb near Point 9,731. The trail now follows a clear jeep road. At mile 4.9 (9,640), follow the road as it bends almost 90 degrees to the southwest (right), climbs steadily to the crest of the hill at mile 5.4, and then rolls southward to the treeless top of a steep hill at mile 6.2 (9,712) where it flattens out.

Enter a wide clearing at mile 7.0 that offers distant views in all directions. At mile 7.5, the CDT descends and curves to the east, intersecting the Ellis Jeep Trail on the left (east) at mile 8.6 (9,460). In 0.2 mile, avoid Forest Route 500 on the right and follow Trail #1101 to the left. This point marks the beginning of the trail's 5.1-mile jaunt along the boundary of the Mount Zirkel Wilderness, which lies north and east of the CDT. At mile 10.2 the trail bends due east (left) and descends to a large beautiful meadow on the left side of the trail at mile 10.7 (9,340). A reliable stream on the east side of the meadow is the first water on this segment, and the edge of the meadow, which is in the wilderness area, makes a peaceful campsite.

After crossing an intermittent stream at mile 11.4 (9,855), the trail proceeds 0.1 mile until it reaches a treeless high point and descends to a grassy valley to the south-east where it is joined by the Manzanares Trail. Stay on Trail #1101 as it trends south of east to a point at 11.7 where a sign indicates the continuation to the northeast of the virtually invisible Manzanares Trail. Stay on the main tread as it bends to the right (southeast) and climbs a steep rocky hill. For a stunning view of the scenic Manzanares Lake valley, walk 100 yards to the left and peer over the ridge.

You'll reach the 10,188-foot high point of this segment at mile 12.0 (N40° 55.13', W106° 49.09'). At mile 13.7, the CDT enters a large clearing where it intersects the Hare Trail, which leads west to Big Red Park. Follow Trail #1101 to its bend to the south at mile 13.9 (10,140), where it leaves the Divide ridge behind for the first time—and with it the Mount Zirkel Wilderness boundary. Views of the magnificent Sawtooth Range and Mount Zirkel Wilderness open up now as the trail passes into a large clearing before a steady descent at mile 14.0. The vista across the Trail Creek valley offers a new perspective on the Divide, which runs across the tops of the ridges to the east (left).

At mile 14.3 (9,600), wet meadows at the bottom of the descent mark the beginning of frequent water along the rest of this segment. Cross a large meadow to the southwest; then follow the trail downhill to the southeast where it meanders through meadows and wetlands before crossing Trail Creek at mile 15.4 (9,430). This should be negotiable throughout the season, but prepare to get your feet wet.

At mile 15.7, avoid the trail created by motorized users through the grass to the southeast. Follow the single-track trail up out of the meadow due east (left). One mile later, the CDT descends sharply through an aspen forest to a well-traveled road at mile 17.1 (8,630). Follow markers to the left (east) for Trail #1101. Walk 30 yards along the road before shooting off on a single-track trail on the right (south). The remainder of the trail does not appear on the 1962 USGS map, but you can find it on Trails Illustrated #116.

Continue south through large pine trees to a good bridge across the North Fork of the Elk River at mile 17.6 (8,560). The pines give way to a beautiful spruce forest before the trail crests a small hill at mile 17.9 above a large idyllic meadow with ponds at its opposite end. At mile 18.6, the trail climbs above and away from the river until it reaches Lost Dog Creek at mile 19.0 (8,280). Here it turns downstream (due west) for 0.1 mile to a crossing on several old logs.

At mile 19.3, the trail returns to the banks of the Elk River, which offer nice camping spots, before continuing through large dry meadows adorned with a variety of wildflowers. After another 0.2 mile, the trail reaches English Creek. A faint path leads upstream 100 yards to a crossing on an old broken log that may have a few years of service left in it. Just after returning to the trail, take its right fork toward Seedhouse Station. At mile 20.1 (8,100), the trail enters a large aspen forest as the campground becomes visible to the right. In 0.1 mile, the CDT reaches Seedhouse Road, a good stopping point for segment hikers or through-hikers needing services. Seedhouse Campground is 0.4 mile to the right (west).

The official Forest Service version of the CDT has it crossing Seedhouse Road here before going through a gate and past a campground to a crossing of the Middle Fork of the Elk River. Unless you are endowed with the faculties of a salmon, I would advise avoiding this high and fast water by turning left (east) onto Seedhouse Road and proceeding 0.5 mile to a right (south) turn onto Forest Route 443 at mile 20.7. Cross the bridge and continue along the road to a point at mile 21.1 (8,090) where there is a pullout on the right and a continuation of the trail trending off to the east (left). Turn onto the trail, pass a sign 25 yards up that says Three Island Trail #1163, and follow several switchbacks into an enchanting forest that sets the standard for the color green. At mile 22.0, the trail crests a hill, flattens out, and then drops slightly before crossing over into an aspen forest on the south (right) side of the ridge at mile 22.4 (8,600). Reach a trail junction 100 yards beyond this where a sign points the way to Three Island Lake. Take the right fork descending into the aspens and reach Forest Route 443, which has looped around from the west, at mile 22.7 (8,385). Turn left (east) and follow the road to the North Lake Trailhead, and the end of this segment, at mile 24.0 (8,465 feet; N40° 45.16', W106° 43.92').

OTHER HIKES

SEVEN LAKES

Approximate one-way distance: 4.5 miles
Difficulty: Moderate

Big Creek Trailhead: See *Access from Colorado Highway 125* at the beginning of this segment.

Seven Lakes sit in an alpine meadow in the shadow of the Continental Divide, which is an easy, 250-foot scramble to the south. From here you may explore the high ridges of the Divide to the south, toward Mount Zirkel, or simply enjoy the views of the stunning Sawtooth Range (also to the south). A map—and the ability to read it—are strongly recommended for hiking on the Divide here. Please remember that this area is within the Mount Zirkel Wilderness.

LAKE KATHERINE

Approximate one-way distance: 3.2 miles
Difficulty: Moderate

Lake Katherine Trailhead: Drive west from the town of Walden on County Road 12W. Follow this road's split to the north (right) and turn left (west) on County Road 16. Follow this road to the trailhead. Supplement these directions with a good road map.

This mystical lake sits at the bottom of an impressive cirque that belies the relative flatness of the Continental Divide plateau 1,000 vertical feet above. The story of Lake Katherine involves references to monsters and the supernatural. Its bottom has never been found, and in one incident two fishermen reported seeing a pair of huge, glowing eyes peering at them from the mist floating on the dark water.

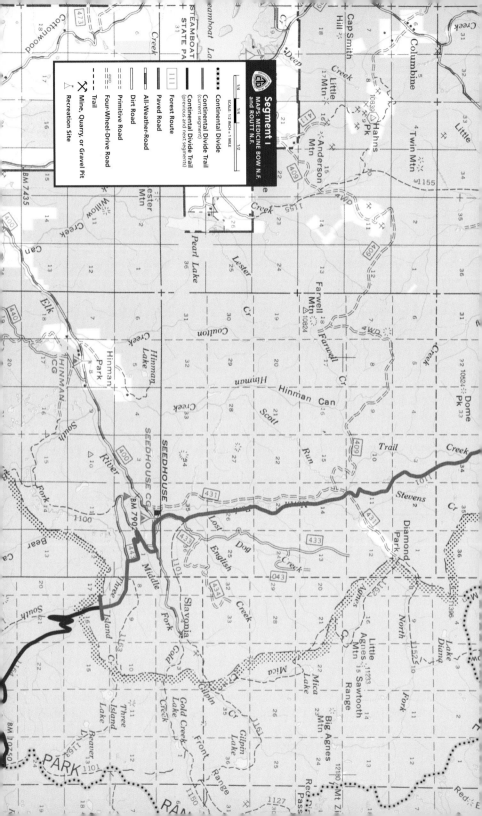

SCALE 1/2 INCH = 1 MILE

1/4   1/4   1/2

• • • • • Continental Divide
━━━━━ Continental Divide Trail
            (current segment)
┅┅┅┅┅ Continental Divide Trail
            (previous and next segments)
│ │ │   Forest Route
━━━━━ Continental Divide
━━━━━ Paved Road
═══════ All-Weather-Road
═══════ Dirt Road
┅┅┅┅ Primitive Road
- - 4WD Four-Wheel-Drive Road
- - - -   Trail
✕   Mine, Quarry, or Gravel Pit
△   Recreation Site

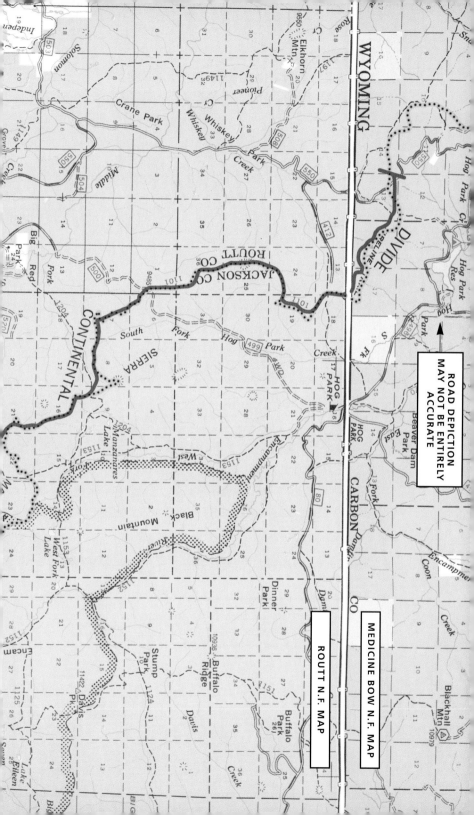

Segment 2
North Lake Trailhead to Buffalo Pass

Near Luna Lake, Mount Zirkel Wilderness

21.6 miles
Difficulty: Strenuous

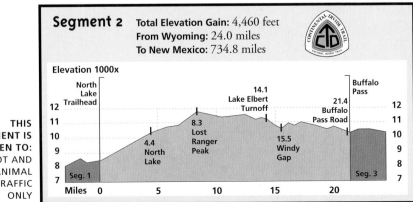

Segment 2   **Total Elevation Gain:** 4,460 feet
From Wyoming: 24.0 miles
To New Mexico: 734.8 miles

CONTINENTAL DIVIDE TRAIL
CDT
NATIONAL SCENIC TRAIL

Elevation 1000x

North Lake Trailhead

14.1 Lake Elbert Turnoff

Buffalo Pass

21.4 Buffalo Pass Road

12
11
10
9
8
7

4.4 North Lake

8.3 Lost Ranger Peak

15.5 Windy Gap

Seg. 1

Seg. 3

Miles   0   5   10   15   20

THIS SEGMENT IS OPEN TO: FOOT AND ANIMAL TRAFFIC ONLY

THE CDT leaves the trees behind on this segment to regain the skyway of the Divide. With sustained exposure to the elements common here, hiking should be timed to avoid crossing high points such as Lost Ranger Peak during the often tempestuous Colorado afternoon. Powerful storms can boil up with little warning.

The stunted spruce trees that often grow in clumps above timberline, called krummholz, are a primary feature of this segment, and they are sometimes the only useful reference points along the trail. Water is plentiful except between miles 5.6 and 13.0, where it is available mostly in the form of still ponds some distance off the trail. The treeless terrain along that interval offers little protection for camping.

Celebrate your completion of this segment with a rejuvenating visit to Strawberry Hot Springs, which boasts large ponds in a beautiful natural setting, as well as cozy cabins for an overnight stay. For more information, see the listing of services in Steamboat Springs in Segment 3 on page 60. For directions to the hot springs, see the description of access to Buffalo Pass at the beginning of Segment 3 on page 59.

As of 1996, there were no CDT markers on this segment.

 MOUNTAIN BIKE NOTES: Biking is prohibited in the Mount Zirkel Wilderness.

MAPS

TRAILS ILLUSTRATED: 116, 117
USGS QUADRANGLES: Mount Zirkel, Mount Ethel, Buffalo Pass
USFS: Routt National Forest, pages 56–57.

ACCESS

 NORTH LAKE TRAILHEAD: From downtown Steamboat Springs, drive north on U.S. Highway 40 1.5 miles to a stoplight at County Road 129. Turn right and continue 17.7 miles to County Road 64 (Seedhouse Road) at a sign for Elk River Guest Ranch. Turn right and proceed 9.8 miles to Forest Route 443 (North Lake Road). Turn right and follow this road 4.8 miles to its end at the North Lake Trailhead. The last mile is very bumpy, but passable. Note that the CDT reaches the north (left) side of Seedhouse Road 0.4 mile east of Seedhouse Campground.

Distance from graded road — 1.0 mile

Thunder is good,

thunder is

impressive;

but it is

lightning

that does

the work.

—Mark Twain

RANGER DISTRICTS:
Hahns Peak
Parks

BUFFALO PASS: See the next segment.

SUPPLIES, SERVICES, AND ACCOMMODATIONS
STEAMBOAT SPRINGS OFFERS ALL SERVICES.
See Segment 3, page 60.

TRAIL DESCRIPTION The trail starts at the south end of the parking area. At mile 0.2, the trail enters the Mount Zirkel Wilderness, where it will remain for 20.9 miles.

WILDERNESS ALERT:

The Mount Zirkel Wilderness was designated in 1964 by federal law to be "an area where the earth and its community of life are untrammeled by man, where man himself is a visitor who does not remain." It covers 160,568 acres of pristine forests and alpine cirques and lakes. Please remember these rules governing wilderness areas: 1. Camp out of sight, at least 200 feet from lakes and streams, on dry, durable surfaces. 2. Use a stove instead of building a fire; use existing fire rings if you must have a fire. 3. Keep water sources pure by washing at least 200 feet from them. 4. Bury human waste six inches deep and 200 feet from lakes and streams. Pack out toilet paper. 5. Hobble or picket livestock at least 200 feet from lakes and streams, and use only treated, weed-free feed and grain. 6. All dogs must be on a leash. 7. No mountain biking. 8. Pack out all trash. Don't attempt to burn it.

After crossing the Elk River South Fork, the CDT begins a steady, switch-backing climb through a nice spruce forest before leveling off at mile 1.1 (9,040) in an enchanted wood where the trees sway to the peaceful strains of a bubbling stream.

The trail resumes a gradual climb to mile 3.8. Then it climbs more steeply to an unmarked fork in a large meadow at mile 4.1. Turn left (east). At mile 4.4 (10,300), the trail passes North Lake, where backpackers may wish to camp and ply the waters for brook trout. There is more good camping at a near-stagnant pond on the left (north) at mile 5.6 (10,750). This is the last guaranteed water for 3.8 miles.

Just beyond the pond a cairn marks the entrance into a large clearing, and it also provides the setting for the trail's intersection with the Continental Divide, which it will follow for the remainder of this segment. From here to Lost Ranger Peak, expect marshy conditions in the spring and after rain.

As the trail disappears here, continue straight ahead to the east toward a post 100 yards across the clearing, and then to a sign 40 yards farther at mile 5.7 (N40° 43.64', W106° 40.14'). Turn right (compass bearing 200°) and walk 160 yards to a rock cairn that marks the continuation of the faint trail. Continue south past a post and into delightful alpine meadows speckled with wildflowers.

NORTHBOUND HIKERS: If you enter some trees and begin climbing for the first time since Lost Ranger Peak, you have missed the turnoff to the left (west).

Now Lost Ranger Peak comes into view, blocking the path and providing the first real alpine ascent for the through-hiker. At mile 6.1 the trail bends slightly left (east) around a spruce grove, and then it fades away as it enters a large clearing. The cairn straight ahead to the south guides you to the faint continuation of the trail as it heads straight toward the peak via occasional posts. At mile 7.0, a small impermanent stream provides the last water before the climb.

Any trace of the trail goes the way of the rapidly disappearing trees at mile 7.3. Continue straight ahead to a cairn and spot a second cairn on the horizon just left of center (compass bearing 150°). Now follow the faint trail up the hill. As you begin the ascent of Lost Ranger Peak, the great plain of North Park becomes visible to the left, while the honed incisors of the Sawtooth Range come into full view behind you.

The trail is unreliable as you ascend, but cairns take up the slack. At mile 8.3 (11,880), the trail flattens on Lost Ranger's high plateau, and then it skirts the true summit's east side. As the CDT begins its descent to the south and you survey the yawning vista before you, it may occur to you that wilderness is defined more by space than by the solid matter it contains.

Now a faint tread and frequent cairns lead across the tundra to the southwest. This rocky alpine ecosystem is actually among the most delicate; please stick to the trail and walk single-file.

At mile 9.3 (11,560), the trail flattens and bears left (south) to circumvent a rocky knob on the right. The CDT's short climb to the top of the ridge may require an easy snow crossing, particularly before July. At mile 9.4, a small pond off the Divide to the east (left) marks the beginning of plentiful water for the next 5.5 miles. The trail continues to follow cairns due south from mile 9.6.

The intersection with the trail to Slide and Roxy Ann Lakes is at mile 10.3 (11,360); follow the CDT as it climbs straight ahead (south). As the trail hops back and forth across the Divide, can you trace the Divide's serpentine path along the ridge?

At mile 11.6 (11,570), the CDT intersects the trail to Lake of the Crags and Luna Lake. If the small, infrequent cairns guiding you up the hill to the southeast are inadequate, simply maintain a path parallel to the steep drop-off on the right (compass bearing 165°). Look for the trail to resume at a cairn at mile 11.8; then proceed to a post supported by a large cairn at mile 12.1 where the trail disappears again. Look across the meadow, under the left-most krummholz on the horizon (compass bearing 165°), for the next cairn 0.1 mile away.

The CDT continues in the same direction to the next cairn at mile 12.3 (11,650), and then it bends downhill to the right (southwest). Luna Lake, a popular hiking and fishing destination, soon comes into view on the right (west). At mile 12.7, the trail descends more steeply through a series of rocky switchbacks until its entrance into a broad green valley at mile 13.0. Plentiful water and good protection make this the first decent campsite since the pond at mile 5.6. Continue to follow cairns to the south. *As you approach a cairn near the streambed* at mile 13.2, look to the left for another cairn at a lone pine tree, marking the trail's sharp swing to the left (east) and then back to the right (south). After climbing out of the streambed, pass a cairn on the flatter part of the tundra and look to the horizon, slightly right of center (compass bearing 210°) for the next cairn near a small growth of trees at mile 13.5 (11,360). Next, a faint trail and more cairns lead you straight ahead. Lake Elbert, soon visible on the right (west), is an ideal spot for a night's rest less than a mile off the trail. Its access trail is 0.6 mile ahead.

Near the bottom of another broad valley, at a cairn at mile 13.9 (11,120), look to the left of the rocky gulch for the next cairn near a lone pine tree. As you crest the next hill near a jeep road, look about 45 degrees to the left for a distant view of the famous rock formations known as the Rabbit Ears.

At mile 14.1 (11,145), cross perpendicular to a trail and an old jeep road and continue south along a faint trail marked by cairns. (If you want to visit Lake Elbert, turn right at this intersection.) The trail begins an uncairned descent into yet another valley near a large boulder at mile 14.2. Look for the road winding its way up the opposing hillside. At mile 14.3 (11,020), regain the trail near the bottom of the descent.

After passing some ponds on the left (east), the trail bends left at mile 14.9 (10,940) to circumvent the steep, rocky descent into an abrupt valley dubbed Windy Gap by local old-timers. At mile 15.5 (10,740), the trail passes through some trees before ascending Windy Gap's south slope. Take the right fork at this point. As the trail cuts a southwest traverse across the slope, try to determine the Divide's path through this area without looking at a map.

The trail tops out at mile 16.0 (11,060), and then it enters a spacious valley— prime elk country—at mile 16.5 (10,940). Crest the next ridge at mile 16.8 (11,050) and continue through a sparse spruce forest, descending to a large meadow at mile 17.2. The edge of the earth beckons from behind the trees on the left, offering a fantastic panoramic view of the Rabbit Ears to the south and mountain range after mountain range to the east. If you don't suffer from vertigo (or existential angst), this is a perfect place to have lunch and read some Nietzsche.

The trail begins a steeper descent at mile 17.7 (10,880) and reaches a large, wildflower-engulfed pond at mile 18.0. One mile farther, a sign points the way to Buffalo Pass, this segment's destination. A climb between miles 19.4 (10,540) and 20.0 (10,740) is this segment's last. Bid farewell to the Mount Zirkel Wilderness at mile 21.1 and turn left (east) onto Buffalo Pass Road at mile 21.4 (10,300). Follow the road's curve to the right (south) around the parking lot on your right. Summit Lake Campground is up the road to the left where tent camping costs $5.00.

Ten yards past the parking lot, take the road s right fork toward Fish Creek Reservoir and turn left into a large parking lot, which marks the end of this segment, at mile 21.6 (10,355 feet; N40° 32.49', W106° 41.04').

OTHER HIKES

PORCUPINE LAKE LOOP/LAKE OF THE CRAGS
Approximate one-way distance: 12 miles
Difficulty: Moderate

Buffalo Pass Trailhead: See *Access* for the next segment, page 59.

For those who want to experience this segment of the Continental Divide without a lot of driving or hiking before reaching it, this is an ideal hike. On the CDT for most of its length, the hike terminates in an area offering many choices for an overnight stay, including the diminutive Lake of the Crags tucked away on a rocky shelf at the base of spectacular cliffs and rock outcroppings. This part of Segment 2 also avoids the exposed relief of the area around Lost Ranger Peak.

Start at Buffalo Pass and hike this segment in reverse, 9.0 miles to the Lake Elbert Trail on the left (west).

POLLUTION AND VISIBILITY IN THE MOUNT ZIRKEL WILDERNESS

In the late 1980s, hikers and Forest Service employees in the Steamboat Springs area began noticing a murky haze in the previously clear, pristine air of the southwest part of the Mount Zirkel Wilderness, a 160,568-acre parcel of federally protected land that straddles the Continental Divide northwest of Steamboat Springs. These individuals reported their observations to Forest Service officials who began monitoring visibility in the area in 1990. They did this by setting up time-lapse cameras near the wilderness area, which confirmed that visibility in the wilderness area was being impaired by some sort of air pollution.

Some observers theorized that the haze might have been the result of pollutants being emitted by coal-fired power plants in the nearby towns of Hayden and Craig, but they were unable to prove this. During the summer of 1992, the Forest Service installed more cameras along the western edge of the wilderness area and situated them so they might be able to pinpoint the source of any observed pollution.

Meanwhile, scientists with the United States Geological Survey were monitoring pollution levels in the wilderness area's snowpack. Through 1993, they found sulphates and acids, pollutants associated with the burning of coal, at levels two to three times greater than anywhere else in the state. In fact, the pollutant levels were the highest ever observed anywhere west of the Mississippi River, and experts said this threatened fish and other aquatic life.

The cameras installed by the Forest Service did show plumes of pollution emanating from very specific sources near the wilderness area. Based on this and other evidence, and under the authority of the Colorado Clean Air Act and the 1964 Wilderness Act, the Forest Service informed the governor of Colorado in July, 1993, that it was reasonable to assume the air pollution and high levels of acid and sulphates were being emitted by the coal-fired power plants in Hayden and Craig. The Forest Service noted that the two power plants combined emitted more than 22,000 tons of the pollutant sulfur dioxide per year, accounting for 99.6 percent of total emissions from stationary sources in three surrounding counties, and 27,000 tons of nitrogen oxides per year, or 91.1 percent of such emissions.

In May, 1996, the plants' operators entered into an agreement with the Sierra Club, an environmental advocacy group, the U.S. Department of Justice, and others, wherein they agreed to pay fines, contribute funds for land preservation and anti-pollution technology, install more modern pollution controls at the plants, and change the way they measured the emission of pollutants. Most of these changes will begin in the spring of 1997 and it will take one year to complete the first phase of modifications, so it is too early to tell if they will have a significant impact on acid and sulphate levels in the Mount Zirkel Wilderness. Experts are optimistic, however, and they add that the kinds and amounts of pollutants observed in the wilderness area are not sufficient to harm humans passing through the area.

Sunrise below Mount Ethel, Mount Zirkel Wilderness

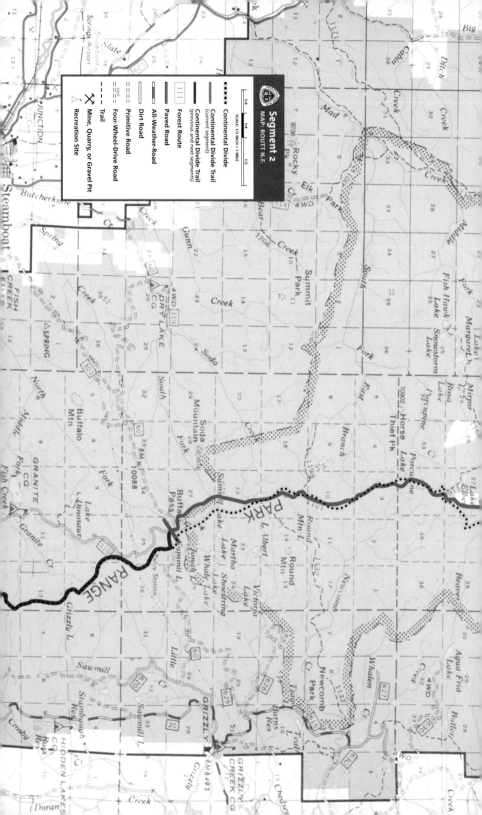

SCALE 1/2 INCH = 1 MILE

1/4   1/4   1/2

········· Continental Divide

········· Continental Divide Trail
(current segment)

Continental Divide Trail
(previous and next segments)

Forest Route

Paved Road

All-Weather-Road

Dirt Road

Primitive Road

Four-Wheel-Drive Road

Trail

Mine, Quarry, or Gravel Pit

Recreation Site

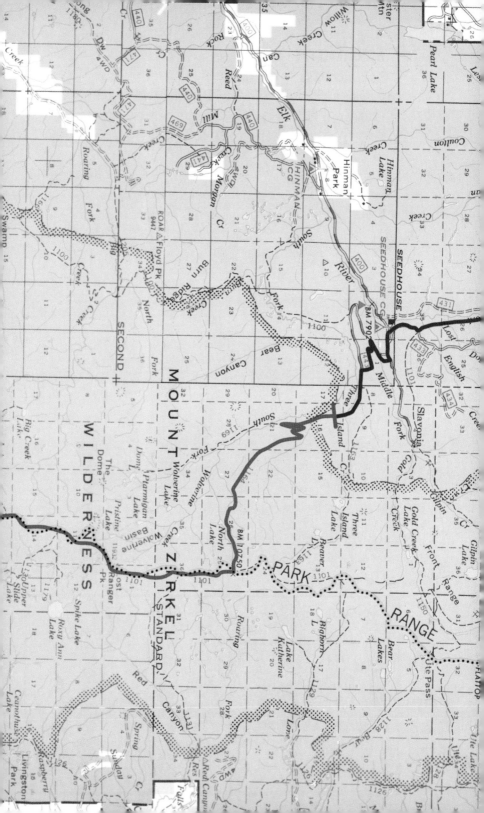

Segment 3
Buffalo Pass to US-40

Along the Divide, Routt National Forest

17.4 miles
Difficulty: Easy

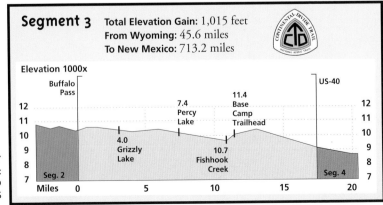

Segment 3   **Total Elevation Gain:** 1,015 feet
From Wyoming: 45.6 miles
To New Mexico: 713.2 miles

**YOU MAY
ENCOUNTER:**
MOTORIZED
VEHICLES

THIS SEGMENT PROVIDES the rare opportunity to walk the Divide without needing the agility of a mountain goat and a backpack full of winter clothing, sun block, and bottles of oxygen. The rigors of the Divide's characteristic above-timberline ridges and lung-busting climbs are not present here, as it meanders over flat ground thick with trees and vegetation.

The well-maintained character of this segment, combined with its relative flatness, make this an excellent—and popular— mountain bike route. Bikes are supposed to yield to hikers, and most bikers are very courteous, but it's not a bad idea to be prepared to hop off the trail on a blind corner. The entire segment is open to mountain bikes, and the first 5.1 miles to the Percy Lake turnoff are open to motorized vehicles.

Water and camping are available all along this segment. There are no CDT markers.

MOUNTAIN BIKE NOTES: This segment offers a nice, easy cruise for bikers. A short ascent at the end is the only challenging section.

MAPS

TRAILS ILLUSTRATED: 117, 118
USGS QUADRANGLES: Buffalo Pass, Mount Werner, Rabbit Ears Peak
USFS: Routt National Forest, page 63.

BEGINNING ACCESS POINT

Smooth road to trailhead

BUFFALO PASS: From US-40 in downtown Steamboat Springs, drive north on Seventh Street for 0.4 mile; then turn diagonally right onto Missouri Avenue. Follow this road for 2 miles as it curves left, then right, then left again, to a right turn (east) onto County Road 38. (To go to Strawberry Hot Springs, skip this right turn and continue straight along the winding dirt road for a few more miles.) Drive approximately 11 miles to the summit of Buffalo Pass. The previous segment joins the road on the left (north) side just before the turnoff to Summit Lake Campground. Follow a curve to the right, away from the campground, and turn right at the intersection toward Fish Creek Reservoir. Proceed less than 0.1 mile and turn left into a large parking lot originally constructed for horse trailers. The CDT climbs away from the south end of the parking lot on a clear single-track trail.

ALTERNATE ACCESS

Distance from graded road 4.5 miles

BASE CAMP TRAILHEAD (N40° 25.78', W106° 39.52'): This is a good place for segment hikers to

I like trees

because

they seem

more resigned

to the way

they have to live

than other

things do.

—Willa Cather,

O Pioneers!

RANGER DISTRICTS:
Hahns Peak
Parks

leave a shuttle vehicle. From the intersection of Highways 14 and 40, proceed west on US-40 4.5 miles to a large parking area at Forest Route 315 (18 miles east of Steamboat Springs). Turn right (north). Continue 1.5 miles to Forest Route 311, distinguished by a large boulder on the left (north). Turn left toward Base Campground and continue straight ahead through a gate, avoiding side roads. After 4.5 miles, look for a small parking area at the Base Camp Trailhead on the right (north) side of the road, marked by several signs, including one that says "Trail 1102."

ENDING ACCESS POINT

 US-40: See the next segment.

SUPPLIES, SERVICES, AND ACCOMMODATIONS

STEAMBOAT SPRINGS is west on Buffalo Pass Road.
Distance from Trail: 13.5 miles
Zip Code: 80477

Bank	Colorado Community First State Bank,	(970) 879-7385
	555 Lincoln Ave.	
Bus	Steamboat Springs Transit	879-3717
Dining	Cuginos Pizzeria, 825 Oak St.	879-5805
	La Montana (expensive and excellent), 2500 Village Dr.	879-5373
Gear	Straightline, 744 Lincoln Ave.	879-7568
	(White gas available at Boggs Hardware, 730 Lincoln Ave.)	879-6250
Groceries	City Market, 1825 Central Park Plaza	879-3290
	(south of town on US-40)	
Information	Steamboat Springs Chamber Resort Association,	879-0880
	1255 S. Lincoln Ave.	
Laundry	Spring Creek Laundromat, 235 Lincoln Ave.	879-5587
Lodging	Nordic Lodge, 1036 Lincoln Ave.	879-0531
	Rabbit Ears Motel, 201 Lincoln Ave.	870-0483
Medical	Routt Memorial Hospital, 80 Park Ave.	879-1322
Post Office	200 Lincoln Ave.	879-0363
Showers	Steamboat Springs Health and Rec., 136 Lincoln Ave.	879-1828

SPECIAL NOTES: Strawberry Park Hot Springs offers relaxation in a low-key, natural setting. Follow signs on Seventh Street east from Lincoln Ave. 7.2 miles. This is just off the road to Buffalo Pass, and hitchhiking is possible. Cabins are available for around $40 (includes springs). Phone: 879-0342.

TRAIL DESCRIPTION   The CDT trends east-southeast as it climbs abruptly away from the parking lot, but it levels off after about 0.5 mile. The trail passes under a power line and turns sharply to the right (southwest) as it briefly joins a jeep road at mile 1.2. Continue 0.2 mile and follow a single-track trail breaking off to the left (south). At mile 4.0 (10,210), you can see Grizzly Lake on the left (northeast).

The trail stays true to the Divide on this rare forested section as it winds through a pleasant spruce ecosystem on its way to the intersection with the Percy Lake/Fish Creek Falls Trail at mile 7.4 (10,155 feet; N40° 28.37', W106° 40.08'). From here, continue straight ahead to the south toward Base Camp Trailhead, as indicated by the sign. Motorized use is prohibited beyond this point, but mountain bikes are allowed on the entire segment.

At mile 8.0, the trail turns 90 degrees to the left (east) to skirt Lake Elmo, a good place for an overnight stay. Turn back to the right (south) and cross a large marshy meadow at mile 8.2 (10,040). At a T intersection at mile 9.5 (9,920), turn right (south) toward Fishhook Lake, which comes into view in 0.1 mile. This is another good candidate for camping and fishing near the trail, particularly at the south end. You'll cross the lake's outlet, Fishhook Creek, at mile 10.0 (9,877).

The CDT now describes a slight climb away from the lake. Then it descends to a point at mile 10.7 (9,727) where it crosses back to the east side of Fishhook Creek. The trail again climbs steadily as it leaves the creek before reaching Base Camp Trailhead at mile 11.4 (10,040 feet; N40° 25.81', W106° 39.49'). This is an ideal place for segment hikers to leave a shuttle vehicle.

Continue along Base Camp road with a turn to the left (east). The trail should not be slighted here simply because it is on a road. The spectacular views to the south and magnificent hillsides bursting with wildflowers will surely please any pedestrian.

At mile 14.4, a side road on the left signals an excellent close-up view of the fabulous Rabbit Ears to the northeast. Avoid this and subsequent side roads as you continue southeast along the main road. At an intersection with a paved road at mile 15.9, turn left (east) onto the paved road and take another look at the Rabbit Ears.

At mile 16.6, walk straight ahead past a barricade and dead end sign, following a dirt road south of east. Descend on this road to US-40, and the end of this segment, at mile 17.4 (9,140 feet; N40° 23.74', W106° 36.27').

IMPORTANT NOTE: This is not an official trailhead and there is no parking here. This is simply the best way for through-hikers to reach US-40. For segment hikers finishing here, cars can be left or pick-ups arranged at one of three locations: Base Camp Trailhead (at trail mile 11.4); a parking area at Dumont Lake Campground just west of the intersection of Forest Routes 315 and 311; or a parking area just north of US-40 about 3.5 miles west of Colorado Highway 14. Hikers aiming for the third location should continue south on a trail when they reach mile 15.9 and proceed about 0.8 mile to the parking area.

OTHER HIKES AND RIDES

BUFFALO PASS-LAKE PERCY BIKE LOOP

Approximate one-way distance: 25.0 miles
Mode of travel: Mountain bike
Difficulty: Moderate

Buffalo Pass/Fish Creek Reservoir Trailhead: See *Access* for this segment.

The mountain biking possibilities are endless in this area. For this loop, start at Buffalo Pass and ride the CDT as described here to the Lake Percy Trail, #1134. Descend on a fun trail to the east; then take Hidden Lakes Road north back to Buffalo Pass Road. This is a long ride, so plan plenty of time.

For a shorter loop, turn right (west) at the Lake Percy intersection and head for Fish Creek Reservoir. A dirt road takes you back north to Buffalo Pass.

FISHHOOK LAKE

Approximate one-way distance: 1.4 miles
Mode of travel: Hiking
Difficulty: Easy

Base Camp Trailhead: See driving directions under *Access* in this segment.

This hike is ideal for a one-night family get-away, and it's an easy way to experience one of the few mellow sections of the trail. Hike the CDT in reverse from the trailhead. Don't forget a fishing rod!

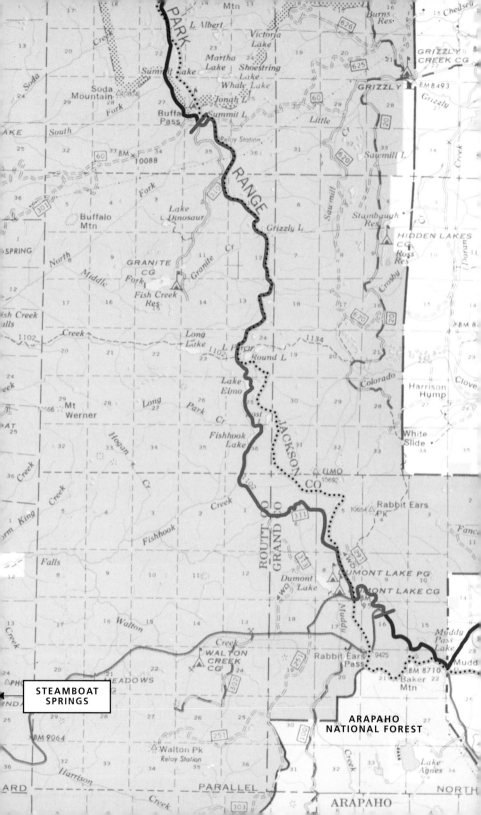

STEAMBOAT
SPRINGS

ARAPAHO
NATIONAL FOREST

Segment 4
US-40 to Forest Route 104

Spruce/fir forest, Arapaho National Forest

**30.0 miles
Difficulty: Easy**

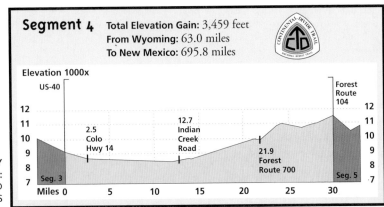

Segment 4   **Total Elevation Gain:** 3,459 feet
From Wyoming: 63.0 miles
To New Mexico: 695.8 miles

Elevation 1000x

US-40

12.7
Indian
Creek
Road

2.5
Colo
Hwy 14

21.9
Forest
Route 700

Forest
Route
104

12

11

10

9

8

7

Seg. 3

Seg. 5

Miles 0   5   10   15   20   25   30

12

11

10

9

8

7

YOU MAY
ENCOUNTER:
MOTORIZED
VEHICLES

THIS IS THE LEAST DESIRABLE SEGMENT of the CDT's entire passage through Colorado. Half of it is on paved highway, and the other half follows motorized dirt roads. This is not a permanent situation, but for now the Bureau of Land Management (BLM) and the Forest Service, the two agencies that manage this area, have no better option. Private property on the east side of Highways 40 and 14 prevents the trail from following the Divide's passage through this area. So for now this segment is included only as a way for through-hikers to link the neighboring segments. Land managers here are engaged in ongoing efforts to route the trail through a more natural, less paved environment.

Even though the final 7.9 miles of this segment are on a four-wheel drive road, it is quiet and there are beautiful panoramic views in all directions.

Grizzly and Indian Creeks provide water on this segment; the trail is dry for about the last 10 miles.

You may park anywhere along the dirt roads on the second half of this segment, as long as there are no "Private Property" or "No Parking" signs. Please park only where the roads accommodate, not off-road on the fragile forest floor. There are no CDT markers.

MOUNTAIN BIKE NOTES: There are a few challenging sections for bikes on the Forest Routes on the second half of this segment.

MAPS
TRAILS ILLUSTRATED: 115, 118
USGS QUADRANGLES: Rabbit Ears Peak, Spicer Peak, Whiteley Peak
USFS: Routt National Forest, pages 68–69

ACCESS

Smooth road to trailhead — This segment begins on US-40 2.5 miles west of its intersection with Colorado Highway 14.

Distance from graded road 9.2 miles + 7.8 miles — **FOREST ROUTE 104:** See the next segment.

SUPPLIES, SERVICES, AND ACCOMMODATIONS
STEAMBOAT SPRINGS HAS ALL SERVICES.
See Segment 3, page 60.

It is unfair

to blame man

too fiercely

for being

pugnacious;

he learned

the habit

from Nature.

—Christopher Morley,

Inward Ho!

RANGER DISTRICTS:
Hahns Peak
Parks

TRAIL DESCRIPTION   From Segment 3's intersection with US-40 (2.5 miles west of Colorado Highway 14), turn left (southeast) onto US-40 and follow its descent to Colorado Highway 14 (mile 2.5; 8,710). Hitchhiking is possible over the entire course of this segment; just be sure to pick a place that provides ample room and visibility for a car to pull over safely.

Turn left (northeast) onto Colorado Highway 14, continue to mile 12.7 (8,520), and turn right (east) at a sign for Indian Creek. At mile 19.4, turn left (east), stay on Forest Route 103, and avoid the numerous side roads. Turn left (north) onto Forest Route 700 at mile 21.9 (9,890). In another 0.2 mile, take the right fork onto Forest Route 104, a rough four-wheel drive road, toward Rabbit Ears Divide.

Now the CDT regains the course of the Divide, which runs along the ridge on the right (south). The road switchbacks up the hill to mile 23.6 (10,890) where it tops out on the Divide ridge. Hyannis Peak comes into view to the northeast at a natural overlook at mile 24.9. Take the left fork of the road as it descends off the ridge in the direction of Hyannis Peak, and enjoy stunning vistas of the Gore Range, Tenmile Range, Mt. Elbert (behind the Gores) and Colorado River Valley to the south, and the Flat Tops Range to the west. This road is occasionally marked by white arrows on sign posts.

At mile 27.6, the bald rocky knob of Hyannis Peak comes into view to the east. Stay on the "main" road, which soon levels out on a wide treeless plateau. At mile 29.6, the road descends for 150 yards before climbing again to a point at mile 30.0 (11,460 feet; N40° 19.83', W106° 18.78') where a marker on the side of the road says "104." This is as far as you can drive, and it is the end of this segment of the CDT. There is no formal parking here, but you have plenty of room to improvise.

OTHER HIKES AND RIDES

No other well-established hiking or biking trails are accessible from this segment.

Hiking near a waterfall

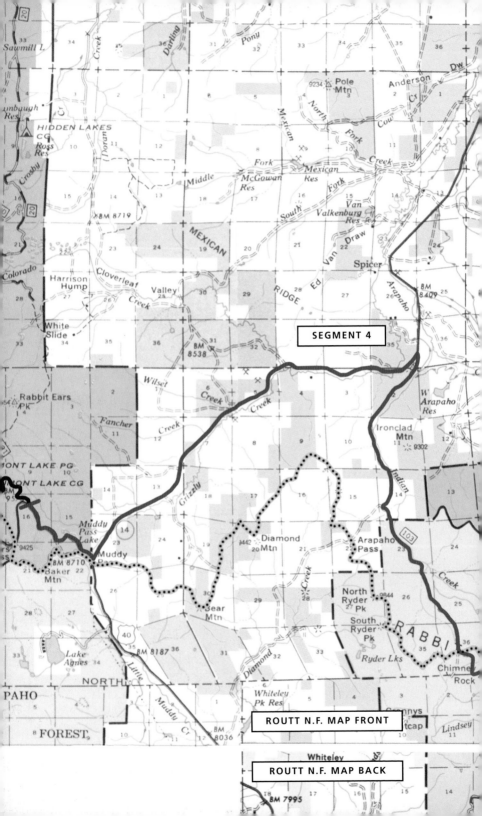

SEGMENT 4

ROUTT N.F. MAP FRONT

ROUTT N.F. MAP BACK

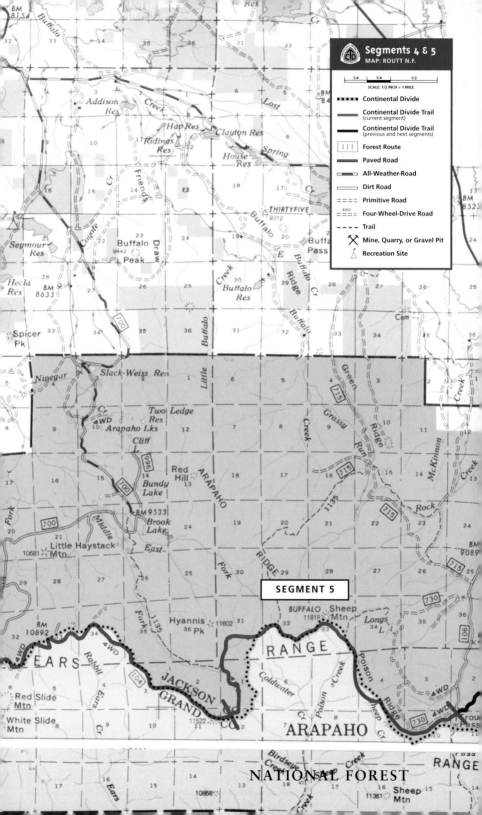

SCALE: 1/2 INCH = 1 MILE

•••••• Continental Divide

——— Continental Divide Trail
(current segment)

——— Continental Divide Trail
(previous and next segments)

111 Forest Route

——— Paved Road

■■■ All-Weather-Road

==== Dirt Road

---- Primitive Road

4WD
==== Four-Wheel-Drive Road

- - - - Trail

⚒ Mine, Quarry, or Gravel Pit

⌂ Recreation Site

SEGMENT 5

NATIONAL FOREST

Segment 5
Forest Route 104 to Troublesome Pass

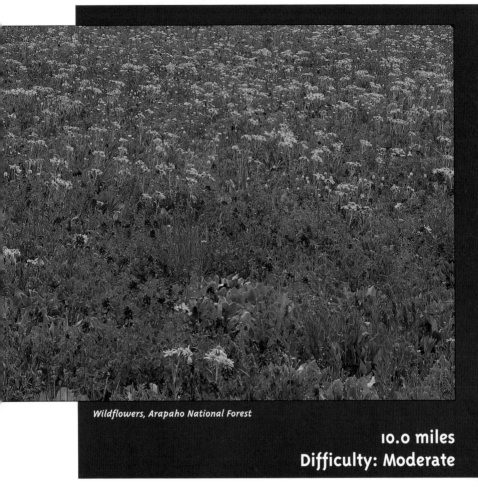

Wildflowers, Arapaho National Forest

10.0 miles
Difficulty: Moderate

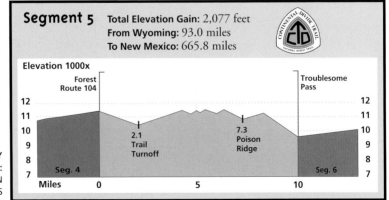

Segment 5 **Total Elevation Gain:** 2,077 feet
From Wyoming: 93.0 miles
To New Mexico: 665.8 miles

CONTINENTAL DIVIDE TRAIL
NATIONAL SCENIC TRAIL

Elevation 1000x

Forest
Route 104

Troublesome
Pass

12

11

10

9

8

7

2.1
Trail
Turnoff

7.3
Poison
Ridge

Seg. 4

Seg. 6

12

11

10

9

8

7

Miles   0   5   10

YOU MAY
ENCOUNTER:
MOUNTAIN
BIKES

DON'T BE FOOLED by this seemingly inauspicious, non-wilderness segment of the trail. It may be one of the least-visited, best-kept secrets of the CDT, as it stays true to the Divide for most of its course, offers stunning views from high treeless ridges, and feels more remote and secretive than many wilderness areas while it takes the hiker into the heart of the Rabbit Ears Range. The area east of Hyannis Peak in particular merits a rest day for the solitude-seeking through-hiker.

After the crossing of the headwaters of Arapaho Creek, at mile 3.1, there is no water until you reach an intermittent stream 12 miles ahead at mile 5.1 of Segment 6. This may be dry in late summer; see the introduction to Segment 6 for more on the scarce water in this area.

MOUNTAIN BIKE NOTES: Biking is possible over parts of this segment, but be prepared to push your bike in some places.

MAPS

TRAILS ILLUSTRATED: 115

USGS QUADRANGLES: Whiteley Peak, Hyannis Peak, Parkview Mountain

USFS: Routt National Forest and Arapaho/Roosevelt National Forests, pages 68–69

ACCESS

Distance from graded road			
9.2 miles	+	7.8 miles	

FOREST ROUTE 104: From US-40, travel 10.2 miles northeast on Colorado Highway 14 and turn right (east) at a sign for Indian Creek. Continue 6.7 miles and turn left (east), staying on Forest Route 103 and avoiding the numerous side roads. After another 2.5 miles, turn left (north) and follow Forest Route 700 for 0.2 mile. Take a right fork onto Forest Route 104 and head toward Rabbit Ears Divide. Now the road becomes rougher and may require a four-wheel drive.

After 2.8 miles, take the left fork of the road as it descends off the ridge. This road is occasionally marked by white arrows on sign posts. Stay on the "main" road for 5 miles; then look for a marker on the side of the road that says "104." This is as far as you can drive. There is no formal parking here, but you'll have plenty of room to improvise.

Distance from graded road
12.0 miles

TROUBLESOME PASS: See the next segment.

Never

does nature

say one thing

and wisdom

another.

—Juvenal,

Satires

RANGER DISTRICT:
Parks

SUPPLIES, SERVICES, AND ACCOMMODATIONS
There are no towns conveniently close to the trail.

TRAIL DESCRIPTION From the 104 sign, face north (left as you approach from the last segment), and walk to a sign that says "711" about 30 yards away. Turn right (east) and follow the trail's departure from the Divide as it descends on an old roadbed. On the third switchback, at mile 0.6, avoid a faint road spur to the right (south) and follow the switchback around to the left. Eighty yards beyond this, take the right (northeast) fork in the road and descend through a thick and healthy spruce-fir ecosystem.

At mile 1.2, the road appears to bottom out in a flat spot and then continue slightly uphill to the north. This is the mischievous work of trail gnomes, however, as the real CDT switchbacks downhill to the left and continues to the southwest. At mile 1.4, resist the temptation to shortcut switchbacks as the road describes a long sweep to the right (north) before following a tributary of Arapaho Creek to the bottom of the valley. The road crosses back over the streambed at mile 1.7. Then it seems to disappear in a clearing next to the stream at mile 2.0. This area offers some of the best camping on this segment. Walk downhill, parallel to the stream (slightly west of north), for about 100 yards to where the road continues into the trees. At mile 2.1 (10,449), just after the road climbs to the northwest away from the stream, turn right (north) onto a single-track trail.

Now the CDT climbs steadily, crossing the streambed under the rocky knob of Hyannis Peak at mile 3.1, then switchbacking up the slope to the east. This is the last reliable water for 12 miles.

The trail fades as it approaches the ridge at mile 4.0. Turn slightly to the right (northeast) and walk 35 yards to a post on top of the ridge. Turn right (east) and spot a faint trail 150 yards away on the left side of the hill. Follow this trail through some trees to the northeast, where the CDT regains the Divide at mile 4.2 (11,500).

The trail follows this ridge for 0.3 mile before descending sharply toward the saddle to the east, which it reaches at mile 4.7 (11,160). Now the trail climbs past a sign for Trail #1135 before it reaches an intersection 0.2 mile farther at a similar sign. Turn right (southeast) and follow the gradually fainter trail toward the top of the ridge. Walk over the hill to the south and pick up the trail as it trends southeast toward the treeless ridge. At mile 5.2 (11,334), the trail fades near a post in the saddle of the ridge; continue straight ahead to the southeast, staying below and left of a knoll. From the crest of the next ridge, look for the trail slightly to the left (due east), traversing across the north slope of Point 11,526.

The CDT bends to the right at mile 5.5 and disappears at a wooden post. Proceed straight ahead 100 yards to another post; then head straight down the hill in front of you. Note the interesting hoodoo rock formations at mile 5.9. At mile 6.0 (11,240), start the steep ascent of the southwest flank of Sheep Mountain. After exiting the last few trees, walk to the second cairn and look slightly to the left (northeast) for a small growth of krummholz. Pass this on the uphill side; then maintain a constant elevation across the rocky slope for 100 yards to where the trail is again visible. Now enjoy your tour of the dry environment of the timberline tundra. Note the proliferation of plant life in the shade of the trees.

You'll pass a gigantic cairn at mile 6.7. A second cairn 100 yards farther marks the point where you can see the next destination, Poison Ridge, to the right (southeast). Follow the CDT's sharp descent to its intersection with the ridge, marked by a cairn at mile 6.9 (11,220). The nearest bald mountain to the east is Haystack Mountain, and just to its left is Parkview Mountain, over which the Divide—and the trail—will pass in a few miles. Follow the CDT down the ridge to the right (south) to where it disappears in a clearing full of standing dead trees at mile 7.3 (10,900). Walk slightly to the left (east) toward a rocky summit to regain the trail. Now the trail climbs until cresting Poison Ridge's south side at mile 8.3 (11,200) where it descends southeast into a spruce-fir forest at mile 8.7. At mile 9.9, you'll reach a jumble of roads at Troublesome Pass where a sign thanking volunteers gives the first indication in some time that this is, in fact, the CDT. Walk to the road, turn 90 degrees to the left (northeast), and walk toward a white road-closure sign across the intersection. This is the beginning of the next segment (mile 10.0; 9,698 feet; N40° 19.96', W106° 12.67').

MOUNTAIN BIKE RIDES

Although the best hiking is on the CDT itself, there are many excellent mountain biking possibilities in this area, particularly for those who prefer dirt roads to single-track trails. A maze of old roads near Troublesome Pass warrant exploration.

POISON RIDGE ROAD
Approximate one-way distance: 6 miles
Difficulty: Moderate

Trailhead: Troublesome Pass. See driving directions under *Access* in the next segment.

Ride or drive to Troublesome Pass and then follow Poison Ridge Road west and south to its remote end near Matheson Reservoir.

You may also wish to explore along the CDT toward Poison Ridge, or take Forest Route 730 north to Longs Lake, which offers loop possibilities.

Segment 6
Troublesome Pass to Willow Creek Pass

Along the trail, Arapaho National Forest

15.6 miles
Difficulty: Strenuous

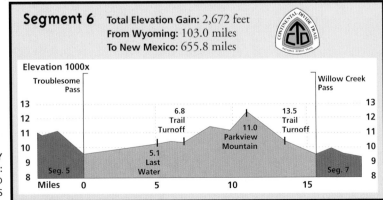

Segment 6   **Total Elevation Gain:** 2,672 feet
From Wyoming: 103.0 miles
To New Mexico: 655.8 miles

Elevation 1000x

Troublesome Pass

Willow Creek Pass

13
12
11
10
9
8

6.8 Trail Turnoff

5.1 Last Water

11.0 Parkview Mountain

13.5 Trail Turnoff

Seg. 5

Seg. 7

Miles   0   5   10   15

YOU MAY
ENCOUNTER:
MOTORIZED
VEHICLES

THIS SEGMENT BEGINS in a maze of roads and trails
that are marked only occasionally with posts. It then follows a
motorized road to the west ridge of Parkview Mountain, and on
to that mountain's summit at 12,296 feet. This rigorous crossing
of Parkview Mountain ends with a steep, rocky descent that leads
eventually to Willow Creek Pass.

There is no water between a stream at the 5.1-mile point
and a stream in the valley at mile 22.4. Both may be dry during
late summer. The next reliable water is another 5.1 miles ahead,
at mile 1.9 of the next segment. In a pinch, there are numerous
streams within one or two miles of the trail, in the drainages
running perpendicular to the Divide. A descent to any of these
should be planned using a map.

 MOUNTAIN BIKE NOTES: The roads around
Troublesome Pass are rideable, but the climb to Parkview
Mountain and the abundant fragile tundra on this segment are
not suited to bikes.

MAPS

TRAILS ILLUSTRATED: 115

USGS QUADRANGLES: Parkview Mountain, Radial Mountain

USFS: Routt National Forest and Arapaho/Roosevelt
National Forests, page 81

ACCESS

Distance from graded road	🚗 12.0 miles

TROUBLESOME PASS: From the summit of
Willow Creek Pass on Colorado Highway 125,
drive north about 5.5 miles to a turnoff on the
left for Willow Creek Road (Forest Route 106). Follow this road
west, then south, about 12 miles to an intersection of several dirt
roads just north of the summit of Troublesome Pass. Parking is
plentiful. The CDT arrives from the west at a sign thanking trail
volunteers, and it departs to the east at a white road closure sign.

Smooth road to trailhead	🚗

WILLOW CREEK PASS TRAILHEAD:
See the next segment.

TRAIL DESCRIPTION From the white road closure sign on
the east side of the intersection, descend to the northeast along

---

Edible, *adj.:*

Good to eat,

and wholesome

to digest,

as a worm to a toad,

a toad to a snake,

a snake to a pig,

a pig to a man,

and a man

to a worm.

—Ambrose Bierce,

The Devil's Dictionary

RANGER DISTRICTS:
Parks
Sulphur

an old road behind the sign. If you are on a road that is open to traffic, you are going the wrong way. The Divide now runs along the top of the ridge to the right (south). Avoid side roads and trails here. At mile 0.7, a post marks a spot where the road appears to switchback to the left; ignore this and continue straight ahead (northeast) to another post on the other side of the road and continue along the single-track trail. Follow a roadcut straight ahead through the trees to another post at mile 0.8. Pass this post on the left and continue along the single-track trail as it descends to the northwest along the crest of the Divide. At mile 0.9, the trail bends sharply left (west) and rejoins an old roadbed after 100 yards, marked by a wooden post. Follow this roadbed west to mile 1.1 where it swings back to the right (northeast). The landscape here is criss-crossed by a network of roads through the forest. The peak dominating the horizon is Haystack Mountain.

At mile 1.7, avoid the intersecting road that climbs away to the right (south), and continue straight ahead (east). The CDT now follows a better road (open to motor vehicles) to the northeast 0.2 mile to a switchback to the left. Avoid this and continue straight ahead (north) past a post where the trail regains an old closed roadbed. Follow its northerly trend past occasional posts to a point at mile 2.4 where it curves back to the left (northwest) and meets a well-graded dirt road. Turn right onto this road and follow its curve to the north.

At mile 3.3, ignore a post on the right and continue straight. Haystack Mountain is now visible to the south. The road bends left and trends generally north-ward at mile 4.4 (10,300). A small intermittent stream, the only source of water on this segment, crosses the road at mile 5.1. The trees open occasionally on the west side of this stretch, revealing tremendous views of Poison Ridge and Sheep Mountain on the previous segment, and of Haystack Mountain to the south. The hiker will gaze down on all of these in just a few miles.

At mile 6.8 (10,460 feet; N40° 21,57', W106° 11.28'), the road curves to the left while a post on the right marks the CDT's departure uphill to the right (northeast). Now the trail turns gradually to the east and then south as it climbs steadily along yet another old roadbed. At mile 7.1, take the right fork as indicated by a wooden post. This segment's first CDT marker, which is tacked to a tree at mile 7.2, indicates a right turn to the southeast into the trees. Follow an overgrown roadbed to its disappearance at a large clearing at mile 7.3. Follow wooden posts to work southeast across the clearing along a faint single-track trail. A series of small fortress-like structures line the ridge to your left (north). Please leave them undisturbed.

Fifty yards past the third post you will be tempted to turn right (south). Don't. Instead, continue straight ahead to the southeast. At the far side of the clearing, at mile 7.5, follow an old roadcut leading up through the trees to the southeast. In 0.1 mile, a CDT marker indicates a right turn (south) along a single-track trail. This is occasionally faint, but it goes straight up the hill slightly east of south. As the trail fades at the top of the hill, walk 15 yards to a flat grassy spot in the trees to the southwest at mile 7.8 (10,972).

Follow posts across the treeless ridge as it trends slightly east of south. Now enjoy a different perspective of Haystack Mountain to the southwest across which the Divide runs on its way to the summit of Parkview Mountain. As you drop into a minor saddle at mile 8.0 (11,100), look for a post high on the horizon straight ahead, still slightly east of south, and eventually climb toward it. Look left (southeast) for the next two posts along the ridge, and regain the Divide at mile 8.5 (11,480). Continue slightly north of east to the next post. Stay on the ridge as it curves to the right (east).

Follow friendly Forest Service posts along the crest of the ridge. From a post at the low saddle at mile 9.8 (11,140), look for a post high on the point to the southeast, which is the next destination. Climb via two intermediate posts halfway up the slope on the right to avoid creating multiple trails. You'll reach the post on the ridge at mile 10.3 where the ridge becomes a little less steep, and where you may be asking yourself, do I really want to hike the CDT? Can this guy use the word "post" one more time in this paragraph? Answer: Follow the posts and the ridge line to the lookout on the summit at mile 11.0 (12,296).

Colorado has a lot of mountains, and you will think you can see them all from here. The volcano-shaped hump to the northeast is Radial Mountain, and beyond that are the skyscrapers of the Never Summer Wilderness. Behind these are the peaks of Rocky Mountain National Park, and further south the Indian Peaks Wilderness. To the west and south, you can see numerous ranges, including the Flat Tops, Gore, Tenmile, Collegiate, Mosquito, and Front Ranges.

The CDT now leaves the Divide, which follows the steep north ridge of Parkview Mountain. Spot a faint trail passing a cairn to the southeast in the direction of the next point, which is 0.3 mile distant and topped by a cairn. Follow the faint trail, but be sure to break off to the left (northeast) and climb to the cairned point that was visible from the summit. Follow more cairns down the steep, rocky slope to the northeast. Don't be seduced by the grassy ridge leading off to the right (south).

After descending a couple of hundred yards, it is easier going on the right (east) side where tundra grass provides better footing than do the rocks. When you reach a cairn just above the krummholz at about 11,800 feet, the trail swings to the left (north) at mile 11.5. Continue to follow cairns north and west into the valley. If at any point during the descent you are unable to see the lookout high on the summit to the left, then you have gone astray.

Near the valley floor, work your way down a steep slope toward what appears to be an old roadbed just on the other side of the bottom of the basin. Reach this roadbed at mile 11.9 (11,080) and follow it as it curves around to the right (east, then south), passing by CDT markers. Descend east along the road to a spot at mile 12.4 where it bends to the north and climbs a small hill to an intersection with another road. Turn right (east) and continue along this road. At mile 13.5 (10,440 feet; N40° 20.42', W106° 6.79') a sign on the right says "Trail" with an arrow pointing to the left, just before a large switchback to the right. Walk 20 yards past this sign and turn left (northeast) onto the intersecting road. A CDT sign on the right at mile 13.8 indicates the trail's split to the right (north) onto an older road. The ridge to the north is the Continental Divide, which the trail now parallels all the way down to Willow Creek Pass.

The CDT now descends to the east in a nice lodgepole forest through which the tiny dot of Parkview Mountain's lookout is occasionally visible behind you to the west. At mile 14.9, follow two CDT markers as the road swings to the right (southeast). At mile 15.4 the CDT describes a gentle curve to the right (south) marking a point where a single-track trail takes off to the left (northeast). Follow this trail to the end of the segment. If you miss this trail, which is difficult to see, you will reach the highway a few hundred yards ahead, where you should turn left and walk to the pass summit.

The trail reaches Willow Creek Pass at mile 15.6 (9,620 feet; N40° 21.01', W106° 5.41'). Cross the road for the beginning of the next segment.

As with Segment 5, there are many dirt roads here for mountain biking.

SUPPLIES, SERVICES, AND ACCOMMODATIONS

RAND is a small town that offers limited services. It is north of the trail on Colorado Highway 125.

Distance from Trail: 10 miles

Zip Code: 80473

Bank	None	
Bus	None	
Camping	None	
Dining	None	
Gear	The Rand Store, P.O. Box 8	(970) 723-4300
	Closed Tuesday. Coleman fuel and snacks. Open 9-6.	
Groceries	The Rand Store	
Information	The Rand Store	
Laundry	None	
Lodging	None	
Medical	None	
Post Office	U.S. Post Office, Rand	723-4434
Showers	None	

SPECIAL NOTES: Regarding hitchhiking, traffic over the pass into Rand is moderate.

OTHER HIKES

PARKVIEW MOUNTAIN

Approximate one-way distance: 2.0 miles with four-wheel drive;
6.0 miles without

Difficulty: Strenuous

Trailhead: About 5 miles south of Willow Creek Pass on Colorado Highway 125, travel west on the Mulstay Jeep Road (Forest Route 258) 4.0 miles to the trailhead.

The climb of the mountain's southeast ridge is straightforward and almost straight up. The Continental Divide runs across the peak's summit, and the views are astounding.

MOOSE IN COLORADO

Moose once roamed much of the area around Colorado's Continental Divide, enjoying relative immunity from predators while basking in the plentiful woodlands and marshes. But their numbers plummeted at the beginning of the 20th century, due to hunting and other human pressures. Colorado remained virtually moose-free until the late 1970s when the Colorado Division of Wildlife consummated its reintroduction program in the northern part of the state.

In 1978 and 1979, 24 moose were transplanted to the Big Bottom area of the Illinois River basin (just north of the Continental Divide). Healthy growth in the population, combined with introductions in the nearby Laramie River basin, have helped the moose expand their range east to Rocky Mountain National Park and south to the areas around and Kremmling and Fraser.

The population has grown to about 525, a level the Division of Wildlife attempts to maintain through hunting. About 100 hunting permits have been issued each year since 1993.

Sightings are not common, but the hopeful wildlife viewer may have good luck near marshes and the calm streams of meadowed areas where moose enjoy a diet of willow trees, water lilies, and other riparian plants. They are more active at night, but you may catch a glimpse of one at any time.

Humans should maintain a healthy distance from these large animals because they are not as predictable as deer and elk. The highly protective cows may charge if they feel their young are threatened, and bulls in rut in the fall may charge anything for no apparent reason. Cows may reach 1,100 pounds—bulls 1,400 — and they can reach speeds of 35 m.p.h. To avoid being hit by the backcountry version of a Mac truck, use common sense in moose country.

Of course, unpleasant moose encounters are less common than lightning strikes, and we are lucky to have this colorful addition to the wildlife along the Continental Divide Trail. Photo opportunities are most likely along the stretch of trail from Colorado Highway 14 east to Grand Lake.

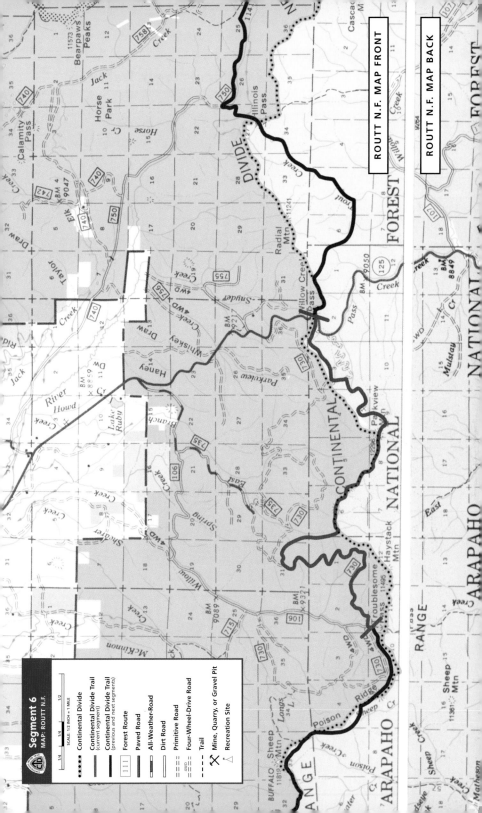

ROUTT N.F. MAP FRONT

ROUTT N.F. MAP BACK

Segment 6
MAP: ROUTT N.F.

SCALE: 1/2 INCH = 1 MILE

1/4   1/2   1

— — — Continental Divide

········· Continental Divide Trail
(current segment)

━━━━ Continental Divide Trail
(previous and next segments)

▭▭▭ Forest Route

━━━━ Paved Road

━━━━ All-Weather Road

━━━━ Dirt Road

— — — Primitive Road

4WD — — — Four-Wheel-Drive Road

— — — Trail

✕ Mine, Quarry, or Gravel Pit

⚠ Recreation Site

Segment 7
Willow Creek Pass to Illinois Creek Trailhead

Aspen forest, autumn in the Arapaho National Forest

9.9 miles
Difficulty: Moderate

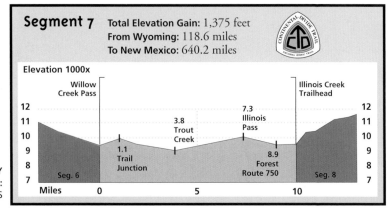

Segment 7   **Total Elevation Gain:** 1,375 feet
From Wyoming: 118.6 miles
To New Mexico: 640.2 miles

Elevation 1000x

Willow Creek Pass

7.3 Illinois Pass

Illinois Creek Trailhead

3.8 Trout Creek

1.1 Trail Junction

8.9 Forest Route 750

Seg. 6

Seg. 8

Miles   0   5   10

YOU MAY ENCOUNTER: MOTORBIKES

THIS SEGMENT WILL APPEAL to those who enjoy the cozy solitude of the woods, as it leaves the Divide in order to follow established trails and remains below timberline for its entire length. It is open to motorbikes, but they seem to be infrequent visitors here, and the delightful forest and meadow areas should not be missed. Water is plentiful, and this is prime moose habitat.

 MOUNTAIN BIKE NOTES: This segment is almost all single-track and occasionally a little rough. It has excellent moderate technical riding.

MAPS

TRAILS ILLUSTRATED: 115
USGS QUADRANGLES: Radial Mountain, Jack Creek Ranch, Mount Richthofen
USFS: Arapaho/Roosevelt National Forests and Routt National Forest, page 85

ACCESS

| Smooth road to trailhead 🚗 | **WILLOW CREEK PASS TRAILHEAD:** Drive 22 miles north of US-40 on Colorado Highway 125 to a pullout on the right (east) side of the road at the summit of the pass. Markers indicate the trail's continuation on both sides of the highway. |

| Distance from graded road 🚗 4.0 miles | **ILLINOIS CREEK TRAILHEAD:** See the next segment. |

SUPPLIES, SERVICES, AND ACCOMMODATIONS

The small town of Rand has limited services. It is north on Colorado Highway 125. (See Segment 6, page 78.)

TRAIL DESCRIPTION The trailhead is marked by a CDT signpost just to the right of the kiosk. The trail begins in a dazzling garden of wildflowers as it climbs immediately to the east, then stays in the northern shadow of the Divide until mile 0.4, where it crosses to the south side to follow the Divide proper to an intersecting trail at mile 1.1 (9,986). Turn right (south) as indicated by a sign, and follow the trail as it descends away from the Divide to the southeast.

Cross a tributary of Pass Creek at mile 1.9 (9,550) and climb steeply out of the valley. Meander through a lodgepole forest to mile 3.8 (9,060) where a CDT signpost next to a large

Silently

one by one,

in the infinite

meadows

of heaven,

blossomed

the lovely stars,

the forget-me-nots

of the angels.

—Henry Wadsworth
Longfellow,
Evangeline

RANGER DISTRICTS:
Sulphur
Parks

meadow indicates the trail's turn to the left (northeast). The trail now ascends along the small, delightfully meadowed valley of Trout Creek.

Avoid the trail splitting off to the right at mile 6.1 and continue straight ahead to the northeast, as indicated by the CDT marker. Up until this point the trail has been open to motorcycles; now it is also accessible to small four-wheel vehicles. When you're lucky enough to avoid the motorized roar, you may spot elk or moose in the large meadow.

The trail now climbs more steeply to cross the Divide at obscure Illinois Pass at mile 7.3 (10,020). As the trail descends from the Divide it soon widens into a road, reaching the Illinois River and well-graded Forest Route 750 at mile 8.9 (9,600). This is a convenient pick-up point for segment hikers (see trailhead access description for Segment 8). Turn right (east) onto the road and continue to the Illinois Creek Trailhead sign on the left (north) side of the road at mile 9.9 (9,650 feet). As you walk up the road, the peaks of the Never Summer Wilderness loom in front of you, steering the Continental Divide north and east toward Rocky Mountain National Park. This is the end of the segment.

MOUNTAIN BIKE RIDES

Although hiking other than on the CDT is limited, there are many possibilities for mountain biking—especially loops.

ILLINOIS PASS AND WILLOW PASS TRAILS

Approximate loop distance:	20 miles
Mode of travel:	Biking
Difficulty:	Moderate

Illinois Pass Trailhead: Drive about 6.0 miles south from Willow Creek Pass and turn left (east) onto Stillwater Pass Road. Continue about 3.5 miles to the trailhead on the left (north) side of the road.

This is a fun ride with some variety. Ride north to the Willow Pass Trail, which is also the CDT. Turn left (south) and continue to a climb through trees to the Divide. Leave the CDT and continue north to Forest Route 755; then follow Colorado Highway 125 south to Stillwater Pass Road. To avoid the highway section, make this into a shuttle or an out-and-back.

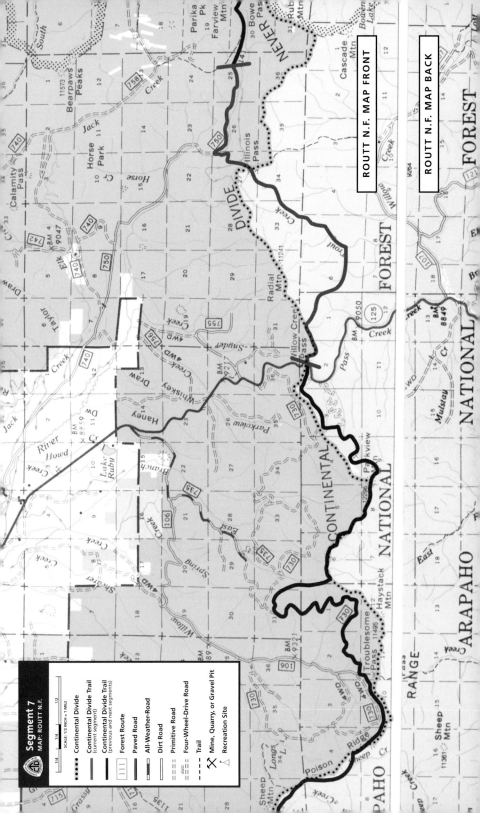

Segment 7
MAP: ROUTT N.F.

SCALE: 1/2 INCH = 1 MILE

1/4   1/4   1/2

····· Continental Divide

──── Continental Divide Trail (current segment)

──── Continental Divide Trail (previous and next segments)

|1 1 1| Forest Route

──── Paved Road

──── All-Weather-Road

──── Dirt Road

═══ Primitive Road

4WD Four-Wheel-Drive Road

──── Trail

⚒ Mine, Quarry, or Gravel Pit

△ Recreation Site

ROUTT N.F. MAP FRONT

ROUTT N.F. MAP BACK

Segment 8
Illinois Creek Trailhead to North Supply Trailhead

Never Summer Mountains

10.7 miles
Difficulty: Strenuous

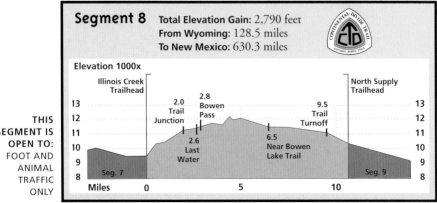

Segment 8 **Total Elevation Gain:** 2,790 feet
From Wyoming: 128.5 miles
To New Mexico: 630.3 miles

Elevation 1000x

THIS
SEGMENT IS
OPEN TO:
FOOT AND
ANIMAL
TRAFFIC
ONLY

THIS SEGMENT CONTAINS the beginning of the CDT's wide sweep far from the actual Divide. This conspicuous detour is a result of the reluctance of the National Park Service to allow the CDT to traverse Rocky Mountain National Park. For now, the trail follows the logging roads, foot paths, and paved roads that skirt the park's southwestern edge. This is somewhat unfortunate because this is a spectacular section of the Divide that traverses peak after rugged peak. Still, I understand the Park Service's desire to ensure the pristine character of this land, and leaving the Divide for a while provides the opportunity to enjoy its magnificence from a distance. We might even be grateful, from this vantage point, to have been spared the arduous task of navigating those sharp crags.

Hikers planning to stay truer to the Divide should be aware of the permit requirements and camping restrictions inside Rocky Mountain National Park. For more information, write to: Rocky Mountain National Park, Backcountry Office, Estes Park, CO 80517; or phone 970-586-2371.

An eight-mile stretch on this segment is devoid of water and offers only limited unexposed camping. Backpackers should read through this section and plan their trip accordingly.

MOUNTAIN BIKE NOTES: Because of the trail's passage through the Never Summer Wilderness, bikes are prohibited on this segment.

MAPS

TRAILS ILLUSTRATED: 115
USGS QUADRANGLES: Mount Richthofen, Bowen Mountain
USFS: Arapaho/Roosevelt National Forests, Routt National Forest, pages 92–93

ACCESS

ILLINOIS CREEK TRAILHEAD: From the summit of Willow Creek Pass on Colorado Highway 125, travel north 8 miles and turn right at a sign that says "Old Homestead." After 0.6 mile, take a right fork and continue 3.4 miles to a large parking area at the trailhead, which is marked by a sign on the left (north) side of the road. Note that one mile before reaching the trailhead, the CDT joins the main road from the right (south) side and continues east along the same road you are driving on.

NORTH SUPPLY TRAILHEAD:
See the next segment.

The whole secret

of the study

of nature

lies in learning

how to use

one's eyes.

—George Sand

RANGER DISTRICTS:
Parks
Sulphur

SUPPLIES, SERVICES, AND ACCOMMODATIONS
The small town of Rand has a few services, but this is not the best segment from which to get there. Follow the road the trailhead is on back to the west and northwest to Colorado Highway 125. Rand is a few miles north of this intersection. Hitchhiking is not an option here.

TRAIL DESCRIPTION   Follow the Illinois Creek Trail (also called Never Summer Trail #1141) up an immediately formidable climb. The CDT crosses a small stream at 0.3 mile and continues its steady climb before leveling off from mile 0.5 to 1.0 (10,400) where it resumes its climb through a series of switchbacks. It's okay to let out a yelp of relief and satisfaction when you pass a sign prohibiting motor vehicles at mile 1.2.

As you enter the meadows at the base of Illinois Creek's beautiful headwater cirque at mile 1.6 (10,800), there is a stream on the left (north) side of the trail and, for the creative camper, a few flat spots to pitch a tent. These meadows offer the last viable campsites before the trail scales Bowen Pass and remains above timberline for several miles. A CDT signpost at mile 2.0 (11,180) marks the intersection with a trail heading to the left (north) around Farview Mountain. Stay to the right.

As the trail turns due south at mile 2.4, you are faced with the barren slopes of Ruby Mountain, up whose northeast ridge you will soon be trudging. The trail descends slightly to a stream at mile 2.6 (11,330), marking the last reliable water for eight miles, so be sure to stock up. Now the CDT begins its sharp ascent to regain the Divide at Bowen Pass. It is advisable to time your hiking so you'll be hiking in the morning before the brewing thunderclouds have had a chance to focus their wrath on this exposed section of the trail. A short prayer to Mounts Cumulus and Nimbus, just northeast of here, couldn't hurt either.

At mile 2.8, the CDT reaches the 11,476-foot summit of Bowen Pass (N40° 21.83', W105° 56.64') and, with it, the Great Divide, whose path to the east (left) leads to Rocky Mountain National Park. The trail leading downhill to the south into an idyllic green meadow in the Never Summer Wilderness is tempting, but the path of the hardy Divide hiker is not so coddling! The CDT turns right (west) and traces the boundary of the Never Summer Wilderness as it follows the Divide's strenuous path up Ruby Mountain. An interesting note: this section of trail is one of only two that follow the Divide in its northerly direction (that is, back toward Wyoming). Thankfully this is the case for only a short distance!

The trail is faint on this rocky slope. It does not cross over Point 11,876, but it follows a contour around the knob's northwest (right) flank, marked by cairns that stand like solitary sentinels on the tundra.

The CDT soon climbs back to the Divide ridge, reaching it at a cairn at mile 3.4 (11,820). A high point 30 yards to the south offers a panoramic view of the crags of the Indian Peaks to the southeast and, to the west and north, much of the Divide that the through-hiker has already covered. The scoured slopes of Parkview Mountain rise to the west, while further north across the sagebrush sea of North Park you can see the peaks of the Mount Zirkel Wilderness. East (right) of these are the tops of the western-most peaks of Rocky Mountain National Park.

The trail now heads almost due south toward Ruby Mountain, which it skirts to the west (right), passing through the mountain's morning shadow at mile 3.8 (11,740). The CDT is again faint here. Watch for cairns, and maintain a roughly even contour as you aim for the saddle between Ruby Mountain and Point 12,198 at mile 4.1. Now the trail is virtually non-existent; please practice low-impact hiking by avoiding the delicate alpine plant life. Climb the steep slope toward the nearest high point directly to the south, which is Point 12,198. Sparsely positioned rock cairns offer occasional reassurance that you are on the true path.

At mile 4.4 (12,140), skirt the rocky summit of Point 12,198 to the right (west), as indicated by the cairns. As you reach the flat plateau at the top of your climb, say good-bye to the Divide for the next 46 miles. (It breaks off along a ridge to the west.) Look ahead for a cairn to the southwest; then follow cairns and a faint trail downhill to the south. The horizon straight ahead is dominated by the awesome peaks of Summit County's Gore and Tenmile Ranges, through which CDT through-hikers will pass in a few weeks.

At mile 4.7, the trail begins a gentle climb around the west (right) side of Cascade Mountain. At mile 5.4 (12,040), as the trail clears the west ridge of this peak, Lake Granby and Shadow Mountain Reservoir come into view to the southeast. The CDT runs along the eastern shores of these lakes, while the Divide itself follows the precipitous path of the high peaks in the background.

Just after this initial view, you'll see a cairn and not much of a trail. Traverse downhill to an obscure cairn to the southeast. Continue in this general direction until you reach another small cairn at mile 5.6. Do not go too low; your direction of travel should be away from the long barren draw that descends into the valley. From this cairn, turn a bit to the east (left) and follow a faint trail past a cairn on the horizon of the ridge. Then head down and away from Cascade Mountain, still punctuated by cairns, to a point at mile 5.9 where the trail becomes, and remains, very visible.

At mile 6.3, take in the view below and to the east (left) of scenic Bowen Lake, a popular fishing destination. The trail fades 100 yards ahead; continue straight ahead and up a hill cleft by a rocky notch. Follow the ridge past the CDT signpost at mile 6.5 (11,520) toward the signs at the other end of the ridge, which mark the intersection with the trail descending to Bowen Lake as well as the CDT's exit, much too soon, from the Never Summer Wilderness.

Follow the CDT to the southeast, straight past the signs. At mile 8.2 (11,280), just before you enter the trees, check out the view to the east (left) of Shadow Mountain Lake, which is the destination of the next segment. At mile 8.4, a trail junction is marked by a sign indicating North Supply down to the left. Even though North Supply is your eventual destination, continue straight ahead along the Wolverine Trail. At mile 9.0, there is an old Forest Service signpost; 60 yards beyond this, avoid the turnoff on the right to Lost Lake via the Wolverine Bypass Trail. Pass a CDT signpost after another 80 yards. At mile 9.5 (11,100 feet; N40° 17.77', W105° 55.94'), turn left (east) at a T intersection, as indicated by a CDT signpost. Now the trail describes a steady descent to this segment's end.

At mile 10.3, reach a gate adorned with an abundance of signs and arrows; simply continue straight along the road to the east. North Supply Creek, at mile 10.6, provides the first water since the ascent to Bowen Pass. The parking lot at North Supply Trailhead, the terminus of this segment, is at mile 10.7 (10,440 feet; N40° 18.00', W105° 55.20').

OTHER HIKES

Please remember that these hikes are in the Never Summer Wilderness.

NEVER SUMMER TRAIL
Approximate one-way distance: 6.0–25.0 miles
Difficulty: Moderate / Strenuous

Bowen/Baker Trailhead: This trailhead is located a short distance north of the town of Grand Lake on the west side of Trail Ridge Road.

The trail climbs through 6.0 miles of old-growth forest, alpine meadows, and impressive peaks with names like Cirrus and Cumulus on its way to the heart of the Never Summer Wilderness. This initial foray will take you to scenic Baker Pass, where you may turn around or continue north for fantastic views above timberline.

For a varied and convenient shuttle hike, leave a car at the Colorado River Trailhead, a few miles north of Bowen/Baker, and take a few days to reach it via Lake Agnes, Michigan Lakes, and Thunder Pass.

FARVIEW MOUNTAIN LOOP
Approximate loop distance: 9.0 miles
Difficulty: Strenuous

Illinois Creek Trailhead: See *Access* for this segment.

Follow this segment's directions along the Illinois Creek Trail to Bowen Pass at mile 2.8. From the pass, turn left (northeast), follow the Divide ridge cross-country to the top of Farview Mountain, and discover why this peak is so appropriately named. Then descend north to the trail. Follow it west, and then south, back to the Illinois Creek Trail.

Camping near a lake

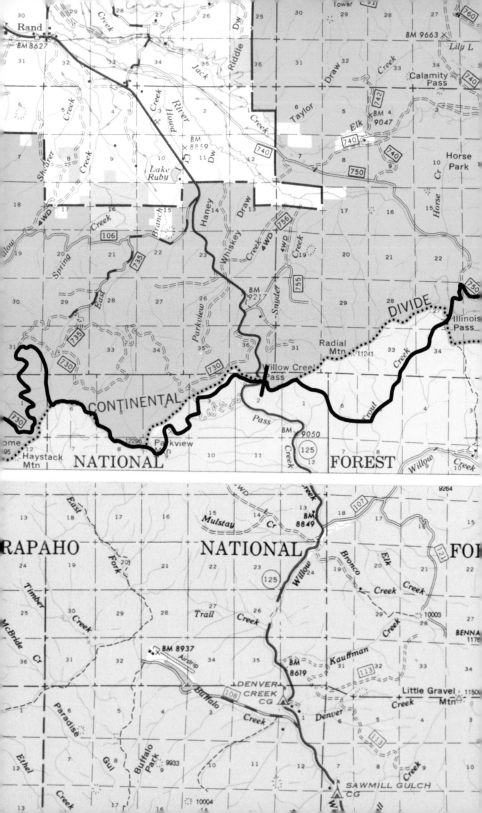

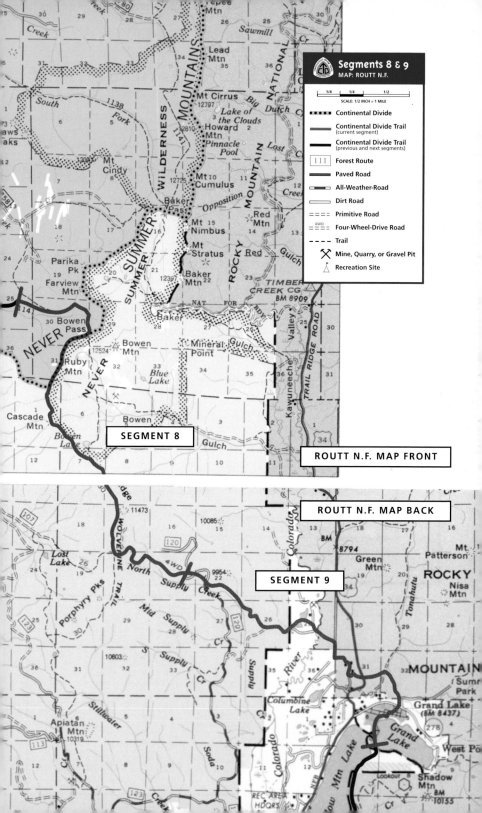

Segments 8 & 9
MAP: ROUTT N.F.

SCALE: 1/2 INCH = 1 MILE

••••••	Continental Divide
▬▬▬	Continental Divide Trail (current segment)
▬▬▬	Continental Divide Trail (previous and next segments)
111	Forest Route
▬▬▬	Paved Road
▭▭▭	All-Weather-Road
=====	Dirt Road
-----	Primitive Road
≡≡≡	Four-Wheel-Drive Road
- - -	Trail
⚒	Mine, Quarry, or Gravel Pit
⌂	Recreation Site

SEGMENT 8

ROUTT N.F. MAP FRONT

ROUTT N.F. MAP BACK

SEGMENT 9

Segment 9
North Supply Trailhead to Grand Lake

Colorado River, Rocky Mountain National Park

10.0 miles
Difficulty: Easy

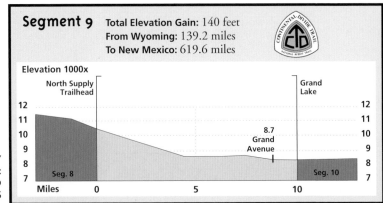

Segment 9   **Total Elevation Gain:** 140 feet
From Wyoming: 139.2 miles
To New Mexico: 619.6 miles

Elevation 1000x

North Supply
Trailhead

Grand
Lake

8.7
Grand
Avenue

	12				12
	11				11
	10				10
	9				9
Seg. 8	8			Seg. 10	8
	7				7

Miles   0   5   10

**YOU MAY
ENCOUNTER:**
MOTORIZED
VEHICLES

THIS SEGMENT may not be interesting to segment hikers, as it begins on an old jeep road, continues onto a heavy-use, graded road, crosses a highway, and reaches its endpoint via a circuitous route along the streets of Grand Lake. More than offering a scenic hike, it provides a link between the wilderness of Segment 8 and the quiet lakeside paths of Segment 10.

You'll pass Rocky Mountain National Park's Kawuneeche Visitor Center at the 6.7-mile point, where water, restrooms, and information are available. It is open every day from 7 a.m. to 7 p.m. during the busy summer season, and 8 a.m. to 5 p.m. from Labor Day to approximately Memorial Day.

Through-hikers may find viable campsites before the 4.3-mile point. The next legal camping is 6.1 miles into the next segment. Please respect the private property through which this segment passes.

 MOUNTAIN BIKE NOTES: A small portion of this segment passes through Rocky Mountain National Park, where bikes are not allowed. The remainder is on jeep or paved roads.

MAPS

TRAILS ILLUSTRATED: 200
USGS QUADRANGLES: Bowen Mountain, Grand Lake, Shadow Mountain
USFS: Arapaho/Roosevelt National Forests, pages 92–93

ACCESS

NORTH SUPPLY TRAILHEAD PARKING LOT: On US-34, drive 4.9 miles south from Grand Lake or 9.4 miles north from US-40 to County Road 4 on the west side of the highway. The turnoff is distinguished by a large sign proclaiming "Storage." Reset your odometer, follow this road 1.8 miles, and bear right at a fork. Proceed to mile 3.0 and turn right again, onto Forest Route 120. Stay on this main road, avoid the many turnoffs, and bear left at the forks at miles 10.6 and 11.5. The parking lot is at mile 12.0.

 GRAND LAKE: See the next segment.

TRAIL DESCRIPTION This segment begins by retracing the last part of its access route. Follow the road out of the east end of the parking lot, walk approximately 100 yards, and turn onto an old jeep road, marked by a sign that says "North Supply Trail," splitting off to the right. At the 1.2- and 1.3-mile points, the trail

Someone said

to Socrates

that a certain man

had grown no better

by his travels.

"I should think not,"

he said;

"he took himself

along with him."

—Michel de

Montaigne

RANGER DISTRICT:
Sulphur

crosses two of the main road's numerous switchbacks. Continue straight across, staying on the jeep road. At mile 1.7 (9,520), the trail reaches the main road for the third time. Cross the road at a 45-degree angle to the right (due south); then turn left (east) onto Forest Route 120.4.

At mile 2.6, take the left fork just after a CDT marker. At mile 3.1, there are some possible campsites on the left. Turn left at the fork at mile 3.7, as indicated by the CDT markers, and follow the trail to an organized camping area near a large RV park at mile 4.3. Stay on the main road as it bears to the north, away from the RV park. For the next 2.3 miles, the trail follows a well-graded, heavily used road that passes through private property. For non-purists, trying to hitch a ride down to the highway may be preferable to breathing the dust of passing vehicles.

At mile 5.0, take a right fork and continue on to US-34 at mile 6.6 (8,700). Cross the highway diagonally to the right and head for the nearby Kawuneeche Visitor Center. Information is available here, as well as an outside water faucet near the women's restroom.

Turn right in front of the Visitor Center and walk to the far (southeast) end of the parking lot where the continuation of the trail is marked by a sign that says "North Inlet and Tonahutu Trailheads." There are no CDT markers here. Follow this wide, well-traveled trail east 0.7 mile to its intersection with an even wider trail at the 7.4-mile point. Turn right (south) toward Grand Lake, and walk 0.1 mile to another fork; follow the path to the left toward Tonahutu Creek.

At mile 8.2 (8,520), the footpath terminates at a parking lot bordered by a large brown building. Walk straight across the parking lot to the southeast and follow a descending dirt road. After 0.2 mile, the road passes ShadowCliff Youth Hostel on the left, a good candidate for a night's lodging. Just past the youth hostel, turn right onto a paved road and proceed 0.2 mile to a stop sign and turn left. Walk down the road into town to a four-way stop at mile 8.7 (8,430). Turn right (west) onto Grand Avenue, the main drag where through-hikers will want to stop for most services.

To complete this segment and reach the beginning of the next one, proceed two blocks along Grand Avenue and turn left onto Vine Street. After another block, turn right at the stop sign; then make an immediate left onto Cairns Avenue. At mile 9.4, follow the road as it bends 90 degrees to the right. Then after another 0.1 mile, turn left onto Jericho Avenue and walk across the bridge. Wind 0.5 mile to the stop sign at Shoreline Landing, turn left, and walk 100 yards to the parking lot at the East Shore Trailhead marking the beginning of Segment 10 at mile 10.0 (8,410 feet; N40° 14.45', W105° 49.50').

OTHER HIKES

There are countless hiking trails offering a variety of experiences in Rocky Mountain National Park. Use Trails Illustrated map #200 and the *Rocky Mountain National Park Day Hiker's Guide,* by Jerome Malitz, to plan your explorations through this gem of the Colorado Rockies.

TONAHUTU-PTARMIGAN POINT-NORTH INLET
Approximate loop distance: 28.0 miles
Difficulty: Strenuous

Tonahutu/North Inlet Trailhead: Drive into the town of Grand Lake on Grand Avenue. The trailhead is less than 0.5 mile north of town at a filtration plant.

This is an excellent hike for anyone disappointed by the CDT's circumvention of Rocky Mountain National Park. It gives you a taste of many aspects of the park, crowned by a visit to the high ridge across which the Continental Divide runs. On its west side, the ridge is flat and accommodating; to the east, it drops off in sheer cliffs, offering views of the many glacier-carved valleys that are rarely, if ever, visited by humans. Use a map to plan this multi-day hike, and remember you can only camp in designated areas, and only by permit.

SUPPLIES, SERVICES, AND ACCOMMODATIONS

GRAND LAKE
DISTANCE FROM TRAIL: 0 miles
ZIP CODE: 80447

Bank	Mountain Parks Bank, 1101 Grand Ave.	(970) 627-8905
Bus	None	
Camping	Elk Creek Campground and RV Park, 0.25 mile north on Hwy. 34, left 1 block on County Road #48	627-8502
Dining	The Terrace Inn, 813 Grand Ave.	627-3097
	Casa del Sol, 825 Grand Ave.	627-8382
Gear	Never Summer Mountain Products, 919 Grand Ave.	627-3642
Groceries	Mountain Food Market, 400 Grand Ave.	627-3470
Information	Visitor Center, 14700 Hwy. 34	627-3402
Laundry	Circle D, 701 Grand Ave.	627-3210
Lodging	ShadowCliff Lodge and Conference Center (Hostel), 405 Summerland Park Rd. (on Segment 9, mile 8.4)	627-9220
	Bluebird Motel, 30 River Drive	627-9314
Medical	in Granby, Timberline Medical Center, 62801 Hwy. 40	887-2503
Post Office	520 Center Drive	627-3340
Showers	Elk Creek Campground and RV Park, 0.25 mile north on Hwy. 34, left 1 block on County Road #48	627-8502

SPECIAL NOTES: Grand Lake marks the west entrance to Rocky Mountain National Park, whose status as a pristine area requiring permits for backcountry camping is the primary reason the trail strays so far from the actual Divide here. To explore the park or the Divide, see *Other Hikes* in this segment or visit the Kawuneeche Visitor Center, 1.5 miles north of town on Colorado Highway 34 (at mile 6.6 on Segment 9).

Segment 10
Grand Lake to Monarch Lake Trailhead

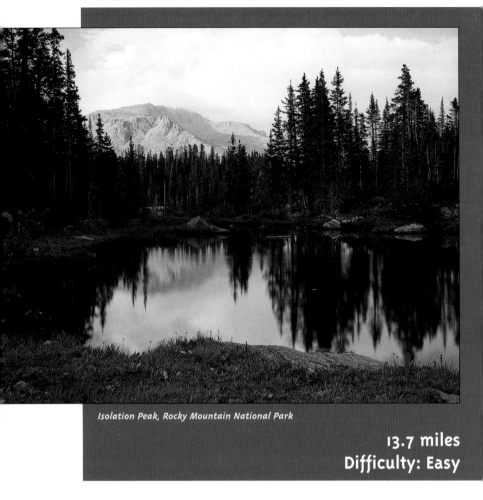

Isolation Peak, Rocky Mountain National Park

13.7 miles
Difficulty: Easy

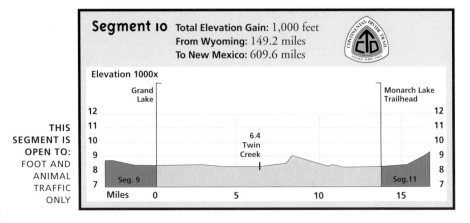

THIS SEGMENT IS OPEN TO:
FOOT AND ANIMAL TRAFFIC ONLY

Segment 10 **Total Elevation Gain:** 1,000 feet
From Wyoming: 149.2 miles
To New Mexico: 609.6 miles

CONTINENTAL DIVIDE TRAIL
NATIONAL SCENIC TRAIL

Elevation 1000x

Grand Lake

Monarch Lake Trailhead

6.4 Twin Creek

Seg. 9

Seg.11

Miles 0   5   10   15

THE TRAIL'S WIDE SWING away from the Divide continues here as it passes through the town of Grand Lake, a recreation mecca nestled between two large bodies of water, Grand Lake and Shadow Mountain Reservoir. Hikers accustomed to life on the coast will appreciate this segment, as the trail hugs the shores of Shadow Mountain Reservoir and Lake Granby for much of its course.

Reminders of civilization are never far off on this section of trail, with its start in town, its proximity to the omnipresent boaters and anglers on the water, and its termination near a popular car camping area on Lake Granby. Still, I encountered few other hikers on a weekend sojourn, and the experience of meandering along the placid water punctuated by frequent forays into quiet meadows and magical pine forests provides tranquility, offering through-hikers a welcome respite from the rigors of above-timberline hiking.

This area's first inhabitants were Ute, Arapaho, and Cheyenne Indians. Legend has it that a terrible storm on Grand Lake claimed the lives of most of the Utes' women and children during a fierce battle with invading Cheyennes. Although ghosts can still be seen hovering above the waters on a misty night, the survivors abandoned the area, leaving it to the Europeans who arrived to hunt and fish in the mid-1800s. Other hunters and trappers soon followed, and Grand Lake's population grew rapidly. What began as vital necessity evolved into popular recreation, and today Grand Lake attracts thousands of recreationists annually, from fishermen and boaters in the summer to snowmobilers and cross-country skiers in the winter. With plenty of opportunities to wet a hook just yards from the trail, anglers should not forget their tackle boxes.

Through-hikers may wish to camp somewhere between miles 6.1 and 7.9, as the only camping beyond this is at the pay campgrounds at Arapaho Bay. No camping is allowed beyond these campgrounds until a point about 1.5 miles into Segment 11.

The CDT briefly crosses land that is part of Rocky Mountain National Park, where camping is regulated by a permit system. For more information, write to: Rocky Mountain National Park, Backcountry Office, Estes Park, CO 80517; or phone (970) 586-2371.

MOUNTAIN BIKE NOTES: A portion of this segment passes through Rocky Mountain National Park, where bikes are not allowed.

A traveler.

I love his title.

A traveler is

to be reverenced

as such.

His profession

is the best symbol

of our life.

Going from—toward;

it is the history

of every one of us.

—Henry David

Thoreau

RANGER DISTRICT:
Sulphur

MAPS

TRAILS ILLUSTRATED: 102 and 200

USGS QUADRANGLES: Shadow Mountain, Strawberry Lake, Monarch Lake

USFS: Arapaho/Roosevelt National Forests, page 103

ACCESS

 GRAND LAKE: From a Conoco station on US-34, drive east into Grand Lake 0.2 mile to Center Drive and turn right. Drive another 0.2 mile to Marina Drive, turn left, and go one block to Shadow Mountain Drive. Turn right and proceed 0.3 mile to Jericho Avenue, turn right across the bridge, and wind 0.5 mile to the stop sign at Shoreline Landing. Turn left, and you'll see the parking area 100 yards ahead.

 MONARCH LAKE TRAILHEAD: See the next segment.

SUPPLIES, SERVICES, AND ACCOMMODATIONS

GRAND LAKE OFFERS ALL SERVICES. See Segment 9, page 97.

TRAIL DESCRIPTION   The trail starts at the east end of the parking lot, reaching a T intersection after 70 yards. Turn right (south) and proceed 0.7 mile along the edge of Shadow Mountain Reservoir to the kiosk marking the entrance to Rocky Mountain National Park. Note that camping in the park is restricted. See this segment's introduction for the park address.

At mile 1.4 (8,430), take the right fork of the trail toward Roaring Fork Campground; then proceed 100 yards farther to a left turn at a second fork, following the East Shore Trail toward Lake Granby. At mile 2.0 (8,390), cross Ranger Creek and enter a large sage meadow where the trail becomes fainter as it meanders west of south for 0.2 mile to a place where the pine trees close in on the trail from both sides. Be alert for deer and elk in these meadows. Enter a second large meadow and travel along its left (east) side for 0.2 mile until reaching the trees at mile 2.4 where the trail is again very clear.

At mile 2.5, enter another sage meadow where the trail is difficult to see; use the clear opening in the sagebrush to find it. After 0.1 mile, the CDT bends to the right (west) and enters a mixed aspen and lodgepole forest. At mile 2.8 (8,440), the trail enters a beautiful small meadow marked by a signpost.

 Don't be tricked by the clear trail leading into the trees on the right; stay along the meadow and follow the faint track through the grass straight ahead.

At mile 3.0, walk straight past the lone pine in the long, narrow meadow and proceed 0.2 mile to a fork and turn left. After another 0.2 mile, at mile 3.4, there is another fork in the trail; again take the left fork and proceed 0.1 mile to the crossing of Pole Creek (8,325).

The trail now trends southeast and meets the mighty Colorado River, at mile 3.7, where vibrant wildflowers thrive in the wet environment. This area is ideal as a lunch destination on a day hike, and anglers may want to dangle a fly on the nearby water.

At mile 4.0, the roar of the Colorado River gives way to the placid waters of Lake Granby's Grand Bay. After another 0.4 mile, the trail forks, but the two branches meet up yards later. Cross Columbine Creek 0.1 mile farther on, and stay to the right, along the bay; then follow the trail as it climbs away from the water 100 yards later.

The trail fades as it reaches an overused camping area at mile 5.1. Walk straight through this area to a ditch on the other side and pick up the trail again as it climbs away from the ditch. The clear trail now follows the east shore of Grand Bay to a small stream crossing at mile 5.7. Then it exits Rocky Mountain National Park at mile 6.1, where there are several nice camping spots. The trail crosses Twin Creek at mile 6.4 (8,300), the last opportunity to replenish water for 4.1 miles. Climb a small hill to a ranger station and a picnic table, which is a good place for lunch for through-hikers looking to complete this segment of trail by evening.

The trail now trends away from the water of the bay as it climbs a moderate hill for 0.2 mile before descending to a sign marking the boundary of the Indian Peaks Wilderness at mile 6.8.

At mile 7.2, use a CDT signpost to work your way through a small grassy meadow; then walk straight through the marshy grass toward a large and lonely lodge-pole pine at the other side of the meadow. Head for the blazed tree beyond the lone pine, and pick up the trail as it ascends out of the meadow to the left. Now enjoy your total immersion in the peculiar quiet of a lodgepole pine forest.

WILDERNESS ALERT:

The Indian Peaks Wilderness was designated in 1978 by federal law to be "an area where the earth and its community of life are untrammeled by man, where man himself is a visitor who does not remain." It consists of 73,296 acres and suffers an inordinate amount of human pressure because of its proximity to Denver and Boulder. For this reason, a camping permit is required. For more information, contact the Sulphur Ranger District, U.S. Forest Service, P.O. Box 10, Granby, CO 80446; or call (303) 887-3331.

Please remember the special rules governing this wilderness area: 1. Camp out of sight, at least 200 feet from lakes and streams, on dry, durable surfaces. 2. Use a stove instead of building a fire. No fires near lakes or east of the Divide. 3. Keep water sources pure by washing at least 200 feet from them. 4. Bury human waste six inches deep and 200 feet from lakes and streams. Pack out toilet paper. 5. Hobble or picket livestock at least 200 feet from lakes and streams, and use only treated, weed-free feed and grain. 6. All dogs must be on a leash. 7. No mountain biking. 8. Pack out all trash. Don't attempt to burn it.

At mile 7.9 (8,680), the trail begins a gradual climb through two switchbacks to a large boulder at the top of the hill, which it reaches at mile 8.2 (9,080). In another 0.2 mile, the trail is faint and somewhat confusing; follow tree blazes as you pass by an aspen forest on your right. Enjoy views of Lake Granby to the south, now 800 feet below the trail. Note also the interesting contrast of two different ecosystems, whose boundary is the trail itself: bright aspen forest on the south-facing slope to the right, and dense lodgepole forest on the north-facing slope to the left. At mile 8.6 the Continental Divide presents itself for a grand photo opportunity for the first time on this segment.

The trail dips off the ridge to the left (north) for 0.5 mile, before regaining the ridge and accompanying views at mile 9.1. At mile 9.4 (9,200), the trail bends to the left and begins a gradual descent through a small aspen forest, then lodgepole, before reaching near-lake level at mile 10.5 (8,340). There is no rest for the weary, however, as the trail again climbs steeply away from the water for 0.2 mile, then descends 0.2 mile to traverse across a steep, sage-covered hillside for 0.5 mile. At mile 11.4, the trail enters the trees and leads to a CDT signpost near lake level at mile 11.5 (8,320).

Meander along the shore until a signpost at mile 11.7 indicates the trail to the right. At mile 11.8, walk across a bridge and proceed straight past the Arapaho Bay Ranger Station and residence on your left. This marks your arrival at the first of three campgrounds. Just past the residence, a CDT signpost on the left indicates the continuation of the trail. You won't have to look for water here; you'll find a faucet right on the trail 0.9 mile ahead. Cross a bridge after 0.1 mile and bear right at the T intersection. Reach a parking area after another 0.1 mile, at mile 12.1, and walk around to the left. Turn left onto a road and follow it straight through another campground after 0.2 mile.

Pass by some private residences and then reach another loop of the campground at mile 12.8. There is a CDT signpost on the left, and fresh water and restrooms on the right; peppy through-hikers should slow to the posted speed limit of 15. Note that this is the last legal camping area for approximately 2.5 miles. Continue 0.1 mile to Road #125 and turn left toward Monarch Lake. Reach the gate at the Monarch Lake trailhead, and the end of this segment, at mile 13.7 (8,350 feet; N40° 6.68', W105° 44.81').

OTHER HIKES

ROARING FORK TRAIL
Approximate one-way distance: 5.5 miles
Difficulty: Strenuous

Arapaho Bay Trailhead: Park near Arapaho Bay Campground. See *Access* to Monarch Lake Trailhead in Segment 11.

This hike takes you through two drainages of crystal clear snowmelt as it climbs 2,440 vertical feet to Stone Lake, nestled in an arching alpine cirque in the shadow of the Great Divide. Because this trail is contained entirely within the Indian Peaks Wilderness, camping permits are required, and all regular wilderness rules apply.

SCALE: 1/2 INCH = 1 MILE

- Continental Divide
- Continental Divide Trail (current segment)
- Continental Divide Trail (previous and next segments)
- Forest Route
- Paved Road
- All-Weather-Road
- Dirt Road
- Primitive Road
- Four-Wheel-Drive Road
- Trail
- Mine, Quarry, or Gravel Pit
- Recreation Site

Segment 11
Monarch Lake Trailhead to Devils Thumb Park

Sunset below Devils Thumb Pass, Indian Peaks Wilderness

13.0 miles
Difficulty: Moderate

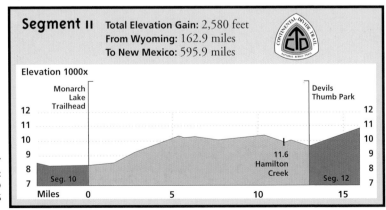

Segment 11 **Total Elevation Gain:** 2,580 feet
From Wyoming: 162.9 miles
To New Mexico: 595.9 miles

YOU MAY
ENCOUNTER:
MOTORIZED
VEHICLES

YOU'LL NOTICE how varied public land use can be here where the trail starts at the recreationally managed Monarch Lake area, passes into the wet and lush seclusion of the Indian Peaks Wilderness, and then climbs into a drier landscape showing signs of recent logging activity and years of road-building. The hiking is never unpleasant, however, and the rapid variation in terrain and ecosystems provides an interesting opportunity for observation and comparison.

Camping is not permitted for the first 1.5 miles, and a permit is required if you intend to camp in the Indian Peaks Wilderness. Permits are available at the ranger station at the beginning of this segment or by writing to the Forest Service. For more information, please see the complete discussion of this wilderness area in Segment 10 on page 102. Water is available here at regular intervals, and campsites are plentiful.

 MOUNTAIN BIKE NOTES: Biking is prohibited where the trail passes through the Indian Peaks Wilderness, but there are some rides at the end of the segment. See "Other Hikes and Rides."

MAPS

TRAILS ILLUSTRATED: 102
USGS QUADRANGLES: Monarch Lake, East Portal
USFS: Arapaho/Roosevelt National Forests, page 110–111

BEGINNING ACCESS POINT

 Smooth road to trailhead **MONARCH LAKE TRAILHEAD:** About 5.5 miles north of US-40 on US-34, turn right (east) onto County Road 6, toward Arapaho Bay Campground. Follow signs approximately 10 miles to a parking area at Monarch Lake Trailhead. Camping is not allowed here.

ALTERNATE ACCESS

Distance from graded road 10.0 miles **JUNCO LAKE TRAILHEAD** (at trail mile 7.6): About one mile south of Tabernash on US-40, turn east onto Forest Route 83. After 0.4 mile, turn left at a T intersection onto County Road 84. About one mile later, turn left toward Meadow Creek Reservoir, which you will pass in 7.5 miles. Continue past the reservoir 2.5 miles to a left turn at a sign pointing the way to Junco Lake Trailhead, which is 0.2 mile beyond the sign. There is ample parking at the trailhead.

One touch

of nature

makes the whole

world kin.

—Shakespeare,

Troillus and Cressida

RANGER DISTRICT:
Sulphur

ENDING ACCESS POINT

Distance from graded road	
	7.5 miles + 0.8 miles

DEVILS THUMB PARK/AQUEDUCT ROAD:
See the next segment.

SUPPLIES, SERVICES, AND ACCOMMODATIONS

GRAND LAKE provides all services. See Segment 9, page 97.

TRAIL DESCRIPTION

From the parking lot at Monarch Lake Trailhead, walk south along the road, through the gate, and 75 yards farther to the ranger station on the right. The ranger station is open every day, 8 a.m. to 5 p.m. It has a primitive restroom, and you can pick up wilderness camping permits here. After 5 p.m., the friendly ranger can be found in his trailer 100 yards past the station, on the left.

Make an immediate right turn after the ranger station and continue along the northwest side of Monarch Lake to a bridge crossing at mile 0.2. The trail now curves left and climbs above and away from the lake to an overlook at mile 0.8. Then it leaves the lake behind and passes into a mysterious spruce forest where the trees are dressed in the misty rags of Spanish moss.

At mile 1.5, the trail enters the Indian Peaks Wilderness, as indicated by a big sign. Walk 40 yards to a fork marked by a CDT symbol, bear right, and avoid the false trail to the left. At mile 1.6 (8,480), another fork marks the beginning of the High Lonesome Trail. Turn right as indicated by the sign, avoiding the bridge over Arapaho Creek.

> **WILDERNESS ALERT:**
> A permit is required to camp in the Indian Peaks Wilderness. Please see the complete discussion of this area in Segment 10, on page 101.

This part is a little tricky. From the signpost, walk 30 yards to a point between two large pine trees. Turn 45 degrees to the right, proceed another 20 yards, and pick up the trail again, passing by some ruins.

Now the trail bends south, following Arapaho Creek upstream, then Mill Creek, through a series of heart-pounding switchbacks. At about mile 2.6, as you climb along the deep gorge of Mill Creek, look to the south for views of Mount Achonee's broad west face, behind which is the Continental Divide. At mile 2.8 (9,160 feet; N40° 05.52', W105° 44.25'), a fork marks the turnoff to Strawberry Lake. Stay left and cross Mill Creek via a series of fallen logs 75 yards farther on. As the CDT now trends due south along Mill Creek, a brief flat section gives way to a moderate, steady climb. At mile 3.7, the trail skirts the creek on its left edge before crossing it 100 yards later.

Mile 4.3 marks the exit from the Indian Peaks Wilderness. Then, 200 yards beyond a ruined cabin at mile 4.7, the trail enters a meadow and becomes faint enough to be marked by cairns. Walk straight past the last cairn, cross the stream, and move into the trees. Pick up the trail again 10 yards to your immediate right. Now the trail climbs into a drier ecosystem with kinnikinnik on the ground and lodgepole pines in the sky. At mile 5.3, follow a CDT marker to the top of the ridge (10,300) and take in the beautiful views of the Indian Peaks and Meadow Creek Reservoir. The peaks in the distance, directly behind the lake, conceal Rollins Pass and the through-hiker's impending return to the Divide.

Now the trail becomes a little confusing, but excellent signage combined with astute guidebook-writing should lead you safely through the coming maze. After descending gradually 150 yards on a dry, sun-drenched hillside, cross an old road, continue past a cairn on the other side for 0.1 mile, and turn left onto a second road. At mile 5.6, avoid another road coming in from the left as the CDT hairpins to the right, where it is occasionally marked by piles of orange-colored rocks. The trail begins to climb again as a CDT signpost on the left at mile 5.8 precedes a second one 30 yards ahead on the right.

 Turn right at the second one, following the piles of orange rocks. This is easy to miss!

From here, look back at the ridge you just descended for a striking example of a burn area that has re-vegetated itself. (Can you guess how long ago the fire struck?) After another 40 yards, the trail meets a much older road and begins a moderate climb up a small hill. Follow cairns and CDT markers up the road as it alternately climbs and flattens out. At mile 6.3 (10,280), the trail veers right (west) around a ridge to a sign marking the High Lonesome Trail's descent away from the road to the left (south). The trail is faint here but delineated by parallel logs on the ground. After a 0.2-mile steady descent, the trail reaches a CDT marker and yet another road. Walk straight onto the road and follow it 35 yards to a T intersection marked by a CDT signpost and turn right. Follow this road for a little more than 100 yards, cross a stream, and turn left onto—you guessed it—another road, as indicated by a CDT marker. A huge fire ring at mile 6.7 marks a good campsite near a meadow, as well as the CDT's transformation into a pleasant single-track trail.

Now the trail enters a deeper and wetter spruce forest where it is essential to follow the Forest Service blazes on the trees. Follow a series of blazes, a cairn, and a CDT marker through daisy-filled meadows and stream crossings along the west side of the meadows. At mile 7.4, you'll reach the south end of a large meadow, which you'll cross to the right by following more cairns and blazes. Now continue to a parking lot at mile 7.6 (10,050). This marks the CDT's intersection with the Junco Lake Trailhead, which is accessible by car (see *Alternate Access* at the beginning of this segment).

From here, follow the CDT south into the willows, as indicated by the trail sign. A path leads to a bridge followed by a CDT marker on the other side of the willows. At mile 8.2, cross a dirt road toward the CDT marker on the other side. Follow the faint trail through a wide meadow at mile 8.5, passing by unmarked posts toward a CDT marker. (This is the last such marker for 3 miles.) In 0.2 mile, the trail enters some trees and then follows the west edge of a meadow for 0.3 mile. Regain the west (right) edge of a large extension of the meadow at mile 9.1; then follow the faint trail left across the meadow at mile 9.2. After another 150 yards, the trail exits the meadow to the right under the patient gaze of the peaks of the Divide looming ever closer to the east.

At mile 9.4, cross the south side of a meadow, bearing left across a stream featuring some very small pools. Then re-enter the trees before crossing a logging road at mile 9.5. The tree blazes soon disappear as the trail begins a moderate climb through a spruce forest at mile 9.8. Keep to the single-track trail as you negotiate many recently built Forest Service routes. At mile 10.2, turn right onto an obvious road, march 35 yards, and pick up the trail again at a tree blaze on the left.

Pass by Point 10,475 and descend along the edge of a large clearcut area on the right (west). Descend through a series of switchbacks marked by tree blazes to a willow meadow at mile 10.8 that offers a fleeting glimpse of the Divide to the south. At mile 11.0, follow a faint trail across a willow meadow; then parallel Hamilton Creek on its west side. Cross the creek on a nice bridge at mile 11.4. Then cross back to the west side at a CDT marker at mile 11.5. Veer to the left on a road at a second CDT marker 40 yards ahead and notice the nice camping area on the left near the stream.

Yet another CDT marker 140 yards later indicates the third crossing of Hamilton Creek, via a wooden bridge to the left (mile 11.6; 9,960). Eighty yards beyond the bridge, follow the trail's left fork to a small stream crossing at mile 11.8. After a short climb to 10,030, you'll start a moderate descent into a lodgepole forest at mile 12.3. Cross a perennial stream at mile 12.9 and reach a trail fork at mile 13.0 (9,690 feet; N39° 59.18', W105° 43.89'). This intersection marks the end of this segment. Through-hikers should turn left (east) here toward Devils Thumb; hikers finishing at the Devils Thumb Trailhead should continue ahead (southeast) 0.1 mile and follow the trail's turn to the right (west), from where the parking area is a 0.7-mile walk.

OTHER HIKES AND RIDES

JUNCO LAKE TRAILHEAD TO DEVILS THUMB TRAILHEAD
Approximate one-way distance: 6.2 miles
Mode of travel: Biking or Hiking
Difficulty: Moderate

Trailheads: See *Alternate Access* for this segment and *Access* for Segment 12.

This route follows the CDT as described here from mile 7.6 to the segment's end. Although perfectly feasible as a day hike, it is more enticing as an excellent mountain bike ride requiring little or no technical expertise. Plan it as an out-and-back or a shuttle. For the latter, leave a car in Fraser and enjoy the primarily downhill ride on a dirt road from the Devils Thumb Trailhead.

COLUMBINE LAKE/CARIBOU PASS
Approximate one-way distance: 2.8 to 4.4 miles
Mode of travel: Hiking
Difficulty: Moderate to Strenuous

Junco Lake Trailhead: See *Access* for this segment.

Columbine Lake is nestled at timberline far below the steep western ramparts of the Continental Divide. Through-hikers might consider this a resting point, and the lake is a good camping destination for hikers parking at Junco Lake Trailhead.

For a more strenuous exploration, take the Caribou Trail cutoff at about 2.0 miles from the trailhead. This trail climbs rapidly into the impressive treeless domain of the Divide. Note that the trail over to the east side is considered by the Forest Service to be hazardous, so proceed only at your own risk. These hikes take you into the Indian Peaks Wilderness where camping permits are required and special regulations apply.

Devils Thumb Lake, Indian Peaks Wilderness

SEGMENT 11

Segment 12
Devils Thumb Park to Rollins Pass

On the Divide, Indian Peaks Wilderness

6.6 miles
Difficulty: Strenuous

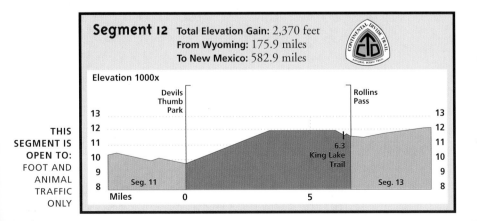

Segment 12 **Total Elevation Gain:** 2,370 feet
From Wyoming: 175.9 miles
To New Mexico: 582.9 miles

THIS
SEGMENT IS
OPEN TO:
FOOT AND
ANIMAL
TRAFFIC
ONLY

THE PARK, PASS, TRAIL, AND LAKE that carry the
Devils Thumb moniker are named for the impressive pinnacle of
rock that protrudes from sheer cliffs near the Continental Divide.
As you ascend the 2,290 vertical feet that define this segment's
first 3.3 miles, the Thumb slowly takes shape against the eastern
sky, growing like a giant stone troll on the horizon. The juxtapo-
sition of this rugged monolith with the vibrant softness of acres
of wildflowers is a rare natural composition.

The pass itself has never been more than a pack trail,
even though it dates back to the mid-1850s. The area had been
proposed as a major highway corridor from the plains into northern Colorado, but nothing ever came of it.

Most of this segment is in the Indian Peaks Wilderness.
Please familiarize the members of your party with the wilderness
regulations in Segment 10, page 102.

There is no immediately accessible water once you leave
the stream at mile 2.4. Sitting like mirrors to the gods in granite
bowls sculpted by retreating glaciers over 10,000 years ago, a few
of this area's many high lakes are a short drop on the east side.
Most notable is King Lake, 230 feet below the CDT at mile 6.3.
Because this is in the Wilderness Area, however, a permit obtained
in advance is required to camp here. A pond 2.9 miles into the next
segment is the next relatively easy water access and is not in designated wilderness, but it too involves a climb of 300 vertical feet.

If you happen to be holding any long, metal objects high
above your head, this would be a good place to set them down.
The CDT is on the exposed ridge of the Divide for 10 miles, so
it is advisable to start hiking as early as possible in the morning,
and to keep in mind possible escape routes toward lower terrain
in the event of lightning.

 MOUNTAIN BIKE NOTES: Bikes are prohibited in
the Indian Peaks Wilderness.

People

from a planet

without flowers

would think

we must be mad

with joy

the whole time

to have such things

about us.

—Iris Murdoch,

A Fairly

Honorable Defeat

MAPS

TRAILS ILLUSTRATED: 102
USGS QUADRANGLE: East Portal
USFS: Arapaho/Roosevelt National Forests, pages 110–111

ACCESS

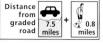

| Distance from graded road | 7.5 miles | + | 0.8 miles |

**DEVILS THUMB PARK/AQUEDUCT
ROAD:** A stone's throw north of the town
of Fraser on US-40, take the first right out

RANGER DISTRICT:
Sulphur

of town (east) onto County Road 8. After 0.2 mile, turn left at the T intersection and proceed 6 miles to a Y intersection. Follow the left fork 1.2 miles to a road coming in from the right that is marked by a sign: "Devil's Thumb CDNST." The trailhead, and ample parking, are 0.3 mile up this road.

ROLLINS PASS: See the next segment.

SUPPLIES, SERVICES, AND ACCOMMODATIONS

WINTER PARK offers a complete range of services. See *Access* for Rollins Pass in the next segment and follow the directions in reverse.

AREA CODE: 970

DISTANCE FROM TRAIL: 12.5 miles

ZIP CODE: 80482

Bank	Norwest, 78515 US-40	(970) 726-5531
Bus	None	
Camping	Idlewild, between the ski area and the town. Call the Clear Creek Ranger District at (303) 567-2901 for more information.	
Dining	La Taqueria, Park Plaza, downtown	726-0280
	Carvers Cafe, behind Cooper Creek Square	726-8202
Gear	Flanagan's, downtown	726-4412
Groceries	Stop 'n Save, Park Place Shopping Center	726-5836
	Safeway, 541 Zerex (2 miles north in Fraser)	726-9484
Information	Chamber of Commerce, 78841 US-40	726-5514
Laundry	Next door to Chamber of Commerce	
Lodging	Winter Park Hostel, 29 Wanderers Way (from $8.50)	726-5356
	Super 8 Motel, 78641 US-40 ($60 to $90)	726-8088
Medical	Seven Mile Medical Clinic, at base of ski area	726-8066
Post Office	78490 US-40	726-5495
Showers	Winter Park Hostel, 29 Wanderers Way	726-5356

TRAIL DESCRIPTION   Through-hikers already at the trail intersection at mile 13 on the last segment can skip ahead to the next paragraph. If you are starting out from the Devils Thumb Trailhead, walk up the trail as indicated by the signs. In 0.7 mile, you will come to Devils Thumb Park, a huge meadow at 9,660 feet. Here the trail bends left (north) to circumnavigate the park before it reaches a trail intersection after another 0.1 mile. Turn right (east) at this intersection, which is marked by a sign for Devils Thumb. *This is the 0-mile point for this segment.* Follow the clear trail's steady climb around and beyond Devils Thumb Park. By mile 2.2, the prolific spruce population

---

WILDERNESS ALERT:

A permit is required to camp in the Indian Peaks Wilderness. Please see the complete discussion of this area in Segment 10, page 101.

gives way to flower-covered alpine meadows. A sign here signals your entry into the Indian Peaks Wilderness. If you don't have a permit to camp in the wilderness, there are a few campsites concealed in the trees outside the wilderness boundary.

Now the land comes alive in a dazzling display of wildflowers, starting with purple aster and yellow senecio; then, as you ascend south away from the stream at mile 2.4, the climb is made a little less demanding as you enjoy ruby-encrusted king's crown along the trail, and saxifrage, dainty blue chiming bells, various shades of paintbrush, sky pilot, and soft white puffs of bistort further afield. The production is capped off by a mesmerizing array of moss campion near the crest of the Divide.

The stream you are leaving behind is the last water on the trail for 10 miles. About 70 yards short of the Divide ridge, the trail fades at two posts with CDT symbols (mile 3.0; 11,750 feet; N39° 58.46', W105° 41.36'). These identify a turn to the right (south; compass bearing 205°), where a third post and cairn are almost invisible against the tundra 160 yards distant. Walk to these, turn a little to the right (compass bearing 210°) and head for a rocky knob in front of which is another cairn at mile 3.3. On the way, pick up a faint tread. There is an intermediate cairn to the left, but there's no reason to go by it.

Follow a faint tread a short distance uphill to the southwest to the edge of a deep cirque (11,980). You can see the runs of Winter Park ski area to the southwest; just to their left is a dip in the ridge, which is Berthoud Pass, Segment 14's endpoint. Now the trail bends to the left (south-southeast). Ignore a line of cairns higher up to the east that join this trail just over the crest of a hill, at mile 3.5. Then *follow* cairns as you descend across a band of talus. Pass a large cairn on the broad slope at mile 3.7, and follow a faint tread into a slight climb.

At mile points 4.1 and 4.7, stay on the tread as the cairns again break off above and to the left (east). As the CDT and the cairn trail converge at mile 5.7 and bend to the left (southeast), Pumphouse Lake comes into view to the south. You'll join the Divide ridge at mile 6.0 and take in views of King Lake. If you need water, continue another 0.3 mile and turn left onto the access trail for a 230-foot drop to the lake. (A permit is required for an overnight stay.) Large snowfields often remain here into August, attracting expert skiers all summer long who can't get enough during Colorado's short, nine-month ski season.

Continue south from this fork on an old road, over a small rise, and out of the wilderness area to this segment's end at the Rollins Pass parking area at mile 6.6 (11,660 feet; N39° 56.06', W105° 40.96').

MOUNTAIN BIKE RIDES

HESSIE-KING LAKE-DEVILS THUMB LOOP OR OUT-AND-BACK
Approximate loop distance: Up to 16.0 miles
Difficulty: Moderate

Hessie Trailhead: Follow County Road 130 west from Nederland and a few miles past Eldora to a left fork to the trailhead.

A short distance west of the trailhead, the trail forks toward Devils Thumb or King Lake. The CDT connects these two points, allowing for a satisfying loop hike through beautiful alpine scenery and along the Divide. Or you may choose to make it a shorter out-and-back hike up either trail. This is an ideal way for folks in the Front Range to enjoy the Divide without having to drive far into the mountains.

Segment 13
Rollins Pass to Rainbow Road

Iceberg Lakes, proposed James Peak Wilderness

13.0 Miles
Difficulty: Strenuous

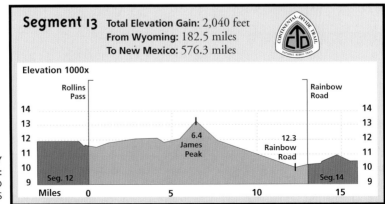

Segment 13 **Total Elevation Gain:** 2,040 feet
From Wyoming: 182.5 miles
To New Mexico: 576.3 miles

CONTINENTAL DIVIDE TRAIL
NATIONAL SCENIC TRAIL

Elevation 1000x

Rollins Pass

Rainbow Road

14
13
12
11
10
9

6.4
James
Peak

12.3
Rainbow
Road

Seg. 12

Seg. 14

**YOU MAY
ENCOUNTER:**
MOTORIZED
VEHICLES

Miles   0   5   10   15

AS ONE OF THE EASIEST ROUTES over the Continental Divide in this area, Rollins Pass has developed a rich history. Native Americans originally used it to move from the plains and foothills into the mountains. It is believed that the Mormons passed here on their way to Salt Lake City. Then, after the U.S. Army improved the route into a viable road, Denver investor and businessman David H. Moffat built a railroad over the pass in 1909. The railroad waged a constant battle against massive snowfall along the route, which would consume up to 40 percent of the total budget. Unable to make a profit, Moffat lobbied the Colorado government to build a tunnel underneath the Divide. In 1927, 16 years after Moffat's death, the Moffat Tunnel opened at a cost three times greater than its originally projected $6 million. The tunnel is still in use today as part of a rail line carrying skiers from Denver to Winter Park. Ruins remain near the parking area at Rollins Pass from the small community of workers who lived here during construction of the pass.

On a continuum with civilization at one end and raw wilderness at the other, this segment takes you to the extremes. Just a few miles after its tortuous climb of James Peak's steep, forbidding north face, the CDT descends 3,000 feet off the Continental Divide to the network of roads surrounding the Fall River valley. This area's proximity to both Denver and the glacial cirques of the Divide make it a popular target for people seeking to escape the urban sprawl of the Front Range. The solitude you can experience on the 13,294-foot summit of James Peak is a sharp contrast to the roads you will soon share with four-wheelers and dirt bikes. Thankfully, the trail's foray into this over-used playground is short; in only a few miles, you are lifted back to the simplicity of the Divide's windswept ridges.

The primary reason for this detour off the Divide is the steep, hand-over-foot section of crumbly rock between James Peak and Mount Bancroft. Also, Forest Service biologists fear a large botanical community would be upset by human presence, and a permanent snowfield on the Divide has a dangerous vertical cornice that lies in wait for the unwary hiker.

For the first 7.0 miles, water and camping are scarce, unless you want to descend to one of the many lakes in the cirques that buttress the Divide ridge on the east side. One such descent is described at mile 2.9. Water is plentiful on the last half of the segment, which is also where you'll find the best campsites. Large fields of talus pose an impossible challenge for pack stock.

> The wind
>
> shows us
>
> how close
>
> to the edge
>
> we are.
>
> —Joan Didion

MOUNTAIN BIKE NOTES: The terrain around James Peak is not rideable.

RANGER DISTRICTS:
Sulphur
Clear Creek

MAPS

TRAILS ILLUSTRATED: 103
USGS QUADRANGLES: East Portal, Empire, Berthoud Pass
USFS: Arapaho/Roosevelt National Forests, pages 122–123

ACCESS

ROLLINS PASS: Drive north on US-40 (west according to the highway signs) from Berthoud Pass 10.6 miles to a turnoff on the right (east) marked by a sign indicating the Moffat Road Hill Route. (This is 1.8 miles south of the Winter Park town proper.) Proceed 14 miles up this road to the summit of Rollins Pass where a kiosk marks the parking lot. The CDT arrives from the north on an old road between the kiosk and some ruins.

RAINBOW ROAD: See the next segment.

SUPPLIES, SERVICES, AND ACCOMMODATIONS

WINTER PARK offers all services. See Segment 12, page 114.

TRAIL DESCRIPTION From the parking area, walk southwest (toward Winter Park) on the Rollins Pass Road 0.5 mile to a CDT marker where the trail leaves the road to the left (east). After about 15 yards, follow the faint trace of a road leading off to the right (south) past a second CDT marker. As the road nears the summit of Point 12,072 at mile 1.2, break off to the right bearing a little west of south, passing high above scenic Arapaho Lakes in the cirque on the left (east). From this point there is no clear trail. Stay near the crest of the Divide, and you can't go wrong.

A large cairn right on the Divide at mile 2.2 (11,880) keeps watch over Crater Lakes. Stay high on the ridge as you continue south, ignoring a few cairns below to the west (right). The CDT soon joins an old road approaching from the west and follows it over Point 12,030 (mile 2.8), offering views of aptly named Iceberg Lakes, whose rocky cradle was carved out by retreating glaciers more than 10,000 years ago. If you need to camp or get water, a cairn at mile 2.9 tops a relatively gentle slope on the left that provides access to a small pond north of Iceberg Lakes, about 300 feet in elevation below the trail.

Infrequent cairns mark the path of the CDT near the steep crest of the Divide. Maintain an even contour as you pass to the right (west) of the next high point above the lakes, at mile 3.5. From here the road to Rogers Pass comes into view in front of you, along with the high point in this area, Point 12,251, a little to the left. Cross over the strands of talus stretching down from the point and walk to a shallow saddle on its southwest (right) flank at mile 4.1. Climb over a small hill and pick up a faint trail, bearing south at mile 4.2 (12,000). James Peak's monstrous north face, up which the CDT soon climbs, now dominates your world.

The CDT reaches Rogers Pass Road at mile 4.5; continue straight, slightly east of south.

N **FOR NORTHBOUND HIKERS,** this is a somewhat obscure intersection. At a faded CDT marker, take the single-track trail breaking off to the right.

Follow the road for only about 150 yards, then split off to the right on a faint single-track trail marked by a cairn next to the road. The trail fades near a second south-facing CDT marker on a post, but it is clearly visible rising along the steep right (west) slope of the precipitous Divide ridge ahead. Those with a fear of heights may be a little squeamish here, as the trail hovers 1,500 feet above the valley below, and then climbs another 1,300 feet to the steep summit of James Peak.

The trail curves up to the crest of the Divide at a flat spot on the ridge, near a CDT marker at mile 5.6 (12,280 feet; N39° 51.58', W105° 41.67'). From here, leave the trail and head straight up the slope to a second CDT marker. Continue beyond this to a series of cairns that lead to the far west (right) edge of the face. The slope angle lessens somewhat at a signless post at the base of a large talus slide (mile 5.8). Numerous springs here are reliable into September. The next cairn (mile 6.0) is barely visible at the top of the talus slope, slightly east of south. You may either turn 45 degrees to the left and angle up to the southeast along a swath of grass, or you can scramble up the talus.

Climb 0.1 mile to a cairn on the horizon up a steep jumble of broken rock above a line of west-facing cliffs, still on the far right edge of the face. Continue in this manner, following cairns and a vague trail to the summit plateau where the summit is marked by a ring of stones (mile 6.4; 13,294 feet; N39° 51.24', W105° 41.53').

About 5 yards north of the summit (back toward Rollins Pass), walk east (right) on a faint trail wandering over the rocky ground toward the very steep eastern edge of the summit plateau, where the trail turns quickly to the right (southeast). The further you go on this trail, the clearer it becomes. For a point-blank dose of rocky mountain high just before the descent, walk 10 yards to a notch near the trail on the left, and gaze into the gaping maw of ancient glacial excavation.

Now the trail bends to the east until a point at mile 6.5 where a hairpin turn leads back to the southwest (right). This is the first of several switchbacks as the trail descends a moderate slope. At mile 6.7, the trail approaches and leaves the steep edge for good in another hairpin to the right. After fading somewhat on a flatter section at mile 6.8, the CDT is marked frequently by cairns as it trends slightly west of south. You will soon cross over several springs and rivulets.

At mile 7.0, just before the terrain steepens considerably, the trail bends to the right (southwest) and cairns lead onto an old road. Turn left onto the road and follow its immediate curve to the left (east). Just after a huge cairn on a large flat-sided rock on the left, look down to the right for another large cairn 60 yards away. Descend southeast (right) to that cairn and turn left (east) onto a clearer road at mile 7.1.

N **NORTHBOUND HIKERS** need to be alert for this turnoff uphill to the right.

Now the CDT turns to the northeast and passes under what is usually a large snowfield at mile 7.4. The slope descends to meet the broad, flat plain below at mile 7.7 (11,960 feet; N39° 50.81', W105° 40.46').

Stop here and look out over what appears to be a cross between a high mountain park and a mesa, dropping gently to the south and southeast. At its far end, the plain rises to two distinct lumps. Bear cross-country for the westernmost of these (the one on the right; bearing 160°), which is labeled on the maps as Point 11,704. Trail construction here is slated to start in 1997.

An underground stream issues from the border between the slope and the plain before it meanders over the land amid a growth of willows. As you descend, stay left (east) of the willows. When you reach their far side, near where the land starts to rise to Point 11,704, turn right (south) onto a very old road at mile 8.3. You will find yourself in an eerie spruce krummholz forest as you descend into the valley toward Fall River and Loch Lomond. The road soon crosses to the west side of the stream and then resumes its plunge to the south. You are entitled to a bit of swagger as you look up to the west for views of the James Peak summit, almost 2,000 vertical feet above. To its left is the saddle that bears the difficult traverse above Ice Lake, and further left is Parry Peak, one of the highest points anywhere on the Divide.

As bristlecone pine take their place around the trail, Loch Lomond comes into view just before the road seems to vanish. Continue straight off the end of the road to the southeast, over a small streambed, and pick up a single-track trail that bends back to the right. Until the Forest Service begins maintaining this trail, you will have to work your way through overgrown vegetation. Descend to the southeast side of Loch Lomond at mile 8.9, cross above some willows to the dam, and cross it 0.1 mile to Forest Route 701.2 (not marked; elevation 11,210). **NOTE:** The dam, the lake, and the surrounding land are on private property. Please respect the owners' generosity in letting us cross here; pass through as inconspicuously as possible (and without stopping). There is another place to stop for water just a few tenths of a mile ahead.

NORTHBOUND HIKERS: As you approach the lake from below, look up on the ridge to the northeast (right) and spot a swath in the trees identified by a large boulder at its top. This is your eventual destination. From the northeast end of the dam, work east into the trees and look for the faint trail or make for the swath in the trees, where you will find the road.

Turn left (east) on Forest Route 701.2 and follow its descent to the south-southeast. Avoid a right fork at mile 11.1, and turn right onto Alice Road at a T intersection at mile 11.4. Continue 0.1 mile to another intersection and again turn right. In 0.2 mile, keep left at a fork and follow the road's steeper descent to its intersection with Rainbow Road at mile 12.3. Turn right (west), follow this road as it climbs through two switchbacks and crosses Fall River, and continue to a parking lot on the left next to a burned-out ruin at mile 13.0 (10,225 feet; N39° 48.75', W105° 40.25').

OTHER HIKES

JAMES PEAK VIA ST. MARY'S GLACIER
Approximate one-way distance: 4.0 miles
Difficulty: Moderate to Strenuous

Trailhead: See *Access* for the next segment. Instead of turning off Fall River Road around the 6-mile point, continue to its end near St. Mary's Glacier Ski Area.

Visit St. Mary's Glacier, one of Colorado's few year-round glacier fields. Then set out to the west-northwest for the climb up James Peak's east ridge or south flank. See the trail description for this segment for more details on the trail here. Views are far-reaching in all directions from the Continental Divide's crossing of the James Peak summit. You can complete this hike easily in a day. You may also follow the Divide south and west to Parry Peak, which is a little higher than James and one of the highest points on the Divide, but remember that sections of this traverse are considered by the Forest Service to be hazardous.

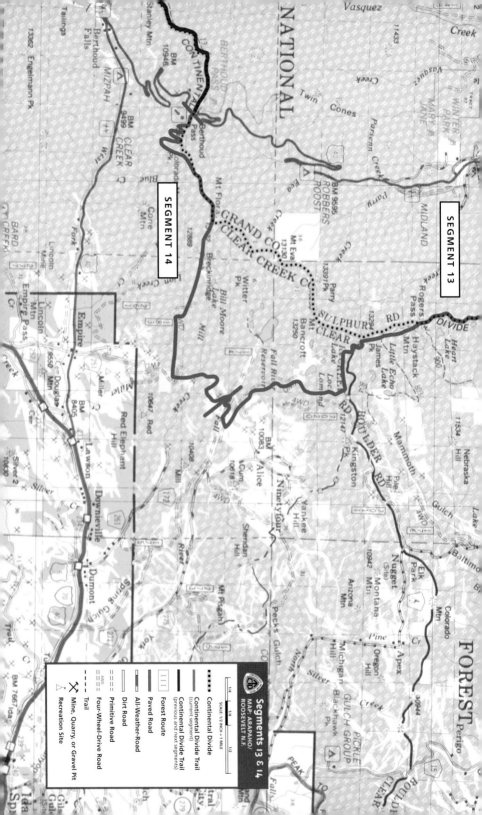

Segment 14
Rainbow Road to Berthoud Pass

On Parry Peak, proposed James Peak Wilderness

12.4 miles
Difficulty: Strenuous

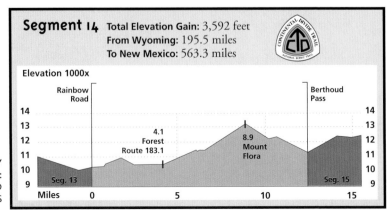

Segment 14 **Total Elevation Gain:** 3,592 feet
From Wyoming: 195.5 miles
To New Mexico: 563.3 miles

YOU MAY ENCOUNTER:
MOTORIZED
VEHICLES

IN THIS SEGMENT, through-hikers complete their tour of a maze of roads open to motor vehicles before climbing back to the serenity of 13,000-foot peaks on the Divide. Recent excavations of active mining claims are evident over the first 2.5 miles, and the roads are popular with backcountry motorists. This changes after mile 6.7, however, when the CDT climbs back to country too rugged for anything not on two or four legs.

After Mill Creek, at mile 2.5, there is no water for 10.0 miles (until mile 0.1 of the next segment). Exposure to weather and lightning is serious from mile 6.8 to 10.0.

 MOUNTAIN BIKE NOTES: The roads on this segment are rideable, but the interesting part from Breckinridge Peak to the Divide is mostly impassible talus.

MAPS

TRAILS ILLUSTRATED: 103
USGS QUADRANGLES: Empire, Berthoud Pass
USFS: Arapaho/Roosevelt National Forests, pages 122–123

ACCESS

 RAINBOW ROAD: From Interstate 70, take Exit 238 toward Fall River Road. Drive 0.2 mile and turn right. After 4.0 miles, the pavement ends for 0.25 mile, then resumes. In another 2.0 miles, take a dirt road straight ahead as the main road makes a sharp hairpin turn to the right. Those without a four-wheel drive vehicle should park here and walk the remaining 2.1 miles to the trailhead. The CDT joins this road in 1.4 miles, in the form of a road coming in from the right (north). Continue 0.7 mile from this point to a parking area next to a burned-out ruin on the left (south).

 BERTHOUD PASS: See the next segment.

SUPPLIES, SERVICES, AND ACCOMMODATIONS

WINTER PARK offers all services and is 12.5 miles north (west according to the highway signs) of Berthoud Pass on US-40. There is plenty of traffic on this road.

TRAIL DESCRIPTION
About 20 yards southeast of the parking area, follow an old road that climbs away from Rainbow Road to the south. This road immediately bends left (southeast) and cuts a narrow corridor through a dense forest of spruce and pine. Avoid side roads as the road climbs to mile 0.5 before it

---

Rocks do not

recommend the land

to the tiller

of the soil, but they

recommend it to

those who reap

a harvest of

another sort—

the artist, the poet,

the walker,

the student and

lover of all primitive

open-air things.

—John Burroughs

RANGER DISTRICTS:
Clear Creek
Sulphur

flattens and begins to descend. A single-track trail departs the right side of the road at mile 0.6 and trends southeast through the trees. Follow the trail for 40 yards until it arrives at some extensive mine ruins. Stop at the near edge of the ruins, turn 90 degrees to the right, and spot a faint trail going straight up the steep hill (compass bearing 210° to 220°). Follow frequent cairns up this trail. Where the trail is little more than a ghost, simply continue straight up the fall line of the hill.

 NORTHBOUND HIKERS will benefit from frequent large tree blazes that face uphill.

Reach a flat saddle on top of the ridge at mile 0.8 (10,500). Watch out for the many mining excavations in this area, some of which are 20 feet deep with vertical sides.

 The trail and cairns disappear now. Turn a little to the right and walk southwest to the other side of the saddle. Bear right, maintaining an even elevation across the gentle slope, bearing about 240°.

Turn right (west-northwest) onto a very clear dirt road in 0.1 mile and follow its persistent climb through trees and meadows to a T intersection at mile 1.6. Turn left (west) and continue as the road tops out in 0.1 mile (10,940), swings back to the south, and descends to Mill Creek and Forest Route 171.3 at mile 2.5 (10,510).

Turn left onto Forest Route 171.3 and walk 50 yards beyond the Mill Creek crossing to a road intersection at mile 2.6. Bear left here (east) and follow the road's climb and eventual curve to the right (south) at mile 3.1. Take a left fork at mile 3.4 and a right fork, onto Forest Route 171.2, at mile 3.5. Descend slightly for 0.6 mile to where Forest Route 183.1 comes in from the right at a 45-degree angle (mile 4.1; 10,520). Turn right and climb to a T intersection at mile 4.8 (11,120). At this and each of the following intersections, follow signs for Forest Route 183.1. Turn left here, and continue straight ahead at a fork in 0.1 mile; then take a left (southwest) fork in another 0.6 mile (mile 5.5). At mile 6.1, the road crests a hill and descends to another intersection at mile 6.2. Stay right at this and the next intersection, where Forest Route 183.1D branches to the left (mile 6.4). Now the road flattens considerably and begins a gradual descent at mile 6.6. Watch for a lone pine tree on the left at mile 6.7, just before the road descends much more steeply. Turn left (west-southwest) at the tree onto a faint, overgrown road that climbs over the tundra.

As the road fades near the top of the ridge at mile 6.8 (11,680 feet; N39° 47.85', W105° 42.22'), bear right (west) and climb directly up the fall line. For the next 3.8 miles, there is not much of a trail, but the Forest Service plans to work on one in 1997. Continue almost due west along the top of the ridge. You are now on Breckinridge Peak, but it might better be named "Mount Sisyphus" for the king in classical mythology whose punishment it was to roll a rock to the top of a hill time after time, only to have it roll back down again. In this case, each time you reach what appears to be the final jaunt to the summit, a new slope of talus appears, leading still higher and farther away.

At a flat area at mile 7.5 (12,600), start bearing slightly more to the right, but don't lose any of your hard-won elevation! Your goal is not the summit of Breckinridge Peak, but the broad, flat saddle just beyond it to the northwest. As you pass under the right (north) side of the summit at mile 8.0 (12,720), the saddle should be visible straight ahead (west). Cross through the saddle at mile 8.3; then continue west-northwest to the isolated summit of Mount Flora at mile 8.9 (13,132 feet; N39° 48.29', W105° 44.08').

The mass of antennas, dishes, and other communication equipment you see to the west-southwest is the next landmark on the CDT. Walk off the back (west) side of Mount Flora on a gentle slope and follow the obvious ridgeline to the southwest. When you reach the deep saddle immediately below and northeast of the summit of Colorado Mines Peak at mile 10.2 (12,145), look slightly south of west (compass bearing 260°) toward the slope reaching down from the top of the peak, and head for a cairn on the horizon. From there, continue to climb across the slope, following its curve around to the left, until you are tracking almost due south. You should intercept a service road at mile 10.6 (12,280); follow it downhill to the south. If you cross under what looks like a power line before reaching the road, turn left (east), and follow the line uphill to the road.

From here, the CDT is visible across US-40, a little north of west, in the form of a ski lift service road climbing west from Berthoud Pass. This is also the course of the Divide.

At mile 11.0, the road switchbacks to the right (north) and continues its descent through four more sprawling switchbacks. Follow it to the large parking lot at Berthoud Pass, and the end of this segment, at mile 12.4 (11,315 feet; N39° 47.90', W105° 46.67').

OTHER HIKES AND RIDES

See Segment 13, page 121, and Segment 15, page 134.

Segment 15
Berthoud Pass to Herman Gulch Trailhead (Interstate-70)

Along the Divide near Jones Pass, Vasquez Peak Wilderness

19.4 miles
Difficulty: Strenuous

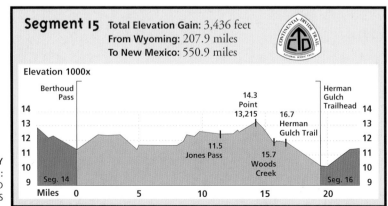

Segment 15   **Total Elevation Gain:** 3,436 feet
From Wyoming: 207.9 miles
To New Mexico: 550.9 miles

Elevation 1000x

Berthoud
Pass

14.3
Point
13,215

Herman
Gulch
Trailhead

14

13

12

11

10

9

16.7
Herman
Gulch Trail

11.5
Jones Pass

15.7
Woods
Creek

Seg. 14

Seg. 16

Miles   0   5   10   15   20

**YOU MAY
ENCOUNTER:**
MOTORIZED
VEHICLES

MUCH OF THE TRAIL on this segment exists only on maps or in the collective consciousness of the Forest Service, so a map, a compass, and this guide will be useful. The CDT was only recently designated here; some of it is still undetermined as this book goes to print. As a result, three different routes are mentioned at one point in this trail description. Note that the elevation profile and mileages are for the proposed Forest Service route (route #2).

Water is available at regular intervals, although it can be several miles between sources, especially over those stretches that follow the Divide proper. When you plan your camping in this area, you should know that the Henderson Molybdenum Mine far down in the valley south of Vasquez Pass emits an inescapable buzz audible from trail mile 3.5 to 14.3. The only respite is a campsite, mentioned at mile 8.4 on route #2, that is protected because it lies on the opposite side of the Divide from the mine. There are no CDT symbols after the first one at mile 0.1.

In spite of the buzzing annoyance, this segment captures the essence of the Divide in many ways. The immensity of two great watersheds is striking. One stretches to infinity across the populated plains to the east; the other undulates westward through the chaotic heart of the state. Here the CDT courses along ridges of barren, broken rock and bald summits buttressed by terrain too steep for humans, diving abruptly to green valley floors thousands of feet below. And, of course, there is that omnipresent vulnerability to the elements, as if we are suspended in the limitless space of the Rocky Mountain sky, at the mercy of the wind, marionettes of the indifferent clouds.

 MOUNTAIN BIKE NOTES: Mountain bikes are prohibited on this segment because of its passage through Vasquez Peak Wilderness.

MAPS

TRAILS ILLUSTRATED: 103, 104
USGS QUADRANGLES: Berthoud Pass, Byers Peak, Loveland Pass, Grays Peak
USFS: Arapaho/Roosevelt National Forests, pages 136–137

BEGINNING ACCESS POINT

 BERTHOUD PASS: Take US-40 14 miles west from Interstate 70 to the summit of Berthoud Pass. There is a parking area on the right (east) side of the highway.

ALTERNATE ACCESS

 JONES PASS ROAD: Take US-40 west from Interstate 70 9.0 miles to a turnoff on the left

---

Thanks

to the interstate

highway system,

it is now

possible

to travel across

the country

from coast to coast

without seeing

anything.

—Charles Kuralt,

On the Road

RANGER DISTRICT:
Clear Creek

(west) for Henderson Mine. Drive 1.7 miles and turn right onto a dirt road marked by a sign for Jones Pass. Continue about 0.75 mile to the unmarked CDT, which arrives via a roadcut in the trees on the right (north) where a power line crosses the road. The CDT now follows the road to Jones Pass. Note that this is one of three possible routes described for this section.

ENDING ACCESS POINT

HERMAN GULCH TRAILHEAD: See next segment.

SUPPLIES, SERVICES, AND ACCOMMODATIONS

WINTER PARK provides all services. Hitchhiking the 12.5 miles north (west according to the highway signs) should not be too difficult. See Segment12, page 114.

TRAIL DESCRIPTION From the parking lot, walk diagonally across the highway to the west toward an old road climbing into the trees from a gate with a CDT marker on it. A small stream, which should be reliable well into August in normal snow years, is just north (right) of the gate. Follow the switchbacking road to the top of a ski lift, behind which the road forms a loop. At the back of the loop (mile 0.8; 11,880), turn left (west) and follow a single-track trail toward a nearby rocky hump. You'll be able to see the trail zigzagging up a ridge to the west. A drainage on the right (north) side will provide reliable water if you're desperate enough to make the half-mile round-trip traverse.

> **WILDERNESS ALERT:**
> The Vasquez Peak Wilderness was designated in 1993 by federal law to be "an area where the earth and its community of life are untrammeled by man, where man himself is a visitor who does not remain." Its 12,300 acres are part of a larger core of primitive land encompassing the nearby Ptarmigan, Byers Peak, and Eagles Nest Wilderness areas. Please remember these rules governing wilderness travel: 1. Camp out of sight, at least 200 feet from lakes and streams, on dry, durable surfaces. 2. Use a stove instead of building a fire; use existing fire rings if you must have a fire. 3. Keep water sources pure by washing at least 200 feet from them. 4. Bury human waste six inches deep and 200 feet from lakes and streams. Pack out toilet paper. 5. Hobble or picket livestock at least 200 feet from lakes and streams, and use only treated, weed-free feed and grain. 6. All dogs must be on a leash. 7. No mountain biking. 8. Pack out all trash. Don't attempt to burn it.

The climb tops out at a sign announcing your entry into the Vasquez Peak Wilderness (mile 1.4; 12,280). The CDT follows the ridge to the right (west), circumnavigating the top of a prominent cirque. Ponds in the valley to the left (south) offer protected camping, but they are a steep 400 vertical feet below the trail. At Point 12,391 (mile 1.7; N39° 48.18', W105° 47.93'), the trail fades; continue around the cirque and along the ridge to the south where the trail is again visible. It soon fades, however, near a large rock that resembles a buffalo at mile 2.0. Strike a course for compass bearing 240°

and drop a little off the Divide proper as you pass to the west (right) of Point 12,424. As you walk, the dominant peak to the right (due west) is Vasquez; the pass of the same name is in the deep cut below and to the left of the peak.

From a shallow saddle at mile 2.5, climb along the faint trail and work your way around the right side of Point 12,507. Continue climbing somewhat, but not directly toward the summit. As you come around the bulk of the point, head for the trail in the distance and ignore the white stakes in this area. After another shallow saddle, you will reach a third saddle at mile 3.3 (12,370), from where a faint tread leads along the ridge line. As the trail fades about 100 yards short of a rocky hump, turn right (southwest) to pass under the hump and much higher Stanley Mountain. Maintain an even contour to the mountain's southwest ridge and follow a series of white posts descending parallel to and below the ridge on its northwest (right) side. Do not descend the very steep slope to the west (right), which leads to Vasquez Pass. At a post near a rocky point at mile 4.0 (12,160), start veering more to the right to pass further north (right) of the next such point. Now you should descend more rapidly toward the trees to the west-southwest. You may pick up a faint trail that switchbacks toward the trees. By now you'll be able to hear the steady hum of the mine in the valley below.

When you reach the first few trees (mile 4.4; 11,600), turn 90 degrees to the right (due north) and follow an intermittent trail 0.4 mile into the valley bottom (11,480). From here you have a choice: You may climb a short distance to Vasquez Pass and then follow the strenuous route that stays true to the Divide, eventually climbing over Vasquez Peak, or you may take one of two lower routes recommended by the Forest Service. For the Divide route (route #1), follow a trail north 0.3 mile to the pass, then turn left (west) and climb steeply up the Divide ridge. After many undulations, the ridge will curve south and meet the Forest Service route at Jones Pass, about 6.0 miles distant.

 NOTE that this option leads high above the trees and far from any water; it is seriously exposed to the elements, and you should not attempt it without map and compass.

For both of the lower Forest Service routes, cross the valley bottom and climb up the opposing slope, bearing a little left (west) across it until you reach the short, stubby trees near timberline at mile 5.0 (11,760). Turn left (southwest) and maintain an even contour as you work your way through patches of dwarf trees. Game trails here may help. You should crest a small ridge near mile 5.2, from where you will see (to the southwest) a steep, rocky ridge plunging into thick trees about 0.5 mile distant. Just short of this ridge, which runs north-south and forms the horizon, you'll see a faint trail slicing through a verdant slope of tundra grass, then climbing onto the ridge. This represents the proposed Forest Service route (route #2), which parallels the Divide for 2.8 miles before regaining it at a shallow saddle just west of Vasquez Peak. There is currently no continuous trail.

The other route (#3) is an optional bypass on established roads and will be offered as an alternative until the proposed route can be built and signed (in 1997). It begins near a flat spot or hump in the trees just below where the rocky ridge meets the timber. If you wish to take it, make a mental note of the flat spot in the trees and continue traversing across the slope you are standing on, maintaining your elevation at or above timberline to avoid the thick tangle of flora slightly lower. As you near the ridge at mile 5.6, drop below a rock outcropping, away from the clear trail that route #2 will take, and follow a bench west-southwest toward the trees, which you should enter at mile 5.8 (11,540). Stay above the slope dropping off sharply to your left (south-southeast) into thick timber and continue about 0.1 mile until you reach the gentler ground of the ridge crest. Turn left (south) and descend along the right side of and parallel to the ridge crest, keeping your eyes open for a somewhat obscure old roadbed less than 0.1 mile distant. It is overgrown with young spruce trees and runs perpendicular to your path. If you reach the steep slopes with views of the mining operations in the valley, you've gone too far.

Turn right (west) onto the road and follow its gentle descent through six switchbacks and over several perennial streams to Jones Pass Road at mile 7.8 (10,200 feet; N39° 46.26', W105° 51.19'). Turn right (west) once again.

N   **NORTHBOUND HIKERS** will recognize this left turn by a power line that crosses the road here; walk under the power line and look for the clear roadcut entering the trees. The main roadbed climbs steadily; avoid the spur roads descending from it.

Bear right at a fork at mile 8.1. Don't get water out of the Clear Creek West Fork when you cross it at mile 8.8; it flows directly out of some mine tailings. Follow many switchbacks to the summit of Jones Pass, at mile 11.5 (12,451).

Route #2 Description: The Forest Service plans to build a trail along this route in the near future. For now it's a bit of a scramble, but more scenic than route #3. Follow a clear trail up onto the treeless ridge (mile 5.7) and scope out, among large boulders and green ground cover 0.4 mile to the southwest, what would be an ideal campsite were it not for the constant hum of the mine. You will cross a few streams as you make the intervening traverse. Then maintain an elevation near timberline as you follow the curve of the ridge to the right, until you are facing a little west of north (mile 6.8, 11,700), where the saddle just west of Vasquez Peak is visible at the head of the valley. Continue in that direction and cross a talus field with car-size boulders at mile 7.2. Climb away from the talus and onto a series of benches that lead to a sizable ravine. Cross near its top, work through stunted spruce trees on gentle terrain, and traverse across a steep slope on a good, level trail at mile 7.9. Continue a short distance north to the saddle, at mile 8.4 (11,940 feet; N39° 47.81', W105° 51.99'). Flat areas north of here combined with a clear pond at mile 8.5 make for nice camping just inside the wilderness boundary.

Turn left (west) and climb past Point 12,316; then follow the roller coaster ridge to Point 12,666, at mile 9.8. Turn left (south) and continue along the Divide ridge to a rocky point just north of Bobtail Peak at mile 10.7. Stay west (right) of this point. Don't be tricked at mile 10.9 into descending to the deep saddle to the west, but continue south over the crest of the ridge and pick up a tenuous path that parallels the Divide ridge from below. Reach Jones Pass, and join route #3, at mile 11.5 (12,451 feet; N39° 46.42', W105° 53.34'). (The distances to Jones Pass for routes #2 and #3 are coincidentally identical.) The remaining references to mileage are based on the proposed Forest Service route (route #2).

The unmarked CDT now follows the Divide ridge south on intermittent trails. Until the Forest Service completes its work here, this is what I found to be the easiest route: Staying on the right (west) side of the ridge line, cross a talus field under Point 12,700 on a faint trail that soon fades. Pass by a saddle, under a second point, and then traverse a steep hillside to a second saddle at mile 12.5 (12,530). Climb south along the ridge 0.3 mile to the top of Point 12,774. Then follow cairns to a saddle and an intervening point before reaching the base of the broken north ridge of Point 13,215 at mile 14.0. You may be distracted by the stupefying views: The Gore and Holy Cross Ranges are stunning in the west, handsome Pettingell Peak surveys its domain from the near horizon, and the headwaters of Clear Creek swirl far below the precipitous drop on your immediate left.

Check your auxiliary parachute as you climb along and just under the ridge on its right (west) side for about 0.1 mile; then climb back to the top to avoid cliffs. Navigate over a rocky dome, boulder-hop your way to gentler terrain, and reach the summit of Point 13,215, which God probably uses for target practice during a thunderstorm, at mile 14.3 (N39° 44.50', W105° 52.87').

Descend due south, bypass a rocky cone, and head toward a mellow saddle at mile 14.8 (12,810 feet; N39° 44.01', 105° 53.17'). You might take a moment before you get too low to look at a map and trace the Divide's circuitous path to Loveland Pass, visible to the south, via the craggy peaks just ahead.

Now the CDT leaves the Divide, which climbs the ragged east ridge of Pettingell Peak. Turn left and walk to the edge of the saddle. Then turn more to the left (due east) and face a bulge in the terrain that forms a bald flat area 400 vertical feet below. There is no trail as you walk to this flat area (mile 15.2; 12,400). Continue to its steep back side, turn right (southwest), and head for the top of the ravine formed by the headwaters of Woods Creek in the valley below. Descend slightly with each step (not too rapidly!) as you traverse above and through krummholz on the steep slope. As you near the valley bottom, look up on the ridge across the valley (compass bearing 160°), and spot a trail climbing to a small saddle. This is your next destination. The dark summit of Torreys Peak, the second highest point on the Continental Divide in the U.S. and Canada, looms directly in the background.

Woods Creek, at mile 15.7 (11,880), is a good source of water, and you may find a camp spot here. From the head of the creek, walk toward a point a little to the right of the target saddle (compass bearing 170°) until you pick up a trail of cairns. This leads to a clear path to the saddle, which is at mile 16.2 (11,950).

N **NORTHBOUND HIKERS** may want to pause here and look to the northwest, where the CDT reaches a saddle on the Divide ridge at the top of a yellow, funnel-shaped area of loose rock. Climbing from the headwaters of Woods Creek, the CDT makes a wide swing to the east, turning once at the flat point at mile 15.2.

Do not follow the trace of a trail that ascends to the southeast, but descend slightly along a small, grassy depression to the southwest for 40 yards; then turn right (west) on a trail that is occasionally vague and overgrown. Crags at the head of the valley define the path of the Divide here. When the trail fades at mile 16.4, continue in the same direction at a constant elevation and watch for cairns and colored flagging that mark the path of a trail the Forest Service plans to build in the near future. Reach the wide and clear Herman Gulch Trail at mile 16.7 (11,800) and turn left (southeast). Herman Lake, a popular hiking destination cradled by the rugged Divide, is 0.3 mile up the trail to the right. It is a gorgeous place to park it for the night.

N **NORTHBOUND HIKERS** should turn right (east) off the trail as it climbs out of the last of the trees into a sloping meadow. Continue at least 100 yards before picking up a trail of cairns and colored flagging.

The Herman Gulch Trail makes a steady descent through meadows and healthy growths of spruce. Late in the season, the enchanting translucent blue of gentian that adorns the trail here is a harbinger of the approaching winter. Take note, through-hikers! At mile 18.3, there may be remnants, even in September, of the previous winter in the form of deep patches of snow, quiet reminders of the fury of an avalanche.

As the trail nears Interstate 70 at mile 19.3, take a right fork switchbacking to the southwest. This segment terminates at the Herman Gulch Trailhead parking lot at mile 19.4 (10,320).

OTHER HIKES

PTARMIGAN TRAIL TO JONES PASS
Approximate one-way distance: 13.0 miles or variable
Difficulty: Moderate

Ptarmigan Trailhead: From Interstate 70, take Exit 205 and turn right into Silverthorne. Turn north onto Rainbow Drive at the Wendy's restaurant and immediately turn right again at a four-way stop. Continue a short distance to another stop sign and make another right turn. Follow this road a short distance to the trailhead at the road's end.

Jones Pass: See *Access* for this segment.

Once a proposed route for the Continental Divide Trail, this trail clears timberline and enters the Ptarmigan Peak Wilderness after only a few miles. It then descends to the Williams Fork River South Fork, joins the South Fork Trail, and climbs into a craggy passage through a spur ridge of one of the Divide's most precipitous areas. The scenery here is incomparable. You may continue on to cross the Divide at Jones Pass, which is accessible to vehicles, and make this a one- or two-night shuttle hike.

HERMAN LAKE
Approximate one-way distance: 3.0 mile
Difficulty: Moderate

Herman Gulch Trailhead: See *Access* for the next segment.

This is an excellent hike if you are short on time or energy but still want to climb into the realm of the Continental Divide. The very clear trail makes a steady ascent covering 1,680 vertical feet. The lake nestles in the eastern shadow of monstrous Pettingell Peak. Most of this hike is on the CDT.

Tarn, Arapaho National Forest

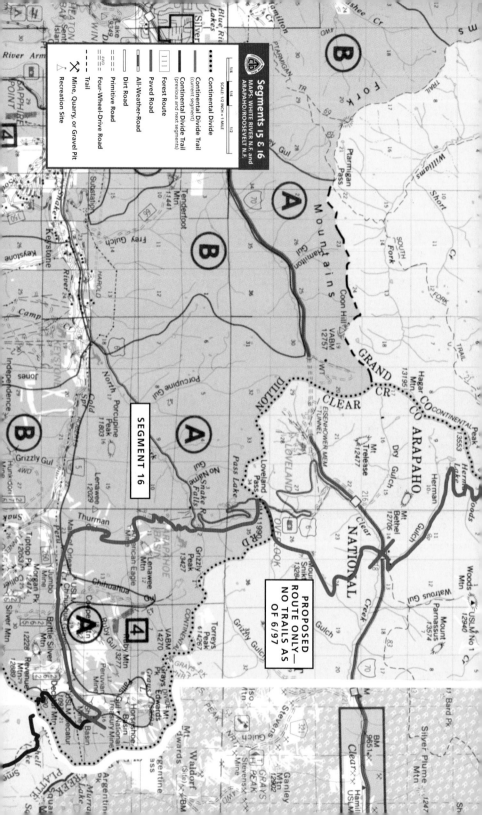

Segments 15 & 16
MAPS, WHITE RIVER N.F. and ARAPAHO/ROOSEVELT N.F.

SCALE: 1/2 INCH = 1 MILE

··········	Continental Divide
———	Continental Divide Trail (current segment)
·········	Continental Divide Trail (previous and next segments)
111	Forest Route
———	Continental Divide
═══	All-Weather-Road
═══	Paved Road
———	Dirt Road
═══	Primitive Road
4WD ──	Four-Wheel-Drive Road
─ ─ ─	Trail
✕	Mine, Quarry, or Gravel Pit
△	Recreation Site

SEGMENT 16

PROPOSED ROUTE ONLY— NO TRAILS AS OF 6/97

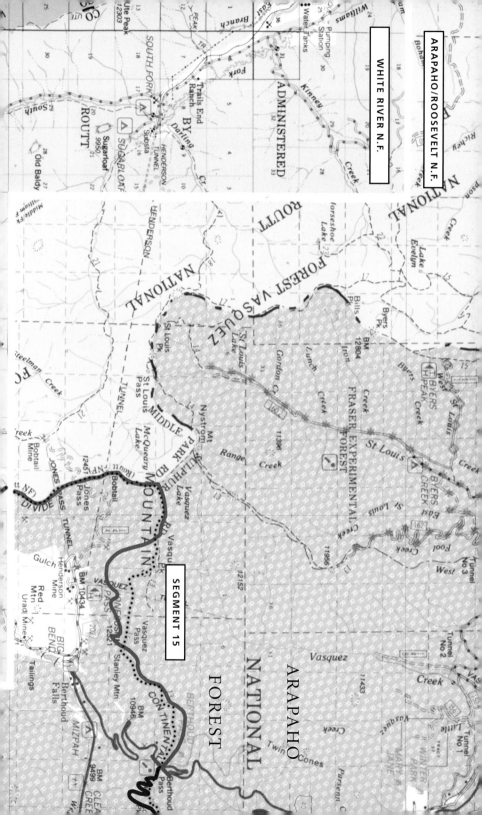

WHITE RIVER N.F.

SEGMENT 15

Segment 16
Herman Gulch Trailhead to Argentine Pass Trailhead

Bristlecone pine below the Divide, Arapaho National Forest

19.5 miles
Difficulty: Strenuous

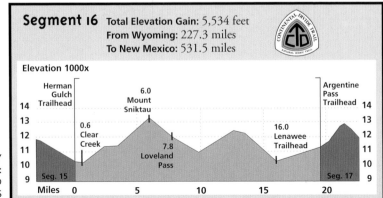

Segment 16 **Total Elevation Gain:** 5,534 feet
From Wyoming: 227.3 miles
To New Mexico: 531.5 miles

Elevation 1000x

Herman
Gulch
Trailhead

6.0
Mount
Sniktau

0.6
Clear
Creek

7.8
Loveland
Pass

16.0
Lenawee
Trailhead

Argentine
Pass
Trailhead

14
13
12
11
10
9

14
13
12
11
10
9

Seg. 15

Seg. 17

Miles   0   5   10   15   20

**YOU MAY
ENCOUNTER:**
MOTORIZED
VEHICLES

THIS SEGMENT CONTINUES the CDT's most recent departure from the Divide. In this case, the trail descends to Interstate 70 to avoid the terrain above Eisenhower Tunnel, which is Colorado's only land bridge from north to south across the interstate. Wildlife experts fear a formal trail here would disrupt animal migration patterns. Additionally, the area is essential wolverine habitat.

Much of the trail over the next two segments has yet to be constructed, so temporary alternative routes are described. Anyone trying to navigate the official proposed routes prior to their construction should be comfortable with a map, compass, and the techniques of Leave No Trace camping. Note that the elevation profile and mileages are for the proposed route, which climbs over Mount Sniktau.

This segment includes a traverse of Arapaho Basin Ski Area, which is generally the last ski area in the country to close, frequently staying open into June and sometimes until the Fourth of July. From there the CDT descends into the area around Montezuma, an authentic Colorado mining town rich in history. A man named D.C. Collier was among the first to mine the abundant silver tucked in seams under the nearby Continental Divide. More fortune-seekers soon arrived and Collier dubbed the resulting settlement "Montezuma" after the gloriously rich Aztec ruler.

Montezuma had the ore, but the fantastic geography that surrounded the community made it difficult or impossible to ship it where someone could actually use it—and pay for it. Stephen Decatur's attempt to put a road over 13,207-foot Argentine Pass (America's highest) proved too costly and dangerous to be useful. In fact, during the construction phase, new workers had to be hired every few weeks to replace the ones who had run off in fear.

Thus the town of Montezuma foundered until roads could be carved out of some of the less severe grades of several surrounding passes, including the one built by enterprising railroad man William A. H. Loveland in 1879. By 1880, the population of Montezuma had swelled to 800. Today, an eclectic post-boom community of 75 hangs on.

Water is regularly available on this segment, although you should avoid drinking from Peru Creek, between miles 16.0 and 19.5, because it is too close to mine tailings.

MOUNTAIN BIKE NOTES: This section is only bike-friendly if you take the bypass route on US-6 over Loveland Pass. The ride from the base of Arapaho Basin to the Lenawee Trail on the other side is excellent.

Inebriate of Air—

am I—

And Debauchee

of Dew—

Reeling through

endless summer

days—

From inns of

Molten Blue.

—Emily Dickinson

RANGER DISTRICTS:
Clear Creek
Dillon

MAPS

TRAILS ILLUSTRATED: 104

USGS QUADRANGLES: Grays Peak, Loveland Pass, Montezuma

USFS: Arapaho/Roosevelt National Forests, White River National Forest, pages 136–137

BEGINNING ACCESS POINT

 HERMAN GULCH TRAILHEAD: Take Exit 218 on Interstate 70 and follow signs a very short distance to the north side of the highway. Then turn right (east) into the parking area.

 LENAWEE AND CHIHUAHUA GULCH TRAILHEADS: These access points are near the town of Montezuma in Summit County, and the latter is the trailhead for a climb of Grays Peak. From US-6 at the east end of Keystone, turn south onto Montezuma Road and drive 4.5 miles to Peru Creek Road, which is on the left as the road makes a sharp turn in that direction. Continue 1.6 miles to where the Lenawee Trail, and the CDT, meet the road on the left (north). The Chihuahua Gulch Trailhead is 0.5 mile farther, across from a parking area on the right. The beginning of the next segment, the Argentine Pass Trailhead, is 3.0 miles beyond this.

ALTERNATE ACCESS

 LOVELAND PASS: Take Interstate 70 to Exit 216 and follow US-6 4.5 miles west to the summit of the pass.

ENDING ACCESS POINT

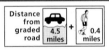 **ARGENTINE PASS TRAILHEAD:** See the next segment.

TRAIL DESCRIPTION

From the Herman Gulch Trailhead, walk 0.2 mile to the stop signs at the interchange and turn left (south). Walk under the highway bridge and turn right onto the eastbound off-ramp. Continue 0.2 mile to where flagging on the left (south) leads down toward the creek. Follow the frequently spaced flagging 0.1 mile and carefully cross the creek on a log (mile 0.6; 10,290). Climb out of the streambed and continue south into the forest a short distance to a man-made corridor running east-west through the trees that is scheduled to become a paved bike path in 1997.

At this point, you have a choice: You may either bushwhack to the summit of Mount Sniktau, which is the proposed Forest Service route, or you can take the temporary bypass on U.S. Highway 6. The latter is easier in terms of route-finding and physical exertion, but it follows the highway most of the way. For that description, skip ahead three paragraphs to "Route #2 Description."

 Proposed Forest Service route (#1): Until a trail is built (scheduled for 1997), the route described here should not be attempted without a compass and the USGS 7.5-minute Grays Peak quadrangle, or Trails Illustrated map #104.

Continue a little west of south into the thick trees and start up a formidable hill, staying on top of a timbered ridge (just west of a small tributary of Clear Creek on the map). After about 0.5 mile, you should reach a small saddle in the trees (10,900). Turn 45 degrees to the left (southeast) and climb diagonally up the steady slope. After

0.2 mile and about 200 vertical feet, start bearing more to the left (east), still climbing, but less rapidly. Clear elk trails here are a big help. If you reach timberline before making this turn to the left, you've gone too high.

Climb up the roughly 15-percent grade 1.0 mile to the east side of Mount Sniktau; then turn south to pass through a flat area immediately west of Point 11,444 (mile 2.3). Continue due south to a bowl with a broad, wet meadow, cross the stream at mile 2.7 (11,470), and bear south of east, maintaining an even contour for about 0.7 mile as you cross to the northeast end of the prominent east ridge of Mount Sniktau. Now climb southwest directly up the ridge toward Point 12,154. Continue to the summit of the mountain at mile 6.0 (13,234 feet; N39° 40.42', W105° 51.41').

Descend as you track a little west of south past Point 13,152 to Point 12,915 (mile 7.0), which is on the Continental Divide. (**NOTE:** From here, you may follow a difficult route that stays on the Divide and rejoins the standard route at mile 0.7 of the next segment. For details, skip ahead two paragraphs to the "Divide Variation.") To remain on the proposed standard route, follow the ridge that descends 0.8 mile west to the summit of Loveland Pass (mile 7.8; 11,990 feet; N39° 39.82', W105° 52.71'). Skip ahead one paragraph to the description from the top of Loveland Pass.

Route #2 Description: To take the bypass route from mile 0.6, turn right (west) onto the bike path corridor and pass under some ski lifts at mile 2.6; then continue 1.0 mile to meet U.S. Highway 6 where it makes a big hairpin curve across from a large stone sign for Loveland Basin. Climb onto the highway, turn left (south), and follow the winding road 4.0 miles to the summit of the pass. If you hitch, ask to be dropped off at the summit or at the Last Chance parking lot on the other side of the pass at the base of the ski area, which leaves you 0.1 mile downhill from the CDT's continuation onto a dirt road on the east side of the highway. **NOTE:** From the top of Loveland Pass, you may follow a difficult route that stays on the Divide and rejoins the standard route at mile 0.7 of the next segment. For details, skip ahead one paragraph to the "Divide Variation."

From the top of Loveland Pass, the proposed Forest Service route descends 2.0 miles along the east side of the creek east of the highway. There are currently some faint trails there, but some bushwhacking will also be required until trail construction is complete (scheduled for 1997). Descend to a dirt road on the east side of the highway next to a highway department storage facility at mile 9.8 (10,990). To avoid this bushwhacking, stay on the highway and descend 3.4 miles to the same dirt road on the left (east). If you hitch, ask to be dropped off at the Last Chance parking lot on the west side of the highway; then walk back uphill 0.1 mile and turn right (east) onto the dirt road. Skip two paragraphs to "Continuation of the standard route from the base of Arapaho Basin."

Divide Variation: The Forest Service has said that the ridgeline from Loveland Pass to Argentine Pass may be used as an alternative to the proposed standard route, which descends to the base of Arapaho Basin. This variation would keep you on the Divide, provide one of the most authentic Divide experiences anywhere, and allow you to traverse the Divide's highest point in the U.S. and Canada. It also involves a measure of danger that should be carefully considered. From Grizzly Peak to Torreys Peak, there is a 2,000-foot face of loose scree with potential rockfall. There is also a difficult knife ridge from Grays Peak to Mount Edwards. In the event of a thunderstorm, escape routes along this entire stretch are almost nonexistent.

 To take this route, use a map to follow the Divide ridge east and south to Argentine Pass, which is at the bottom of the USGS 7.5-minute Grays Peak quadrangle. From Argentine Pass, follow a trail south along the west side of the Divide, and pick up the standard route at mile 0.7 of the next segment, where the trail on which you are descending swings abruptly to the right (northwest).

Continuation of the standard route from the base of Arapaho Basin: Pass through a gate and follow the dirt road as it winds up the slopes of the ski area, trending south. You'll cross a reliable stream at mile 10.2. Turn right (west and north) when the road forks at mile 10.6. Follow the road south past the top of the Exhibition ski lift at mile 10.9. As the road climbs above timberline, take a look at the steep slopes all around you. In winter, this is all open to skiing, including, when conditions are right, the rocky chutes on the wall to the east (left).

At mile 12.4, near the top of the mountain, the road reaches a T intersection. Turn left (east) and continue straight ahead past the top of the Lenawee chairlift, and cross the trailless tundra toward a shallow saddle at mile 12.6 (12,460). Look to the left (east) for the continuation of a clear trail going up the side of the ridge. Dillon Reservoir comes into view to the west, backed by the splendid peaks of the Gore Range.

At mile 12.7, the single-track trail reaches the crest of a short ridge, just short of a rocky point. Follow the trail's turn to the left (northeast) and descend steadily around a bowl above the Thurman Gulch drainage. The CDT breaks out of the bowl at mile 13.5 (12,240) and rolls south and southeast across the open tundra for 0.5 mile before bending back to the right (northwest). The trail soon enters the trees, descending via many switchbacks before striking a consistent rate of descent to the east and crossing over several small streams. Follow the clear trail to the Lenawee Trailhead at mile 16.0 (10,340) and turn left (east) onto Peru Creek Road.

You will pass the trailhead to Chihuahua Gulch and Grays Peak at mile 16.5. For information on climbing Grays, the Continental Divide's highest point in Canada and the U.S., see *Other Hikes* at the end of this segment.

Continue up the road to mile 19.5 (11,280 feet; N39° 36.80', W105° 47.77') where the CDT reaches the single-track Argentine Pass Trail on the right (east), and the end of this segment. Note that the parking area for this trailhead is 0.4 mile back down the road at mile 19.1.

OTHER HIKES

GRAYS AND TORREYS PEAKS
Approximate one-way distance: 5.0 miles
Difficulty: Strenuous

Chihuahua Gulch Trailhead: This is located at mile 16.5 on this segment. For driving directions, see *Access* at the beginning of this segment.

Follow a four-wheel drive road up Chihuahua Gulch; then use a map to follow Ruby Gulch Road south of Grays Peak to its end at some mine ruins. Climb to the southwest ridge and take it to the summit. You may also follow the Continental Divide north a short distance to Torreys Peak; then choose your route down.

LOVELAND PASS INTERPRETIVE LOOP TRAIL
Approximate one-way distance: 3.5 miles
Difficulty: Easy

Loveland Pass Trailhead: See *Access* for this segment. The trail is on the west side of the pass.

This trail is slated for formal construction by the Forest Service in 1997 to offer non-CDT hikers a chance to experience the unique alpine environment of the Continental Divide. You'll find a heavily used, informal trail here. Please stay on the trail to avoid damaging the sensitive plant growth.

SUPPLIES, SERVICES, AND ACCOMMODATIONS

KEYSTONE provides limited services. For a more complete array, see Silverthorne below. Silverthorne is about 6.0 miles past Keystone on US-6. The small community of Grant is 5.0 miles down Guanella Pass Road to the east. There is not much there, but if you need food and/or lodging, it's worth the walk or hitch to the friendly Platte River Inn, at the intersection with US-285. Phone: (303) 838-4975.

DISTANCE FROM TRAIL: 6.5 miles

ZIP CODE: 80435

Bank	None; see Silverthorne below	
Bus	Summit Stage	(970) 453-1241
Camping	None	
Dining	Raz's, next door to grocery; breakfast and lunch only	468-9454
Gear	None; see Silverthorne below	
Groceries	Keystone Grocery, 21801 U.S. Highway 6	468-1102
Information	Keystone Lodge, U.S. Highway 6	468-2316
Laundry	None; see Silverthorne below	
Lodging	No affordable lodging; see Silverthorne below	
Medical	Snake River Health Services, near the ski area base	468-1440
Post Office	Next door to grocery	468-4510
Showers	None; see Silverthorne below	

SILVERTHORNE

DISTANCE FROM TRAIL: 9.0 miles

ZIP CODE: 80498

Bank	1st Bank, 160 U.S. Highway 6	(970) 468-8000
Bus	Summit Stage	453-1241
Camping	See Frisco, Segment 19, page 161	
Dining	Sunshine Cafe, Summit Place Shopping Center	468-6663
Gear	Wilderness Sports, Summit Place Shopping Center	468-5687
Groceries	City Market, U.S. Highway 6	468-2363
Information	409 Main Street, FRISCO	668-5800
Laundry	Laundromat, Summit Place Shopping Center	
Lodging	Alpen Hutte, 471 Rainbow Dr. (dorm style, $13)	468-6336
Medical	See Frisco, Segment 19, page 161	
Post Office	390 Brian Ave.	468-8112
Showers	Suds 'Ur Duds, Summit Place Shopping Center	

OTHER NOTES: The Silverthorne Recreation Center has a hot tub and showers for one low fee and is on the bus line. It is at 430 Rainbow Dr. Phone: 468-0711.

Segment 17
Argentine Pass Trailhead to Gibson Lake Trailhead

Mount Guyot, along the Divide

21.5 miles
Difficulty: Strenuous

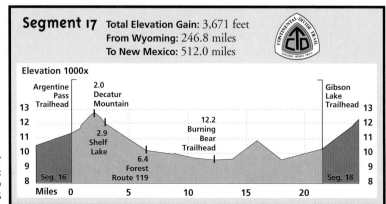

Segment 17   **Total Elevation Gain:** 3,671 feet
From Wyoming: 246.8 miles
To New Mexico: 512.0 miles

Elevation 1000x

Argentine Pass Trailhead

2.0 Decatur Mountain

2.9 Shelf Lake

6.4 Forest Route 119

12.2 Burning Bear Trailhead

Gibson Lake Trailhead

Seg. 16

Seg. 18

Miles   0   5   10   15   20

YOU MAY ENCOUNTER: MOTORIZED VEHICLES

THE LACK OF TRAIL CONSTRUCTION on the last
segment continues on the first 2.9 miles of this one, so pay close
attention to the directions. Between miles 6.8 and 12.2, similar
vigilance is required as the CDT follows a maze of connector trails
that are clearly established but not marked with CDT symbols.

The dominant feature on this segment is 12,890-foot
Decatur Mountain, named for Stephen Decatur, whose real name
was Bross. (A nearby fourteener was named after his brother
William, a former governor of Illinois.) The enigmatic Decatur
was a hero of the Mexican War, a polygamist with several Native
American wives, and an enterprising businessman who built the
precarious, often deadly, and ultimately unprofitable road over
Argentine Pass. The traverse of Decatur Mountain, from about
mile 1.0 to mile 3.0, is well above timberline and exposed, so
avoid this section during afternoon thunderstorms.

Water and campsites are plentiful on this segment. There
are no CDT markers.

MOUNTAIN BIKE NOTES: The first 6.4 miles of this
segment are not rideable. The remainder, however, offer
some good moderate riding. The winding downhills of the Burning
Bear Trail, near the end of the segment, are particularly fun.

MAPS

TRAILS ILLUSTRATED: 104 (The 1996 edition of this map
does not include the section of trail on the USGS 7.5-minute
Jefferson quadrangle. Trails Illustrated plans a revision for
future editions.)

USGS QUADRANGLES: Montezuma, Mount Evans, Jefferson

USFS: Arapaho/Roosevelt National Forests, White River National
Forest, pages 150–151

BEGINNING ACCESS POINT

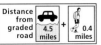

ARGENTINE PASS TRAILHEAD: From
US-6 at the east end of Keystone, turn
onto Montezuma Road and drive 4.5 miles
to Peru Creek Road, which is on the left as the road makes a sharp
turn in that direction. Turn left and continue about 4.7 miles to
a parking area for the Argentine Pass Trail. Walk 0.4 mile up the
road to the trailhead, which is marked by a sign on the right side
of the road. This is at trail mile 6.4.

ALTERNATE ACCESS

Distance from graded road	3.5 miles

SMELTER GULCH/SHELF LAKE TRAILHEAD:
From Denver, take US-285 to the small hamlet
of Grant and turn right (north) onto Guanella

Sweet

is the breath

of morn,

her rising sweet,

With charm

of earliest birds.

—John Milton,

Paradise Lost

RANGER DISTRICTS:
Dillon
South Platte

Pass Road. The Burning Bear Trailhead, part of the CDT, is on the left 5.0 miles from US-285. Continue 1.8 miles beyond this point and turn left (northwest) onto a road 10 to 20 yards before a sign for Duck Creek Picnic Ground and Geneva Park Campground. This is Forest Route 119, which offers camping on both sides 0.3 to 0.6 mile from the turnoff. At mile 3.1 from the turnoff, the CDT joins Forest Route 119 where Forest Trail 600 comes in from the left. Continue to mile 3.5, where two large boulders block a road forking to the right (northwest). This is Forest Trail 634, the path of the CDT from Shelf Lake. There is room for one or two cars to park here.

ENDING ACCESS POINT

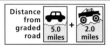

GIBSON LAKE TRAILHEAD: See the next segment.

SUPPLIES, SERVICES, AND ACCOMMODATIONS

The small town of Grant is 5.0 miles from the trail on US-285. There is nothing there except the friendly motel/restaurant called the Platte River Inn Restaurant and Lounge (303) 838-4975.

TRAIL DESCRIPTION
Follow the single-track Argentine Pass Trail as it passes through willows, crosses a small stream, and climbs through some trees. After about 0.5 mile, as you approach a power line, take note of the deepening gully on the right (south) side of the trail.

At mile 0.7 (11,760 feet; N39° 36.39', W105° 47.36'), just before the trail makes a sharp switchback to the left (north), drop off to the right and cross above the top of the gully, bearing due south toward the opposing ridge across the valley. Cross under the power line and then, just upslope from it, reach a reliable stream at the base of the ridge (mile 0.8; 11,880).

NORTHBOUND HIKERS can opt for the more difficult route that stays true to the Divide all the way to Loveland Pass. At mile 0.7, follow the trail as it climbs to the north. Be sure to refer to the discussion of the "Divide Variation" in the previous segment.

Climb a short distance south to the crest of the ridge. Now you may turn a little to the left (still south) and follow the ridge to the top of Decatur Mountain's north summit. Or you may look down along the west side of the ridge for an old trail winding up to a saddle just northeast of the mountain's true summit. The Forest Service should be improving this trail in 1997. In either case, when you reach the top, turn right (southwest) and follow this high ridge a short distance toward the summit of Decatur Mountain. You'll see Shelf Lake at the bottom of the steep cirque on your left. Pass between the summit and a precarious, twisted snow cornice on the left (east) at mile 2.0 (12,870 feet; N39° 35.65', W105° 47.69'). Stroll 30 yards to the flat summit of the mountain for 360-degree views.

Bear to the left (southeast), away from the summit and along the steep, narrow ridge, keeping the deep azure of Shelf Lake on your immediate left. After you reach a saddle at mile 2.3, cross over a rocky hump to another saddle at mile 2.4 and around the left (northeast) side of another rocky hump to a third saddle at mile 2.5 (12,500). From here, drop off the ridge to the left (east). The south end of Shelf Lake, which comes into view after a few yards, is the next destination of the CDT. Work your way to the right (northeast) around the top of a ravine and descend toward a less steep, grassy slope in that direction. Follow that slope's descent to the east. About two-thirds of the way down, at mile 2.7, be sure to turn back to the left (northwest) in order to reach the flat area near the south end of Shelf Lake at mile 2.9 (12,000). This area offers nice camping.

Continue toward the lake's outlet until you reach, at right angles, the trail that descends through the willows and away from the lake. Turn right (east) and follow the trail's descent. After the trail crosses the stream at mile 4.0, a lush spruce forest offers sheltered camping for the next mile. The CDT reaches unmarked Forest Route 119 at mile 6.4 (10,138). Turn left and continue southeast 0.4 mile to Forest Trail 600, which is marked.

Now it is especially important to follow the directions carefully. Turn right (southwest) onto this trail and cross over a stream in 0.1 mile; then follow the trail's bend to the left (south). Continue 0.6 mile and pass by two ponds on the left (east). Then go another 0.1 mile to a fork where the path to the right is marked as Forest Trail 600, and the path to the left is unmarked (mile 7.6; 9,995 feet; N39° 32.94', W105° 45.53'). Take the left (southeast) fork and pass by what looks like a developed, commercial summer camp area in 0.1 mile. Continue to a small stream crossing at mile 7.9. In another 0.3 mile, turn left (southeast) onto a road that soon becomes a single-track trail. Continue 0.5 mile to an obscure but important trail fork at mile 8.7 (9,930 feet; N39° 32.35', W105° 44.92') and turn right (south). After a 0.1-mile hill climb, turn left (southeast) onto a road in the midst of a garden of huge boulders. In another 0.2 mile, the road joins another road and turns to the right (south), and passes by a corral before it enters a large park at mile 9.5 (9,825 feet; N39° 31.70', W105° 44.81'). The Forest Service intends to construct a trail from here south through Geneva Park to the Burning Bear Trail. For now, continue east 0.9 mile to Guanella Pass Road and turn right (south) at the unmarked intersection. Follow the road 1.8 miles and turn right (southwest) onto the trail at Burning Bear Trailhead (mile 12.2; 9,605).

At mile 12.4, the trail turns to the left (south) and crosses over Geneva Creek, where you'll find a nice campsite. When other trails occasionally fork off, follow signs that say "Trail." The trail approaches Burning Bear Creek at mile 13.1 and parallels it upstream, crossing it at mile 13.8. Now follow a gradual ascent up the stream and cross back to the left (south) side at mile 14.7. After several switchbacks, you'll reach the top of the climb at mile 15.9 (10,860). Descend the other side, crossing a tributary of Lamping Creek in 0.5 mile and continuing to the south. Camping is available in this area.

The trail crosses the creek two more times before turning abruptly to the right (southwest) at mile 17.6. Follow its 0.4-mile descent to County Road 60 (9,560) and turn right (west). Campsites are plentiful here, particularly after mile 19.7, but you should not drink the water until you are past the contaminated tributary of the South Platte River North Fork at mile 20.1. Continue 3.5 miles from the Burning Bear Trail to the Gibson Lake Trailhead parking area, which is on the left side of the road at a sign that says "Park Straight In." A sign at the far end of the parking lot identifies this as the trail to Gibson Lake. This marks the end of this segment (mile 21.5; 10,316 feet; N39° 29.51', W105° 49.35').

MOUNTAIN BIKE RIDES

WEBSTER PASS ROAD TO SAINTS JOHN or TIGER ROAD VIA SWANDYKE
Approximate distance: 14.0 mile loop or 18.0 miles one-way
Difficulty: Strenuous

Webster Pass Trailhead: Park in the town of Montezuma at a lot on the west side of the road at the intersection with the road to Saints John.

Tiger Road: See the driving directions for Middle Fork Road under *Access* for the next segment.

Ride to a turnoff for Webster Pass Road on the left. After about 3.5 miles, take a right fork onto the Radical Hill Jeep Trail. The road climbs near the Divide. In about 3.0 miles, a right fork will take you through Saints John and back to Montezuma via some very demanding riding. For a shuttle ride, continue to the south and descend steeply to the site of Swandyke, a short-lived mining camp. This road becomes Tiger Road and descends to Colorado Highway 9. There are numerous places to leave a shuttle vehicle all along Tiger Road.

WHAT IS THE DIVIDE'S HIGHEST POINT?

The highest point on the Continental Divide in the U.S. and Canada is Colorado's Grays Peak. At 14,270 feet in elevation, Grays presides over the Divide's southernmost reach in the Front Range before it swings back to the west toward the mighty Sawatch Range. Since the Continental Divide National Scenic Trail does not cross over Grays Peak, it finds its highest point much further south, but still in Colorado, on 13,334-foot Coney Summit.

Given the many higher peaks of Alaska and Canada, it may seem odd that the relatively medium-sized Grays should hold this lofty distinction. But the Divide seems to have had a mind of its own in the determination of its course. It is remarkable that, of Colorado's 54 mountains that tower above 14,000 feet, the Continental Divide reaches the summits of only two of them. Grays is one; nearby Torreys Peak, at 14,267 feet, is the other.

But, since this Divide is continental, to be fair we must consider its path through all of North America. This involves adding Mexico and Central America, where you may not expect the land to rise above Colorado's famed fourteeners.

But Mexico has several high volcanoes, and one of them lifts the Divide to an astounding 17,925 feet above sea level. As the fifth-highest peak in all of North America, Popocatépetl (po-po-cuh-TEP-etl) rises into air whose thinness renders it incapable of holding enough heat—even at this balmy southern latitude—to melt the permanent glaciers that encrust the volcano's upper reaches. In fact, its icy high-altitude environment has for years attracted aspiring mountain climbers practicing for more challenging ascents elsewhere in the world.

But just as the Divide and the natural elements that surround it are unpredictable in our area, so it is in Mexico. In December, 1994, Popocatépetl began spewing smoke and ash into the air and onto the surrounding towns and cities. Through 1996, climbing on the mountain was not possible. "Popo" usually quiets down after a few years, but it does have a history of erupting with catastrophic results every couple thousand. If the mountain heats up enough to melt the glaciers, a deluge of mud and water will race down the steep slopes with apocalyptic force, inundating the surrounding area. The 30 million people within the volcano's reach, many of whom live in Mexico City, are understandably keeping a wary eye on this smoldering giant.

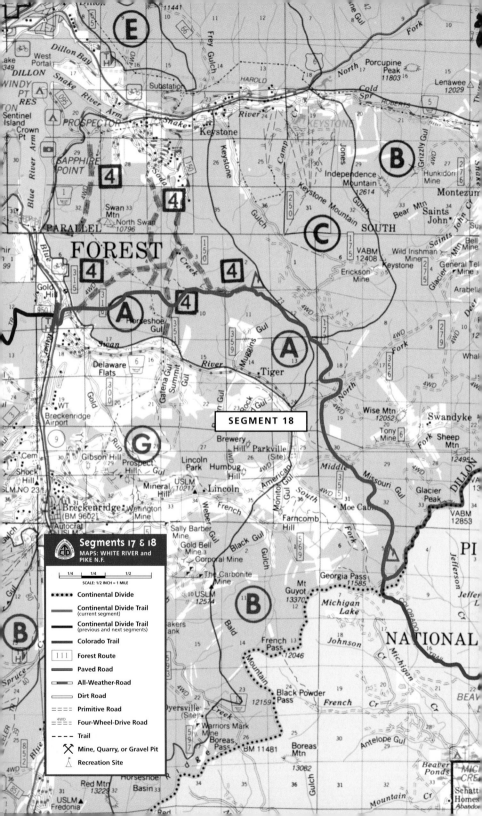

SEGMENT 18

Segments 17 & 18
MAPS: WHITE RIVER and PIKE N.F.

1/4	1/4	1/2

SCALE: 1/2 INCH = 1 MILE

•••••• Continental Divide
——— Continental Divide Trail (current segment)
——— Continental Divide Trail (previous and next segments)
——— Colorado Trail
|111| Forest Route
——— Paved Road
▭▭▭ All-Weather-Road
▭▭▭ Dirt Road
==== Primitive Road
4WD
- - - Four-Wheel-Drive Road
- - - Trail
✕ Mine, Quarry, or Gravel Pit
⛺ Recreation Site

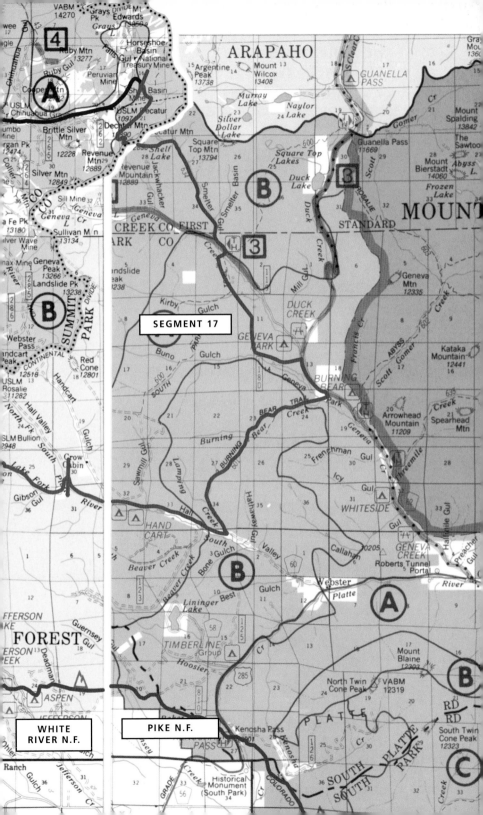

SEGMENT 17

Segment 18
Gibson Lake Trailhead to Gold Hill Trailhead (Colorado Highway 9)

Autumn colors, Arapaho National Forest

29.2 miles
Difficulty: Moderate

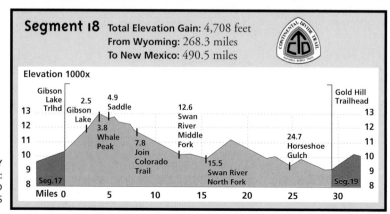

Segment 18 **Total Elevation Gain:** 4,708 feet
From Wyoming: 268.3 miles
To New Mexico: 490.5 miles

CONTINENTAL DIVIDE TRAIL
CDT
NATIONAL SCENIC TRAIL

Elevation 1000x

Gibson Lake Trlhd — 2.5 Gibson Lake — 4.9 Saddle — 3.8 Whale Peak — 7.8 Join Colorado Trail — 12.6 Swan River Middle Fork — 15.5 Swan River North Fork — 24.7 Horseshoe Gulch — Gold Hill Trailhead

Seg.17   Seg.19

Miles 0   5   10   15   20   25   30

13 12 11 10 9 8

YOU MAY ENCOUNTER:
MOTORIZED VEHICLES

FOUR MILES OF THIS SEGMENT follow the Continental
Divide along its southwest bend away from the Front Range,
continuing its foray deeper into the next tier of the Colorado
Rockies. This is also the last stretch of Divide the trail will actually
follow for a while, as it joins the tamer Colorado Trail to avoid miles
of trailless ridges along the Divide between here and Chaffee
County a considerable distance to the south.

Colorado's rich history of demanding routes over the
Divide continues here with Georgia Pass. Ute and Arapaho
Indians were the first to frequent the pass, and their presence
often caused white settlers to use more dangerous detours. In
1859, miners flowed through this passageway to the rumored
riches of the Blue River Valley. For a while it was also used as a
toll road.

Water is available at regular intervals on this stretch of
the CDT, but one of those intervals is 10.1 miles long, from Gibson
Lake to Missouri Gulch Creek. Between Gibson Lake at mile 2.5,
and the spot where the trail quits the Divide ridge at mile 7.8,
there is no suitable camping and also no clear trail. Following
these directions in conjunction with a map is recommended.

Exposure to lightning is a serious concern on and near
the Divide. Motor vehicles are not allowed on this segment, except
for a short section of road near Glacier Peak. After mile 7.8, the
trail follows a popular mountain bike route that attracts droves
of fat-tire enthusiasts.

 MOUNTAIN BIKE NOTES: Approximately the first
7.0 miles of this segment are not rideable, but the
remaining 22.2 miles provide excellent biking.

The wind blows

where it chooses,

and you hear

the sound of it,

but you do not know

where it comes from

or where it goes.

—John 3:8

MAPS
TRAILS ILLUSTRATED: 104, 108, 109
USGS QUADRANGLES: Jefferson, Boreas Pass, Keystone, Frisco
USFS: Pike National Forest, White River National Forest,
pages 150–151

BEGINNING ACCESS POINT
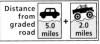 **GIBSON LAKE TRAILHEAD:** Drive
3.3 miles south of the small town of Grant
on US-285 and turn right (northwest) onto
County Road 60 (Forest Route 120). In 3.0 miles, the CDT joins
the road in the form of the Burning Bear Trail at a small pullout
on the right. Continue 3.5 miles beyond this point to the Gibson
Lake Trailhead parking area, which is most easily recognized by a

RANGER DISTRICTS:
South Platte
Dillon

sign on the left side of the road that says "Park Straight In." The trail begins at a sign at the far side of the parking lot giving the distance to Gibson Lake.

ALTERNATE ACCESS

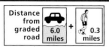

SWAN RIVER NORTH FORK: From Interstate 70, take exit 203 onto Colorado Highway 9 south. Drive 6.5 miles and turn left (east) onto Tiger Road at a sign for the Breckenridge Golf Club. Continue 5.9 miles and turn left at a post indicating North Fork Road. There is ample parking 0.6 mile up this road. Walk 0.2 mile farther to where the CDT, marked by Colorado Trail signs, crosses the road at trail mile 15.8.

You may also stay on Tiger Road and continue 2.4 miles to another intersection with the CDT, where the road is referred to as Middle Fork Road, at trail mile 12.7. Both spots offer water and camping.

ENDING ACCESS POINT

GOLD HILL TRAILHEAD: See the next segment.

SUPPLIES, SERVICES, AND ACCOMMODATIONS

The Summit Stage provides convenient transportation all over Summit County. Use it to go to Frisco, 5.0 miles north on Colorado Highway 9, (see Segment 19, page 161). For a more complete selection of camping gear, or for a hot tub at the Silverthorne Recreation Center, continue 4.0 more miles to Silverthorne (see Segment 16, page 143).

TRAIL DESCRIPTION

Follow the trail past the sign, through some willows, and over the South Platte River North Fork; then climb immediately through a moist spruce forest. The clear trail trends west-northwest, climbing past timberline at mile 1.8. After crossing the headwaters of the river's Lake Fork, climb slightly until the trail fades. Continue straight ahead (west) a short distance to where Gibson Lake comes into view at mile 2.5 (11,870). This is the last water for 10.1 miles.

Because there is no clear trail for the next 5.3 miles, you should use a map in conjunction with reading these directions.

Look across the lake at the high ridge to the southwest and spot two saddles next to each other. The smaller one on the right is your immediate destination, but no trail had been constructed at the time of this writing. Look for a mine tailing a little to the left (south), just above lake level. Climb the slope along the tailing's right edge and pick up an intermittent trail that begins a gradual climb toward the small saddle, bearing a little south of west. As you cross over some fingers of talus stretching down through the tundra, aim for a switchbacking trail visible near the top of the climb.

Reach the top of the ridge at mile 3.3 (12,550). Turn right and follow a faint trail along the crest of the ridge, passing after a short while to the left of the jumbled rock of what appears to be Whale Peak's summit. Then climb parallel and to the right of a deep, usually snowy ravine. Reach the broad expanse of the peak's summit plateau at mile 3.8 (12,990), where you rejoin the Continental Divide for the next 4.0 miles. Continue straight ahead to the west-northwest as numerous mountain ranges come into view. Follow an intermittent trail along the ridge west and then south to a major saddle at mile 4.9 (12,620).

Now look up on the ridge in front and slightly to your right (southwest) and spot a road high on the north flank of Glacier Peak. Angle diagonally up the slope to pick up that road at mile 5.5 (12,750). Follow the road's bend to the left (southwest) around the crest of the ridge and its subsequent sharp drop from Glacier Peak. Now look down the slope in front of you to a flat saddle where the road forks. Descend and take the left fork (mile 6.0; 12,300), which stays high atop the Divide ridge as it trends to the south.

After 1.1 miles, the CDT begins a sharp descent to a broad saddle where several roads intersect at mile 7.6 (11,785). Continue in about the same direction on the lower road on the right (west) until the Colorado Trail crosses the road at mile 7.8. Join the Colorado Trail by turning sharply to the right and following the single-track trail east-northeast, parallel to the road you just left. This may seem the long way around, but please use it to avoid creating multiple trails.

As the trail descends gradually into the trees, it becomes clearer and swings to the left until it is heading north-northwest. Then it winds its way through the trees, breaking into occasional clearings until it crosses a narrow, overgrown road at mile 10.7 (10,900). Now the CDT crosses over to the right (north) side of the ridge it has been descending along and crosses over another trail at mile 11.1. After more switchbacks, you'll reach Missouri Gulch Creek, the first water in 10.1 miles. You'll cross the Swan River Middle Fork 50 yards later at mile 12.6 (10,166). Climb 100 yards to the Middle Fork Road, turn right (east), walk 25 yards, and turn left (north) onto the continuation of the trail, which is marked by a Colorado Trail symbol. You can choose from a number of good campsites along the road.

At mile 13.8 (10,230), the trail tops out in the anomalous wasteland left by a timber clearcut before it descends to cross the Swan River North Fork on a very nice bridge at mile 15.5 (9,930). The trail parallels the stream to the northeast and becomes a little undefined after passing by an established campsite. When the faint trail splits at mile 15.7, take the left fork due north to cross the North Fork Road 0.1 mile later. Colorado Trail symbols mark this intersection.

The CDT climbs steadily now, twice crossing over a tributary of the river before trending north and northwest to a high point on a flat ridgetop at mile 18.2 (11,220), from where the runs of Keystone Resort ski area come into full view. The clear trail soon veers more to the west and descends via many switchbacks to a low point at mile 22.1 (9,950). Climb briefly to where the trail passes through an interesting phenomenon of lodgepole pine forest growth known as doghair. Doghair is characterized by innumerable skinny, tightly spaced trees, some of which may be 100 hundred years old. Doghair growth is the result of a survival adaptation in pine trees called serotiny. In this process, instead of dropping seeds when they are mature, like most tree species, several kinds of pine will retain their seeds in tightly sealed cones that remain attached to the branches for many years. Then, in the event of a fire or other disturbance, the cones open and disperse their seeds while the fire destroys other species that compete with the pine. The ground is inundated with seedlings and the resulting huge number of sprouts prevents any one individual from getting the nutrients or space it requires for normal development. The dense, impenetrable forest of uniform shapes and patterns that follows induces an eerie claustrophobia in the forest traveler.

Descend to a power line at Horseshoe Gulch (mile 24.7; 9,450), which has the first reliable water since the Swan River North Fork. Another brief climb leads to the final descent on this segment, where the trail hits a rocky road at mile 28.3. Turn left (southwest) and pass through a gate and onto a cement sidewalk at mile 28.4 (9,180).

Brace yourself for the tidy surreality of a trailer/RV park. There are no trail markers here. Turn right onto a paved street, walk about 100 yards, and turn left (southwest) onto another street, which is marked a short distance ahead as Peak Three Drive. Pass by the tennis courts and clubhouse, follow the 90-degree turn to the left and turn right onto Peak One Drive at mile 28.7. Continue through a gate and across a parking lot 0.1 mile to a stop sign and turn right (south-southwest). A short distance beyond, turn right (north) onto Colorado Highway 9, continue 0.2 mile, and cross the highway to the Gold Hill Trailhead and parking lot at mile 29.2 (9,190 feet; N39° 32.46', W106° 02.49') where this segment ends.

N NORTHBOUND HIKERS departing from Gold Hill Trailhead will walk 0.2 mile south on Colorado Highway 9, then turn left at a sign for Tiger Run RV Resort. Continue 0.1 mile and turn left into the parking lot for RV check-in, pass by a gate, and follow the trail description in reverse. Note that the trail is disguised as a cement sidewalk for a few yards at mile 28.4.

MOUNTAIN BIKE RIDES

GEORGIA PASS BIKE RIDE
Approximate one-way distance: Up to 21 miles
Difficulty: Moderate

Gold Hill Trailhead: This is the best place to leave a car. See *Access* for the next segment. Follow this segment's directions in reverse to reach the single-track trail just behind an RV and trailer park.

This is an excellent, demanding mountain bike ride with some of the smoothest sustained downhills in the state. You can go as far as you want toward Georgia Pass. For added variety, explore the dirt roads leading up the three forks of the Swan River, or make it into a loop by following Tiger Road west back to the highway.

GOLD HILL TRAILHEAD TO KEYSTONE GULCH SHUTTLE BIKE RIDE
Approximate one-way distance: 18.0 miles or variable
Difficulty: Moderate

Gold Hill Trailhead: See *Access* for the next segment.
Keystone Gulch Trailhead: From Interstate 70, take US-6 east to Keystone and turn right (south) onto Keystone Road. Turn immediately left; then turn right onto Soda Ridge Road. Keystone Gulch Road is about 0.4 mile ahead on the left (south) side.

Start as for the Georgia Pass ride described above, but approximately 10 miles into the ride, look for a spur trail breaking off to the northeast (left). Use a map to follow this route into Keystone Gulch, where you can explore the ski area service roads before descending northwest along the dirt Keystone Gulch Road to the trailhead.

Resting at the campsite

Segment 19
Gold Hill Trailhead to Copper Mountain

Dillon Reservoir from the Tenmile Range

13.1 miles
Difficulty: Moderate

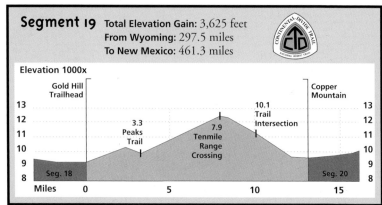

Segment 19 **Total Elevation Gain:** 3,625 feet
From Wyoming: 297.5 miles
To New Mexico: 461.3 miles

CONTINENTAL DIVIDE TRAIL · NATIONAL SCENIC TRAIL

Elevation 1000x

Gold Hill
Trailhead

Copper
Mountain

13		10.1	13
12		Trail	12
11	3.3	Intersection	11
10	Peaks	7.9	10
9	Trail	Tenmile	9
8	Seg. 18	Range	Seg. 20	8

Crossing

THIS
SEGMENT IS
CLOSED TO:
MOTORIZED
VEHICLES

Miles   0   5   10   15

THE CDT CONTINUES to stray further from the Continental Divide as it follows the path of the Colorado Trail. The Divide is occasionally visible on the peaks and ridges to the south, where it dips to such historic passes as Boreas, Hoosier, and Fremont.

This segment takes you through the heart of ski country, as it starts near the runs of Breckenridge and climbs over the Tenmile Range for a comprehensive view of Copper Mountain Resort. The route is never far from people or trailheads, traveling as it does between Colorado Highways 9 and 91. But the thick forests here offer some solitude and conceal wildlife, including elk and deer, and the views from atop the Tenmile Range are far-reaching.

Water is plentiful from mile 3.3 to 6.4. You'll find the best camping between miles 3.6 and 6.4. The first 3.6 miles are popular with mountain bikes. Severe thunderstorms often light up the above-timberline section here, especially in the afternoons of July and August.

 MOUNTAIN BIKE NOTES: This is a steep and difficult ride with sections where you will have to walk your bike.

MAPS

TRAILS ILLUSTRATED: 108, 109
USGS QUADRANGLES: Frisco, Breckenridge, Copper Mountain, Vail Pass
USFS: White River National Forest, pages 162–163

ACCESS

 GOLD HILL TRAILHEAD: From Exit 203 on Interstate 70, follow Colorado Highway 9 south 6.0 miles to a parking area on the right (west) where a sign marks the trailhead.

 COPPER MOUNTAIN: See the next segment.

TRAIL DESCRIPTION A very clear trail begins across the dirt road from the parking area and climbs immediately through lodge-pole pine punctuated with meadows of sage. Watch for mountain bikes. The ski runs of Breckenridge's four mountains are soon visible to the left (southwest), as is the Tenmile Range, which extends north from Breckenridge and over which the trail will soon climb. The CDT makes a gradual climb to mile 1.0 (9,680) where it brushes an old road. Stay to the left, following Colorado Trail signs to the southwest into what initially looks like a dense spruce forest, but which soon gives way to lodgepole pine.

Passing through

your wonderful

mountains and

canyons I realize

that this state

is going to be

more and more

the playground

for the entire

Republic.

You will see

this as the

real Switzerland

of America.

—Theodore Roosevelt,

on Colorado

RANGER DISTRICT:
Dillon

The trail passes by two timber clearcuts before crossing perpendicular to a road at mile 1.6 (9,960). You'll reach old roadbeds at miles 1.7 and 1.9; turn right (north) in both cases. A short distance ahead, the trail passes through a large clearcut, characterized by several gray piles of slash left by the logging operation. The twin peaks of Grays and Torreys are visible to the right (east-northeast). Look a little south of these peaks along the Continental Divide to see Mounts Baldy and Guyot.

About 80 yards after the clearcut, take a left fork. In 0.2 mile, there is a striking example of the phenomenon of doghair tree growth on the right side, where many pine tree trunks are only a few inches in diameter.

The CDT tops out on a small knob at mile 2.4 (10,290), from which several of the peaks of the Tenmile Range are visible to the west, including the sharp point of Peak 1. Now the trail descends the rocky ground to the west, crosses one more logging road at mile 2.8, which is marked by cairns and Colorado Trail symbols, and reaches the Peaks Trail intersection in a flourish of monkshood at mile 3.3 (9,915 feet; N39° 32.23', W106° 04.89'). Turn left and ascend along the trail, which is fanatically popular with mountain bikers, to a right (west) turn onto Miners Creek Trail at mile 3.6. The trail soon crosses over the reliable water of Miners Creek and bends left (southwest) to ascend along a small tributary. After two more crossings and a hard swing to the right (north) over about 0.6 mile, the CDT follows a contour along the slope. It soon turns left (southwest) and continues climbing along the edge of a ridge that drops off steeply to the north.

At mile 4.9 (10,560), the trail passes through a parking area (accessed by a four-wheel drive road) and continues at a sign for the Miners Creek Trail. Cross Miners Creek and follow the trail 0.6 mile into a very large avalanche path covered with beautiful wildflowers including aster, paintbrush, and bistort. The force of Nature is soon visible in a second avalanche path where thick logs have been snapped and crushed to splinters. After brief flat and descending sections, the CDT climbs steeply, following a thin finger of trees between huge, elongated piles of rock left by receding glaciers thousands of years ago. After the trail curves left (south) and heads for a low saddle, Dillon Reservoir, which quenches much of Denver's thirst, is visible to the northeast. Cairns and several steep switchbacks lead to the low saddle at mile 6.6 (11,840). (The erosion along the switchbacks is a result of people taking shortcuts.)

As you crest the saddle, the town of Breckenridge comes into view directly ahead in the valley. Continue along the very clear trail and look up to the right at snow cornices that remain well into August, and imagine them at their peak winter stature of up to 10 times higher than what you see in summer.

The trail bends right (west) to reach the top of the ridge at mile 7.9 (12,440 feet; N39° 30.30', W106° 06.87'). Straight out to the west is the vast expanse of Copper Mountain Resort, backed by the peaks of the Holy Cross Wilderness. Colorado Highway 91 climbs the valley to the left (east) of Copper Mountain to Fremont Pass on the Continental Divide, passing by mine tailings from the Climax Molybdenum Mine, which are also visible. The next segment of the trail follows a gulch on the far right (west) side of the ski area.

Cairns on the relatively flat top of the ridge will guide you over faint sections —or through snow—as the CDT bends left (southwest) and descends slightly along the ridge. After an equally slight climb to a rocky knob, the trail crosses a flat spot on the ridge, reaching a cairn at another rocky area at mile 8.3 (12,360).

Now the trail jumps off the ridge to the right (west) and descends to the south before following regular-sized cairns down the side of the ridge to a gigantic one, where there is a 90-degree turn to the right (west-southwest). After a short distance, the trail reaches the edge of the trees and turns abruptly back to the left (south) on a clear tread.

At an intersection at mile 10.1 (11,240), turn 180 degrees to the right (northwest) onto the Wheeler Trail and follow a steady descent to mile 12.1 where the trail turns left (west) and crosses under a power line. Just before a bridge at mile 12.2 (9,740), turn right (north) onto a jeep road toward Wheeler Flats and follow Tenmile Creek's east side. There are plenty of campsites here if you don't mind the proximity to Colorado Highway 91 and Interstate 70. After passing behind a Conoco station and a sewage treatment plant, cross Tenmile Creek on a cement bridge and reach a paved bike path at mile 13.1 (9,680 feet; N39° 30.55', W105° 08.51'). You will be facing precisely the wrong direction, so turn left (southwest) and cross the small tributary of Tenmile Creek on a wooden bridge. The parking lot here marks the end of this segment.

OTHER HIKES AND RIDES

No other well-established hiking or biking trails are accessible from this segment.

SUPPLIES, SERVICES, AND ACCOMMODATIONS

FRISCO is 5.0 miles north of the trail on Colorado Highway 9. For a more complete camping gear selection (or a soak in the Silverthorne Recreation Center's hot tub) continue an additional 4.0 miles to Silverthorne. The Summit Stage provides efficient transportation in this area. Copper Mountain, right on the trail at the end of this segment, has limited services, including a grocery store and a post office.

DISTANCE FROM TRAIL: 5.0 miles

ZIP CODE: 80443

Bank	WestStar, Seventh and Main	(970) 668-5353
Bus	Summit Stage	453-1241
Camping	Heaton Bay (primitive), about 1.5 miles out of Frisco on the Dam Road	
Dining	Golden Annie's, 603 Main	668-0345
	The Moose Jaw, 208 Main	668-3931
Gear	Antler's Trading Post, 908 N. Summit Blvd.	668-3152
Groceries	Safeway, 715 N. Summit Blvd.	668-5144
Information	409 Main	668-5800
Laundry	Frisco's Washtub, 406 Main	668-3552
Lodging	Snowshoe Motel, 521 Main ($37–$45)	668-3444
	New Summit Inn, 1205 N. Summit Blvd. ($64)	668-3220
Medical	Summit Blvd. and School Road	668-3300
Post Office	35 W. Main	668-5505
Showers	None	

SPECIAL NOTES: For an enchanting massage or hot tub, try Bodyworks Spa, 101 Forest Drive, 668-5859.

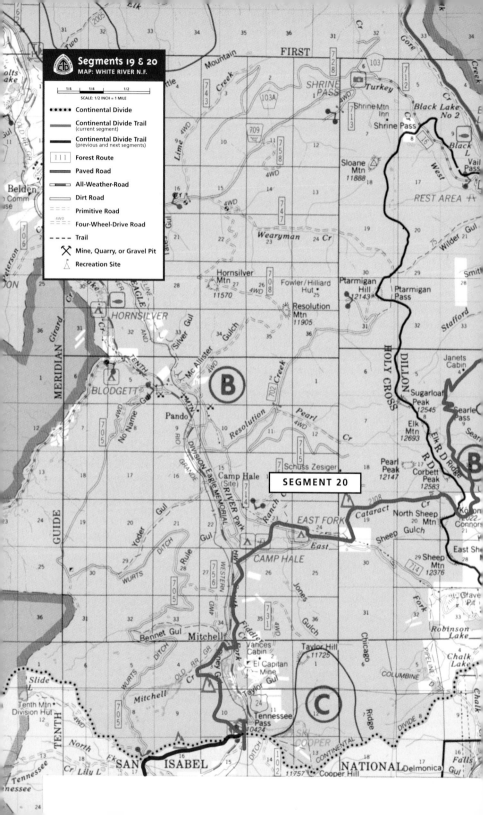

Segments 19 & 20
MAP: WHITE RIVER N.F.

SCALE: 1/2 INCH = 1 MILE

••••	Continental Divide
	Continental Divide Trail (current segment)
	Continental Divide Trail (previous and next segments)
|||	Forest Route
	Paved Road
	All-Weather-Road
	Dirt Road
- - -	Primitive Road
4WD	Four-Wheel-Drive Road
– – –	Trail
✕	Mine, Quarry, or Gravel Pit
⛺	Recreation Site

SEGMENT 20

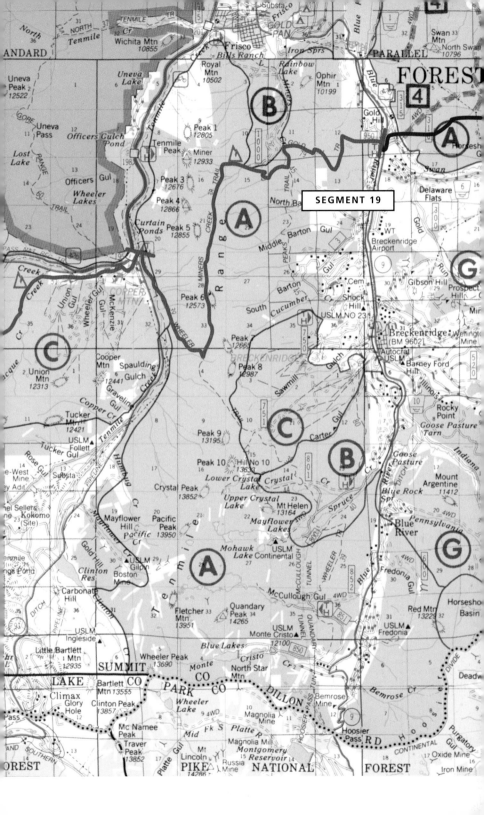

SEGMENT 19

Segment 20
Copper Mountain to Tennessee Pass

Indian paintbrush near Searle Pass, Arapaho National Forest

24.3 miles
Difficulty: Moderate

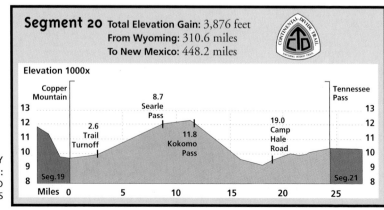

Segment 20 **Total Elevation Gain:** 3,876 feet
From Wyoming: 310.6 miles
To New Mexico: 448.2 miles

CONTINENTAL DIVIDE TRAIL · NATIONAL SCENIC TRAIL

Elevation 1000x

Copper Mountain

2.6 Trail Turnoff

8.7 Searle Pass

11.8 Kokomo Pass

19.0 Camp Hale Road

Tennessee Pass

Seg.19

Seg.21

Miles   0   5   10   15   20   25

YOU MAY ENCOUNTER: MOTORIZED VEHICLES

THIS SEGMENT'S WIDE SWING away from the Divide
provides a compelling view from a distance. Perhaps the most
notable feature visible from the vantage point of the CDT is
the Climax Molybdenum Mine, part of which sits squarely on
the Divide. Climax is the culmination of a rich mining history
in this area that started in the 1860s with some unremarkable
placer mining. But then, late in the next decade, two prospectors
financed by Leadville investor George B. Robinson discovered
impressive veins of silver in the Tenmile Valley (which today
guides Colorado Highway 91 south from Interstate 70 along
the east side of Copper Mountain). Word of the strikes spread
quickly, and by 1880 there were 2,000 men living in the upstart
town of Robinson, rivaling the little boomtown just over the
Divide called Leadville. Some 10,000 miners were living in
the Tenmile mining district when the Denver and Rio Grande
Railroad made its way from Leadville over Fremont Pass in 1881.

The boom died down, and Robinson was a virtual
ghost town 10 years later, but mining for minerals like silver
and zinc would continue in fits and starts well into the 1940s.
At the same time, interest would rise in another ore excavated
from nearby Bartlett Mountain. Charles J. Senter discovered this
intriguing gray mineral in 1879, but it would be 21 years before
anyone identified it as molybdenum, a hardening agent for steel
that proved its value during World War I. The Climax Molybdenum
Company was born near the end of the war. The mine would
become the largest producer of "moly" in the world, even as it
went through its own booms and busts, always dragging econom-
ically dependent Leadville along for the ride. The Climax mine
is still in operation today.

The CDT continues to follow the Colorado Trail here.
The route is popular with mountain bikers, particularly the first
8.7 miles to Searle Pass. Water and camping are available at regular
intervals, although you won't want to camp in the Copper Mountain
Resort area in the first 2.6 miles of this segment. Also, you will be
near or on roads accessible to motorized vehicles after mile 16.0.

MOUNTAIN BIKE NOTES: This is a very popular mountain bike trail with some truly technical riding. The determined rider will enjoy the moderate challenge. The entire length
of this segment is rideable.

To make a prairie

it takes a clover

and one bee,

One clover,

and a bee,

And revery.

The revery alone

will do,

If bees are few.

—Emily Dickinson

MAPS

TRAILS ILLUSTRATED: 108, 109
USGS QUADRANGLES: Vail Pass, Copper Mountain, Pando
USFS: White River National Forest, pages 162–163

RANGER DISTRICTS:
Dillon
Holy Cross

ACCESS **WHEELER FLATS PARKING LOT:** From Interstate 70, take Exit 195 onto

Colorado Highway 91 south. Just after the overpass, turn left toward a Conoco gas station. Bypass it and continue 0.4 mile to the parking lot at Wheeler Flats.

Smooth road to trailhead

TENNESSEE PASS: See the next segment.

SUPPLIES, SERVICES, AND ACCOMMODATIONS

COPPER MOUNTAIN offers limited supplies and services. Don't count on lodging unless you are prepared to pay resort prices. Leadville has all services and can be reached by hitching south on US-24 from Tennessee Pass.

DISTANCE FROM TRAIL: 0 miles

ZIP CODE: 80443

Bank	None (ATM in The Center Building)	
Bus	Summit Stage	(970) 453-1241
Camping	None	
Dining	Creekside Pizza, 760 Copper Rd.	968-2033
Gear	Imperial Palace, Village Square	968-6688
Groceries	Corner Grocery, Village Square (trail mile 1.1)	968-2882
Information	Welcome Center, at base of American Eagle lift	968-2882
Laundry	Available only with lodging	
Lodging	Copper Mountain Resort	(800) 458-8386
	(be prepared for resort prices)	
Medical	See Frisco, Segment 19, page 161	
Post Office	West Lake Lodge Building (trail mile 1.2)	968-2882
Showers	Available only with lodging	

TRAIL DESCRIPTION Leave the parking lot by following the paved road south 0.4 mile back to Colorado Highway 91. Watch for cars approaching at high speeds from the right as you cross the highway. Continue through the entrance to Copper Mountain and follow the main road (Copper Road) west through the resort. At mile 1.1, you will reach the very large Chapel Parking Lot, on the west side of which a cluster of buildings conceals a small grocery store. The CDT continues along the main road and passes by the building that houses the post office in 0.1 mile. Stop in and say hi to Vi, the friendliest postperson in the world. Continue through the resort to a point at mile 1.5 (9,800), just past Beeler Place, where a paved bike path leaves the road on the right (west) near the Club Med shuttle stop. Turn onto the bike path and beware the many bikes, pedestrians, horses, and ski area vehicles in this area.

At mile 2.6 (9,960), turn left and follow a Colorado Trail symbol across a bridge. Climb along Guller Creek, where the riparian valley separates a north-facing spruce forest from the lodgepole pine ecosystem on the right. Wildflowers are abundant here. The CDT crosses the creek, and then it crosses a tributary named Jacque Creek at mile 4.0. Nice camping areas will occasionally present themselves between here and timberline. The trail soon crosses back to the north side of the creek and passes timberline at mile 7.5 (11,600), where it flits through a yellow sea of wildflowers with purple islands of aster. You will reach Searle Pass at mile 8.7 (12,030 feet; N39° 27.47', W106° 13.71') near a garden of red sandstone. You'll be able to see Clinton Reservoir in the valley to the southwest. The craggy peaks behind it carry the Continental Divide through this area. Avoid the trail descending in that direction and take the one more to the right, which climbs slightly to the south. Open mine shafts between here and Kokomo Pass could ruin your day if you leave the trail and stumble into one.

A faint tread follows posts and cairns across the tundra under the steady gaze of Jacque Peak on the other side of the valley. That peak's other side cradles the snow that attracts hundreds of thousands of visitors to Copper Mountain Resort each year. As the trail nears Kokomo Pass, it turns right (west) in one last switchback and tops out on Elk Ridge at mile 11.3 (12,280). This point offers one of the best views anywhere of the extensive strip mining operation at Climax Molybdenum Mine to the southeast, whose voracious appetite has taken a sizeable bite out of Bartlett Mountain. Some of the buildings there sit precisely on the Continental Divide, which descends from the sharp peaks behind the mine to course east-west over the gentler hills below you.

The trail descends to reach Kokomo Pass at mile 11.8 (12,022 feet; N39° 25.75', W106° 13.59'). As the CDT swings northwest to descend into the Cataract Creek valley, you can take in stunning views to the west of Mount of the Holy Cross and its surrounding peaks. A mesmerizing impressionist tableau comes to life in the foreground in the largest sea of crimson and pink paintbrush you may have ever seen.

The CDT passes by viable campsites at the rate of about one per mile during its steady descent. A post at mile 15.3 (10,110) indicates a left turn off of the main trail to a creek crossing on several logs. A steep descent leads to a fork at mile 16.0 (9,675); turn right (north) and cross Cataract Creek a short distance ahead.

Now the trail descends parallel to Forest Road 714 before joining it at mile 16.9 and leaving it again at mile 17.1. These intersections are marked by Colorado Trail symbols on posts. The trail continues west for another 0.6 mile before veering back into the road. Turn right on the road and continue 200 yards to where another road comes in from the left (south). Turn onto it and continue south into historic Camp Hale.

The trail passes by some concrete bunkers left over from the glory days of this facility where soldiers in the Tenth Mountain Division trained before going to fight in the mountains of Italy during World War II. Cross the Eagle River East Fork on a good bridge at mile 18.1 (9,318). Of a few treads visible on the ground, follow the clearest one straight off the bridge and follow its slow curve to the right (southwest). Continue into a spruce forest via two switchbacks up a steep hill, which is followed by a mosaic of aspen, spruce, and pine. The trail crosses Camp Hale Road at mile 19.0 (9,665). Follow the trail's continuation on the other side, where it occasionally parallels the road below and to the right and rolls through meadows and trees. Small streams are frequent here. Follow the trail to a crossing of busy US-24 at mile 20.9 (10,000 feet; N39° 23.33', W106° 19.11').

On the other side of the highway, follow a short driveway to the railroad tracks, cross them, and continue west across a meadow about 130 yards to a small stream. Cross the stream, make a sharp right turn, and continue a short distance to where the trail bends back to the left (southwest) to meander along the meadows of Mitchell Creek. At mile 22.1 (9,980), the trail climbs away from the meadow to the left (southeast) and joins a jeep road in 0.3 mile. Turn left (east) and follow the road's bend to the south and then east again, all the way to the parking area at Tennessee Pass (mile 24.3; 10,424 feet; N39° 29.27', W106° 18.63'). This point marks the trail's first intersection with the Continental Divide in 59.0 miles. The Divide descends from Cooper Hill Ski Area, discreetly crosses the highway, and continues west over timbered hills. This is the end of this segment; the next one begins closer to the highway at a sign marked with the Colorado Trail symbol.

OTHER HIKES

CLINTON RESERVOIR
Approximate one-way distance: 2.0 miles
Difficulty: Moderate

Clinton Creek Trailhead: This parking area is immediately south of Clinton Reservoir, about 2.5 miles north of Fremont Pass on Colorado Highway 91 between Leadville and Copper Mountain.

No part of this trail is on the Continental Divide Trail, nor even close enough for a CDT hiker to access it. But for a day-hiker looking for a slightly different experience of the Divide, this is an excellent choice. The CDT in this area strays some distance from the Divide, while this hike puts you directly in the Divide's clutches. The trail climbs moderately, passes by many mine excavations, and terminates in the maw of massive Clinton Amphitheatre, whose back walls are defined by the Divide.

OLD-GROWTH FORESTS

As you hike Colorado's Continental Divide Trail, you will encounter a variety of eco-systems and environments ranging from dry meadows of sage to the windswept tundra of alpine ridges. One of the rarest of these ecosystems is old-growth forest, of which very little remains in Colorado. Still, there are several places along the CDT where you will encounter the magical richness of this special place.

At times it might sneak up on you—old growth is not particularly conspicuous unless you are looking for it. You might be sauntering along when you notice a different feel—a different character—in the surrounding forest. The light is a bit dimmer, the cool air is a little more moist, and a peculiar timeless quality prevails that can lull you into slowing your pace, perhaps even stopping a while.

A thick canopy of dark green boughs hangs high overhead, and some of the lowest branches are 40 feet off the ground. Sunlight streams through in thin beams, casting speckles on the forest floor like the obscure mosaic cast by stained-glass windows in an airy old cathedral.

Colorado old growth is made up almost exclusively of two species: Engelmann spruce and subalpine fir. These trees thrive in the cold, harsh climate of higher altitudes extending from about 9,000 feet to timberline (up to 12,000 feet). Trees in all stages of life, death, and rebirth intertwine on and above the forest floor. Standing dead trees, or snags, provide homes for birds, insects, and other small animals. Those trees that have fallen form an intricate and often impassable maze of logs in various stages of decay. Moss, lichens, and fungi carpet these logs, returning their nutrients to the soil from which tiny saplings spring forth. Young trees in various stages of development stand like attentive disciples around those centerpieces of the old-growth forest, the huge, ancient skyscrapers whose thick canopy forms a living ceiling high above the fertile ground. These old trees are so thick you can scarcely get your arms halfway around them, bulging as they do up to 10 feet around. They climb 120 feet into the sky; some are old enough to have taken root before Columbus set sail for the New World.

The closed canopy blocks out direct sunlight, and moisture is trapped in the forest, nurturing a variety of water-loving plants. These include blueberry, Colorado currant, and high-bush cranberry, and flowers with names like pipsissewa, wood nymph, and curled lousewort. Particularly wet areas harbor delicate orchids such as lady's slipper and twayblade.

The effects of decay are everywhere, with mosses and fungi forming a soft, green carpet on the debris that litters the forest floor. You may see small, magical gardens of odd mushrooms growing in beds of moss, all protected inside a hollow stump. Their pungent odor mingles with the reminiscent sweetness of the spruce.

This is an old-growth forest, one small part of a larger whole dotting the western edge of North America. It is also a diminishing resource — only 10 percent of the old growth that once thrived on the planet still stands.

It is a privilege to know these trees. They began to grow here long before we were born, and will remain long after we are gone. To me, that's eternity. It's overwhelming and cosmic and full of secrets we can't comprehend. I hope we are not so shortsighted that we eradicate all these messengers of eternity, reminders in various forms that there are things on this Earth that are much more lasting, and perhaps more important, than we.

Segment 21
Tennessee Pass to Timberline Lake Trailhead

Skiing the trail near Homestake Peak, White River National Forest

13.3 miles
Difficulty: Moderate

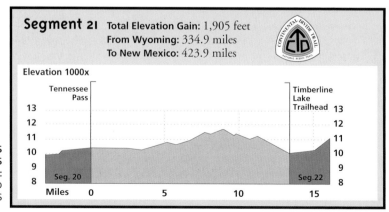

Segment 21 **Total Elevation Gain:** 1,905 feet
From Wyoming: 334.9 miles
To New Mexico: 423.9 miles

Elevation 1000x

Tennessee Pass

Timberline Lake Trailhead

THIS SEGMENT IS CLOSED TO: MOTORIZED VEHICLES

EVEN THOUGH THE TRAIL is not precisely on the Divide in this segment, it is much closer than in the previous few segments, and it offers some stunning perspectives on the Divide's course through the Holy Cross Wilderness. It takes a few miles for the trail to escape the more developed feel of the Tennessee Pass area, but once it does, the ambiance shifts rapidly to the other end of the spectrum as you approach, and finally enter, the wilderness. The solitude of this little corner of raw nature belies the proximity of such developed diversions as Turquoise Lake Recreation Area and the backcountry huts that have grown almost exponentially in popularity in the last decade. Two of these huts, "Uncle Buds" and "Tenth Mountain," lie within a mile of the trail. Backcountry travelers, mostly cross-country skiers, use them in the winter to access the beauty of the remote, snow-covered wilderness.

Don't count on Wurts Ditch for water, even though it is shown on the maps as a perennial aqueduct. The first reliable source is West Tennessee Creek at mile 3.4, after which water is common. Camping is available over most of the segment. Expect mountain bikes on the first 5 or 6 miles.

 MOUNTAIN BIKE NOTES: Bikes are prohibited where the trail passes through the Holy Cross Wilderness. However, the first 6.7 miles are open to bikes and offer strenuous, but non-technical, riding.

MAPS

TRAILS ILLUSTRATED: 109, 126
USGS QUADRANGLES: Leadville North, Homestake Reservoir
USFS: White River National Forest, San Isabel National Forest, pages 174–175

BEGINNING ACCESS POINT

 TENNESSEE PASS: From Colorado Highway 91 a short distance north of Leadville, take US-24 north about 9.0 miles to the summit of Tennessee Pass. The parking area is on the left (west) side of the highway.

You can also reach Tennessee Pass by taking Interstate 70 to Exit 171, just west of Vail, and traveling south on US-24.

ALTERNATE ACCESS

WURTS DITCH ROAD (Trail mile 2.7): Take Colorado Highway 91 to Leadville and turn north onto US-24, heading toward Minturn. Continue 7.2 miles to an unmarked dirt road turnoff on the left side, just before the highway makes a wide turn to the right. The only sign, on the left after you make the turn, is for Tenth Mountain Hut parking. After about 1.0 mile, turn right onto Forest Road 100 toward Wurts Ditch. Continue 0.4 mile to where a Colorado Trail sign marks the trail's crossing of the road. There is room for two cars here.

Summer afternoon—

summer afternoon;

to me

those have

always been

the two most

beautiful words

in the

English language.

—Henry James,

quoted in

Edith Wharton's

A Backward Glance

RANGER DISTRICT:
Leadville

ENDING ACCESS POINT

TIMBERLINE LAKE TRAILHEAD: See the next segment. You'll find the trailhead at a signboard marked with the Colorado Trail

SUPPLIES, SERVICES, AND ACCOMMODATIONS

LEADVILLE has all services and can be reached by hitching south on US-24 from Tennessee Pass.

DISTANCE FROM TRAIL: 9.0 miles

ZIP CODE: 80461

Bank	Commercial Bank of Leadville, 400 Harrison Ave. (ATM)	(719) 486-0420
Bus	None	
Camping	SugarLoafin' Campground, off US-24 at mile post 177, 3.5 miles northwest on County Road 4, near Turquoise Lake	486-1031
Dining	Golden Burro, 710 Harrison Ave.	486-1239
	Mom's Place, 612 Harrison Ave.	N/A
Gear	Bill's Sport Shop has Coleman fuel and limited stock, 225 Harrison Ave.	486-0739
Groceries	Safeway, 1900 Hwy. 24 North	486-0795
Information	Greater Leadville Area Chamber of Commerce, 809 Harrison Ave.	486-3900
Laundry	Leadville Laundromat, 1707 Poplar	486-3447
Lodging	Delaware Hotel, 700 Harrison Ave.	486-1418
	Silver King Motor Inn, 2020 N. Poplar	486-2610
Medical	St. Vincent General Hospital, 822 W. 4th at Washington	486-0230
Post Office	130 W. 5th	486-1667
Showers	Available at laundromat (see Laundry), or Lake County Recreation Center, 1000 W. 6th at McWethy Drive	486-2564

SPECIAL NOTES: Leadville has ridden the roller coaster of mining's legacy of boom and bust. For an authentic look at life in the heyday of Colorado mining, check the Chamber of Commerce for information on tours and sights. Of particular interest are Tabor's Matchless Mine and the Healy House, an 1899 boarding house.

TRAIL DESCRIPTION

symbol on the southwest side of the parking area, near the highway. The trail begins by undulating gently to the southwest as it parallels the Divide, which is on an indistinct ridge on the right. Cross Wurts Ditch at mile 2.5 (10,400). This waterway is not controlled by Mother Nature; consider it unreliable. Cross over Wurts Ditch Road in about 0.2 mile and continue at a sign for the Tenth Mountain Hut route.

Cross the road to Lily Lake at mile 3.0; then take a side road on the left a very short distance to another fork of the main road. Turn left, walk about 50 yards, and turn onto a tread leading into the lodgepole forest on the right. Regain the road at mile 3.4 (10,330) and turn right to cross the West Tennessee Creek North Fork.

NORTHBOUND HIKERS will be looking for an obscure left (northwest) turn marked by a cairn and a Colorado Trail symbol on a tree in the distance, 90 degrees to the left. If you hit the meadow, you've gone too far.

Continue to mile 3.5 and ford West Tennessee Creek. A single-track trail leads a short distance upstream to a good crossing on some logs. Less than 100 yards later, the road curves to the left while the CDT leaves it to follow a single-track straight ahead to the south-southwest. This marks the beginning of a steady climb that soon turns to the west-southwest, following old roads to a high point at mile 5.2 (10,880). Descend for about 0.5 mile into Longs Gulch before climbing gently along the meadows there.

WILDERNESS ALERT:

The Holy Cross Wilderness was designated in 1980 by federal law to be "an area where the earth and its community of life are untrammeled by man, where man himself is a visitor who does not remain." It guards 122,037 acres that rise to the Holy Cross Ridge and culminate in 14,005-foot Mount of the Holy Cross. Please remember these rules governing wilderness areas: 1. Camp out of sight, at least 200 feet from lakes and streams, on dry, durable surfaces. 2. Use a stove instead of building a fire; use existing fire rings if you must have a fire. 3. Keep water sources pure by washing at least 200 feet from them. 4. Bury human waste six inches deep and 200 feet from lakes and streams. Pack out toilet paper. 5. Hobble or picket livestock at least 200 feet from lakes and streams, and use only treated, weed-free feed and grain. 6. All dogs must be on a leash. 7. No mountain biking. 8. Pack out all trash. Don't attempt to burn it.

You will enter the Holy Cross Wilderness at mile 6.7 (10,940). Pass a stream in about 125 yards and begin a sharp climb to a beautiful, broad saddle that contains some ponds and excellent camping at mile 7.6 (11,480). The Divide runs along the ridge atop the towering walls of the impressive glacial cirques here. The CDT crosses Porcupine Creek and curves to the east before climbing to a timbered saddle at mile 8.8 (11,685). Follow its descent onto a road and continue down to a point at mile 9.6 where the CDT briefly leaves the wilderness.

After reentering the wilderness, follow an old road west-northwest to a steep, rocky slope where the trail seems to disappear. Descend past several inviting lakes and ponds (11,060); then climb to a ridge at mile 11.2 (11,290) that provides a photo-op of Mount Massive to the south. Follow a consistent descent through lodgepole pine, out of the wilderness area, and twice under a power line. A little over 0.1 mile beyond the power line, this segment ends at a bridge over Mill Creek at mile 13.3 (10,060 feet; N39° 17.11', W106° 26.70'). Just before the bridge (east), a trail leads 100 yards southeast to the small parking area at the Timberline Lake Trailhead on Turquoise Lake Road.

OTHER HIKES

WEST TENNESSEE LAKES
Approximate one-way distance: 4.5 miles (from CDT)
Difficulty: Moderate

Tennessee Pass Trailhead: See *Access* at the beginning of this segment.

From Tennessee Pass, follow the trail directions to mile 3.0. Turn right (west) onto the road to Lily Lake. Continue on the trail at the end of the four-wheel-drive road near Lily Lake.

These high alpine lakes are on the flanks of the Divide, above timberline, and protected by the surrounding Holy Cross Wilderness. Through-hikers may wish to plan a day of respite at this pristine setting. A permit is not required.

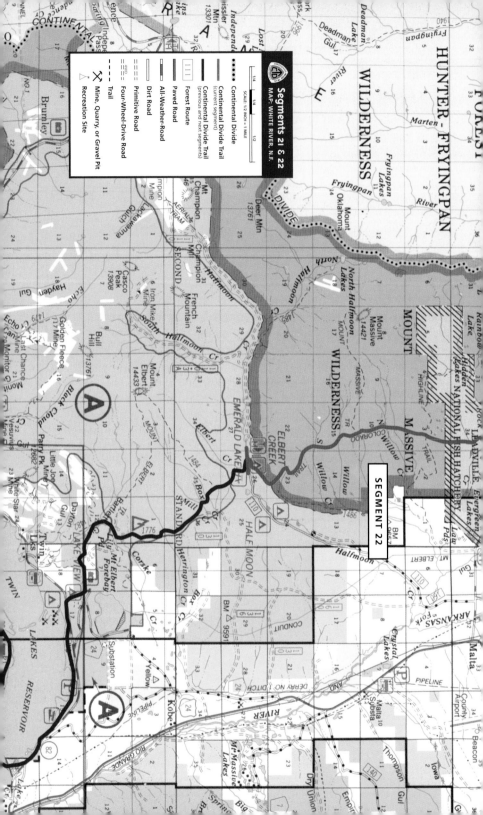

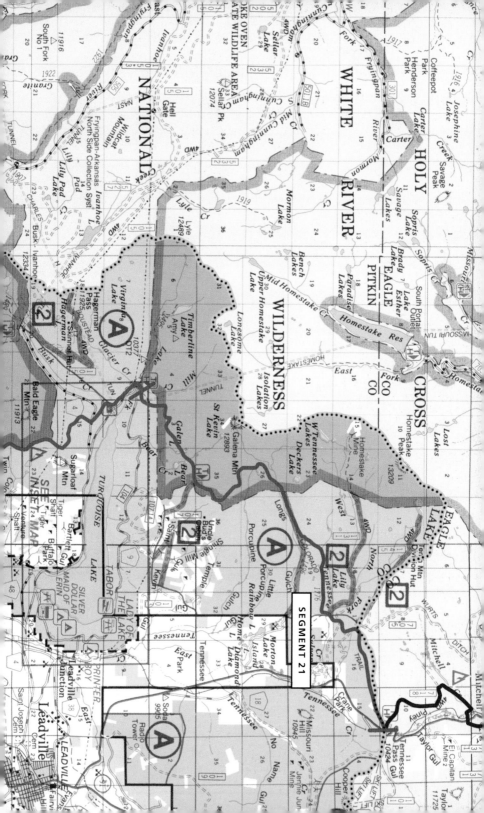

Segment 22
Timberline Lake Trailhead to Mount Massive/Mount Elbert Trailhead

Mount Massive, Mount Massive Wilderness

12.9 miles
Difficulty: Moderate

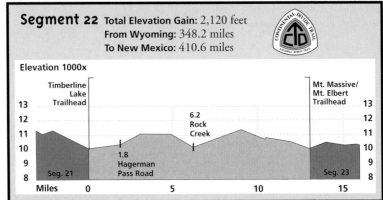

Segment 22 **Total Elevation Gain:** 2,120 feet
From Wyoming: 348.2 miles
To New Mexico: 410.6 miles

THIS
SEGMENT IS
CLOSED TO:
MOTORIZED
VEHICLES

THE CDT CONTINUES to follow the Colorado Trail here, drawing you away from the actual Divide. This mostly timbered section rambles along the eastern flanks of Colorado's highest peaks, Mount Massive and, in the next segment, Mount Elbert, whose towering masses block any view of the Divide. These top prizes of the fourteener cult attract gobs of people, especially on weekends.

Sections of this trail are popular with mountain bikers, particularly the first 3.1 miles. For most of the ensuing 9.8 miles, however, the CDT passes through the Mount Massive Wilderness, where bikes are not allowed.

This segment crosses streams at regular intervals, and campsites are plentiful.

 MOUNTAIN BIKE NOTES: Bikes are prohibited in the Mount Massive Wilderness.

MAPS

TRAILS ILLUSTRATED: 126, 127
USGS QUADRANGLES: Homestake Reservoir, Mount Massive
USFS: White River National Forest, pages 174–175

BEGINNING POINT ACCESS

Smooth road to trailhead **TIMBERLINE LAKE TRAILHEAD:** From US-24 in Leadville, turn west onto Mountain View Drive on the south side of Safeway, following signs for Turquoise Lake. After 2.6 miles, turn right at a T intersection and proceed another 0.5 mile to where the roadway splits into three forks. Take the left fork over the railroad tracks toward Turquoise Lake and proceed 0.5 mile to another T intersection. Turn right and drive 6.9 miles to a hairpin curve to the left. The small, unsigned parking area for the trailhead is on the right side of the curve. Additional parking is available at May Queen Campground, just around the bend to the left. Follow the trail 100 yards to the north, up the right side of the stream, to a bridge that marks the intersection of the CDT.

ALTERNATE ACCESS

Smooth road to trailhead **HAGERMAN PASS ROAD (TRAIL MILE 1.8):** The parking area described above is small. If you prefer a different access point, drive around the hairpin curve to the left and continue 1.9 miles to the turnoff to Hagerman Pass Road (#105) on the right. The CDT, along with the Colorado Trail, crosses the road 0.9 mile beyond the turnoff. No formal parking is provided.

There can be no

very black melancholy

to him who lives

in the midst

of nature

and has his

senses still.

There was never yet

such a storm

but it was

Æolian music

to a healthy

and innocent ear.

—Henry David

Thoreau,

Walden

RANGER DISTRICT:
Leadville

ENDING ACCESS POINT

Distance from graded road	6.5 miles

MOUNT MASSIVE/MOUNT ELBERT TRAILHEAD:
See the next segment.

SUPPLIES, SERVICES, AND ACCOMMODATIONS

LEADVILLE is about 10.5 miles from the Timberline Lake Trailhead. Traffic from anglers and other recreationists is moderate throughout the week. If you plan to hitchhike, it would be best to schedule a trip into town at a better-traveled road crossing. See Segment 21, page 172.

TRAIL DESCRIPTION
Cross the bridge, follow the trail down the hill past a bulletin board, and follow Colorado Trail symbols along the two-track road. Cross another bridge at mile 0.1 and turn right (west) onto a rocky road. Walk up the road 100 yards and turn left (south) at a road closure sign. Now enjoy the moderate walk through trees and over streams to a gradual climb that steepens before you reach Hagerman Pass Road at mile 1.8 (10,360). This is the alternative access point described at the beginning of this segment.

The CDT continues on the other side of the road, about 30 yards to the left, at a Colorado Trail marker. A steep climb for 0.2 mile leads to a meadow that offers beautiful views. As the trail parallels the Mount Massive Wilderness boundary, a less abrupt climb leads to an old road at mile 3.1 (11,065), marked by a Colorado Trail sign. Cross the road and continue on the single-track trail to the south, which leads immediately under a power line and into an area that has been heavily logged. This artificial opening offers views of the Arkansas River Valley to the east and of Galena Mountain straddling the Divide to the north.

> **WILDERNESS ALERT:**
> The Mount Massive Wilderness was designated in 1980 by federal law to be "an area where the earth and its community of life are untrammeled by man, where man himself is a visitor who does not remain." Its 30,540 acres contain few trails, and the CT/CDT route comprises about half of the total trail mileage here. Because of the popularity of Mount Massive, this wilderness receives a lot of pressure. Please remember these rules governing wilderness areas: 1. Camp out of sight, at least 200 feet from lakes and streams, on dry, durable surfaces. 2. Use a stove instead of building a fire; use existing fire rings if you must have a fire. 3. Keep water sources pure by washing at least 200 feet from them. 4. Bury human waste six inches deep and 200 feet from lakes and streams. Pack out toilet paper. 5. Hobble or picket livestock at least 200 feet from lakes and streams, and use only treated, weed-free feed and grain. 6. All dogs must be on a leash. 7. No mountain biking. 8. Pack out all trash. Don't attempt to burn it.

The trail enters the Mount Massive Wilderness at mile 3.2. Cross a stream on two old logs 0.3 mile later and look through a window in the trees to the east for a view of the Mosquito Range on the other side of the valley. After crossing two cascading

Segment 23
Mount Massive/Mount Elbert Trailhead to Winfield/South Clear Creek Trailhead

Colorado columbine, San Isabel National Forest

27.1 miles
Difficulty: Strenuous

AFTER 107.7 MILES of following the same path, the CDT diverges from the Colorado Trail in this segment, setting the stage for a return to the Divide in the next segment. But first the two trails roll together over the tame east slopes of Mount Elbert, Colorado's highest peak. Elbert's popularity as the highest four-teener draws thousands of hikers every summer. You will see fewer people if you avoid this segment on weekends. The peak is named for Samuel Elbert, the unremarkable statesman who came to Colorado as secretary to the governor of the Colorado Territory in 1862. Elbert was himself appointed governor in 1873, a post he held for less than one year. Mount Elbert's summit has seen everything from bicycles to a helicopter to the highest snowshoe race in the country. Some people advocate building a road to the summit, further proof that we are responsible for most of our own tragedies.

The trail passes a short distance from Twin Lakes, a sleepy little town whose most visible livelihood is its last-chance-for-services position on the highway to the 12,095-foot crossing of the Continental Divide on Independence Pass. But this appearance belies a history involving millionaires, fancy hotels, and a national reputation as one of the most exclusive resorts in the country. The town started as a crossroads for travelers head-ing over the demanding pass to Aspen, and as the center of a large mining area covering more than 50,000 acres. But it was not long before the newly monied residents of Leadville were attracted by the charm and serenity of the area and started pouring their considerable mining wealth into lakeside cottages, hotels, and lodges. By 1883, the area was recognized as a posh resort from coast to coast. The biggest and most famous of the hotels was called Interlaken, of which several well-preserved

Never did we plan

the morrow,

for we had learned

that in the wilderness

some new and

irresistible distraction

is sure to turn up

each day

before breakfast.

—Aldo Leopold

RANGER DISTRICT:
Leadville

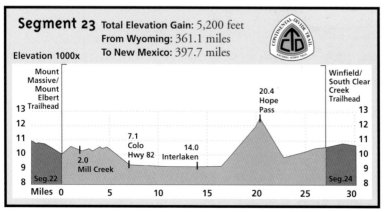

Segment 23 Total Elevation Gain: 5,200 feet
From Wyoming: 361.1 miles
To New Mexico: 397.7 miles
Elevation 1000x

Mount Massive/ Mount Elbert Trailhead
13
12
11
10
9
8
Seg.22

2.0 Mill Creek

7.1 Colo Hwy 82

14.0 Interlaken

20.4 Hope Pass

Winfield/ South Clear Creek Trailhead
13
12
11
10
9
8
Seg.24

Miles 0   5   10   15   20   25   30

THIS SEGMENT IS CLOSED TO: MOTORIZED VEHICLES

buildings still stand at trail mile 14.0. The area's popularity slowly died away after the turn of the century when a dam built on one of the lakes drowned the pleasant trees and foliage around the shores and made access to the area more difficult. Many of the rich second-homeowners moved away in disgust.

Water and places to camp are frequent here. Lakeview Campground offers semiprimitive camping with water, toilets, and the ubiquitous picnic table. Note that there are no services in Winfield, Vicksburg, or Rockdale.

 MOUNTAIN BIKE NOTES: Most of the trail over Hope Pass is too steep or rough to ride.

MAPS

TRAILS ILLUSTRATED: 127, 129
USGS QUADRANGLES: Mount Massive, Mount Elbert, Granite, Winfield
USFS: White River National Forest, pages 188–189

BEGINNING ACCESS POINT

Distance from graded road	🚗 6.5 miles

MOUNT MASSIVE/MOUNT ELBERT TRAILHEAD: 3.5 miles south of Leadville on US-24, turn west onto Colorado Highway 300. Drive 0.7 mile and turn left (south) onto a dirt road marked by a sign to Halfmoon Campground. Continue 1.2 miles to a right turn; then follow a bumpy road 5.3 miles to the Mount Massive/Mount Elbert trailhead parking area on the right (north) side of the road.

ALTERNATE ACCESS

Smooth road to trailhead	🚗

LAKEVIEW CAMPGROUND TRAILHEAD: About 15 miles south of downtown Leadville on US-24, turn right (west) onto Colorado Highway 82. Proceed 4.0 miles to a turnoff on the right to Lakeview Campground. Drive 1.0 mile on County Road 24 to the campground entrance on the left. There is a parking area near the trailhead in the campground. There is also a parking area just past the campground on the same side of the road. A trail descending west from this lot intersects the CDT in about 100 yards.

ENDING ACCESS POINT

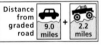

Distance from graded road	🚗 9.0 miles	🚙 2.2 miles

WINFIELD/SOUTH CLEAR CREEK TRAILHEAD: See the next segment.

TRAIL DESCRIPTION

From the parking area, cross the road and walk back to the east 40 yards to where the CDT leaves the road on the south (right) side. This is a popular starting point for Mount Elbert-bound hikers. The trail soon bends due west, fords a boot-topping tributary of Halfmoon Creek at mile 0.1, and crosses Elbert Creek 0.3 mile beyond. A steady climb ensues to mile 1.0 (10,610); then a descent leads to an intersection at mile 1.4 with the trail to Mount Elbert's summit. The CDT stays left and descends to cross Box Creek at mile 1.7 and Mill Creek at mile 2.0 (10,290). After passing a stream and a CT marker at mile 2.3, the trail enters a marshy area, followed by a mixed aspen/lodgepole pine forest. Cross Herrington Creek at mile 3.2 (10,280).

A steep ascent lifts you out of the stream valley and into a denser aspen community. The ensuing hypnotic effect caused by the repetitive patterns of these trees is not broken until a series of ponds at mile 4.2 (10,440). At a trail junction just above the ponds at mile 4.6 (10,600), bear right (west) and continue 50 yards to the junction with another trail to Mount Elbert. Turn left (south) and proceed to a stream crossing on two planks of wood at mile 4.9. Immediately after this, take the trail's right fork, walk 50 yards, and cross another stream where the trail becomes a four-wheel drive road that trends south.

Avoid occasional primitive side roads as you progress to a stream crossing on three logs (10 yards upstream) at mile 5.3 (10,280). After another 100 yards, the aspens open onto beautiful views to the south of the Collegiate Peaks Wilderness, Twin Peaks, and Mount Hope. Some prime campsites at mile 5.7 provide views of Twin Lakes as well. At mile 6.2, take the road's left (east) fork, as the occasional Ponderosa pine starts popping up. Avoid a right turnoff 0.2 mile farther, continuing straight ahead to the east. After another 0.2 mile, at mile 6.6 (9,640), look for the Colorado Trail marker on the right side and take the single-track trail leading away to the southeast. Avoid the many side trails winding through the sagebrush as you follow the trail's descent to a trailhead at mile 6.7 in Lakeview Campground.

Continue through the campground and descend 0.4 mile to a tunnel under Colorado Highway 82 (9,320). Follow the trail east through some peaceful Ponderosa pines before breaking out into a sea of sagebrush. The trail is occasionally obscure or poorly marked here, but as long as you roughly follow the perimeter of Twin Lakes Reservoir (around its east end, over the dam, and back to the west on the reservoir's south side), you can't go wrong.

Cross the dam at mile 10.9 (9,200) and follow a dirt road's curve to the west around the water. At mile 11.4, the CT leaves the road and skirts the edge of the inviting trees, winding along the pleasant south shore. You will reach the remnants of Interlaken at mile 14.0 (9,220). This resort thrived as a destination for Colorado's burgeoning upper and middle classes in the late 1800s.

Now the trail veers away from the reservoir to the southwest. Continue west-southwest along an occasionally faint trail and watch carefully for an old road at a sign that says "Closed To All Vehicles" at mile 16.5 (9,295). Turn left and climb about 0.3 mile to where a trail continues on the left (east). Follow this trail's southerly trend along Willis Gulch Creek. At mile 17.7, avoid a right fork and continue straight ahead (south). A generally clearer trail leads out of the trees and past a nice lake with good camping at mile 19.7 (11,780). From here, the trail climbs 750 feet over 0.7 mile and tops out on Hope Pass at mile 20.4 (12,540), where you are rewarded with views of the Collegiate Peaks to the south.

Descend rapidly along Sheep Gulch and follow Colorado Trail signs as the trail merges with a road at mile 22.6. Walk 0.1 mile to County Road 390, which is where the CDT and the Colorado Trail split (9,870). Turn right (west) and follow the road 2.2 miles to the little town of Winfield at mile 24.9 (10,240). Turn left (south) onto road 390.3 at a sign for "Restrooms," walk 1.7 miles to a fork, and bear left. Continue 0.5 mile to the end of this segment at the South Clear Creek Trailhead (mile 27.1; 10,600 feet; N38° 57.44', W106° 27.64').

SUPPLIES, SERVICES, AND ACCOMMODATIONS

TWIN LAKES offers limited supplies, but you can use its post office (in the General Store) to mail a package to yourself before beginning your hike. The town is about 1.0 mile west of the trail on Colorado Highway 82, at trail mile 7.1.

DISTANCE FROM TRAIL: 1.0 mile

ZIP CODE: 81251

Bank	None	
Bus	None	
Camping	Lakeview Campground (Forest Service)	
Dining	Twin Lakes Nordic Inn, 6435 Hwy. 82	(719) 486-2196
	Twin Lakes Expeditions Coffee Shop/Deli	486-3928
Gear	None	
Groceries	Twin Lakes General Store, in the heart of town	None
Information	See Leadville Information	
Laundry	Win-Mar Cabins, 4.0 miles east on	None
	Colorado Highway 82 at US-24	
Lodging	Twin Lakes Nordic Inn, 6435 Hwy. 82	486-1830
	Mount Elbert Lodge, 4.5 miles west	486-0594
	of Twin Lakes on Hwy. 82	
Medical	See Leadville	
Post Office	Twin Lakes General Store, in the heart of town	486-2196
Showers	Win-Mar Cabins, 4.0 miles east on	N/A
	Colorado Highway 82 at US-24	

OTHER HIKES

MOUNT ELBERT VIA HALFMOON CREEK AND NORTHEAST RIDGE
Approximate one-way distance: 2.4 miles (from intersection with CDT)
Difficulty: Strenuous

Mount Massive/Mount Elbert Trailhead: See *Access* for this segment.

Follow the directions for the first 1.4 miles of this segment; then turn right (west) onto the Mount Elbert Trail. The popular trail is quite clear from here as it climbs 3,920 feet to the 14,433-foot summit. Elbert is the highest point in the Rocky Mountains and runs a close second for highest in the lower 48 states. Immediately beyond the peaks and ridges visible to the west lie the Divide and its intersection with Colorado Highway 82 at Independence Pass.

MOUNT ELBERT VIA MOUNT ELBERT TRAIL
   Approximate one-way distance: 6.2 miles (from Lakeview Campground)
                     Difficulty: Strenuous

Mount Elbert Trailhead: See *Access* for Lakeview Campground at the beginning of this segment.

Begin by hiking this segment of the CDT in reverse (north) for 2.3 miles to a left (west) turnoff for Mount Elbert. Follow a clear trail 3.9 miles and 4,000 vertical feet to the summit.

LOST MAN SHUTTLE HIKE
   Approximate one-way distance: 23.0 miles
                     Difficulty: Strenuous

Lost Man Trailhead: Drive about 4.0 miles west from the summit of Independence Pass on Colorado Highway 82. The trailhead is on the right (north) side of the road.

This trail is an outstanding one if you want to get a better feel for the essence of the Divide in this area. It is not on, nor accessible to, the CDT, but it is well worth the effort. Most of the trail is well above timberline, immersed in the raw beauty of the Divide and the surrounding peaks and rocky ridges.

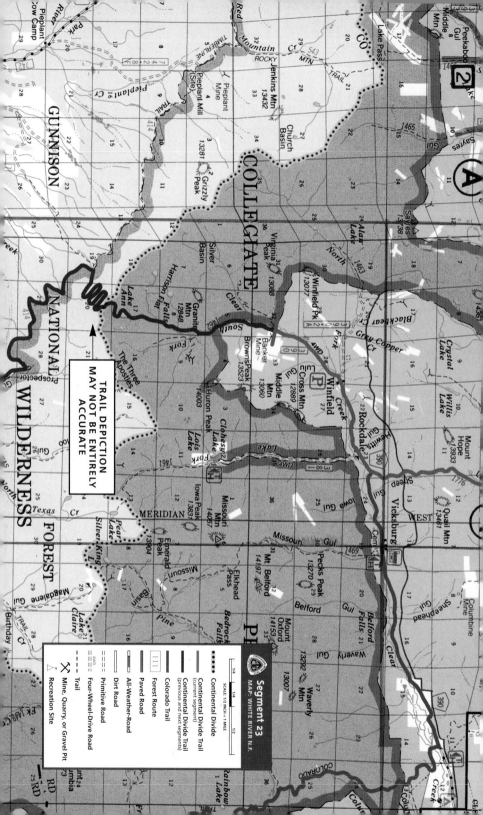

TRAIL DEPICTION
MAY NOT BE ENTIRELY
ACCURATE

Segment 23
MAP: WHITE RIVER N.F.

SCALE: 1/2 INCH = 1 MILE

Continental Divide
Continental Divide Trail
(current segment)
Continental Divide Trail
(previous and next segments)
Colorado Trail
Forest Route
Paved Road
All-Weather-Road
Dirt Road
Primitive Road
Four-Wheel-Drive Road
Trail
Mine, Quarry, or Gravel Pit
Recreation Site

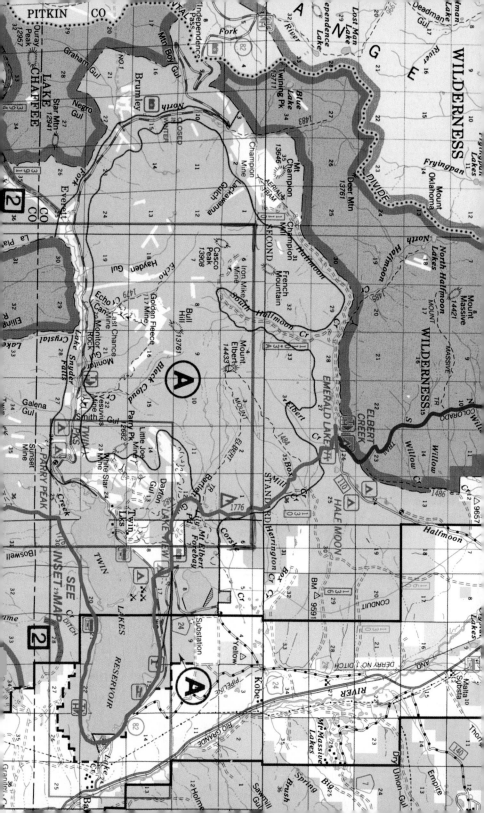

Segment 24
Winfield/South Clear Creek Trailhead to Cottonwood Pass Road

Along Texas Creek, Collegiate Peaks Wilderness

17.9 miles
Difficulty: Strenuous

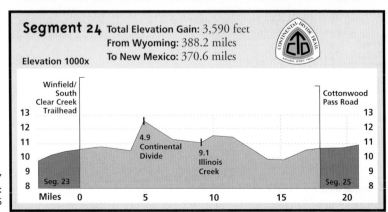

Segment 24 **Total Elevation Gain:** 3,590 feet
From Wyoming: 388.2 miles
To New Mexico: 370.6 miles

CONTINENTAL DIVIDE TRAIL
NATIONAL SCENIC TRAIL

Elevation 1000x

Winfield/
South
Clear Creek
Trailhead

Cottonwood
Pass Road

13
12
11
10
9
8

4.9
Continental
Divide

9.1
Illinois
Creek

Seg. 23

Seg. 25

13
12
11
10
9
8

Miles   0   5   10   15   20

**YOU MAY
ENCOUNTER:**
MOTORBIKES

THIS SEGMENT PROVIDES the CDT's first contact with the Divide since Tennessee Pass, some 68.2 miles to the north. For day hikers, it offers relatively quick access to the Divide along a beautiful trail with stunning views of Colorado's highest concentration of fourteeners. Another highlight is a steep climb to an awesome, cornice-covered pass well above timberline.

Winfield, near the trailhead for this segment, was a mining camp founded in the early 1880s by a group of Leadville prospectors heading for the Gunnison Basin. Legend has it that when the men went to pack their burros, which had wandered off during the night, they discovered an outcropping of promising silver-bearing ore and never left. There were more than 200 miners here at one time, plying the nearby streams and valley walls. Some buildings are still standing (and in good condition) largely because of the efforts of the Clear Creek Canyon Historical Society of Chaffee County.

Water is plentiful here, with the exception of the 4.3-mile stretch from the headwaters of Clear Creek at mile 2.8 to the Timberline Trail at mile 7.1. Note that the moderate flow of Texas Creek must be forded at mile 15.0, either via narrow logs or by wading. There are plenty of places to camp in the first three miles, as well as in the Texas Creek valley at mile 14.0.

The last 10.8 miles of this segment are open to motorbikes. Horses are not recommended on this segment because of the steep pass south of Lake Ann.

MOUNTAIN BIKE NOTES: Most of the trail is too rough to ride, and it passes through the Collegiate Peaks Wilderness where bikes are prohibited. However, part of this segment is on a trail that offers miles of excellent single-track. See *Other Hikes and Rides* at the end of this segment.

MAPS

TRAILS ILLUSTRATED: 129
USGS QUADRANGLES: Winfield, Tincup
USFS: Gunnison Basin Area, pages 196-197

BEGINNING ACCESS POINT

Distance from graded road: 9.0 miles

WINFIELD: From downtown Leadville, follow US-24 south 19.5 miles (or about 15.0 miles north of Buena Vista) to a turnoff to Winfield on the west side, on Clear Creek Canyon Road (County Road 390). At mile 9.4, the CDT and the Colorado Trail join this road from

---

In those

vernal seasons

of the year,

when the air is calm

and pleasant,

it were an injury

and sullenness

against Nature

not to go out

and see her riches,

and partake

in her rejoicing with

heaven and earth.

—John Milton,

Of Education

RANGER DISTRICTS:
Leadville
Taylor-Cebolla

the right (north). Continue 2.2 miles past this point and turn left (south) onto road 390.3 at a sign announcing "Restrooms." Those with non-four-wheel drive vehicles will want to park in the lot here.

Distance from graded road	2.2 miles

FOUR-WHEEL DRIVES can continue on this bumpy road, staying on Forest Road 390. Drive 1.7 miles from the last parking lot, bear left at a fork, and continue 0.5 mile farther to a small parking area.

ALTERNATE ACCESS

Distance from graded road	9.0 miles

TEXAS CREEK ROAD (trail mile 14.0): About 1.5 miles north of Cottonwood Pass Road on Taylor River Road, turn right (east) onto Texas Creek Road (Forest Road 755). Follow it about 8.0 miles to where the CDT departs the road to the south (right). Continue 0.9 mile to a parking area where the CDT arrives from the north.

ENDING ACCESS POINT

Smooth road to trailhead	

COTTONWOOD PASS/TIMBERLINE TRAIL: See the next segment.

SUPPLIES, SERVICES, AND ACCOMMODATIONS

BUENA VISTA is about 24 miles east of the CDT on Cottonwood Pass Road (which becomes Main Street in town). Hitching may be difficult on this slow-moving tourist route popular for its scenery.

DISTANCE FROM TRAIL: 24.0 miles

ZIP CODE: 81211

Bank	Collegiate Peaks, 105 Centennial Plaza	(719) 395-2472
Bus	None	
Camping	Crazy Horse Camping Resort	(800) 888-7320
	5 miles north of Buena Vista at 33975 Hwy 24 N.	
Dining	Marti's, 708 Hwy. 24 South	395-9289
	Evergreen, 418 Hwy. 24 North	395-8984
Gear	Trailhead Ventures, 707 Hwy. 24 North	395-8001
Groceries	Circle Super, Hwy. 24 South	395-2431
Information	Chamber of Commerce, 343 Hwy. 24 South	395-6612
Laundry	Morrison's, 410 Hwy. 24	N/A
Lodging	Coronado Motel, 517 Hwy. 24 North, $21–$65	395-2251
	Vista Court Cabins and Lodge, 1004 W. Main, $45	395-6557
Medical	Mountain Medical Center of Buena Vista, 36 Oak St.	395-8632
Post Office	112 Linderman Ave.	395-2445
Showers	Community Center, 7 blocks east of	N/A
	Hwy. 24 on Main St.	

SPECIAL NOTES: On the way from the trail to Buena Vista, you'll pass by Cottonwood Hot Springs Inn and Spa about 6 miles west of town. The facility offers lodging, a sauna, soaking pools, jacuzzi, and massage. Not a bad place to take a day off from the trail! Call (719) 395-6434.

TRAIL DESCRIPTION Begin by walking south 100 yards beyond the parking area to the gate at South Clear Creek Trailhead. Continue to a Collegiate Peaks Wilderness sign at mile 0.1, avoiding the single-track trail here on the left. The trail actually enters the wilderness area at mile 0.9, where you can enjoy views of the west side of 14,003-foot Mount Huron to the left (east) and the craggy monoliths of the Three Apostles straight ahead.

At mile 1.6, take a right fork toward Lake Ann, as indicated by a sign. The CDT crosses the creek in a few yards and parallels it to another fork at mile 2.6. Bear right and follow a new Forest Service trail into the trees to the southwest. (As of summer 1995, this trail was incomplete but well-flagged. It should be complete and very clear by now.)

The trail climbs more steeply as it leaves the trees, offering views of Lake Ann below. Lake Ann has seen heavy use in the last few years, and the Forest Service asks you to avoid camping here. The meadows in the trees prior to the CDT's climb to this point offer excellent camping.

Follow a cairned series of switchbacks through boulders and talus as you climb more aggressively to the summit of the pass south of Lake Ann. This area holds snow well into July in some years. Note that the trail crosses the large cornice at the top on its left (east) side. Watch your footing on the unpredictable snow! This area seems to be a magnet for very severe storms.

You will reach the pass summit and the Continental Divide at mile 4.9 (12,580). Pause here to take in the masterpiece of natural scenery that surrounds you. Two fourteeners, La Plata Peak and Mount Huron, are visible behind you to the north. You can see Taylor Park Reservoir far below to the southwest while the San Juan Mountains linger much farther in the distance. The rugged peaks to the north are those of the Aspen area, many of which are part of the beautiful Maroon Bells-Snowmass Wilderness.

WILDERNESS ALERT:

The Collegiate Peaks Wilderness was designated in 1980 by federal law to be "an area where the earth and its community of life are untrammeled by man, where man himself is a visitor who does not remain." With 166,654 acres encompassing eight 14,000-foot peaks, this is likely the country's highest wilderness area. Please remember these rules governing wilderness areas: 1. Camp out of sight, at least 200 feet from lakes and streams, on dry, durable surfaces. 2. Use a stove instead of building a fire; use existing fire rings if you must have a fire. 3. Keep water sources pure by washing at least 200 feet from them. 4. Bury human waste six inches deep and 200 feet from lakes and streams. Pack out toilet paper. 5. Hobble or picket livestock at least 200 feet from lakes and streams, and use only treated, weed-free feed and grain. 6. All dogs must be on a leash. 7. No mountain biking. 8. Pack out all trash. Don't attempt to burn it.

Plenty of switchbacks descending the steep south side of the pass now define the CDT. This area's glacial history is evident in the overlapping moraines in the basin below. The trail gains the trees and continues its serpentine path toward this basin before reaching a sign for the wilderness boundary at mile 7.0 (11,200). Continue straight across the creekbed (north) and follow the trail as it bends left (east) up the opposing hillside. A signed T intersection 0.1 mile later marks the Timberline Trail, onto which the CDT turns left (east). This trail, which forms the southwest boundary of the Collegiate Peaks Wilderness all the way to Cottonwood Pass, is popular with motorcyclists. This presents an interesting irony: When you move uphill off the trail to let the riders pass, you are stepping onto ground that is itself legally protected from the tread of the bikes buzzing by you.

Water is plentiful now as the trail rolls over a series of parallel ridges jutting south from the Divide. At mile 9.1 (11,010), a sign marks an intersection with the Gunnison loop of the Colorado Trail and a crossing of Illinois Creek. Avoid this trail, which heads off to the right (west), and continue into the willows to the south. You'll find a good place to camp at a small stream crossing at mile 9.4. At mile 11.5 (11,400), the trail reaches the steep hillsides of Prospector Gulch, which it soon follows downhill before exiting to the left (east) at mile 13.4. Reach the Texas Creek valley floor at a parking lot 0.6 mile later (9,960).

User-friendly camping is available all along this valley. Follow the road out of the parking lot as it curves to the right (west) along the meadow, then straight through a fork at mile 14.4 where the CDT continues to the west. At mile 14.9, look for an illegible white sign with a green border tacked to a tree on the left. (If you pass a pond on the left, or if the road widens substantially before you see this sign, you've gone too far.) Turn left (southeast) onto an old jeep road here that is the continuation of the Timberline Trail. At mile 15.0, follow a path down through the willows to Texas Creek, which has no bridge. On the right (west) edge of the sandbar, spot some precarious-looking old logs and use them to cross the creek. The less-daring hiker may wish to find a place to wade. Where the logs reach the opposite bank, turn 90 degrees to the left (slightly east of south) and walk through a small stand of dead trees 20 yards away. On the other side of this grey grove, turn right (south) onto a very clear trail and follow it through the willows to the other side of the meadow. Ignore the old bridge on the right, and find the trail in the dense trees at mile 15.2 (9,880) near an old grey stump.

The trail, which is still open to motorbikes, climbs steadily through a spruce forest to its intersection with Cottonwood Pass Road at mile 17.4 (10,585). For mosquito hunters, this forest offers some formidable trophies. Turn left (east) onto the road and continue to this segment's end at a parking lot on the right at mile 17.9 (10,705 feet; N38° 50.68', W106° 26.76').

OTHER HIKES AND RIDES

There are many fourteeners in this area, including Huron Peak, Missouri Mountain, and Mounts Belford and Oxford. La Plata Peak is described here because it is most accessible from the CDT.

LA PLATA PEAK
Approximate one-way distance: 4.5 miles
Method of Travel: Hiking
Difficulty: Strenuous

West Winfield Trailhead: See *Access* for Winfield at the beginning of this section. From Winfield, walk (or drive) a very short distance north; then turn west onto a rough road and continue about 0.6 mile to where the road worsens. Vehicles should park here.

Walk west on the road for about 1.0 mile and turn right (north) onto another road in a meadow. Continue 0.2 mile to a gate. Head north, climb onto the mountain's southwest ridge, and follow it to the 14,336-foot summit.

CLOYSES LAKE-SOUTH CLEAR CREEK LOOP
Approximate loop distance: 30 miles
Method of Travel: Hiking
Difficulty: Strenuous

Pear Lake Trailhead: Drive as for the South Clear Creek Trailhead in this segment's *Access*, but turn left (south) about 2.0 miles short of Winfield at the Rockdale townsite onto Cloyses Lake Road. Continue approximately 3.5 miles to the trailhead.

This rugged hike, which circumnavigates the regal Three Apostles as it winds through the Collegiate Peaks Wilderness and crosses the Divide at two steep, rocky passes, was suggested by a wilderness ranger as one of her favorites—rare, privileged information indeed! Please note the special rules governing travel in wilderness areas.

From the trailhead, continue south over the Divide to Pear Lake. Then follow an informal trail down North Texas Creek to a trail at Texas Creek. Continue west-southwest on Trail #416 to an unmarked intersection with the Continental Divide Trail (see the text of this segment at mile 14.0), follow it north over the Divide to Winfield, and then walk east and south to the trailhead. This is a long, strenuous hike recommended for experienced backpackers only. You can cut off about 8 miles by making it into a shuttle from the Pear Lake Trailhead to the South Clear Creek Trailhead.

TIMBERLINE TRAIL BIKE RIDE
Approximate loop distance: Variable up to 30 miles
Method of Travel: Biking
Difficulty: Moderate or Strenuous

Trailhead: You may start anywhere on this trail. One prominent trailhead is at Texas Creek, as described in this segment's *Access*. The trail actually starts on Red Mountain Road, just off of Taylor River Road about 6.0 miles north of Cottonwood Pass Road.

Mirror Lake: See *Access* for Segment 26, page 204.

The Timberline Trail covers more than 30 miles as it forms much of the southwestern boundary of the Collegiate Peaks Wilderness before it heads over Cottonwood Pass Road to terminate at Mirror Lake near Tincup. At least 20 miles of it define the CDT. It is extremely popular with motorbike enthusiasts, but it is still an excellent single-track bike ride. Try a shuttle ride of the entire trail, or make a very long loop via Texas Creek and Cottonwood Pass Road or Cottonwood Pass Road and Mirror Lake Campground.

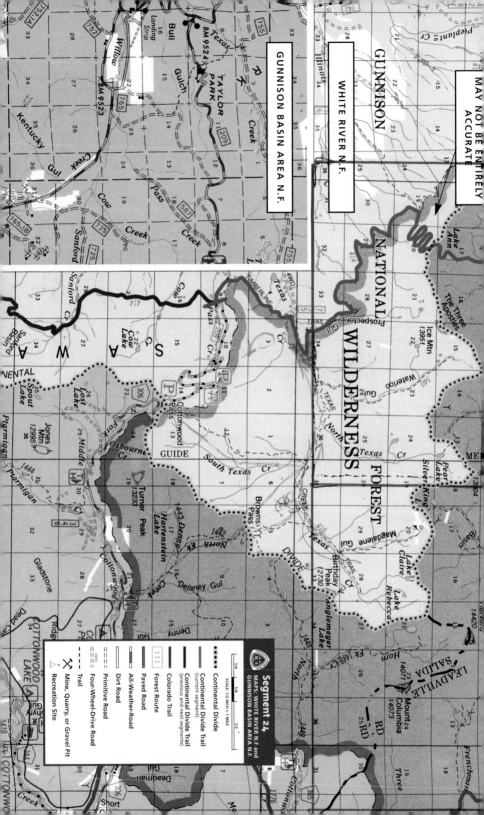

Segment 25
Cottonwood Pass Road to Mirror Lake

Near Tincup Pass, San Isabel National Forest

11.4 miles
Difficulty: Moderate

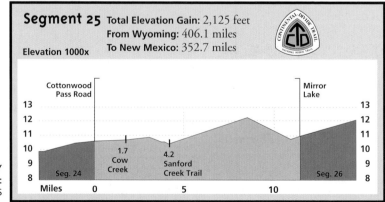

Segment 25 **Total Elevation Gain:** 2,125 feet
From Wyoming: 406.1 miles
To New Mexico: 352.7 miles

CONTINENTAL DIVIDE TRAIL
NATIONAL SCENIC TRAIL

Elevation 1000x

Cottonwood
Pass Road

Mirror
Lake

13

12

11

10

9

Seg. 24

1.7
Cow
Creek

4.2
Sanford
Creek Trail

Seg. 26

Miles   0   5   10

13

12

11

10

9

8

**YOU MAY
ENCOUNTER:**
MOTORBIKES

THE MOST NOTABLE HISTORICAL FEATURE near this segment is the town of Tincup, named for a miner who carried his gold dust in just such a vessel. During the mining boom of the 1880s, people west of Colorado's Continental Divide could not rely on law and order for justice or protection. There were few places where this was more of a problem than in Tincup. The thugs who ran the town made it clear to the sheriff that an arrest of the wrong man would have dire consequences. As a result of this edict, the first lawman lasted only a few months; the second appeased the underworld bosses by avoiding arresting anyone for anything worse than drunkenness; number three was shot and killed by the saloon keeper; the next sheriff committed suicide; and the fifth poor soul led by fate to the dubious post was killed in a gun battle. If a magazine had been around in 1882 to rate the country's worst jobs, sheriff of Tincup would most certainly have topped the list.

By 1882, Tincup was producing more silver than any other camp in the region, and its population swelled to more than 6,000. In spite of this, the railroads never saw fit to lay track up the valley from Gunnison, so ore was carted over steep and snowy Tincup Pass (the CDT's route in the next segment) or other Divide crossings like Cottonwood, Taylor, and Williams Passes. The town, which is located about 3 miles south of Mirror Lake, had dwindled considerably by 1912, and today only a few buildings (and even fewer permanent residents) remain. Tincup today is simply a rustic mountain get-away.

This segment is open to motorcycles, but they seem rare, especially during the week. Water is frequent except from mile 7.0 to mile 10.0. Great camping spots abound.

MOUNTAIN BIKE NOTES: This is an excellent mountain bike ride of mostly moderate difficulty. Do it as an out-and-back, a long loop, or a shuttle. See *Other Hikes and Rides* at the end of the previous segment.

MAPS

TRAILS ILLUSTRATED: 129, 130

USGS QUADRANGLES: Tincup, Cumberland Pass

USFS: Gunnison Basin Area, page 201

BEGINNING ACCESS POINT

Smooth road to trailhead | **COTTONWOOD PASS ROAD/TIMBERLINE TRAIL:** Take US-24 to Buena Vista and turn west at a stoplight on Main Street (County Road 306). Drive 18 miles to the summit of Cottonwood Pass. This marks the intersection with the Continental Divide, but to reach the CDT itself, continue 5.7 miles down the other side of the pass to a sign on the left (south) side indicating the Timberline Trail (#414). Ample parking is provided. The previous segment reaches Cottonwood Pass Road 0.5 mile farther down the road to the west, and it is marked by an identical sign on the right (north).

Night hath

a thousand eyes.

—John Lyly,

The Maides

Metamorphosis

RANGER DISTRICT:
Taylor-Cebolla

ALTERNATE ACCESS

Smooth road to trailhead 🚗 **FROM THE WEST:** From Gunnison, proceed as in the description to Mirror Lake Campground (Segment 24), but ignore the turnoff to Tincup at Taylor Park Trading Post and continue a few more miles to the turnoff on the right (east) toward Cottonwood Pass.

ENDING ACCESS POINT

Smooth road to trailhead 🚗 **MIRROR LAKE:** See the next segment.

SUPPLIES, SERVICES, AND ACCOMMODATIONS

BUENA VISTA is about 24 miles east on Cottonwood Pass Road (which becomes Main Street in town). Hitching may be difficult on this slow-moving tourist route popular for its scenery. Tincup, which offers limited services, is a 3-mile walk south from Mirror Lake Campground.

TRAIL DESCRIPTION

The trail exits the parking lot at its east end, crosses Pass Creek, and then it bends west and south. It ascends gradually for the first 0.6 mile before rolling gently through a lodgepole forest dotted with pretty meadows. You'll reach Cow Creek at mile 1.7 (10,720).

As the trail begins a descent through a forest of aspens at mile 3.2 (10,840), it is joined by a jeep road. Continue straight (south) along the path. You'll reach a wide, muddy meadow that looks like it was the site of a recent convention of motorcycle enthusiasts at mile 3.6. There is a dry route through this bog about 100 yards downstream (west).

At mile 4.2 (10,365), the CDT forms a diagonal intersection with the Sanford Creek Trail on the right, marking the beginning of a 4.3-mile ascent. Continue straight ahead (east). Meadows near timberline at mile 6.3 offer excellent camping. At mile 7.0 the trail switchbacks to the right (west) and crosses Sanford Creek, which provides the last reliable water for 3 miles. The CDT eases above timberline at mile 7.6, offering great views to the west and north. Then it cuts a mellow traverse along the bare ridge before cresting it at mile 8.7 (12,080). The Continental Divide is now in full view as defined by the peaks to the left (east). The trail will soon begin a steady descent to this segment's destination, Mirror Lake, which lies in the valley straight ahead. In the next segment, the CDT continues beyond the lake and over Tincup Pass to the south.

The trail describes a wide bend through Garden Basin, the cirque to the east, before beginning its descent and widening into a clear jeep road. Avoid the left fork at mile 9.6 and continue downhill to the right. A small stream offers water at mile 10.0 just after a big swing to the southwest. Start thinking about campsites if you don't want to pay for one at Mirror Lake.

Next to an outhouse at mile 10.9 (10,800), turn left (east), walk 100 yards to Mirror Lake Road, and turn left again. The road passes the campground at mile 11.3 and forks to a parking lot on the right (west) that marks the end of this segment (mile 11.4; 10,970 feet; N38° 44.77', W106° 25.85').

MOUNTAIN BIKE RIDES

This entire segment makes an excellent mountain bike ride. It can be combined with the preceding and/or succeeding segments to make a long and varied outing. After mile 5.9 of the next segment, the CDT becomes too rough for bikes. Stay on Tincup Pass Road and ride into the old mining town of St. Elmo.

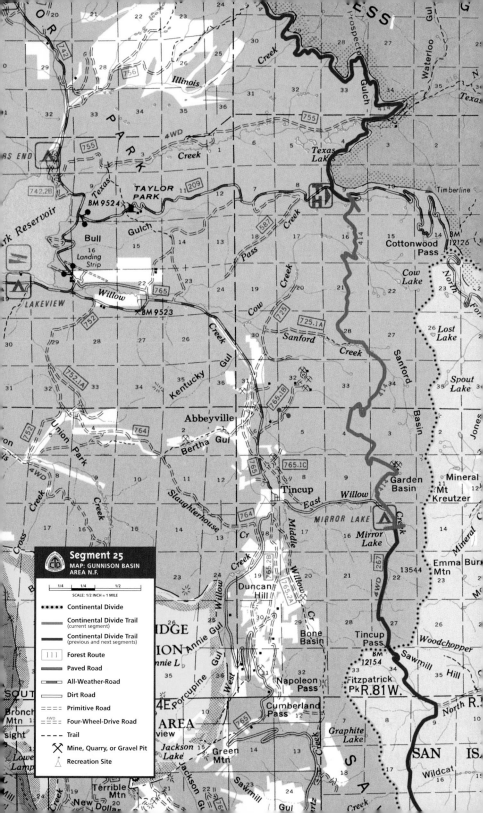

Segment 25

MAP: GUNNISON BASIN
AREA N.F.

SCALE: 1/2 INCH = 1 MILE

1/4	1/4	1/2

- **● ● ● ●**   Continental Divide
- **━━━**   Continental Divide Trail (current segment)
- **━━━**   Continental Divide Trail (previous and next segments)
- ⌐111⌐   Forest Route
- **━━━**   Paved Road
- **━━━**   All-Weather-Road
- **━━━**   Dirt Road
- = = = =   Primitive Road
- 4WD - - -   Four-Wheel-Drive Road
- - - - -   Trail
- ✕   Mine, Quarry, or Gravel Pit
- ⛺   Recreation Site

Segment 26
Mirror Lake to Hancock

Clearing storm near Hancock, San Isabel National Forest

13.5 miles
Difficulty: Strenuous

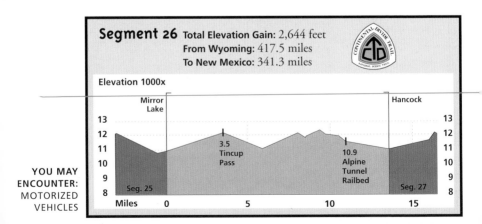

Segment 26 **Total Elevation Gain:** 2,644 feet
From Wyoming: 417.5 miles
To New Mexico: 341.3 miles

Elevation 1000x

Mirror Lake

Hancock

13 — 13
12 — 12
11 — 11
  3.5
  Tincup
  Pass
10 — 10.9 — 10
  Alpine
  Tunnel
9 — Railbed — 9
Seg. 25 — Seg. 27
8 — 8

Miles   0   5   10   15

**YOU MAY
ENCOUNTER:**
MOTORIZED
VEHICLES

THIS SEGMENT BEGINS by climbing to the summit of Tincup Pass, the historic route that was once used to cart ore over the Continental Divide from the lawless mining town of Tincup. On the other side of the pass is the somewhat more civil town of St. Elmo, a rail stop on the Denver and South Park line that eventually climbed to the Alpine Tunnel. St. Elmo was the largest town in the area in the 1880s and 1890s when a population of 3,000 provided a haven for rail travelers and miners from the surrounding area. The town supported many businesses, including hotels, saloons, two general stores, a drug store, and a newspaper—the *St. Elmo Mountaineer*. The town went into decline early in the 20th century, shadowing the demise of the railroad.

The CDT leaves Tincup Pass Road about 4.0 miles before the road reaches St. Elmo. The trail then parallels the Divide to the south, follows it over the Alpine Tunnel bore at trail mile 10.5, and then descends off the Divide ridge to a point very near the northern end of the tunnel.

The result of some very ambitious engineering and financing, the Alpine Tunnel was the highest in the world. And it was expected to be 1,800 feet long. In the late 1870s, the Denver, South Park, and Pacific Railroad of former Colorado Governor John Evans was locked in a race with the rival Denver and Rio Grande to cross the Great Divide and reach the burgeoning market in the Gunnison Basin. Evans anticipated the impossibility of going over the Divide and began constructing a tunnel through it late in 1879. Because of the dangerous conditions and continual problems with avalanches, rockslides, and the steep grade, worker turnover was high. In all, some 10,000 men are believed to have worked on the tunnel.

Construction costs soared for other reasons as well. The rock turned out to be porous, requiring expensive beams of imported California redwood for support. And the constant threat of avalanche necessitated large snowsheds. In fact, this was one of the most expensive transportation construction projects ever, with the tunnel alone costing more than $2.4 million in today's dollars, and the rest of the line averaging $1 million per mile. This huge drain initiated the demise of the rail company, and post-construction problems didn't help. The costs of snow removal were exorbitant. Avalanches constantly roared down over the tracks despite the snowsheds, one of which was longer than two football fields. In one tragic accident, 13 passengers were buried. In 1910, a cave-in killed several people, and the tunnel was never re-opened.

> Every formula
>
> which expresses
>
> a law of nature
>
> is a hymn of praise
>
> to God.
>
> —Maria Mitchell

RANGER DISTRICTS:
Taylor-Cebolla
Salida

And what of the race to Gunnison? A train finally reached Gunnison via the Alpine Tunnel in September, 1882. But the Denver and Rio Grande, using the more benign Marshall Pass to the south, had already been running trains there since August, 1881—thus winning the race by more than a year.

Water is plentiful on this segment. For camping, I recommend waiting until after mile 5.9, where a single-track trail leaves the vehicle-accessible road. Once the CDT leaves the trees at mile 6.9, it is above timberline for some 4.0 miles with few routes to shelter.

Watch for dangerous old mineshafts if you go exploring around here, especially near St. Elmo.

 MOUNTAIN BIKE NOTES: Tincup Pass Road, from Mirror Lake to St. Elmo, is rideable, but it is also open to four-wheel drive vehicles. The section of CDT from that road to the railroad bed at the Alpine Tunnel is not suitable for riding. The rocky trail is not clear, and riding here would seriously damage the fragile tundra. But see *Other Hikes and Rides* at the end of this segment for a challenging ride over two airy Divide passes.

MAPS

TRAILS ILLUSTRATED: 130
USGS QUADRANGLES: Cumberland Pass, St. Elmo
USFS: Gunnison Basin Area, San Isabel National Forest, pages 208-209

BEGINNING ACCESS POINT

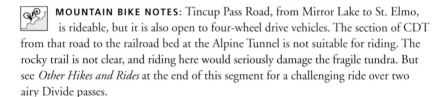 **MIRROR LAKE:** From Gunnison, go north on Main Street (Highway 135) 10.3 miles to Almont. Turn right at the sign to Taylor Reservoir onto Forest Road 742. Travel 23.3 miles along the Taylor River to the turnoff on the right to Tincup (at the Taylor Park Trading Post). Follow an easy dirt road 8.0 miles to the only stop sign in Tincup. Turn left at the stop sign and drive 3.0 miles to Mirror Lake Campground. You'll find a parking area just past the campground on the right.

ALTERNATE ACCESS

 TINCUP PASS ROAD: Proceed as in the description to Hancock (Segment 27), but continue into the town of St. Elmo. Turn right (north) at the sign to Tincup Pass followed by an immediate left (west) onto County Road 267. Continue 4.0 miles to the trailhead, which is marked by a kiosk with a blue CDT symbol on the left side of the road. This is trail mile 5.9. The pass summit is 2.4 miles farther along the CDT route at trail mile 3.5.

ENDING ACCESS POINT

 HANCOCK: See next segment.

TRAIL DESCRIPTION Follow the old jeep road south along the east (left) side of Mirror Lake and cross East Willow Creek at mile 0.5. At mile 1.9, take a right fork as it curves around to the northwest and then switchbacks to the south. As you climb toward Tincup Pass, note the Divide's path as it descends from the Sawatch Range on the left (east) to intersect the CDT at the summit of Tincup Pass.

The trail reaches the pass summit at mile 3.5 (12,154) and continues south on the jeep road down the other side. At mile 4.7, follow the trail as it bends to the right (west) around Sawmill Hill, avoiding a tangle of improvised roads.

At mile 5.9 (11,080), the road exits the trees into a wide, willow-covered meadow on the valley floor. A kiosk on the right (southwest) marks the CDT's departure from the road. Turn onto the trail here as it forms a 45-degree angle with the road and set out on the first nonmotorized section since the CDT exited the Collegiate Peaks Wilderness in Segment 24.

The trail passes through a growth of willows and exits them at a post at mile 6.1 where the trail becomes obscure. Continue straight ahead about 30 yards to an obvious stream crossing on the left (south) and cross the creek on a bridge. Follow a clear trail that turns back to the southwest and enters the trees.

The CDT climbs to a point at mile 6.8 where it veers left (southeast) before turning 90 degrees to the right (west-southwest) and exiting the trees at mile 6.9 (11,720). Cross a small stream, follow frequent cairns 0.2 mile through the willows, and swing to the left (south). Climb toward a flat, unnamed pass between Wildcat Gulch and the Chalk Creek North Fork drainage. Turn due south (right) and continue climbing along a trail of cairns through a small growth of willows. You won't find any visible tread until mile 7.9 where the CDT turns left (southeast) and climbs 0.1 mile to a shallow saddle (mile 8.0; 12,100). Look just east of south to where two saddles on the horizon are separated by a distinct ridge. The CDT will cross through the one on the left (east), which is approximately at compass bearing 160° from this point.

The tread is intermittent as cairns delineate a descent to the southeast. At mile 8.4 (11,880), the trail bottoms out near some streams and willows and resumes climbing again to a small ridge. Another short descent leads to a streambed at mile 8.6 (11,960). In a fragile alpine environment like this, the conscientious hiker will stay on the trail, hike single-file, and, in the absence of a tread, try to hike on durable surfaces like rocks as much as possible.

From here, a trail seems to lead south toward the westernmost (right) of the two saddles observed from mile 8.0. The CDT, however, climbs to the one on the left (east). Work your way around the left side of the ridge jutting toward you from between the saddles and climb south-southeast along an intermittent trail to a cairn on the pass summit at mile 9.3 (12,290 feet; N38° 39.53', W106° 25.10'). Note that the trail alignment on the USGS Cumberland Pass quadrangle is wrong from here to the Alpine Tunnel.

Follow a visible trail that descends to the south. Where you see two trails, take the one on the right until the tread disappears at a cairn after only 100 yards. Walk straight through some willows (just east of south) to the far end of a flat part of the ridge and follow a trail of cairns downhill. Tunnel Lake soon comes into view down to the left (east) at mile 9.4. Continue through the willows, still east of south, on a faint tread along a bench above the lake's west side. Cross the inlet stream at mile 9.6 (12,020) and follow a faint tread southeast along a fairly even contour. Do not descend into the valley or lose much elevation.

Stay on this clear trail as it rolls along the ridge to the southeast. At mile 10.5 (11,940), the trail fades at a flat, saddle-like area before a high rocky point. Continue a few more yards to a very clear trail running perpendicular to your path. Turn left (north) and begin a 0.4-mile descent through several switchbacks to the old railbed (11,580 feet; N38° 38.98', W106° 24.22') that used to carry the Denver, South Park, and Pacific line to the Alpine Tunnel. A post marks the intersection with this wide, flat, obvious road. To view the collapsed remains of the tunnel, turn left off the CDT and walk 130 yards north to where the road turns into a single-track. The caved-in tunnel entrance is visible in the rock wall on the left.

N **NORTHBOUND HIKERS** will be looking for a single-track trail at a post on the left (south) side of the road ascending sharply across a field of talus. If the railbed turns into a single-track in the trees before you make this left turn, you've gone too far by about 130 yards.

Follow the roadbed's gradual descent to the east to a road-closure gate at mile 13.3. The townsite of Hancock marks the end of this segment at mile 13.5 (11,040 feet; N38° 38.36', W106° 21.65'). There are no buildings here and no indication that this was once a town. You will recognize this point as the parking area where the road to the Alpine Tunnel meets a vehicle-accessible road. A sign marks the route to the tunnel. The next segment does not continue to descend north along the road (which leads to near St. Elmo), but it turns right (south) to climb along Forest Road 295.2, a four-wheel drive road.

SUPPLIES, SERVICES, AND ACCOMMODATIONS

TINCUP offers limited supplies at a small grocery. A restaurant and lodging are also available. The nice proprietors of the businesses here will hold a package mailed to you, but call them first: Greg and Eleanor McAuliffe, 1713 County Road 55, Almont, CO 81210. Phone (970) 641-1400.

TINCUP DISTANCE FROM TRAIL: 3.0 miles.

Bank	None
Bus	None
Camping	Available
Dining	Frenchy's Cafe
Gear	Tincup Store (limited supplies, including white gas)
Groceries	Tincup Store (limited)
Information	Tincup Store
Laundry	Tincup Store
Lodging	Cabins are available.
Medical	None
Post Office	None, but contact Eleanor McAuliffe about sending packages.
Showers	Tincup Store

OTHER HIKES AND RIDES

From Hancock, the day hike to the Alpine Tunnel is short, flat, and easy. However, the loop described below offers a much better feel for the surrounding terrain, as well as the lengths to which men went to push the railroad up to—and through—the Divide.

WILLIAMS PASS-ALPINE TUNNEL LOOP

Approximate loop distance:	9.0 miles
Mode of travel:	Hiking or biking
Difficulty:	Moderate (Strenuous for bikes)

Hancock Trailhead: See *Access* at the beginning of the next segment.

Crossing the Divide twice, this impressive hike above timberline traces part of the old route of the train on the south side of the Alpine Tunnel, including the harrowing section called "The Palisades" where rail workers had to construct a shelf of rock across the steep southwest slopes of Mt. Poor.

Hike the CDT in reverse from Hancock a short distance to where the trail to Williams Pass departs on the left. Follow this steady climb over the pass to Alpine Tunnel Road, turn right, and follow it to a single-track back over the Divide to the flat rail bed at the tunnel's north end. Now refer to the CDT description in this segment at trail mile 10.9.

IMPORTANT NOTE: This trail may be closed well into the summer. Call the Taylor-Cebolla Ranger District (see Appendix A) before planning a hike or ride. It is advisable to use a map for this hike.

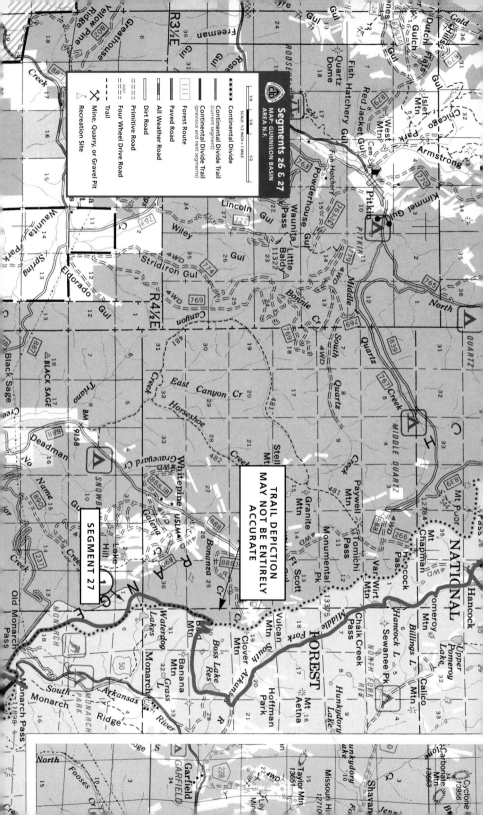

SEGMENT 26

FOSSIL RIDGE RECREATION MANAGEMENT AREA

SAN ISABEL

GUNNISON BASIN AREA N.F.

SAN ISABEL N.F.

Segment 27
Hancock to Monarch Pass

Sunrise along the Divide, San Isabel National Forest

19.3 miles
Difficulty: Strenuous

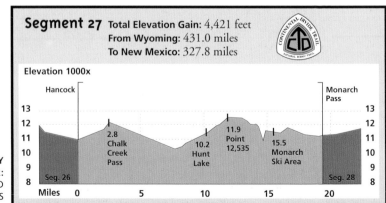

Segment 27 **Total Elevation Gain:** 4,421 feet
From Wyoming: 431.0 miles
To New Mexico: 327.8 miles

Elevation 1000x

Hancock

Monarch Pass

2.8 Chalk Creek Pass

10.2 Hunt Lake

11.9 Point 12,535

15.5 Monarch Ski Area

Seg. 26

Seg. 28

Miles   0   5   10   15   20

YOU MAY ENCOUNTER: MOTORIZED VEHICLES

THIS SEGMENT STARTS at the site of Hancock, a ghost town that existed almost entirely to serve the Alpine Tunnel, both during construction and after completion. (See the previous segment for information on the Alpine Tunnel.) Although miners worked around Hancock, its population of more than 1,000 in the 1880s and '90s was mostly made up of railroad employees. The tunnel's closing in 1910 sparked Hancock's decline. By 1926, only a few hopeful miners hung on. The ruins in the area, most notably the mine at mile 0.5, are from the old town.

Water is plentiful for the first 11.1 miles of this segment, and it is non-existent on the remaining 8.2 miles to Monarch Pass. (The Monarch Crest store has water inside, but it closes at 7 p.m. in the summer and is closed all winter.) There are no services in Hancock or St. Elmo.

 MOUNTAIN BIKE NOTES: On about 3 miles of trail surrounding Chalk Creek Pass, just south of Hancock Lakes, the terrain is too steep or rough to ride, and you would spend most of your time pushing. The ride from US-50 north toward the pass combines jeep road and single-track trail. You cannot ride from Boss Lake Reservoir to Monarch Pass (mile 7.7 to 19.3) because of steep grades, rocky terrain, and lack of a trail. See *Other Hikes and Rides* at the end of this segment.

MAPS

TRAILS ILLUSTRATED: 130, 139
USGS QUADRANGLES: St. Elmo, Garfield, Pahlone Peak
USFS: Gunnison Basin Area, San Isabel National Forest, pages 208-209

BEGINNING ACCESS POINT

 HANCOCK: Drive 7 miles south of Buena Vista on Highway 285 and take County Road 162 west toward St. Elmo. After driving 14.7 miles, turn left onto Forest Route 295 just before you reach St. Elmo, and proceed 5 miles to a sign indicating your arrival in Hancock. Drive past the sign and over a small bridge to the parking lot. The trail starts up the left fork of the jeep trail at a sign indicating Hancock Lake and Hancock Pass. The final steps of the previous segment come down the right fork, which is the road to the Alpine Tunnel.

ALTERNATE ACCESS

 BOSS LAKE TRAILHEAD (trail mile 7.7): Drive 12 miles west on US-50 from Poncha Springs and turn right on Forest Route 230 near the Monarch Lodge. Reset your odometer and continue straight over an intersecting

Joy in the universe, and keen curiosity about it all— that has been my religion.

—John Burroughs

RANGER DISTRICTS:
Salida
Taylor-Cebolla

road at mile 0.1. At mile 1.4 , follow a sign for the Boss Lake Trail onto a spur road on the left. Continue about 50 yards and park.

ALTERNATE ACCESS

CHALK CREEK PASS TRAILHEAD (trail mile 5.4): Start as for the Boss Lake Trailhead (see above), but continue past the Boss Lake turnoff to mile 3.7 (from US-50) where the road ends. The trailhead is at the northeast corner of the parking area. The 2.3-mile stretch from here to the Boss Lake Trail is the CDT.

Distance from graded road — 3.7 miles

ENDING ACCESS POINT

MONARCH PASS: See the next segment.

Smooth road to trailhead

TRAIL DESCRIPTION   Begin by ascending south on Forest Road 295.2, a rough four-wheel drive road. Pass by a mining ruin at mile 0.5 and turn left at a fork at mile 0.9. The road ends in a cul-de-sac at mile 1.6. Follow a single-track trail south and pass to the west (right) of Hancock Lake at mile 1.8 (11,680). (The 1992 revision of Trails Illustrated map #130 incorrectly shows the trail passing east of the lake.) The grassy saddle to the south-southeast is Chalk Creek Pass, over which the CDT will pass into the South Arkansas River Middle Fork drainage. Cross the Hancock Lake inlet streams at miles 2.2 and 2.3, follow an obscure trail left (east) of Upper Hancock Lake, and start the sharp climb to the pass at mile 2.5 (11,760).

You will reach the top of the pass at a CDT marker on a post at mile 2.8 (12,160). This is not the Continental Divide, which runs south along the higher ridge on the right (west). Stay to the right of something that may once have been a pond as you start down the other side on a faint tread. For the next few miles, orange flagging marks the trail route, but the Forest Service will remove the flagging when they have finished building the trail (probably in 1997). Pass a post at mile 2.9, avoid a trail forking to the right, and continue to another post in a flat area near some willows at mile 3.0. Now the trail bends right (due south) and passes two more posts before turning left (southeast) to cross a small stream at mile 3.2. Follow an immediate curve back to the right (south), descend along the stream's left (east) edge for less than 100 yards, and veer off to the left again, making sure to avoid a faint tread that tries to draw you straight down the slope under a rocky point of krummholz. Follow posts around the top of the rocky point and down to the left (east) side of the willow-choked valley (mile 3.3; 11,700).

A faint tread marked by cairns parallels the edge of the willows and disappears into a talus field. Cross the talus and pick up the same kind of trail on the other side at mile 3.4. Pass along the left edge of some mud flats, through the willows, and into the trees.

The CDT descends into a broad, flat valley of willows and meadows at mile 3.8 (11,400). Follow an increasingly clearer tread to the trailhead and parking area for this trail at mile 5.4 (11,210). Descend along the road and respect the privacy of the residences at mile 6.4. Avoid side roads until you reach the obscure turnoff on the right (south) for the Boss Lake Trailhead at mile 7.7 (10,400 feet; N38° 33.90', W106° 18.77'). A sign for the Boss Lake Trail marks this point, but it faces east, away from you.

After you complete this turnoff's 180-degree turn, walk about 100 yards to where the road veers left into the trees and continue straight ahead about 20 yards. Turn left (south) again, cross the stream on a good bridge, and ascend steeply on a good trail

SUPPLIES, SERVICES, AND ACCOMMODATIONS

GUNNISON provides all services, but it is 45 miles from the trail. The Monarch Crest store at the top of Monarch Pass is right on the trail and has a small snack bar, restrooms, water, and a phone. All of these are inside the building, which is open during the summer from 7 a.m. to 7 p.m., seven days a week.

Only 13 miles from the trail, the small roadside community of Sargents offers limited services. Both Gunnison and Sargents are west on US-50, which sees a lot of traffic.

DISTANCE FROM TRAIL: 45 miles from Monarch Pass, 38 miles from North Pass (Colorado Highway 114)

ZIP CODE: 81230

Bank	Gunnison Savings and Loan, 303 N. Main St.	(970) 641-2171
Bus	None	
Camping	Mesa Campground, 36128 W. Hwy 50,	641-3186
	(3 miles west of Gunnison)	
Dining	Cafe Silvestre, 903 N. Main (Mexican)	641-4001
	Mario's Pizza, 213 W. Tomichi Ave.	641-1374
Gear	Gene Taylor's, 201 W. Tomichi Ave.	(800) 253-1463
Groceries	Safeway, 112 S. Spruce & Tomichi Ave.	641-0787
Information	Chamber of Commerce, 500 E. Tomichi	641-1501
Laundry	Hi-Country Service & Laundry,	641-3894
	700 N. Main at Denver Ave.	
Lodging	Bennett's Western Motel, 403 E. Tomichi Ave.	641-1722
	Gunnison Super 8 Motel, 411 E. Tomichi Ave.	641-3068
Medical	Gunnison Valley Hospital, 214 E. Denver Ave.	641-1456
Post Office	200 N. Wisconsin Ave.	641-1884
Showers	Mesa Campground, 36128,	641-3186
	W. Hwy. 50 (3 miles west of Gunnison)	

SARGENTS

DISTANCE FROM TRAIL: 13 miles

ZIP CODE: 81248

Bank	None	
Bus	None	
Camping	None	
Dining	Elks Run	(970) 641-5605
Gear	None, but white gas is available in the Elks Run store.	
Groceries	Elks Run has a limited convenience store.	
Information	Elks Run	
Laundry	None	
Lodging	Elks Run has cabins available.	
Medical	None	
Post Office	Sargents Post Office	641-1418
Showers	Elks Run	

to Boss Lake Reservoir at mile 8.5 (10,890). Turn left, walk across the dam, and go around the reservoir on its south side. At mile 8.8, the trail turns into Boss Lake Road, which forks 0.1 mile later. Bear right (south), climb steadily to the west, and reach Hunt Lake at mile 10.2 (11,480). The road ends here, and a single-track trail continues to the west, passing a shallow pond at mile 11.1 (11,980). This is a good area to camp and the last reliable water for 8.2 miles.

The trail soon climbs very steeply through many switchbacks to return to the Divide at the summit of Point 12,535 at mile 11.9. Now the trail disappears. Simply follow the Divide ridge west of south to some very large cairns. The views are superb, and you'll see Monarch Pass, this segment's terminus, to the southeast. The trail is again visible at mile 12.2 as it leaves the Divide to skirt the west of Bald Mountain. It regains the Divide ridge at mile 12.9 (12,500) and promptly disappears at a large cairn. More cairns parallel the Divide ridge to the south. Continue through a couple of descents and watch for Waterdog Lakes below the Divide on the left (east). These are rumored to conceal some big fish.

The trail flattens considerably at mile 13.6 and resumes climbing toward a power line at mile 14.0. Follow cairns veering to the right (west) of a point and crest a side-ridge of the Divide at a cairn at mile 14.1 (12,060). Turn left (southeast) onto a single-track that descends across the steep ridge for 0.2 mile. Stop at mile 14.8 to read about the prehistoric game drive there, of which there is still some visible evidence.

Follow the clear trail to the right (west) of the high points on the ridge and enter the Monarch Ski Area boundary, which is marked by a series of tall poles at mile 15.5. The CDT soon reaches a dirt road at the first of several CDT symbols spread over the rest of the segment. The road turns right to track south along the ridge and descends to an intersection with another road at a small saddle at mile 15.9. Turn right and climb a 0.5-mile hill to the top of the Panorama ski lift. Descend the other side to an intersection at mile 17.1 (11,580). Stay to the right (southeast) and follow the main road through a few switchbacks to a wide, well-graded dirt road at mile 17.8. Walk straight across this road and pick up the single-track Crest Trail (#531), which leads down the hill to the south before winding generally eastward through the trees between US-50 and the Continental Divide.

At mile 18.9, you can see the store at the Monarch Pass summit across US-50. Continue 0.2 mile to where the trail reaches the paved road at a CDT symbol. Turn left (north), cross the busy highway, and join the tourists at the Monarch Crest store, which is the end of this segment at mile 19.3 (11,312 feet; N38° 29.81', W106° 19.48').

OTHER HIKES OR RIDES

HANCOCK PASS BIKE RIDE

Approximate one-way distance:	Variable
Mode of Travel:	Biking or Hiking
Difficulty:	Strenuous

Hancock Trailhead: See *Access* for this segment.

From Hancock, ride toward the Alpine Tunnel, but turn left onto Hancock Pass Road after a short distance. You may simply go to the top of the pass, continue over the top and explore precipitous Tomichi Pass, or you can combine this ride with the Williams Pass or Alpine Tunnel routes for a great loop. (See *Other Hikes and Rides* for the previous segment.) This is almost all on dirt roads. It is advisable to use a map for this ride.

Alpine tarn, Sawatch Range

Segment 28
Monarch Pass to Marshall Pass

Sunset on Mount Ouray, San Isabel National Forest

11.5 miles
Difficulty: Easy

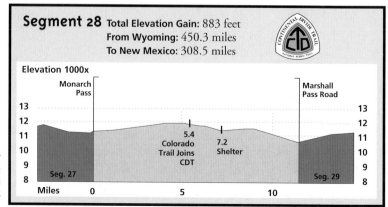

Segment 28 Total Elevation Gain: 883 feet
From Wyoming: 450.3 miles
To New Mexico: 308.5 miles

Elevation 1000x

Monarch Pass

Marshall Pass Road

5.4 Colorado Trail Joins CDT

7.2 Shelter

Seg. 27

Seg. 29

Miles   0   5   10

YOU MAY ENCOUNTER:
MOUNTAIN BIKES

THE RICH HISTORY surrounding so many Colorado landmarks seems to have evaded Monarch Pass. As far as historians know, there was nothing there until the current road was built specifically for motorized vehicles in 1939. However, there were two prior Monarch Passes a short distance to the west along the Divide. The first was built in 1880 as a stage road to serve miners in the Gunnison Basin. A second Monarch Pass used a slightly different route and was designed for automobiles as part of a transcontinental route in the 1920s. It was replaced by the current pass.

An ambitious state highway engineer named Charles Vail overcame strong opposition to build what is now called Monarch Pass. Then he named it after himself, complete with a sign on the summit. Irate locals vandalized the sign, and the name was soon changed. But that was not the end of Mr. Vail's highway career. He had to wait a while, but his dream of geographic immortality came true when he lent his name to a quiet little pass (and a town and a ski area and a valley…) some distance to the north.

This is a nice segment for those who wish to hike along the Divide without having to climb 2,000 vertical feet to get there. It has few ups and downs, and the two passes at its endpoints provide easy access. The payoff of fantastic views is well worth the minimal effort.

This segment follows a popular mountain bike route called the Crest Trail. If you don't want to step off the trail every few minutes to let bikers pass, then it would behoove you to schedule this segment for a weekday. If you do find yourself here on a weekend, you may avoid most of the bike traffic by waiting until after about 11 a.m. In any event, please be courteous. The mountain bikers claimed this trail before it was designated as the CDT. In fact, if you want to have some fun, you might consider grabbing a bike and joining them.

Almost the entire segment is above timberline, so be ready to head for lower ground if you hear the cranky grumble of thunder. Camping spots are not abundant between miles 1.2 and 7.2. The shop at Monarch Crest offers the last water for 7.5 miles. If you are relying on this stop, don't forget that the water is inside and the shop is open 7 to 7, seven days a week, and only during summer.

MOUNTAIN BIKE NOTES: If you've done any biking in Colorado, you've probably heard of the Crest Trail. Its non-technical Continental Divide access, nice single-track trail, and stunning views make it a very popular ride. If you're feeling

For my part,

I travel not

to go anywhere,

but to go.

I travel

for travel's sake.

The great affair

is to move.

—Robert Louis Stevenson, *Travels with a Donkey*

RANGER DISTRICT: Taylor-Cebolla

particularly ambitious, use the surrounding roads to make a loop out of it. Most people ride southbound from Monarch to Marshall Pass.

MAPS

TRAILS ILLUSTRATED: 139
USGS QUADRANGLES: Pahlone Peak, Mount Ouray
USFS: San Isabel National Forest, pages 220–221

ACCESS

 MONARCH PASS: The parking area is at the top of the pass near a tourist stop called Monarch Crest. It is on US-50 about 18 miles west of Poncha Springs and 45 miles east of Gunnison.

 MARSHALL PASS: See the next segment.

SUPPLIES, SERVICES, AND ACCOMMODATIONS

See notes for Gunnison and Sargents in the last segment. The shop at Monarch Pass, called Monarch Crest, has a small snack bar, restrooms, and water (all inside). It is open during the summer from 7 to 7, seven days a week. If you plan to pass through here before Memorial Day or after Labor Day, you should call to see if the shop is still open, (719) 539-4091.

TRAIL DESCRIPTION

From the parking area near the Monarch Crest store, walk behind (northeast of) the gondola terminal and continue east on a dirt road. After a brief climb, turn at a sign for the single-track Crest Trail on the right (south) at mile 0.4. Follow this to an intersection with a jeep road at a saddle at mile 1.2 (11,380). This spot offers one of the few flat spots to camp in this area.

Turn right (south) onto the road and follow it to a sign at mile 1.8 for Marshall Pass. Follow this sign onto a very clear single-track on the right. The trail climbs gently until it reaches the top of the ridge, which is also the Continental Divide. Flattening out at approximately 11,860 feet, the trail offers far-reaching views in all directions. At mile 5.4 (11,900), the South Fooses Creek Trail brings the Colorado Trail back to the domain of the Divide, and the CDT and CT will share the same tread for the next 122.3 miles. Continue east (straight) and make a gradual descent as the trail follows the Divide's jog to the south before veering abruptly back to the east at mile 6.3 (11,860). Now the CDT guides you over to the Atlantic side of the Divide, into a cool spruce forest, and down to a trail intersection where you should stay right. A short distance later, you'll find an open-air shelter that could house a few people in a surprise rainstorm (mile 7.2; 11,505).

The trail turns sharply to the right (south) and temporarily leaves the Divide, which cruises to the top of Chipeta Mountain to the east. In 0.3 mile, you will pass by a spring (coming out of a pipe) that seems to be perennial. As the trail climbs again, the milder terrain of hills and timber to the south comes into view, offering the first hint of the rolling Cochetopa Hills. At mile 8.5 (11,720), continue straight south past an intersecting trail that marks your passage under timberline, where the trail will remain for most of the next 70 miles. Pass two more seemingly perennial springs at miles 9.8 and 10.2. Halfway between these springs, a trailhead marks where the CDT widens into a road open to motorized vehicles. Look to the northeast (left) to catch an occasional glimpse of the hulking mass of Mount Ouray, which just missed being a fourteener by 29 feet.

Follow the road to where it bends sharply to the left (north) at mile 11.3 and continue 0.1 mile to an intersecting road. Turn 180 degrees to the right (southeast) and walk to Marshall Pass Road at mile 11.5 (10,830 feet; N38° 23.73', W106° 14.80').

N **NORTHBOUND HIKERS:** This may be an easy one for northbound hikers to miss. Look for the left turn onto an intersecting road 0.1 mile after leaving Marshall Pass Road. You should not hit a single-track for 1.4 miles.

This segment ends in the parking lot across the road from this trailhead. You'll find restrooms in the parking lot and some nice informal camping spots down the bank behind it. To continue on to the next segment, turn right from the trailhead (south) and continue 0.2 mile south to a deep roadcut in the ridge. A road breaking off to the left (south) at the near end of the roadcut is the path of the next segment.

OTHER HIKES AND RIDES

No other well-established hiking or biking trails are accessible from this segment.

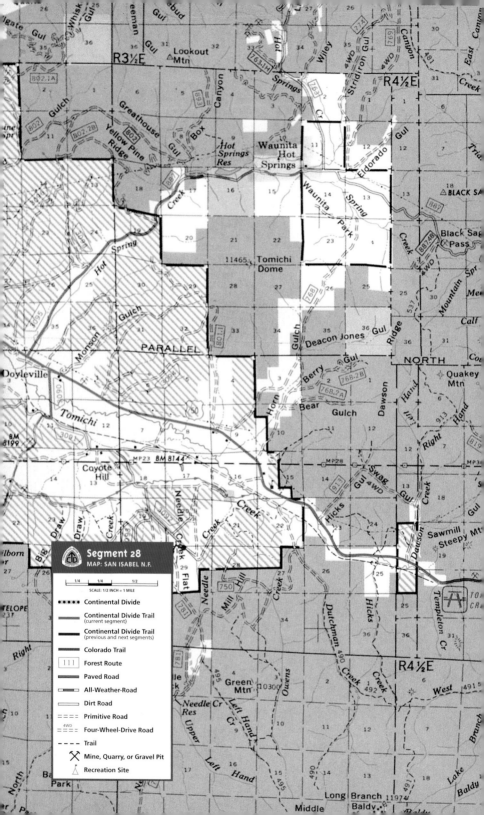

Segment 28
MAP: SAN ISABEL N.F.

SCALE: 1/2 INCH = 1 MILE

- •••• Continental Divide
- —— Continental Divide Trail (current segment)
- ▬▬ Continental Divide Trail (previous and next segments)
- ▬▬ Colorado Trail
- |1 1 1| Forest Route
- ▬▬ Paved Road
- ▭▭ All-Weather-Road
- ▭▭ Dirt Road
- ==== Primitive Road
- ==== Four-Wheel-Drive Road
- - - - Trail
- ✕ Mine, Quarry, or Gravel Pit
- ⌂ Recreation Site

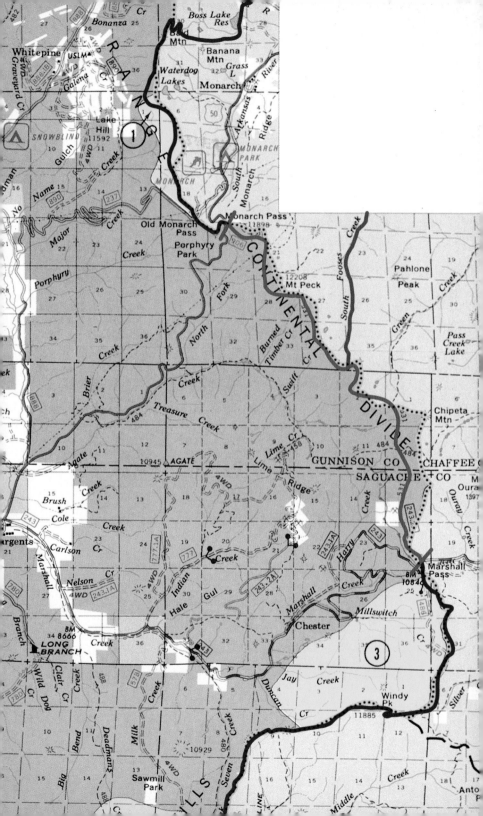

Segment 29
Marshall Pass to Colorado Highway 114

In the Cochetopa Hills, Gunnison National Forest

35.4 miles
Difficulty: Moderate

MARSHALL PASS is the trail's transition point from the massive Sawatch Range to the smaller and much less imposing Cochetopa Hills. A third mountain range, the Sangre de Cristo, has its roots near here and trends off to the southeast.

The pass is named for Army Lieutenant William L. Marshall, who came down with a bad toothache while doing survey work in the San Juan Mountains in 1873. In his haste to get to the nearest dentist, who was a few hundred miles away in Denver, he found his own way over the Continental Divide instead of taking the extra time to go over the well-established Cochetopa Pass farther south. After a successful repose with the dentist, Marshall claimed his improvised route saved him four days and 125 miles.

Eight years after the toothache, two railroad companies were locked in tight competition to lay track across the Divide to the Gunnison area, whose growing ore production required faster and more efficient transport to the market on the Eastern Slope. One line (the Denver, South Park and Pacific) bored under the Divide near the towns of St. Elmo and Hancock, creating the Alpine Tunnel. The other line (the Denver and Rio Grande) raced over Marshall Pass. The latter proved to be the better plan as the railroad reached Gunnison more than a year before its subterranean rival to the north.

This segment is open to motorized vehicles, which mainly take the form of the occasional dirt bike. The only reliable water sources are Silver Creek (350 vertical feet below the CDT at mile 4.0), Tank Seven Creek at mile 11.9, Baldy Lake (0.5 mile off the CDT at mile 22.1), and Lujan Creek at approximately mile 34.8.

Conservation

is a state

of harmony

between men

and land.

—Aldo Leopold,

A Sand County

Almanac

RANGER DISTRICTS:
Taylor-Cebolla
Saguache

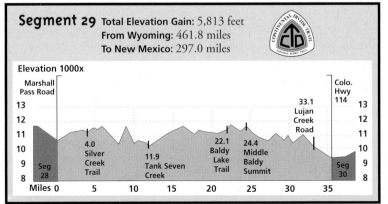

Segment 29 Total Elevation Gain: 5,813 feet
From Wyoming: 461.8 miles
To New Mexico: 297.0 miles

Elevation 1000x

Marshall Pass Road — 33.1 Lujan Creek Road — Colo. Hwy 114

13, 12, 11, 10, 9, 8

Seg 28 — 4.0 Silver Creek Trail — 11.9 Tank Seven Creek — 22.1 Baldy Lake Trail — 24.4 Middle Baldy Summit — Seg 30

Miles 0   5   10   15   20   25   30   35

YOU MAY ENCOUNTER: MOTORIZED VEHICLES

MOUNTAIN BIKE NOTES: This segment is well-suited to riding, although it is almost without exception non-technical. The riding is smooth and easy. You might consider trying other loops in this area as well. The Silver Creek Trail, at trail mile 4.0, offers more challenging riding and loop possibilities.

MAPS

TRAILS ILLUSTRATED: 139

USGS QUADRANGLES: Mount Ouray, Bonanza, Chester, Sargents Mesa, West Baldy, North Pass

USFS: Gunnison Basin Area, San Isabel National Forest, Rio Grande National Forest, pages 228–229

ACCESS

MARSHALL PASS: Drive south from Poncha Springs on US-285 about 5 miles and turn right (west) toward Marshall Pass. Continue 13.0 miles to a parking area on the left (east) side of the road next to some restrooms near the summit of the pass. The trailhead where the CDT arrives from the last segment is just across the road. The trail continues up the road to the south, heading toward a deep roadcut in the ridge.

There are other ways to access the trail in this segment. Most require driving long distances on bumpy dirt roads. If you choose to give it a try, use a good map to pick your route. You can also refer to Randy Jacobs' guide to the Colorado Trail for an access point at Sargents Mesa.

 COLORADO HIGHWAY 114: See the next segment.

SUPPLIES, SERVICES, AND ACCOMMODATIONS

SARGENTS: The small community of Sargents and its limited services are about 18 miles west on the Marshall Pass road. The moderate traffic on this road may not be conducive to hitchhiking. See Segment 27, page 213.

TRAIL DESCRIPTION From the parking lot, walk south 0.2 mile on the Marshall Pass road to a deep roadcut in the ridge. At the near end of the roadcut, turn left (south) onto a dirt road and continue 0.1 mile. Turn left (east) onto the single-track trail for Silver Creek and follow a gentle climb through a spruce forest. At mile 1.5 (11,200), the CDT flattens and switchbacks briefly to the northwest before bending back to the south and west. Continue to mile 2.8 (11,160) and turn left (south) onto a logging road at a well-signed intersection. Climb steadily to mile 3.1. In another 0.1 mile, turn right onto an old jeep road disguised as a wide single-track that tunnels through thick trees to the south. A gentle climb to mile 3.6 leads to a lookout on the left with views of Sheep Mountain to the east-southeast. After a gradual descent, the trail leaves the trees. The turnoff to Silver Creek on Trail 1356 is on the left at mile 4.0 (11,250). For water or a nice place to camp with commanding close-up views of Antora Peak, turn here and descend a few hundred vertical feet.

The CDT continues south and climbs along an old jeep track to a grassy saddle at mile 4.4 (11,415). You'll be able to see the high peaks of the Sawatch Range to the north. The road turns left (west) and continues to climb. Just before it enters the trees at mile 4.6, turn onto a single-track trail on the right (northwest). This trail quickly turns back to the west and levels off in about 100 yards on the north side of the ridge in a cool spruce forest. You'll pass a small spring of questionable reliability at mile 4.8, followed by a climb that ends in a clearing at mile 5.1 (11,540). Now descend into a saddle and pass through a gated fence in 50 yards. The trail follows the line of the Divide for about 0.1 mile and bottoms out in the saddle at mile 5.3 (11,460) just east of Windy Peak. It then climbs through two switchbacks and tops out on the south side of the ridge at mile 5.9 (11,710 feet; N38° 21.06', W106° 16.01'). From here the CDT descends to the south-southwest into a markedly drier lodgepole pine forest.

At mile 7.1, you will pass through an interesting phenomenon of lodgepole forest growth known as doghair. It is characterized by innumerable skinny, tightly spaced trees, some of which may be 100 hundred years old—as old as full-sized trees. In doghair growth, there are so many trees that no individual gets the nutrients or space it requires for normal development. The resulting dense forest of uniform shapes and patterns induces an eerie claustrophobia.

At mile 7.3, the trail crosses the road to Jay Creek at a poorly marked inter-section. Continue to descend southwest on a single-track trail. The snowy West Elk Mountains are visible to the west-northwest from mile 7.6 where the trail jogs briefly to the left (south) at a ravine. After a short climb, the trail reaches the top of the steep Divide ridge at mile 8.3, which offers great views to the east, north, and west. Continue over relatively flat terrain, climb to mile 8.8 (10,470), and follow the CDT's sharp turn to the left (south) at mile 9.0 to follow a natural gas pipeline easement for 70 yards. Then look for the trail burrowing back into the taller trees on the right (southwest).

Descend 0.2 mile and follow the CDT as it shadows the Divide's curve to the left (south). Enter a bright, refreshing aspen forest at mile 10.5. In 1.0 mile (10,590), the CDT veers off the ridge to the right (southwest) and descends to Tank Seven Creek. The trail crosses the creek at mile 11.9 (10,280). Turn left onto the Tank Seven Creek Trail and watch for Colorado blue spruce, the state tree, along the creek as you ascend. What a difference some water makes! The forest is thicker, and the thriving spruce trees rise from a variety of foliage, lush grasses, and wildflowers.

At mile 12.7, enter the east end of sunny Cameron Park, continue to its upper end, and bear left toward two dilapidated cabins at mile 13.2 (10,785). As it crosses a logging road (#578) at right angles, the trail passes between the two cabins. The Forest Service slogan "Land of Many Uses" is an understatement here. Hikers and bikers join motorized vehicles on logging roads zigzagging through grazing allotments. The trail follows Cameron Park's swing to the south and passes into a spruce forest at mile 13.4.

At mile 14.0, the trail crosses another dirt road and continues as a single-track to the west-southwest. It climbs gradually through spruce stands and meadows until mile 14.3 where it turns right (north) at the source of Tank Seven Creek and flattens out in a huge meadow. In 0.1 mile, the CDT turns left (west) and fades. Well-placed carsonite posts will lead you to a faint trail that continues the bend to the left around a wet meadow. Follow the trail across the meadow to the southwest onto a faint jeep road, Forest Route 486, which soon passes through open meadows surrounded by stands of spruce. In contrast to the hullabaloo of multiple use around Cameron Park, this area is pristine and peaceful.

Continue straight ahead (west of south) at the intersection with the trail to Big Bend Creek at mile 15.0. As you ascend here, take in excellent views of the Sawatch Range to the north and part of the Sangre de Cristo Range to the east. You can see the large Pinnacle Mine on the opposing slope to the northeast. Cross over a road from the southeast at mile 15.6 and continue on Forest Route 850.

Follow a gentle climb to the broad plateau of Sargents Mesa at mile 16.3 (11,720). As the trail bends slightly to the right to go around the north side of a low, charred knob, it reenters the forest for several miles. Descend to mile 17.7 where the trail curves left until it is facing due south. In another 0.1 mile, be alert for cairns and Colorado Trail symbols on the right (west) side of the road that mark a turn onto a faint single-track trail (11,160 feet; N38° 16.96', W106° 24.67'). Continue through a saddle and straight (west) past a large cairn that marks the Long Branch Trail. Climb out of the saddle and follow the gentle undulations to an intersection with the Baldy Lake Trail at mile 22.1 (11,495). At a spot 0.2 mile before this point, if you walk a little to the right (north) where the trees open, you can see Long Branch Baldy's steep east face, at the base of which is the lake. Campsites abound in this area.

To reach the reliable water of Baldy Lake, leave the CDT by turning right (north) and descending 0.5 mile. You'll find places to camp there just off the trail (N38° 19.12', W106° 28.11').

The CDT continues west and climbs through two switchbacks to mile 22.5 (11,788). In another 0.2 mile, the trail exits the trees and offers sweeping views to the southwest of the San Juan Mountains where the last leg of Colorado's CDT waits. The impressive peaks in the foreground are the La Garita Mountains. Now descend to a saddle and climb to the flat area that is the summit of Middle Baldy at mile 24.4 (11,680). In 0.2 mile, the trail descends to the west on a treeless slope, beginning a 2.0-mile departure from the Divide. This opening offers views of the Gunnison Basin and the West Elk Mountains to the northwest. Pass by the trail to Dutchman Creek at mile 25.1 and follow the CDT to the left (southwest). Enter a large park in 0.1 mile (11,280 feet; N38° 18.88', W106° 30.82').

Descend southwest and south through the meadow and enter sparse trees at mile 25.6. Ignore a left fork and stay on the clear tread. At mile 25.8, the trail crosses to the other side of Razor Creek, which, at this point near its source, is nothing more than a few shallow puddles by July. At mile 26.1 (10,900), enter some trees and bend left (east) toward the Summit Trail. Follow a sign straight ahead onto the Razor Creek Trail. A gradual descent continues as you enter an enchanting spruce forest and regain the nondescript Divide ridge a short distance later. The CDT continues south past an intersection at mile 27.8. In 0.1 mile, pause at an area on the left that was cut for a timber sale and compare the feeling you get there with that of the spruce forest you just left. From here the trail follows the Divide's undulations through three climbs separated by two saddles. The climbs (210, 277, and 460 vertical feet, respectively) lead to an old roadcut at mile 31.6 (11,000). Turn left onto the roadcut and follow Colorado Trail symbols in a 100-foot climb to the southwest. At mile 31.7 (11,100), the trail tops out on the ridge, descends due south along the Divide, and drops via a series of switchbacks to an intersection with Lujan Creek Road at mile 33.1 (10,336).

Turn right (west) onto the road and curve north through a fence in 0.1 mile. In another 0.1 mile, follow Forest Road 785 as it turns left (south) away from a spur road that continues straight ahead. At mile 33.7 (10,150), the road crosses over to the west side of Lujan Creek, which may be dry for the first mile or so. The La Garita Mountains loom in the near distance just west of south.

You will reach Colorado Highway 114 at mile 35.0 (9,720). Turn right (west) and continue along the highway to mile 35.3 where you'll find a large pullout on the other (south) side of the road. Walk to an old gate in the fence at the southwest corner of the pullout, which is also the end of this segment, at mile 35.4 (9,600 feet; N38° 13.40', W106° 35.47'). Carsonite posts mark the CDT's continuation on the other side of the gate.

OTHER HIKES AND RIDES

No other well-established hiking or biking trails are accessible from this segment.

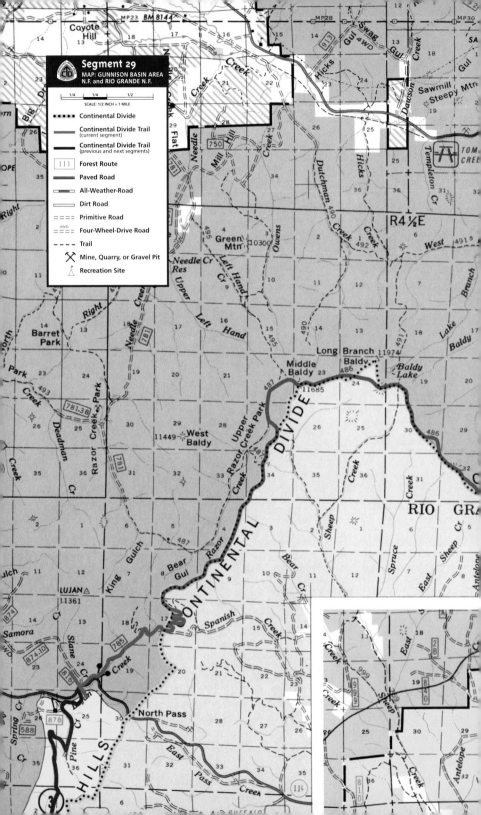

Segment 29

**MAP: GUNNISON BASIN AREA
N.F. and RIO GRANDE N.F.**

SCALE: 1/2 INCH = 1 MILE

- ••••••• Continental Divide
- ▬▬▬ Continental Divide Trail (current segment)
- ▬▬▬ Continental Divide Trail (previous and next segments)
- ||| Forest Route
- ▬▬▬ Paved Road
- ▭▬▭ All-Weather-Road
- ▭▭ Dirt Road
- ==== Primitive Road
- - - - Four-Wheel-Drive Road
- - - - Trail
- ✕ Mine, Quarry, or Gravel Pit
- △ Recreation Site

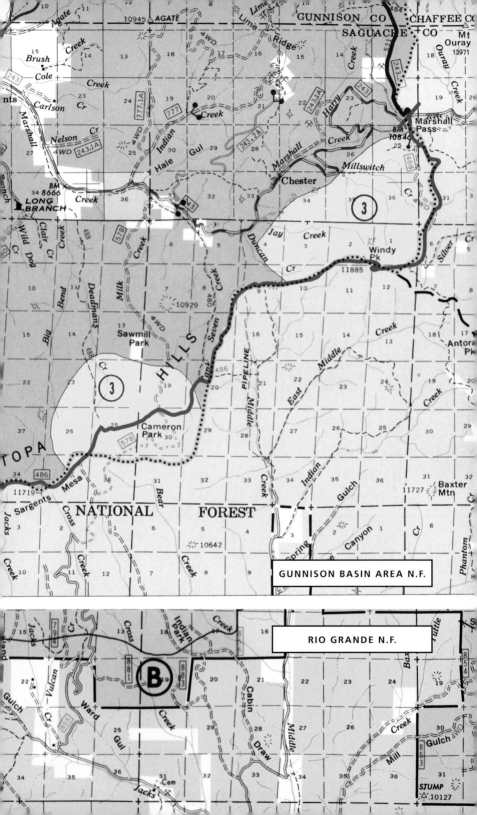

GUNNISON BASIN AREA N.F.

RIO GRANDE N.F.

Segment 30
Colorado Highway 114 to Saguache Park Road

In the Cochetopa Hills, Gunnison National Forest

13.3 miles
Difficulty: Easy

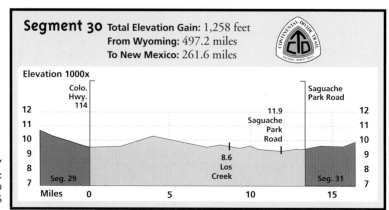

Segment 30 Total Elevation Gain: 1,258 feet
From Wyoming: 497.2 miles
To New Mexico: 261.6 miles

Elevation 1000x

Colo.
Hwy.
114

Saguache
Park Road

12

11.9
Saguache
Park
Road

12

11

11

10

10

9

8.6
Los
Creek

9

YOU MAY
ENCOUNTER:
MOTORIZED
VEHICLES

8

Seg. 29

Seg. 31

8

7

7

Miles   0   5   10   15

THE CDT'S COURSE THROUGH the Cochetopa Hills continues on this segment. This area has important historical significance because it is one of the first places regularly used by humans to cross the Continental Divide. We know that the Ute Indians used this low gap as early as 400 years ago, as the Anasazi probably did centuries earlier. It was the Utes who named the passage Cochetopa, their word for the buffalo they hunted here.

This is also one of the first stretches of the Continental Divide north of New Mexico ever to be viewed by a European. That person was Juan Bautista de Anza, governor of the Spanish colony of New Mexico, who set out to the north in 1779 to pursue a band of Comanche Indians who had been troubling Spanish colonists in New Mexico. He spotted this conspicuous low point on the Divide, and his Ute Indian guides explained that they had been using it as an easy, year-round route to the Gunnison Basin for as long as anyone could remember. De Anza dreamed of making the pass an important part of a vast Spanish empire stretching from the Rockies to the Pacific Ocean. But those plans never materialized, and Cochetopa Pass played only a minor role in the settlement of the West.

Water is scarce, and it isn't the fresh stuff that has spoiled the through-hiker to this point. The small flows of Lujan (mile 0.1), Pine (mile 1.8), and Los Creeks (mile 8.6) should be reliable.

 MOUNTAIN BIKE NOTES: This segment provides easy riding, almost entirely on dirt roads.

MAPS

TRAILS ILLUSTRATED: 139
USGS QUADRANGLES: North Pass, Cochetopa Park
USFS: Gunnison Basin Area, Rio Grande National Forest, page 233

ACCESS

 COLORADO HIGHWAY 114: From the summit of North Pass on Colorado Highway 114, drive northwest and west 1.4 miles to a large pullout on the left (southeast) side of the road. The trail starts at the gate in the southwest corner of the pullout.

 SAGUACHE PARK ROAD: See the next segment.

SUPPLIES, SERVICES, AND ACCOMMODATIONS

GUNNISON: You can reach Gunnison by traveling west and north on Colorado Highway 114 and west on US-50, but it is a long way and not recommended.

A road

is a dagger

placed in the heart

of a wilderness.

—William O. Douglas,

as quoted in

Ghost Grizzlies

RANGER DISTRICT:
Taylor-Cebolla

TRAIL DESCRIPTION Pass through a gate in the fence at the southwest end of the pullout on Colorado Highway 114. Follow a clear trail to the south past carsonite posts into the Lujan Creek drainage. The trail soon turns right (west) at mile 0.3 to parallel the edge of the trees. A tread soon develops a short distance south (left) of the line of posts and crosses Pine Creek at mile 0.6. Don't follow this across the stream! Just before the near edge of Pine Creek, turn left (south) and spot more posts leading upstream along the east side of the water. A faint tread soon develops along this route.

Lupine, wild geraniums, and other bursts of floral fecundity adorn the sides of the trail. Potentilla, rabbitbrush, and willow add color to this arid section of the trail. As an obscure roadbed materializes under the CDT, stay in the drainage along the left side of the streambed until the road crosses over to the right (west) side of the stream at mile 1.8 (9,675). In 0.1 mile, get into the exit lane, take an off-ramp away from the stream to the right, and follow it through a 100-yard U-turn that ends up pointing north. The CDT follows a clear logging road (Forest Route 878.1C) out of the drainage and curves back to the south (left) at mile 2.7 (9,940). The road ends in 1.0 mile as a clear single-track continues to the south via a stout, 0.3-mile climb. This ends at a gate at mile 3.9 (10,260). At mile 4.1, turn left (southeast) off the single-track onto another roadbed (Forest Route 876, unmarked). This descends gradually to the south to a gate at mile 6.4 and reaches Cochetopa Pass Road at mile 6.8. Turn right (west), descend through two switchbacks, and turn left (southeast) onto a jeep road at mile 7.3 (9,630).

The CDT bends to the right (south, then west) as it climbs gradually to a small stand of trees and a gate at mile 8.1 (9,810). This begins a slight descent into the Los Creek drainage on an idyllic country lane. Stay on the right fork of the main road at mile 8.2 and reach Los Creek at mile 8.6. Follow the road along the creek 0.8 mile to a small pond (9,555) where it forks again. Follow the left fork over Los Creek to the west and climb to mile 9.9 (9,705) on Forest Route 787.2A where you will have your first views of the great expanse of Cochetopa Park.

Descend into the park and pass through a gate at mile 11.6. In another 50 yards, stay on Forest Route 787.2A by turning right at a fork. You will reach the well-maintained Saguache Park Road at mile 11.9 (9,352). Turn left (south) and continue to a cattle guard in a wooded saddle at mile 12.8 (9,510). From here the road curves west (right), then south, and reaches the intersection with Forest Route 787.2D, a spur road on the right (southwest) at mile 13.3 (9,525 feet; N38° 7.88', W106° 41.79'). This marks the end of this segment.

OTHER HIKES AND RIDES
No other well-established hiking or biking trails are accessible from this segment.

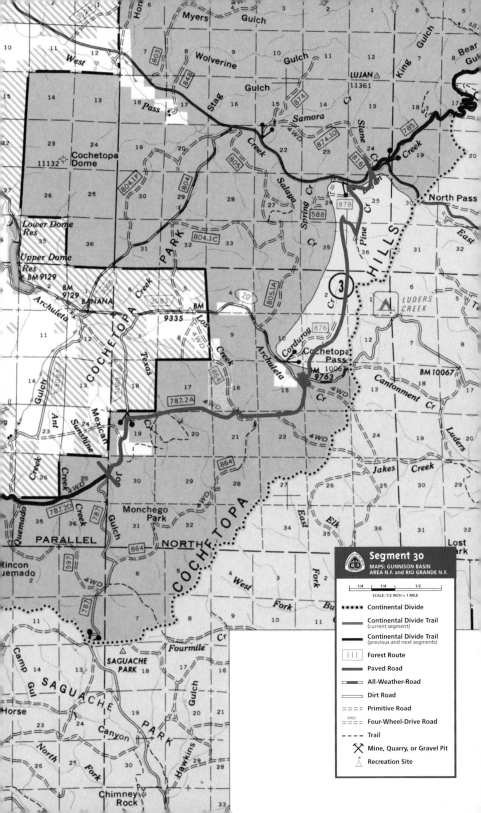

Segment 30

MAPS: GUNNISON BASIN
AREA N.F. and RIO GRANDE N.F.

| 1/4 | 1/4 | 1/2 |

SCALE: 1/2 INCH = 1 MILE

•••• Continental Divide

━━━ Continental Divide Trail
(current segment)

━━━ Continental Divide Trail
(previous and next segments)

|111| Forest Route

▬▬▬ Paved Road

▭▭▭ All-Weather-Road

▭▭▭ Dirt Road

==== Primitive Road

4WD Four-Wheel-Drive Road

- - - Trail

✕ Mine, Quarry, or Gravel Pit

⛺ Recreation Site

Segment 31
Saguache Park Road to San Luis Pass

Sunrise along the Divide, La Garita Wilderness

25.7 miles
Difficulty: Strenuous

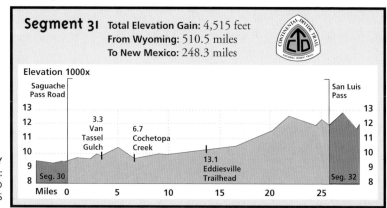

Segment 31 **Total Elevation Gain:** 4,515 feet
From Wyoming: 510.5 miles
To New Mexico: 248.3 miles

Elevation 1000x

Saguache Pass Road

San Luis Pass

13

12

3.3 Van Tassel Gulch

6.7 Cochetopa Creek

11

10

9   Seg. 30

13.1 Eddiesville Trailhead

Seg. 32

8

Miles 0   5   10   15   20   25

YOU MAY ENCOUNTER: MOTORIZED VEHICLES

AFTER SEVERAL DAYS of toiling through the dry, vehicle-accessible Cochetopa Hills, the through-hiker is amply rewarded here as the CDT climbs back above timberline to the cool air and pure, plentiful water of the mountains. The La Garita Mountains stand like a fortress, repelling all but the determined few who are willing to take up a pack and walk among the rocks and clouds. All the rest are left behind, bound to the pavement and dusty roads.

But first there is a little more of the low country to get through. Many of the streams that are shown to be perennial on the map are dry. The first reliable water is a pond near Cochetopa Creek at mile 6.6. From that point on, water is plentiful. Motorized vehicle enthusiasts seem to like the roads leading to the pond, but they are prohibited from driving beyond it.

A sign at the base of the climb into the wilderness warns against taking horses over the unnamed pass near San Luis Peak.

 MOUNTAIN BIKE NOTES: Most of the first 9.8 miles of this segment are on roads easily accessible to mountain bikes; however bikes are prohibited in the designated wilderness, which begins at the 10.4-mile point.

MAPS

TRAILS ILLUSTRATED: 139
USGS QUADRANGLES: Cochetopa Park, Saguache Park, Elk Park, Halfmoon Pass, San Luis Peak
USFS: Gunnison Basin Area, Rio Grande National Forest, pages 240–241

BEGINNING ACCESS POINT

Smooth road to trailhead **SAGUACHE PARK ROAD:** Drive 5.0 miles west of the summit of North Pass on Colorado Highway 114 and turn left onto County Road 17GG. After 5.3 miles, turn left (east) onto County Road NN14, continue 1.1 miles, and turn right (south) onto County Road 17FF. Proceed 2.2 miles to a cattle guard and a Gunnison National Forest sign. This point marks the CDT's arrival from the north, in the form of Forest Route 787.2A. The trail continues along County Road 787 straight ahead to the south. Follow it 1.4 miles to its intersection with Forest Route 787.2D, a spur road on the right. This segment of the CDT starts here and continues southwest on Forest Route 787.2D.

ALTERNATE ACCESS

Smooth road to trailhead **EDDIESVILLE TRAILHEAD** (trail mile 13.1): From the summit of North Pass on Colorado

Do not look

to the ground

for your next step;

greatness lies

with those

who look

to the horizon.

—Norwegian Proverb

RANGER DISTRICTS:
Taylor-Cebolla
Divide

Highway 114, drive west about 5.0 miles and turn left (south) on County Road 17GG. Continue another 5.0 miles to County Road NN14 and turn right (west). (Historic Cochetopa Pass is up this road to the left.) Drive 1.4 miles to County Road 15GG and turn left (south). Continue about 21 miles to the trailhead at the end of the road.

ENDING ACCESS POINT

 SAN LUIS PASS: See the next segment.

SUPPLIES, SERVICES, AND ACCOMMODATIONS

CREEDE has all the basics, but it is a 22-mile round-trip walk. You might consider hitchhiking into Lake City on Colorado Highway 149, which is at the end of the next segment. You can reach Creede by walking south from San Luis Pass at trail mile 25.7. Follow the trail until it turns into a road (Forest Route 503). Avoid side roads and continue southeast and south until the road becomes Main Street in Creede.

DISTANCE FROM TRAIL: 11 miles

ZIP CODE: 81130

Bank	First National Bank of Creede, 117 N. Main St.	(719) 658-0700
Bus	None	
Camping	No campgrounds within walking distance.	
Dining	Old Miner's Inn Pizza Parlor, on Main St.	658-2767
Gear	San Juan Sports, 102 Main St.	658-2359
	White gas at Tomkins Hardware, 511 Main St.	658-2240
Groceries	Kentucky Belle Market, 156 Creede Ave.	658-2526
Information	Creede Ave. & Second St.	658-2374
Laundry	Creede Laundromat, 101 E. Fifth	None
Lodging	Snowshoe Motel, 1 block south of gas station on Hwy. 149	658-2315
	Blessing Inn, S. Main St.	658-0215
Medical	None	
Post Office	10 S. Main St.	658-2615
Showers	Snowshoe Motel, 1 block south of gas station on Hwy. 149	658-2315

SPECIAL NOTES: Creede was one of the wildest mining towns in Colorado history, boasting at one time a population of 10,000. The two museums here offer an exciting glimpse into the not-so-distant past.

TRAIL DESCRIPTION   Start out to the southeast on Forest Route 787.2D. Just after 0.1 mile, leave this road to follow a fainter one to the left (southwest). The CDT soon passes a majestic Ponderosa pine and begins a good climb to mile 0.6. After passing through some trees, the trail breaks out again into sprawling Cochetopa Park and meanders along its southern edge. You will cross the Quemado Creek drainage, which is usually dry, at mile 2.1 (9,775). A side road branches off to the left (south) to follow this drainage upstream. Avoid this, stay to the right, and follow the faint road's curve

0.2 mile northwest to Forest Route 787.2D, which is more clear. Turn left (west), cross the Quemado Creek drainage, and begin a gradual climb. The trail tops out at mile 2.9 (9,960). Pass through a gate and descend into the dry Van Tassel Gulch. Cross to the west side of the gulch at mile 3.4 (9,830) and continue 0.1 mile to a road. Turn left (south) and climb steadily through a winsome aspen forest that explodes with color and light in September. Top out in a clearing at mile 5.1 (10,410).

Descend along the road in a slow curve to the right (west, then north) to mile 6.3 where it exits the trees and turns sharply to the left (southwest). Continue 0.3 mile to where several jeep roads converge near a pond. Follow the one farthest left (south) along the edge of the pond and then descend steeply as the road curves to the right (west). At the bottom of this brief descent, look for a very faint trail breaking off to the left (southwest) at mile 6.7 (9,720). If you miss this and end up at the road's end in a grassy cul-de-sac, walk southeast and pick up the single-track trail where the flat valley bottom meets the steeper hillsides.

This is a good place to get water out of Cochetopa Creek, which the CDT now parallels upstream on mostly good trails. Fishing for brook and brown trout is reportedly good here, and you'll find plenty of good campsites along the valley. Aspen forests are still prolific and put on quite a colorful show in the fall.

The single-track soon turns into a jeep road. Where it appears to fork at mile 8.5, take the clearer track that bears left (southeast) behind some spruce trees. In 0.2 mile, the CDT climbs steeply to a bench, beginning a series of climbs and descents above the valley floor. At mile 9.8 (9,945), one last steep descent takes you to a ford of Cochetopa Creek. Before you descend, look across the stream to the right to spot one of the posts that mark the crossing. Work through the willows, cross where you can, and pick up the trail on the other side.

WILDERNESS ALERT:

The La Garita Wilderness was designated in 1964 by federal law to be "an area where the earth and its community of life are untrammeled by man, where man himself is a visitor who does not remain." In spite of its single fourteener, San Luis Peak, the La Garita Wilderness has managed to avoid heavy pressure from humans and has thus maintained a pristine character in most of its 129,626 acres. Please help keep it that way by remembering these rules: 1. Camp out of sight, at least 200 feet from lakes and streams, on dry, durable surfaces. 2. Use a stove instead of building a fire; use existing fire rings if you must have a fire. 3. Keep water sources pure by washing at least 200 feet from them. 4. Bury human waste six inches deep and 200 feet from lakes and streams. Pack out toilet paper. 5. Hobble or picket livestock at least 200 feet from lakes and streams, and use only treated, weed-free feed and grain. 6. All dogs must be on a leash. 7. No mountain biking. 8. Pack out all trash. Don't attempt to burn it.

Continue south to mile 10.4 where the trail crosses Nutras Creek and enters the La Garita Wilderness. Then the CDT temporarily exits the wilderness at a gate at mile 13.1 (10,320 feet; N38° 01.55', W106° 50.11'). This leaves you at the Eddiesville Trailhead.

Continue to a road branching off to the left (south) and cross Stewart Creek near some good car camping sites. Continue to a fence at mile 13.4 that protects private property. Turn right (southwest), walk 0.1 mile, and turn left (southeast) to follow the Skyline Trail along a barbed wire fence. Please respect the private property here. The CDT soon crosses Cañon Hondo, which is dry, and then it crosses a small brook at mile 14.0. The brook is shown as intermittent on the USGS map, but I found a good flow here in August.

The trail leaves the fence at mile 14.4, passes through a gate, and reenters the La Garita Wilderness. A short distance later, the trail still resembles a jeep road as it turns right (south) to continue following the upstream path of Cochetopa Creek. At mile 14.7 (10,360), a sign indicates a left turn toward the Continental Divide. Do not mistake this for the CDT, which continues straight ahead to the south. Although the valley is relatively flat here, it does not have much to offer in the way of campsites, especially if you like privacy. That changes when the trail enters a stand of trees at mile 16.4, where there are a few nice spots to choose from.

The impressive chasm called Cañon Diablo gapes from the ridge across the valley as you pass through a gate and enter a meadow at mile 16.8 (10,640). The Divide runs erratically along the precarious ridges at the back of the canyon. Numerous small springs soon cross the trail, giving rise to a moist environment supporting lush communities of lodgepole pine, Engelmann spruce, subalpine fir, aspen, willow, and the vibrant green of countless plants and shrubs. As the CDT rises through this smorgasbord of contagiously healthy trees, the valley narrows, the timber thickens, and the placid murmur of Cochetopa Creek's lower reaches gives way to the roar of cascading water-falls at mile 17.3. There is an idyllic campsite at mile 17.5, but it violates the at-least-100-feet-off-the-trail rule. There is another nice spot, however, concealed 100 yards up the slope to the right (north) at the top of a swath through the trees, just behind a dead tree leaning at a 45-degree angle.

You'll discover many suitable campsites as the CDT climbs moderately through meadows and spruce stands. At mile 20.0, the trail reaches some willows and turns sharply to the left (southeast). You can see San Luis Peak from here as a somewhat unremarkable ridgeline at the head of the valley to the west. The saddle on its left side is the path of the CDT. At mile 20.6, the trail passes a sign for Stewart Creek and then crosses Cochetopa Creek. As the trail clears the trees and you pass through willows adorned with bright red paintbrush, look back to the northeast for awesome views of Organ Mountain. The trail wanders north and then south-southwest as it steepens for the final leg to the pass. The occasional cairn or post marks the way in those places where the trail fades.

The trail reaches the saddle south of San Luis Peak at mile 21.8 (12,620). It then turns left (south) and traverses across the slopes of a large cirque high above the Spring Creek drainage. Note the "hoodoo" formations—tall, contorted pillars of hardened lava containing large chunks of volcanic debris—near the saddle. There is a second saddle at mile 23.2 (12,380), and the trail again descends to the left (south) around a wide bowl. Avoid the Bonholder Trail, which descends to the right (north) at mile 23.5, and continue along the CDT when it makes a sudden right turn and descends moderately to the west. A picturesque stream at mile 23.9 begins its long journey to the Pacific Ocean a short distance above the trail.

The trail reaches a low point at mile 24.5 (11,920) before the demanding climb to the ridge above San Luis Pass. From here, your progress to the west offers a different perspective on San Luis Peak. Now in the northeast, buttressed by its precipitous south and west flanks, the barren throne dominates the valley, the surrounding peaks, and even the Continental Divide.

Brilliant yellow wildflowers are a prelude to the magnificent views as the trail reaches one last saddle, and the Continental Divide, at mile 25.1 (12,340). The CDT continues straight over the pass onto a faint tread to the northwest. Ignore the post up the ridge to the right (north) and follow the trail downhill toward San Luis Pass. Note the high point across the valley to the west, Point 13,111. The CDT will skirt its north (right) side after it climbs out of San Luis Pass.

You will reach the pass at mile 25.7 (11,940 feet; N37° 58.28', W106° 58.33') at a conglomeration of signs for various destinations. A marshy area just south of the pass has a small brook flowing through it. You'll also find a reliable stream a little farther away on the north side of the pass. This is the end of the segment.

OTHER HIKES AND RIDES

No other well-established hiking or biking trails are accessible from this segment.

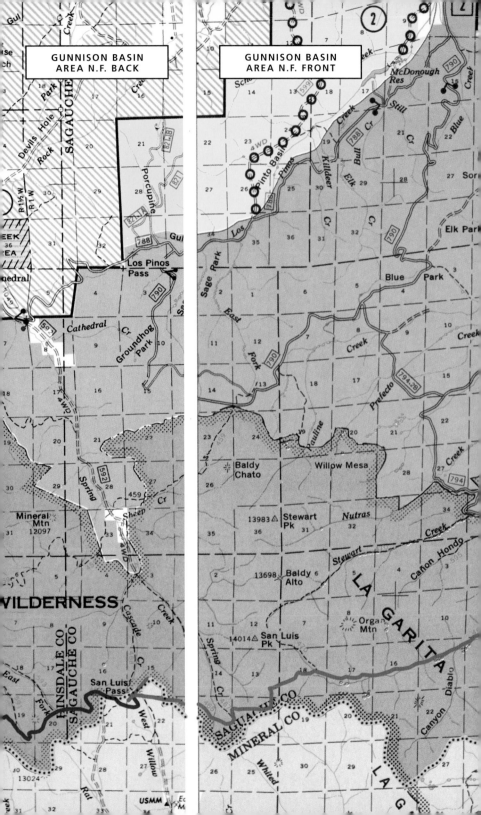

GUNNISON BASIN
AREA N.F. BACK

GUNNISON BASIN
AREA N.F. FRONT

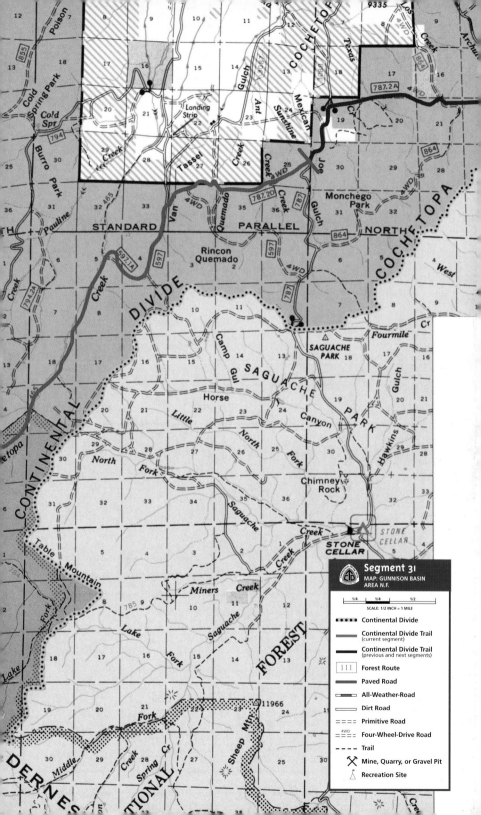

Segment 31
MAP: GUNNISON BASIN
AREA N.F.

| 1/4 | 1/4 | 1/2 |

SCALE: 1/2 INCH = 1 MILE

•••••• Continental Divide

━━━━ Continental Divide Trail
(current segment)

━━━━ Continental Divide Trail
(previous and next segments)

111 Forest Route

━━━━ Paved Road

━━━━ All-Weather-Road

━━━━ Dirt Road

==== Primitive Road

4WD
= = = Four-Wheel-Drive Road

- - - Trail

✕ Mine, Quarry, or Gravel Pit

⛺ Recreation Site

Segment 32
San Luis Pass to Spring Creek Pass

Sunrise on Snow Mesa, Rio Grande National Forest

14.5 miles
Difficulty: Strenuous

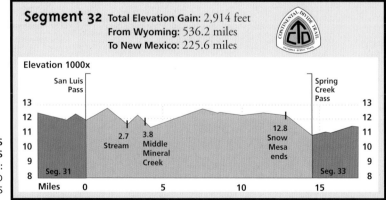

Segment 32 **Total Elevation Gain:** 2,914 feet
From Wyoming: 536.2 miles
To New Mexico: 225.6 miles

THIS
SEGMENT IS
CLOSED TO:
MOTORIZED
VEHICLES

THIS IS ONE OF THE MOST BEAUTIFUL SEGMENTS
on the Continental Divide Trail anywhere in the country.
Because of its wilderness designation and demanding access
routes, the area does not suffer too much human pressure. Its
jumble of impressive peaks, deep drainages, and inspirational
expanses of mesas—all sprinkled with pockets of old-growth
forest—remain in a state of pristine beauty that should inspire
us to keep such sacred areas protected.

The La Garita Mountains are one of several "satellite"
ranges of the massive dome that was pushed up by internal pressure to become the San Juan Mountains about 72 million years
ago. Around 48 million years later, the satellite ranges took shape
as molten rock was forced into the sediments along the margins
of the dome. Evidence of this volcanic activity is common here,
particularly in the formations that show solid chunks of volcanic
debris embedded in masses of hardened lava. These are called
breccias, and there is an excellent close-up example of them at
mile 21.9 on the previous segment.

Water is plentiful on this segment. Much of the trail
offer little protection from lightning, rain, or snow. Getting an
early start is a good strategy. You can take advantage of restrooms
and non-fee camping at Spring Creek Pass.

MOUNTAIN BIKE NOTES: Biking is prohibited
here because of the trail's passage through the La Garita
Wilderness.

> I do not own
>
> an inch of land,
>
> But all I see
>
> is mine.
>
> —Lucy Larcom

MAPS

TRAILS ILLUSTRATED: 139
USGS QUADRANGLES: San Luis Peak, Baldy Cinco,
   Slumgullion Pass
USFS: Gunnison Basin Area, Rio Grande National Forest,
   pages 248–249

ACCESS

Distance from graded road	🚙 8.5 miles	+	🚶 1.5 miles

FROM CREEDE: Follow Main Street out
of town to the north where it abruptly
becomes steep and rocky as Forest Route
503. Only a few non-four-wheel drive vehicles will make this
climb. About 0.5 mile out of town, avoid a right fork onto Forest
Route 502. Continue straight ahead 6.5 miles to a parking area
at Equity Mine. From here on, a four-wheel drive is required.
Drive or hike 1.5 miles north on Forest Route 503 to where the

RANGER DISTRICTS:
Taylor-Cebolla
Divide

road veers left (west) and begins a steep climb. Continue on foot up the valley to the north 1.5 miles to San Luis Pass.

 SPRING CREEK PASS: See the next segment.

SUPPLIES, SERVICES, AND ACCOMMODATIONS

CREEDE is 11.0 miles south of San Luis Pass on trails and roads. See *Access,* above, and follow the directions in reverse. Lake City is on Colorado Highway 149, 17 miles north of Spring Creek Pass, this segment's endpoint. For information on Creede see Segment 31, page 236; for Lake City see Segment 33, page 252.

TRAIL DESCRIPTION Follow the Skyline Trail west toward East Mineral Creek. Walk straight across the trailless rise of San Luis Pass 0.1 mile to a post and continue 25 yards west to a second post down a hill in some willows. Look west of south (compass bearing 220°) for a white and green Colorado Trail marker nailed to a tree that may be obscured by the morning shadow. Walk about 35 yards to the tree and turn left (south), follow a trail through a clear swath in the willows, and begin to climb through a captivating conflagration of color from paintbrush, bluebells, elephant-head, and delphinium. At mile 0.4, the trail swings to the right (west) and vanishes as posts and cairns pop up to guide your ascent. Pass a large cairn on a flat knoll at mile 0.6 (12,375 feet; N37° 58.00', W106° 58.58') and continue west toward Point 13,111.

The CDT reaches a tall slender post with a Colorado Trail marker at mile 1.0 and begins to bend right (northwest) to pass around the far side of Point 13,111. Climb to the flat ridge crossing at mile 1.4 (12,860 feet; N37° 58.28', W106° 59.32'), where the trail bends back to the left (west-southwest) and offers awesome panoramic views. To the north, look for the Elk Mountains near Crested Butte. Majestic and solitary, San Luis Peak rises to 14,014 feet to the east. The sharp peaks of the Big Blue Wilderness near Lake City, which include some fourteeners, jut skyward at compass bearing 290°. And at 230°, you'll see the Needle Mountains in the Weminuche Wilderness, which through-hikers will soon witness much more closely.

Now brace yourself for one of the most beautiful basins in the country. Follow posts and cairns straight down the hill to the west until the trail reaches the left (south) edge of a steep, barren gully at a post at mile 1.6. Turn left and descend to another cairn on a hillside covered in snowy white alpine sandwort. A tread soon develops as you descend steadily to the south. The trail curves around the upper edge of the floor of a gigantic cirque, bending right until it is tracking west. You'll pass a reliable spring just below the trail at mile 2.1 (12,110). This is followed by a flat campsite surrounded by thick spruce trees. Next is a vibrant garden of red paintbrush, chiming bells, aster, dandelions, and larkspur. A short distance beyond this, at mile 2.5, several trails seem to fork off; stay on the lower trail and pass into the enchantment of an old-growth forest. Pause to enjoy the primeval murmur of 400-year-old trees.

At mile 2.6, the CDT intersects the East Mineral Trail. Continue straight ahead to the southwest. Idyllic meadows are the setting for another tributary of the creek at mile 2.7 (11,720). From here the trail climbs west and south to a saddle at mile 3.3 (12,180) where it curves right (west) and descends via a straight line of posts and a faint tread to the Middle Mineral Creek drainage. Pass through trees and nice meadows in the shadow of some imposing cliff faces whose elegant lines will tantalize technical rock climbers. Campsites here are plentiful. Cross perennial Middle Mineral Creek at mile 3.8. This is the last water near the trail for 5.5 miles. The trail turns right to follow the creek's plunge to the northwest for 0.4 mile. Then it bears left (west) and climbs via a steep snow avalanche path to a saddle at mile 4.8 (11,860). This climb provides a good view of the aspen forest on the east slopes of the Middle Mineral valley, which puts on a vivid show of color in the autumn.

Instead of descending the other side of the saddle, the CDT continues to climb through the trees to the south. Recent deadfall has resulted in the creation of a decoy trail leading off to the right. Don't be fooled here; stay high after the deadfall and continue a gradual climb on a good trail marked by Forest Service blazes on the trees. At mile 5.3, the trail bends left (south) to work through a unique cliff band. A steeper climb leads to a post on the ridge at mile 5.6 and flattens considerably. At a post at mile 6.0, the trail jogs left (south) for 100 yards on a faint tread and then back to the right (west) at a second post. A sign indicates the intersection with the Mineral Creek Trail at mile 6.1. Don't descend here toward posts and cairns, but continue straight on the Skyline Trail on a faint tread toward the prominent saddle on the ridge to the southwest.

Aim for a post in the middle of the saddle at mile 6.3 (12,290 feet; N37° 56.92', W107° 02.71'). Turn a bit to your right (compass bearing 330°) and follow a series of posts up the hillside. At a flat area at mile 6.7, the trail bends left until it is facing almost due south on a much clearer tread that traverses in a steady climb up the east side of a grassy ridge. At mile 7.0, the trail bends back to the right (west-southwest) to complete its circumnavigation of Point 12,813. Now you'll enjoy expansive views of the Rio Grande valley to the south, and the most notable feature in the immediate foreground, Table Mountain, has a flat top that is offset by a 180-degree cirque of sheer cliffs.

Prepare your senses for overload as you continue climbing and turning gradually to the right. As you clear the ridge, take in the awesome view of Snow Mesa, whose stretch into infinity appears to be stopped only by the craggy peaks of the San Juan Mountains rising behind it. The deep, white erosion gullies in the valley at your feet are carved out of volcanic ash deposited many millions of years ago.

The trail peaks very subtly at mile 7.5 (12,780) and begins a moderate descent. Look at the opposing ridge across the bowl; the CDT is a thin ray etched diagonally across it. The descent takes you over a foot-jarring rockslide and past a side trail at a saddle at mile 8.2 (12,550). From here the CDT veers to the left (south) and climbs slightly at mile 8.4. Chess players may notice a knight (the horse) stationed like a stony sentinel high on the ridge to the right. After you pass the knight and round a rocky bend, walk a couple hundred yards and turn around to view another chess piece: the rook (or castle). Apparently, the giants who once lived here used the broad, flat plateau of Snow Mesa as a chess board. Continue like a pawn, slow but steadfast, down to the mesa at mile 9.3 (12,320 feet; N37° 56.53', W107° 04.38').

Now the trail follows the course of an old stock driveway that was once marked with two lines of parallel cairns up to a few hundred yards apart. You may find some of its remaining cairns confusing. For that reason, the following directions are particularly precise.

The tread disappears at this point. Follow posts and cairns around the far side of the pond. From a lone carsonite post on the south side of the pond, look to the west toward a hill on the mesa that obscures part of the mountainous horizon far in the distance. Walk around the right side of that hill and look west for a white Colorado Trail emblem on a carsonite post perched on some rocks.

Negotiate a wet area and reach this post at mile 10.0. Look over a small draw to the near horizon and walk 0.2 mile to the next post at compass bearing 290°. Continue a few paces ahead (west), and you will spot a faint tread slightly to the right (north of west). Pick this up and follow it until it fades. Climb a hill to a cairn at mile 10.7 and follow posts slightly north of west.

The mountains to the left (south and southwest) are the San Juans, which carry the Divide back to the east after its current trend to the west ends in a giant U-turn. Through-hikers will become quite familiar with those beautiful mountains in less than two weeks. For now, the Divide runs along the top of the ridge to the right (north).

At a post at mile 10.9 (12,290 feet; N37° 56.33', W107° 05.90'), just short of a small drainage and in the shadow of steeper terrain straight ahead, follow the CDT's bend to the left (west-southwest) along a faint tread marked by posts. You will top out at mile 11.4 (12,375) with panoramic views of the mountainous ends of the earth for almost 360 degrees. From here the trail resumes its westerly trend via posts, cairns, and no tread. At mile 12.7, on a low hill at the far western edge of the mesa, you'll spot a cairn with a short wooden post and Colorado Trail symbol. Look to the left (southwest; approximate compass bearing 240°) for a large rift in the mesa on the edge of which you'll see a post with an orange marker. This is where the trail leaves Snow Mesa and begins its steady descent to Spring Creek Pass (mile 12.8; 12,220 feet; N37° 56.09', W107° 07.82').

A rocky but clear trail descends rapidly and passes the first few trees at mile 13.1. The denuded ground in the trees, a result of this area's use as a stock migration route, renders the path somewhat ambiguous. Follow cairns and white Colorado Trail symbols as the trail alternately enters meadows and stands of trees. The ridge that the trail joins at mile 13.7 is the Continental Divide. At mile 14.3, a few final switchbacks take you down through the trees to one last hill that deposits you unceremoniously on the pavement of Colorado Highway 149. Cross the road to the pass parking area. To continue to the next segment, turn right (north) and walk through the parking lot to a paved loop. Go left at the loop, follow the pavement for about 100 yards more, and turn left (west) onto a dirt road at mile 14.5 (10,900 feet; N37° 56.45', W107° 9.57'). This marks the end of this segment.

OTHER HIKES

MINERAL CREEK TRAIL
Approximate loop distance: 19.0 miles
Difficulty: Moderate

Mineral Creek Trailhead: From Colorado Highway 149 between US-50 and Lake City, drive south beyond Powderhorn on County Road 27. Just after you pass through the Cebolla State Wildlife Area, avoid a left fork that climbs to Los Pinos Pass and continue a few miles to a brown Forest Service sign for the Mineral Creek Trailhead. Turn left (south) here, pass through two gates (be sure to close them—this is an easement through private property), and continue a short distance to the trailhead.

This single trailhead allows for a variety of hiking opportunities along one of the most stunning stretches of the Continental Divide. The most exciting may be a loop where you hike south along Mineral Creek for approximately 7 miles to the East Mineral Creek Trail on the left (east). This trail climbs and meets the Continental Divide Trail (at CDT mile 2.6), which you can follow 1.6 miles west to the Middle Mineral Creek drainage. Turn north on the trail here and follow it back to the main trail that leads downstream to the trailhead.

Since the Mineral Creek Trail branches to follow the three forks of the creek, many different loop or out-and-back variations are possible. Don't forget this is in the wilderness and special regulations apply.

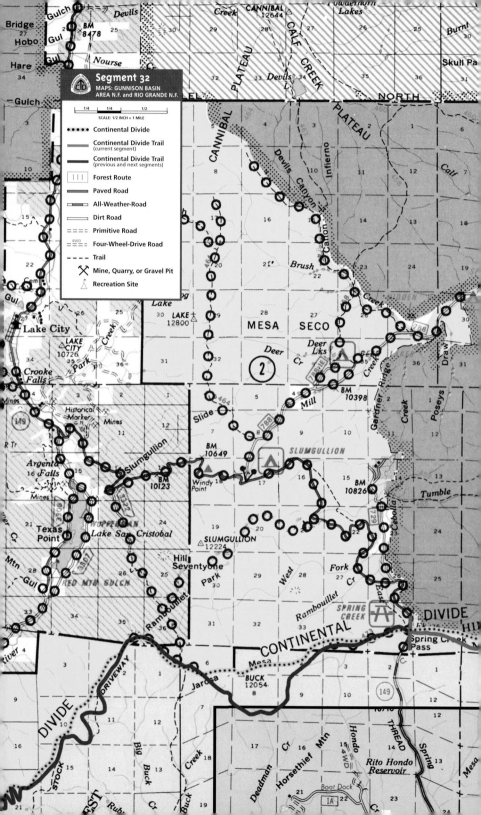

1/4   1/4   1/2

SCALE: 1/2 INCH = 1 MILE

•••• Continental Divide

━━ Continental Divide Trail
(current segment)

━━ Continental Divide Trail
(previous and next segments)

|┃┃┃| Forest Route

━━ Paved Road

▭ All-Weather-Road

▭ Dirt Road

==== Primitive Road

4WD
---- Four-Wheel-Drive Road

- - - Trail

⚒ Mine, Quarry, or Gravel Pit

⛺ Recreation Site

CANNIBAL

Bridge
27
Hobo

Devils

Creek

CANNIBAL
12644

Powderhorn
Lakes

27   26

25

Burnt

BM
8478

25

30

29

28

PLATEAU

CALF   CREEK

Skull Pa
30

Hare
34

Nourse

32

33

Devils

34

NORTH

31

Gulch

36

PLATEAU

CANNIBAL

Devils Canyon

Infierno

11   12   Calf
7

10

15

8

16

14   13   18

22

Cem

420

27

21

Brush

23   24   19

Creek
22

Gul

Lake

28   27   Creek

30   30

Lake City

LAKE
12800

MESA   SECO

788

LAKE
CITY
10726

Deer
Cr

Deer Lks

788

36   31

34
35

Park

31

32

2

BM
10398

Gardner Ridge

Poseys

Crooke
Falls

Slide

464

5

Mill

4

12

Mines

Historical
Marker

Mines

7

788

8   9   10   11

149

R Tr

Slumgullion

12

BM
10649

SLUMGULLION

788

BM
10123

Windy 18
Point

17   16   15   13
BM
10826

Tumble

Argenta
Falls

322

Mines

327

Lake San Cristobal

19   20   21   22   24

329

Cebolla

Texas
Point

330?

RED MTN GULCH

SLUMGULLION
12224

West   Fork

23

3301

Hill
Seventyone

Park
30

29   28   Cr
27   26   25

Mtn

Gul

Rambouillet

31   32

Rambouillet

33

SPRING
CREEK

⛺

DIVIDE

HI

33   34   35

DRIVEWAY

CONTINENTAL

Mesa

BUCK
12054

Spring Creek
Pass

149

DIVIDE

3

Jaroca

8

9   10   2
1

C

9

10

stock

16

Big   Buck

Creek

17   18

Cr

Deadman

Horsethief Mtn

16 4WD
Hondo

Rito Hondo
Reservoir

THREAD

Spring

Mesa

13

12

21
22   23   24

Boat Dock

1A

ᎬFOREST

Rub

Cr

19

20

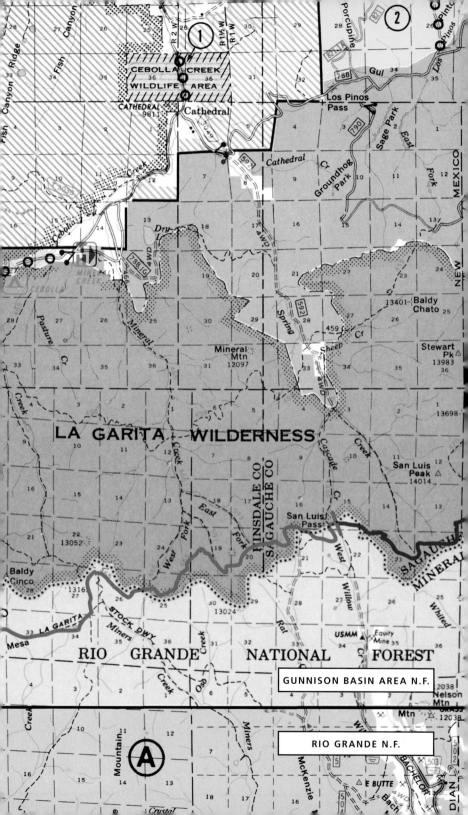

Segment 33
Spring Creek Pass to Carson Saddle

Sunrise along the Divide, Rio Grande National Forest

19.2 miles
Difficulty: Strenuous

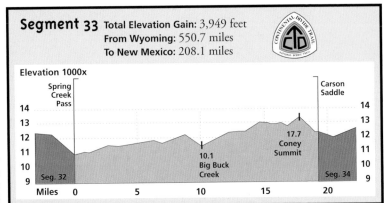

Segment 33 Total Elevation Gain: 3,949 feet
From Wyoming: 550.7 miles
To New Mexico: 208.1 miles

Elevation 1000x

Spring Creek Pass

Carson Saddle

17.7 Coney Summit

10.1 Big Buck Creek

Seg. 32

Seg. 34

Miles 0   5   10   15   20

YOU MAY ENCOUNTER: MOTORIZED VEHICLES

THIS SEGMENT carries the Continental Divide Trail to its highest sustained altitudes so far and its highest point anywhere in the country atop 13,334-foot Coney Summit. The trail is almost entirely above timberline here, so pay attention to the weather and be ready to dash to lower elevations in the event of lightning.

The views along this stretch of the CDT are outstanding. You will see Sunlight and Handies Peaks, both fourteeners, very near the trail to the west; the sharp, tortured summit of Uncompahgre Peak farther away to the northwest; parts of the impressive Needle Mountains in the Weminuche Wilderness to the west; and the heart of the San Juan Mountains, which convey the Divide on its lofty course through the Weminuche, to the south.

Most of this segment is open to motorized vehicles, although its remoteness seems to deter many of them. The trail stays on the crest of the Divide for this entire segment, and water is scarce. Big Buck Creek at mile 10.1 should be reliable. There are some permanent ponds a short distance off the trail at mile 13.7, and you'll find more ponds a little farther away at mile 16.8. The next water is at a tributary of Lost Trail Creek, 1.3 miles into the next segment.

MOUNTAIN BIKE NOTES: This segment makes for challenging riding, not because of its technical difficulty but because the rough ground and lack of trails after about mile 10.0 impede any effort at sustained riding. Still, this segment should not be missed by anyone, with its far-ranging views and invigorating ascent to well above 13,000 feet. If you don't mind pushing your bike over a few long stretches, you will be amply rewarded for your efforts here.

I have been one

acquainted with

the night.

I have walked

out in rain—

and back in rain.

I have outwalked

the furthest city light.

—Robert Frost,

"Acquainted with

the Night"

MAPS

TRAILS ILLUSTRATED: 139, 141

USGS QUADRANGLES: Slumgullion Pass, Lake San Cristobal, Finger Mesa

USFS: Gunnison Basin Area, Rio Grande National Forest, page 255

ACCESS

SPRING CREEK PASS: Drive to the summit of Spring Creek Pass on Colorado Highway 149 by traveling south from Lake City or north from Creede. The trailhead, which is not marked, is at the northwest corner of the parking lot on the west side of the highway.

RANGER DISTRICTS:
Divide
Taylor-Cebolla

Distance from graded road **5.0 miles**

CARSON SADDLE: See the next segment.

SUPPLIES, SERVICES, AND ACCOMMODATIONS

LAKE CITY is 18.0 miles north on Colorado Highway 149; Creede is 34.0 miles south, see Segment 31, page 236. They have a similar selection of services.

Bank	First National Bank of Lake City and Creede,	(970) 944-2242
	Third and Silver Streets	
Bus	None	
Camping	Castle Lakes Campground Resort,	944-2622
	11 miles SW of town on Cinnamon Pass Road. $11-$15	
Dining	G & M Smokehouse, downtown across from the caboose	944-2282
	The Happy Camper Sports Grille,	944-2494
	Gunnison Ave. and Third Street	
Gear	The Sportsman, 257 N. Hwy, 149.	944-2526
Groceries	Country Store Grocery, 916 N. Hwy 149	944-2387
Information	Tourist Information Center, 306 N. Silver	944-2527
Laundry	The Wash of Lake City, 325 Silver Street	944-2655
Lodging	Silver Thread Village Cabins, 3rd and Hwy. 149. $35-$85	944-2236
	Lake City Resort, 307 S. Gunnison Ave. $35-$75	944-2866
Medical	Lake City Area Medical Center, 700 N. Henson	944-2331
Post Office	803 Gunnison Ave.	944-2560
Showers	The Wash of Lake City, 325 Silver Street	944-2655

SPECIAL NOTES: Lake City is one of Colorado's largest Historical Districts, with over 75 buildings from the late 1800's. Visit the museum or schedule a tour of the various Victorian buildings.

TRAIL DESCRIPTION The trail starts at the northwest end of the parking area on a dirt road that ascends gradually through a spruce forest to the west. As this book was being written late in 1996, there was talk of moving the trail off the road onto a single-track trail to the north (right). Contact the Taylor/Cebolla Ranger District for more information. As you enter a large meadow, Jarosa Mesa comes into view across an intervening drainage in front of you. At mile 1.0 (11,120), near the southwest edge of the meadow, you can see the distinctive Rio Grande Pyramid to the south-southwest hunkered solidly in the heart of the Weminuche Wilderness. About 100 trail miles distant, the CDT follows the Divide to the pyramid and then breaks off as the Divide climbs steep ridges to cross the mountain's commanding 13,821-foot summit.

After a slight descent, follow an even contour around a basin to a gradual climb up Jarosa Mesa. The CDT turns a little to the left to enter a small stand of trees at mile 2.2. The trail exits the trees with a 90-degree turn to the right (southwest). It winds uphill through sparse trees, passes a meadow at mile 2.6, and soon flattens on a plateau notable for the uniform vegetation that covers it. You are soon solidly above timberline, and the views are tremendous.

The CDT curves south and then west to trace the southern edge of Jarosa Mesa. A gentle climb leads to the wide, flat, featureless expanse near the top of the mesa at mile 5.0 (11,840), where the trail bends north-northwest on what is still a clear road. At mile 6.2, you will pass by a series of posts and turn right (just west of north), following Forest Route 547. At mile 6.6, there is a small tarn followed by some cairns on the right (southwest). Ignore the cairns and follow the road to the bottom of a shallow valley at mile 7.0 (11,700), where you'll discover several forks in the road. Take the one on the left (west) as indicated by a Colorado Trail marker, and follow the trail's bend to the left (south) in 100 yards.

 Note that the depiction of the route on the USGS Lake San Cristobal quadrangle is mostly inaccurate. Refer instead to Trails Illustrated map #139 or Colorado Trail series map #22.

Climb along the south slopes of Point 12,305 to a saddle at mile 8.5 (12,050). Swing to the left (south) to climb to a cairn on the next point along the Divide, where there are great views of 14,001-foot Sunshine Peak immediately to the west (mile 8.7; 12,260). As you descend, you can see a deep gorge reminiscent of the Swiss Alps across the valley to the west. This gash separates Sunshine from Handies Peak, another fourteener.

The trail descends steadily into the trees and bottoms out as it curves to the right (west) near Big Buck Creek at mile 10.1 (11,480). Climb along the creek and turn left (south) onto a single-track trail at a Colorado Trail marker just before the road reaches a saddle (mile 10.6; 11,720). The trail is faint, but a dilapidated post across the meadow confirms your route. From this second post, turn slightly to the left and spot a Forest Service blaze on a tree about 50 yards away (almost due south). Pass the tree and continue on a badly rutted trail into a peaceful forest.

The trail exits the trees at mile 11.3, and a carsonite post marks the way through a field of short willows. Follow frequent posts as the trail winds its way up to the barren ridge to the west and levels out at mile 12.3 (12,340). In 0.6 mile, there are several confusing forks. Take a right fork climbing to the southwest toward a post on the horizon. As the tread fades, follow posts and the obvious Divide ridge. Snow in this area may cover the trail into July. The ponds in the valley to the left (south) are a good source of water. At mile 13.7, you'll enjoy nice views to the north of Lake San Cristobal, Colorado's second largest natural lake.

A clear trail follows cairns up a steep, rocky ridge that tops out at mile 14.6 (13,040). The trail makes a gradual turn to the right (south-southwest) as it passes two carsonite posts and reaches a small rocky ridge at mile 14.9. Work your way through the rocks, bearing a little right (west). Continue across the wide, grassy plain—without the benefit of trail, post, or cairn—toward the high points on the next horizon.

As a steep, grassy hillside comes into view in front of you at about mile 15.2, aim for a trail cutting diagonally across it. If you do not suffer from vertigo, walk over to the edge of the cliffs on your right for an incredible panoramic view. Cairns on your left (east) are part of the La Garita Stock Driveway, which the CDT joins just before a saddle at mile 15.7 (12,840). Stop here to look at Lake San Cristobal to the north. The yellow earth just beyond it is the Slumgullion Earthflow, which slid into the valley several hundred years ago to dam the river and form the lake. Look for the swirls and patterns suggesting the movement of a liquid.

N AS NORTHBOUND HIKERS climb out of this saddle and the trail traverses to the right (east), they should bear more to the left, closer to the cliffs, and go straight over the ridge.

Follow the CDT's traverse up a hillside to the south and reach the top at mile 16.2, where the trail bends to the southwest and rolls along the Divide ridge toward a high point that is Coney Summit. Soon, as you follow a clear tread, you may notice a line of Colorado Trail markers up the slope about 100 yards to the right (west). There is no tread where the markers are, so you may choose to save some elevation gain and avoid contributing to the creation of a new trail by staying on the existing path.

As you descend toward the last saddle before Coney Summit, you can see the road to Carson Saddle far below to the southwest. The trail curves to the right (southwest) and crosses through a section of loose rock before a switchback turns back to the left (south) to point you in the right direction. Pass through the saddle at mile 16.8 (12,850) and continue straight ahead (south) via carsonite posts. If you prefer to tackle the climb to Coney Summit first thing in the morning, you may want to camp at some ponds in the basin 400 vertical feet below the trail on the left (southeast).

Where the terrain steepens considerably at mile 17.3, stay to the right as the stock driveway veers off to the left (east). Snow may cling to these steep slopes well into summer, making for a hazardous ascent. Choose a route you are comfortable with, use a stick or a pole if you carry one, and plant each step deliberately. Don't climb above the very steep drop-off on the west side (right).

Follow carsonite posts and a series of switchbacks to a flatter area at mile 17.6 where the trail disappears. Continue 0.1 mile to the summit, the highest point anywhere on the Continental Divide Trail at 13,334 feet. Most of Creation unfolds before you as you gaze to distant horizons in all four directions.

Walk south along Coney's ridge toward a cairn 0.1 mile distant. Pick up a jeep road, which is still in use by four-wheel drive tour companies in Lake City, and descend to the saddle just south of Coney at mile 18.2 (13,100). Several roads come together here. Turn right and follow the road that descends rapidly into the valley to the west. At mile 19.0 (12,310), join a second road at a T intersection and turn right (west). You will reach Carson Saddle, which is not so named on the maps, at another intersection of several roads at mile 19.2 (12,340).

OTHER HIKES

CAMP TRAIL
Approximate one-way distance: 5.4 miles
Difficulty: Moderate

Camp Trailhead: From Lake City, drive south 2.2 miles on Colorado Highway 149 and turn right (southwest) toward Lake San Cristobal. Continue 7.1 miles to the trailhead on the left (east) side of the road.

The trail ascends from Williams Creek Campground on Trail #474 through spruce forest before passing timberline and reaching the Divide in 5.4 miles. A yurt at this point is part of the Hinsdale Hut Route, which cross-country skiers use in the winter. The yurt is not open to hikers. Mile 10.6 of the Continental Divide Trail is 0.2 mile to the east at the head of a meadowed valley.

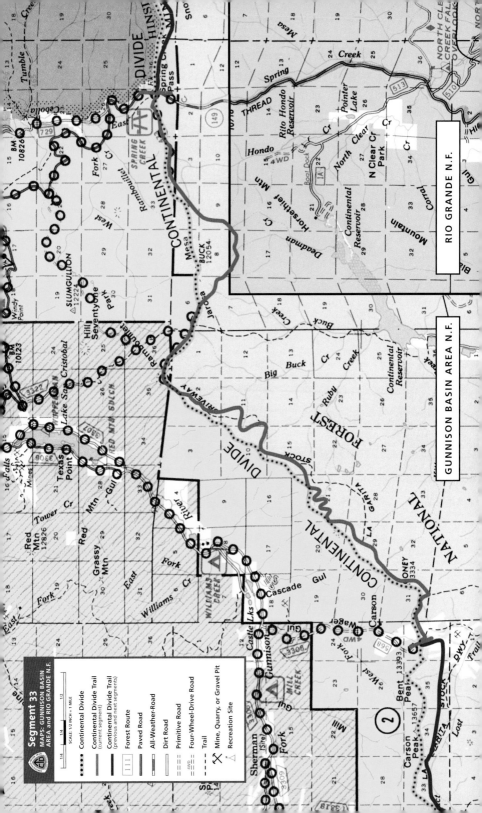

Segment 34
Carson Saddle to Stony Pass

Natural bridge along Pole Creek, Rio Grande National Forest

18.0 miles
Difficulty: Strenuous

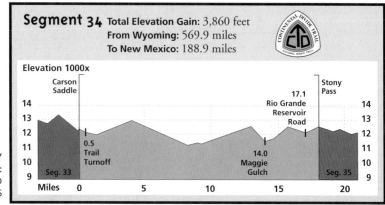

Segment 34 **Total Elevation Gain:** 3,860 feet
From Wyoming: 569.9 miles
To New Mexico: 188.9 miles

YOU MAY ENCOUNTER:
MOTORIZED VEHICLES

THIS SEGMENT LEADS deeper into the remote, rugged terrain of the San Juan Mountains and delivers you to the least-used gateway of the incredible Weminuche Wilderness. There are a few places where the route may be confusing; be sure to pay extra attention when you see the compass symbol.

The town of Carson, near where this segment begins, was notorious as an isolated, snowbound outpost situated high on the Divide at 12,000 feet. The area boasted some productive gold and silver mines, but its severe winters and dangerous, often impassable access roads made it difficult to get supplies in and ore out. Mining work was hampered by heavy snow that lingered for much of the year. Still, up to 500 men worked the area around the turn of the century, and some of the claims were quite lucrative for their owners. In the end, Mother Nature won out, and the town succumbed to the relentless winter.

Water and campsites are plentiful from start to finish along this segment.

 MOUNTAIN BIKE NOTES: Most of this segment crosses impassable terrain or fragile tundra that can't resist the damage caused by fat tires. You may opt to ride the Colorado Trail to Rio Grande Reservoir Road, which leads northwest to Silverton via Stony Pass.

MAPS

TRAILS ILLUSTRATED: 141
USGS QUADRANGLES: Finger Mesa, Pole Creek Mountain, Howardsville
USFS: Gunnison National Forest, Rio Grande National Forest, San Juan National Forest, pages 262–263

ACCESS

Distance from graded road — 5.0 miles. **CARSON SADDLE:** From Lake City, drive south on Colorado Highway 149 2.2 miles and turn right (southwest) toward Lake San Cristobal. Follow this road for 9.0 miles and turn left onto County Road 36 (Wager Gulch Road). Continue approximately 5.0 miles along this very rough road to Carson Saddle, which is also 1.2 miles past the Carson townsite. After the final climb to the saddle, the terrain flattens abruptly. The CDT continues straight along the road to the south.

Distance from graded road — 20.0 miles + 13.0 miles. **STONY PASS FROM CREEDE:** See the next segment.

I chatter, chatter,

as I flow,

To join the

brimming river,

For men may come

and men may go,

But I go on forever.

—Alfred, Lord

Tennyson,

"The Brook"

RANGER DISTRICTS:
Divide
Columbine

SUPPLIES, SERVICES, AND ACCOMMODATIONS

LAKE CITY AND CREEDE: See Creede in Segment 31, page 236; Lake City in Segment 33, page 252.

TRAIL DESCRIPTION
From the preceding segment, turn left (south) onto an intersecting dirt road and pass the ruins of the Carson mining operations on your left. Avoid the steep jeep road climbing along the Divide to the west. Just past the last ruin, which is also the closest one to the road, the road disappears over a hill. A few yards before that point, a single-track trail marked by a carsonite post takes off to the right (mile 0.5; 12,170). Climb along this trail above and parallel to Lost Trail Creek. There is a reliable stream at mile 1.3 (12,000). The CDT climbs more steeply as it follows cairns and erosion pathways into a jumble of rocks at mile 2.0 (12,300). From a large cairn at mile 2.1, you can see a sizable ridge plunging into the valley perpendicular to the path of the trail. Watch for the snow that its formidable shadow may nurture well into the summer. The CDT angles up the ridge and flattens at mile 2.3, where the rest of the Lost Trail Creek valley opens before you to the west.

Cross a small stream at mile 2.6 and follow the trail west toward the head of the valley. After the CDT flattens briefly and fades at mile 3.6, work around snowfields as you resume climbing. Look for the trail slightly to the right (a little north of west) up the hill. At mile 3.7, the trail makes a straight shot to the southwest and reaches the saddle at mile 4.0 (12,910). A pond on the Divide here is an unexpected surprise. Mother Nature defies prediction: The last place you would expect to find a body of water is squarely on the Continental Divide. Yet, over much of its course through the San Juan Mountains, the Divide is dotted with small ponds so high and reflective that it is difficult to tell where the water stops and the sky begins.

Now the CDT makes a gradual descent southwest along the Pole Creek drainage as a new and different postcard-perfect landscape surrounds you. The Needles of the San Juan Mountains loom ever closer to the south-southwest. About 0.1 mile after the trail passes a small pond, don't miss a somewhat obscure fork at an old post at mile 5.5 (12,510).

Take the left fork and descend into the Pole Creek valley to the southwest. This area may be covered by snow as late as July. If you start curving to the right and end up descending north toward Cataract Lake under a prominent cliff face, you have missed the turnoff. The area just before the fork offers a few camping spots.

The trail follows cairns and posts through a marshy area at mile 5.7 and then descends steadily along the west side of Pole Creek on a generally good tread. Where it fades in marshy areas, just continue to parallel the creek. The valley narrows into a small gorge at mile 7.3, and the trail crosses to the east side of the creek at mile 7.5 (11,470). This is a formidable crossing during high run-off; large rocks 10 yards downstream may be helpful. Cross back to the west side of Pole Creek 0.2 mile later. With some creativity, you can keep your feet dry. At this point, a few large, vaguely familiar green things start popping up along the edges of the valley. My plant book identifies them as "trees."

The CDT describes a short, slight climb along a steep hillside before descending rapidly into a huge meadowed area where another valley and an obscure trail come in from the northwest (mile 8.0). Continue past this trail junction and descend a small bank of grey earth that is devoid of vegetation. A trail fork at the bottom of this marks the final split with the Colorado Trail, which goes to the left and crosses Pole Creek. For the Continental Divide Trail, take the right (south) fork, continue 120 yards, and cross the Pole Creek North Fork at mile 8.2 (11,230 feet; N37° 48.48', W107° 28.09'). After it climbs steeply out of the streambed, the trail trends southeast through a meadow. At mile 8.4, you will pass through a large, dusty area of completely denuded ground. About 0.1 mile beyond this, turn onto an intersecting trail at a sharp angle to the right (northwest). If you miss this turn, you will descend back to Pole Creek, cross it, and rejoin the Colorado Trail a short distance ahead.

 It is important to follow directions carefully over most of the rest of this segment.

Climb to where this new trail fades in about 200 yards near an exceptionally soft-looking meadow on the left (west). Cross the meadow's upper end and pick up a clear trail about 20 yards left (south) of a lone spruce tree in some willows. The trail immediately climbs steeply up a hill and fades. Continue to climb straight up (west) and a little to the left. When the slope steepens even more after a short distance, turn left (south) and walk to a flat area on a hump at mile 8.8 (11,400). Look up on the hill to the south-southwest (compass bearing 210°) for a couple of lone pine trees and aim for a low point just to their right. The prominent peak behind the trees is 13,220-foot Greenhalgh Mountain. Top out at a beautiful meadow backed by the rolling green slopes of Point 12,654. Work around a small pond at the meadow's far (south) end to a tall post on the other side at mile 9.0 (11,490). Follow a trail contouring around the hillside to the southwest. The pleasant valley of the Pole Creek West Fork greets you with approximately 2,000 different shades of green.

The CDT meanders upstream on the north side of the valley. At mile 10.5, it reaches the level of the stream and disappears in a marshy area. Ford where you can toward a post on the other side (southwest). Continue to another post near the trees to the southwest and pick up a trail. The distinct, mountain-shaped high point directly in front of you to the west is Point 12,972. The second saddle to its right (north) is where the CDT passes over the Divide.

As the trees fall away behind you and to your left, you will reach a tiny streambed where the trail once again disappears. Continue slightly south of west (approximate compass bearing 255°) directly toward Point 12,972, and climb slightly as you pass between several large rocks. When you reach a large growth of willows, walk around them to the right, pick up a clear trail at mile 11.0, and follow its descent to cross a stream. If you look up to the right, below the saddle over which the trail crosses the Divide, you can see a trace of the trail on a hillside near the top of a long stand of spruce trees.

After you cross the stream, ignore a faint trail shooting off to the right and follow the clearer high route along a sometimes muddy path into a sea of willows. Cross another stream at mile 11.5 (11,760) and begin a moderate ascent up the slope to the west. Cross Pole Creek above an impressive gorge at mile 11.8. Climb a short, steep hill 0.1 mile to a flat spot where the trail is obscure until it reappears a short distance to the northwest. The valleys and meadows beyond this point should be in the campsite hall of fame.

Sheep Mountain, the highest peak to the south, is distinguished by a huge deposit of talus (or moraine) left by the glacier that carved its impressive north cirque.

 NORTHBOUND HIKERS should avoid the many trails climbing south (right) toward Sheep Mountain. Your destination is instead the broad valley below to the east-southeast.

Cross a fairy-tale stream at mile 12.2 and climb steeply to the Divide at mile 12.9 (12,650), where there is another of those ponds that hover on the Divide, defying division into either ocean.

Follow a clear trail down the other side into a green alpine landscape that could easily be the setting for "Heidi." Ignore side trails as the trail fades near a ruined cabin at mile 13.2 (12,300). Descend to cross the stream under the ruins and pick up the trail on the opposing bank. Follow a gradually descending traverse across a steep hillside away from the stream to the northwest. At mile 13.7, the trail reaches a small gorge and descends southwest via several steep switchbacks to the road in the bottom of Maggie Gulch (mile 14.0; 11,670).

NORTHBOUND HIKERS will make a sharp right turn here at a small cairn on the side of the road.

Turn left (south) and continue 0.1 mile to a fork in the road. Go left and climb a hill to the southeast. The road ends at a small parking area at mile 14.6 (11,840) near some mining ruins.

Note that there is not one continuous trail to the top of this valley, but several possible routes. The driest one, which follows intermittent trails as much as possible, is described here. Look south-southwest to the high point at the back of the valley. That is Canby Mountain, and the trail will cross the saddle on the mountain's east (left) side.

Follow a single-track trail out of the parking area straight up the hill to the east. Follow a curve to the right (southeast) around some willows to an erosion gully. Walk a short distance up the erosion gully to the left (east). Cut to the right (south) and head for two large rockslides about 0.25 mile distant on the left (east) side of the valley. There is now no clear path, but game trails and erosion gullies lead in the right direction. You will steadily gain elevation as you walk through a marshy area. When the slope flattens somewhat at the base of the steep slopes on the east side of the valley, bear more to the right (due south) and pick up a faint trail at the base of the second (southernmost) rockslide, which is also the largest of the two (mile 14.9; 12,100).

When this trail splits into several game paths, stay high to the left (east). Note that the trail will pass to the left (east) of the prominent cliff face in the middle of the valley. As the trail fades, climb the steepening slope to the southeast and pick up a very clear trail that goes above an abandoned mine shaft and then below another. As the trail fades again after a few hundred yards, bear southwest toward the summit of the high point in that direction, Canby Mountain, and reach a flat grassy bench above the cliffs at mile 15.2. Traverse the grassy bench to its far (west) side and pick up a faint trail that curves left (south) where the saddle that is your destination comes into view to the south. Continue in that direction and try to stay on some semblance of a trail to avoid damaging the fragile tundra. You will reach the saddle at mile 15.7 (12,650). Be careful not to mistakenly head for a higher saddle on the left (east). Welcome back to the Atlantic side of the Divide.

 NORTHBOUND HIKERS should aim for the dirt road in the bottom of the valley, but stay on the right (east) side while descending.

As you start down the other side, don't blink at mile 16.0 and miss your crossing of the mighty Rio Grande River. The small stream here constitutes that waterway's highest headwaters. Follow a clear trail that descends steadily to the south before it levels out at mile 16.1 and contours along the steep side of the valley. Stay on the highest of several parallel trails. At mile 16.6, the trail curves right (west) around a hillside and descends into a small rocky streambed. Of several trails leading out of here, pick up the most prominent one on the left and follow it over a grassy knob on the east (left) edge of a small meadow. About 30 yards before the trail makes its final descent into a large meadow, turn right (southwest) and follow a grassy bench around the corner and across the bottom of a large pile of rocks. Continue southwest, drop into the meadow, and work slightly west of south through an opening in some sparse willows as you maintain a roughly even elevation.

Continue past the willows and look for a cairn with a post high on the hill to the right and an orange sign farther down to the left. Strike a course for a point about one-third the distance from the sign to the cairn. As you crest a final small hill, follow a faint trail through a wide opening in some willows and continue 100 yards to Rio Grande Reservoir Road at mile 17.1 (12,160). A sign on the road gives the distances to West Ute Creek Trail and Ute Creek Trail.

 NORTHBOUND HIKERS: This sign is the cue to turn left (northeast).

The views south into the Weminuche Wilderness, a taste of things to come, are sublime. The Grenadier Mountains stand like sentries at some hidden gate concealed beyond the rolling green ridges of the Divide.

Turn right (northwest) and climb to an obscure single-track trail on the left (south) at mile 18.0 (12,540 feet; N37° 47.68', W107° 32.82') that descends to the ruins of a cabin. This is the end of the segment. There is a pullout on the left side of the road 50 yards ahead, or 0.1 mile east of the summit of Stony Pass.

OTHER HIKES AND RIDES

There are no other well-established hiking or biking trails available in this segment.

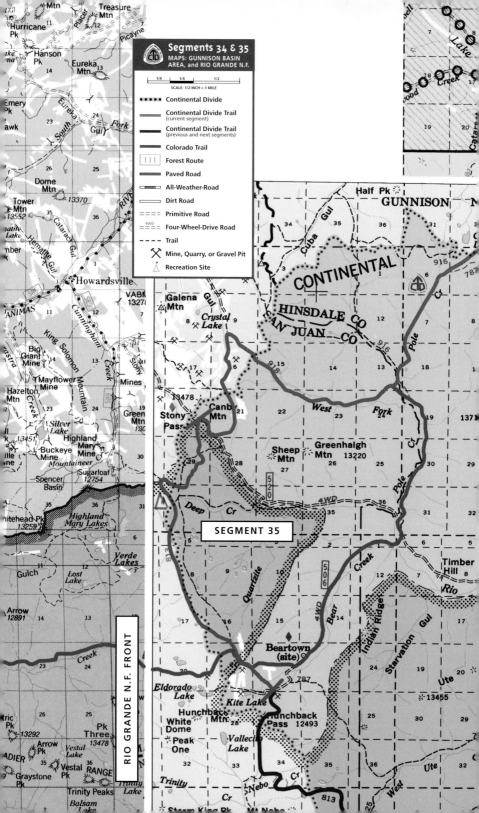

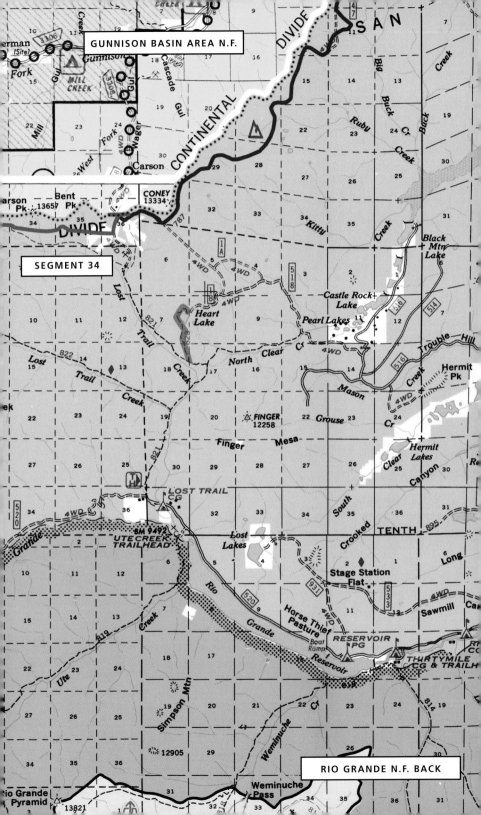

GUNNISON BASIN AREA N.F.

SEGMENT 34

RIO GRANDE N.F. BACK

Segment 35
Stony Pass to Beartown Road

Indian paintbrush above Beartown, Weminuche Wilderness

8.9 miles
Difficulty: Moderate

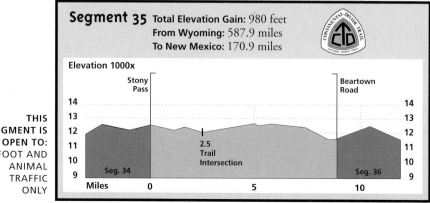

Segment 35 Total Elevation Gain: 980 feet
From Wyoming: 587.9 miles
To New Mexico: 170.9 miles

Elevation 1000x

Stony Pass

Beartown Road

14   14
13   13
12   12
11   11
10   10
9   9

2.5
Trail
Intersection

Seg. 34

Seg. 36

Miles   0   5   10

THIS
SEGMENT IS
OPEN TO:
FOOT AND
ANIMAL
TRAFFIC
ONLY

IF YOU DON'T ENTER the Weminuche Wilderness with an air of humility and reverence, you will almost certainly leave it with one. The scenery, solitude, and ambiance here are beyond compare; it feels as if not much has changed since volcanoes shaped this land 28 million years ago.

With beauty and federally protected wilderness come isolation and great physical distance. It is 94.6 miles with more than 16,000 feet of total elevation gain from Stony Pass to Wolf Creek Pass, and many who set out on this stretch are forced to stop prematurely. Once you enter the Weminuche, there are no easy ways back to civilization. In some places, you may be up to 15 miles from the nearest trailhead, and the trailheads are many more miles from any well-travelled roads or highways. As a result, self-sufficiency and perseverance are of utmost importance for anyone contemplating a through-hike of this vast land. Planning for fewer than 10 days of hiking leaves little room for error—or the unexpected—regarding weather, equipment, physical endurance, etc. Of course, planning for much more makes the burden on your back almost prohibitively heavy. The best course may be to schedule resupply points along the route where someone hikes in to meet you with provisions, but this of course requires a reliable friend and precise timing.

> The clearest way
>
> into the Universe
>
> is through a
>
> forest wilderness.
>
> —John Muir

The first 2.5 miles of this segment may be the most deceptive and difficult of the entire length of the CDT in Colorado. The uniform rolling hills that build on each other like soap bubbles separated by a maze of deep ravines and gullies might confound even an experienced outdoorsperson. Add to this wildly folded terrain the lack of a clear trail and frequent decoy paths—which seem placed almost as if by design to lead hikers astray—and you see the importance of supplementing this written trail description with a map and a compass (and the ability to use them). The trail depicted on the 1955 USGS Howardsville quadrangle shows the best route through the area, even though most of the actual trail no longer exists. To preserve the orienteering challenge, this book provides only the GPS coordinates for the beginning and ending points of the segment.

Many cairns in this area mark the route of an old stock driveway that the CDT follows. It is generally best to aim between cairns, since they are arranged in two parallel lines that sandwich the actual route. There is, however, the occasional cairn located right on the trail. The text mentions the most important of these.

Stony Pass, this segment's starting point, was used by Ute Indians for generations before a man named Hamilton built

RANGER DISTRICT:
Divide

a toll road for wagons in 1872. The road soon became popular with social travelers because it did not pass through Ute Indian territory (they had since been moved), and it was the shortest route from the San Luis Valley to Silverton. It also had its charming features, like a cozy road house tucked in spruce trees on the east side of the pass. The actual Divide crossing, however, was a different story. Wagons had to be disassembled and hauled over on mule trains. The west side was steep and rocky, and it is said that once a mule lost its footing, it wouldn't stop until it hit Cunningham Creek 2,000 feet below. The pass faded into oblivion when the railroad reached Silverton by a different route in 1882.

Water is plentiful on this segment.

MOUNTAIN BIKE NOTES: Bikes are prohibited in the Weminuche Wilderness. However, the ride from Rio Grande Reservoir to Silverton or Lake City, via Stony Pass, would provide an excellent multi-day bike trip in the vicinity of the Continental Divide.

MAPS

TRAILS ILLUSTRATED: 140

USGS QUADRANGLES: Howardsville, Storm King Peak

USFS: San Juan National Forest, Rio Grande National Forest, pages 262–263

ACCESS

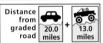

STONY PASS FROM CREEDE: Follow Colorado Highway 149 north from Creede (toward Lake City) 20 miles and turn left (west) onto Rio Grande Reservoir Road. Bear left at a fork 0.5 mile from the highway and continue 19.5 miles to a stream crossing, staying on Forest Road 520 and avoiding the various turnoffs. This stream should be considered the end of the road for non-four-wheel drive vehicles. There is no formal parking here.

Four-wheel drives can continue on this road if they are up to the numerous stream crossings. It is about 7.0 miles from here to a place where the road descends into a broad, breathtaking valley through which the Rio Grande River flows. Drive to the bottom of the valley and follow a sign toward Stony Pass, which will lead to a crossing of Pole Creek. It is about 6.0 miles to Stony Pass, where there is a pullout on the south side of the road. The trail starts about 50 yards back down the road (east) at a single-track trail that descends south past an old cabin.

Stony Pass is also accessible from Silverton, but that side of the pass is much rougher.

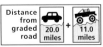

BEARTOWN ROAD: See the next segment.

SUPPLIES, SERVICES, AND ACCOMMODATIONS

SILVERTON: There are no towns near the trail in this segment. Creede is about 53 miles east. It is 10 miles to Silverton, which you can reach by descending the west side of the pass and traveling west on Colorado Highway 110. Traffic over the pass is not reliable enough for hitchhiking.

DISTANCE FROM TRAIL: 10 miles

ZIP CODE: 81433

Bank	Citizens State Bank, 1218 Greene St.	(970) 387-5502
Bus	None	
Dining	Miner's Tavern, 1069 Greene St.	387-5337
	Rusty Cowboy BBQ and Steakhouse, 1323 Greene St.	387-5508
Gear	Outdoor World, 1234 Greene St.	387-5628
Groceries	Greene Street Grocery, 717 Greene St.	387-5652
Information	Silverton Visitor Center, 414 Greene St.	387-5654
Laundry	Wash Tub, 959 Greene St.	N/A
Lodging	Prospector Motel, 1015 Greene St.	387-5466
	Teller House Hotel, 1250 Greene St.	387-5423
Medical	Silverton Clinic, 1450 Greene St.	387-5502
Post Office	12th and Reese Streets	387-5402
Showers	Silverton Lakes Campground,	387-5721
	on Hwy. 110 just out of town to the north.	

SPECIAL NOTES: To experience Colorado history in a different way, take a tour bus to Durango and return on the Durango & Silverton Narrow Gauge Railroad. Phone 387-5416.

TRAIL DESCRIPTION This segment starts on a single-track trail that heads south from Stony Pass Road about 0.1 mile east of the pass summit and 50 yards east of a pullout in the road. Follow the trail past the ruins of a cabin and enter the Weminuche Wilderness (unmarked) . At mile 0.4, there are several parallel trails traversing across a slope. Stay on what looks like the main trail, which is the lower one, and follow it to the crossing of a small streambed. Pick up a faint trail that curves to the left (east) and climbs a short hill before turning back to the right (south). Pass by a large cairn with a yellow sign on it at mile 0.5. You should ignore cairns high on a hill to your right, which mark an old stock driveway. Continue on a faint but discernible trail through rocks, tundra, and what must be a marmot preserve, until mile 0.7 where you pass within 10 feet of a tiny pond on the right (west). There are some good campsites here. The Continental Divide runs ambiguously along the hills to the right (west).

The CDT continues to the southwest across the top of a beautiful, green plateau on the left (east) and promptly disappears. Continue straight to the southwest and crest a tiny rise in the terrain about 30 yards ahead. Then turn left (slightly east of south) and follow a series of eroded patches of ground that lead down the hill. Cross a small streambed at mile 0.9 and descend the other side of the hill on similarly

WILDERNESS ALERT:

The Weminuche Wilderness was designated in 1975 by federal law to be "an area where the earth and its community of life are untrammeled by man, where man himself is a visitor who does not remain." With 488,544 acres, it is the state's largest wilderness area. It is also the most popular, and for that it has suffered. Please remember these rules governing wilderness areas: 1. Camp out of sight, at least 200 feet from lakes and streams, on dry, durable surfaces. 2. Use a stove instead of building a fire; use existing fire rings if you must have a fire. 3. Keep water sources pure by washing at least 200 feet from them. 4. Bury human waste six inches deep and 200 feet from lakes and streams. Pack out toilet paper. 5. Hobble or picket livestock at least 200 feet from lakes and streams, and use only treated, weed-free feed and grain. 6. All dogs must be on a leash. 7. No mountain biking. 8. Pack out all trash. Don't attempt to burn it.

eroded ground. Cross another streambed where you'll see the faint trace of a trail trending south from the opposing bank before it disappears. Continue in a straight line across a flat, grassy area to the edge of a deep ravine. You can see two trails climbing the opposing bank: a clear one to the left and a more obscure one to the right (just west of south). Work your way carefully down the steep bank of the ravine and cross it at mile 1.2 (12,200). Take the trail on the right as it climbs steeply to some willows and disappears. Resist the urge to veer left (southeast) into the meadow.

Continue straight (due south) along a line of willows toward a high hill. At the base of the hill, pick up a trail that moves around its right side (west). Ascend steeply, slightly west of south, along the left (east) side of a depression that holds snow well into mid-season. The faint trail levels as it exits the depression at its top. Continue straight ahead to the southwest above the head of another deep ravine on the left (east). Now aim straight ahead (just west of south) across two small ravines to a shallow saddle at mile 1.6 (12,400). Pick up obscure trails that lead down the ravine to the south. As the valley opens before you, the trail descends to the bottom of the ravine on the right (southwest), crosses it, and continues on an even contour on the opposing bank. Take care as you cross a very steep side ravine that is filled with either gooey mud or slippery snow. Now several parallel trails develop. Pick one of the higher ones and take it around to the right through a very small saddle. Then follow a clear trail that descends slightly into a rolling green valley to the west. When the trail fades, take the course that flowing water would, following the slope downhill until you reach a large flat meadow. Now you can see the trail trending west past the right side of a high, prominent hump in the landscape. A small cairn at mile 2.2 (12,190) marks the trail's right-angle intersection with the Continental Divide. You are now officially in the middle of nowhere. This area has some of the rarest land and scenery in the world, and you are one of only a handful of humans to see it.

The CDT continues to the west side of the hump where it descends to an intersection with a much clearer trail at mile 2.5 (12,060). Turn left (southeast) and follow the new trail across a streambed. Now begin a steady climb on a much clearer tread into a whole new landscape, a primitive one in which solid rock still holds out in large part against the persistent probing of the seeds of life.

At mile 3.3, the trail reaches a very large cairn and descends steeply through a section that may be obscured by snow well into mid-season. Use your best judgment to pick a path through this section. After this brief descent, the trail climbs more vigorously. A post at mile 4.0 (12,530) marks another intersection with the Continental Divide.

Magnificent views of the Grenadier Range begin to dominate the horizon in front of you to the south. At mile 4.5, a trail breaks off to descend along a deep ravine that opens on the right (west). Stay on the clearer trail that climbs gently onto a wide, flat, grassy ridge. This part of the trail props you up in the sky with little cover and no escape routes except at the near and far ends of the ridge, 3.5 miles apart. This area probably appears as a bullseye to passing thunderstorms, so plan accordingly. If there is much hint of a storm, it may be worth the loss of time to hunker down in the lower country that precedes the ridge.

The many parallel trails in this area are not from vehicles, as they appear to be, but from the millions of hooves of stock that have been driven through. This segment's subtle peak is at mile 5.8 (12,700). After the trail descends to a group of ponds at mile 6.2 (12,500), look far to the southeast for a view of the unique formation on the Divide known as "The Window." As the trail winds deeper into the Weminuche Wilderness, it will pass much closer to The Window.

A few yards after you pass very close to a pond on the left (east) side of the trail at mile 6.4, turn left at an unmarked fork onto the clearer of the two trails. Descend gently to cross a stream at mile 6.8 and follow the trail's curve to the right to climb out of the streambed to the southwest under a steep slope. Climb briefly to a high point at mile 7.4 (12,460), where the trail forks at a post with rusty metal arrows on it. Ignore the arrows and briefly link up with the Colorado Trail as you follow the left fork's descent into a ravine. This marks the CDT's temporary departure from the Weminuche Wilderness. In 0.2 mile, the ravine opens into a cozy valley that could easily pass for a Monet painting. Bear right at a fork at mile 8.0 (the Colorado Trail follows the left fork).

The trail descends rapidly to Bear Creek at mile 8.5 (11,700) and flattens out. This stream is tough to cross without completely inundating your feet. Cross a pleasant meadow for 0.2 mile and continue to an intersection with the road to Kite Lake at mile 8.8. Turn sharply right (west) onto the road and climb 0.1 mile to a kiosk on the left at the Hunchback Pass Trailhead. This is the end of the segment (mile 8.9; 11,720 feet; N37° 42.76', W107° 30.94').

OTHER HIKES

HIGHLAND MARY LAKES

Approximate one-way distance: 3.0 miles

Difficulty: Moderate

Highland Mary Mill Trailhead: From Silverton, drive 4.25 miles north on Colorado Highway 110 to a right turn onto Forest Route 589, which ascends along Cunningham Gulch. The road to Stony Pass is on the left in about 2 miles. Continue 4.0 miles from Colorado Highway 110 to the Highland Mary Mill. Park here.

With a minimal amount of hiking, this trail puts you at a group of beautiful lakes very near the Divide on its west side. Please note that this is in the wilderness area. Walk up the jeep road about 0.3 mile and wade across Cunningham Gulch Creek. Continue south along the creek and follow a steep single-track trail to the lakes.

Segment 36
Beartown Road to Twin Lakes

Headwaters of Ute Creek, Weminuche Wilderness

11.9 miles
Difficulty: Strenuous

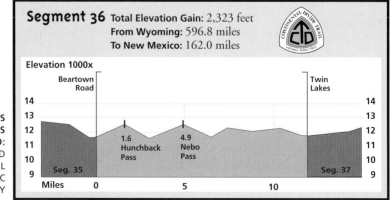

Segment 36 Total Elevation Gain: 2,323 feet
From Wyoming: 596.8 miles
To New Mexico: 162.0 miles

CONTINENTAL DIVIDE TRAIL
CID
NATIONAL SCENIC TRAIL

Elevation 1000x

Beartown
Road

Twin
Lakes

THIS
SEGMENT IS
OPEN TO:
FOOT AND
ANIMAL
TRAFFIC
ONLY

14
13
12
11
10
9

1.6
Hunchback
Pass

4.9
Nebo
Pass

Seg. 35

Seg. 37

14
13
12
11
10
9

Miles   0   5   10

A SHORT DISTANCE down the road to the northeast along Bear Creek is the site of Beartown, a once-thriving mining camp that has all but disappeared today. A rich strike in this area attracted hundreds of prospectors in 1893, and mining lasted well into the 20th century. A 275-pound grizzly bear that had been preying on domestic sheep was trapped and killed near here in 1951.

The hiking difficulty in this segment is notched up to strenuous because it has three significant climbs and two crossings of the Divide well above 12,000 feet. The views are worth the effort, with great close-ups of the granite monoliths of the chaotic Grenadier Range and sweeping vistas of the Rio Grande Pyramid and beyond. The Grenadiers are composed of some of the oldest rock in the state, dating more than one billion years old.

This segment lies entirely within the Weminuche Wilderness. Please review the discussion of regulations governing wilderness travel in Segment 35, page 269. Please respect the special closure at West Ute Lake: You must camp at least 300 feet from the shore. People hiking up Middle Ute Creek from Rio Grande Reservoir should not camp at Black Lake, but they can pitch a tent in the meadow 0.5 mile south of the lake. Black Lake is recovering from overuse. The meadow is a good stopping point after one day of a multi-day hike.

This segment is not well-marked with CDT symbols, but the trail is clear throughout. Water is plentiful.

MOUNTAIN BIKE NOTES: Bikes are prohibited in the Weminuche Wilderness. The ride from Stony Pass Road to Kite Lake is open and challenging, but non-technical. See the directions under *Access* for a description of this route.

MAPS

TRAILS ILLUSTRATED: 140
USGS QUADRANGLES: Storm King Peak, Rio Grande Pyramid
USFS: San Juan National Forest, Rio Grande National Forest, pages 274–275

ACCESS

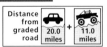

Distance from graded road		
🚗 20.0 miles	+	🚙 11.0 miles

BEARTOWN ROAD: The roads to Beartown and beyond are not in the wilderness, but they might as well be. In fact, this area feels so remote, anyone meeting you here for a food drop might be better off to just hike the trail with you to this point. But for those hardy souls with a Hummer and a day to kill, here's how you do it:

Twenty miles north of Creede on Colorado Highway 149 (toward Lake City), turn left (west) onto the Rio Grande

The land is like

poetry: it is

inexplicably coherent,

it is transcendent

in its meaning,

and it has

the power

to elevate

a consideration

of human life.

—Barry Lopez,

"The Country

of the Mind"

RANGER DISTRICTS:
Columbine
Divide

Reservoir Road, bear left at a fork 0.5 mile from the highway, and continue 19.5 miles to a stream crossing, staying on Forest Route 520 and avoiding the various turnoffs. This stream is the end of the road for non-four-wheel drive vehicles. There is no formal parking here, but you should have no trouble improvising.

Four-wheel drives can continue on this road if they are up to the numerous stream crossings. It is 7.0 rough miles from here to a place where the road descends into a broad, breathtaking valley through which the Rio Grande River runs. Drive to the bottom of the valley and turn left (south) at the sign for Beartown. The Rio Grande must be forded at this point. It is not a huge torrent here, but it is still formidable, especially in the spring. From here it is about 5 miles to a kiosk on the left (south) side of the road at the trailhead for this segment.

 UTE CREEK TRAILHEAD TO TWIN LAKES: See the next segment.

SUPPLIES, SERVICES, AND ACCOMMODATIONS

There are no towns near this segment.

TRAIL DESCRIPTION   Begin by hiking east from the kiosk on a clear trail that climbs immediately and reaches Hunchback Pass—and the Continental Divide—at mile 1.6 (12,493). The trail continues into a steep valley that offers incredible close-up views of The Guardian in the Grenadier Range immediately to the south. The trail follows a stream until shortly after it reenters the trees at mile 2.8. There it swings sharply to the left (southeast) and reaches a trail intersection marked by a wooden post that says nothing about the Continental Divide Trail (mile 3.0; 11,600). Turn left (east) and climb back out of the trees to where the trail fades near Nebo Creek at mile 3.3. (This trail does not appear on the USGS 1964 Rio Grande Pyramid quadrangle or on the 1991 Trails Illustrated map #140.) The tread seems to continue upstream through willows, but it may be flooded until mid-season. An alternative is to cross the stream here, work your way past willows on the south side, and pick up the trail again on the other side of a boulder field.

Cross the stream again at mile 3.8, follow the trail's curve to the right (south), and cross for a third time in 100 yards. Switchbacks lead west to the top of a steep slope that offers inspirational views of Mount Nebo's dark north face. An explorer named Franklin Rhoda scared up a grizzly bear near that mountain's summit in 1874, and then he lamented the animal's invasion of his solitude! He wrote: "It is ever thus: when you feel you are treading a path never trod by a living thing before … some beastly quadruped needs must break the previous solitude and scatter your air castle to the winds. To show our utter disgust—we yelled and threw stones after the bear—." Thus did Beartown and Bear Creek receive their names.

Now the trail trends southeast and climbs steadily through alpine meadows and rocky peaks toward the Nebo Pass summit. Ponds and a lake at the base of Mount Nebo at mile 4.6 (12,400) offer an otherworldly camping experience. You will reach the summit of the pass at mile 4.9 (12,480).

As you crest the pass, the magnificent Rio Grande Pyramid dominates the horizon. The Window, a huge notch in the Continental Divide, is just south (right) of the peak. The trail ambles down the east side of the pass, aiming for the upper limit of the trees on the right (south) side of the valley. Just after you cross a stream at mile 6.1, you will enter a magical old-growth forest of Engelmann Spruce. The CDT soon climbs south out of the trees, fords West Ute Creek, and meets West Ute Creek Trail at mile 6.5 (11,790). Turn right (south) and follow this trail a few yards to West Ute Lake. This is a nice place to stop, but a special regulation prohibits camping within 300 feet of the lake.

The trail climbs out of the lake basin 400 feet to a rolling ridge that over-looks a highland paradise of deep blue lakes, lush valleys, deep forests, and, quite often, elk grazing lazily in the meadows. As you circle west around the top of a small drainage, keep an eye out for an obscure post at mile 7.7 that marks a trail forking off to the right (west). If you start descending steadily to the east, you've missed the turnoff. Follow a trail of cairns that maintains a roughly even contour as it bends to the southwest. You'll see an intermittent tread lower down the slope, but the Forest Service encourages hikers to use the higher route. Middle Ute Lake soon comes into view, and you will pass above it at mile 8.8. Instead of trying to camp here, continue 0.5 mile south to some ponds near the trail.

At mile 9.1, a clear tread replaces the cairns. You will see Twin Lakes down the valley to the east from around mile 9.9. The CDT intersects the Rock Lake Trail at an obscure intersection at mile 10.3 (12,280). Turn left (north) and descend to Twin Lakes on a trail that often doubles as a streambed. Pass Twin Lakes at mile 11.6 and reach the intersection with the Middle Ute Creek Trail, and the end of this segment, at mile 11.9 (11,780 feet; N37° 38.52', W107° 27.40').

N **FOR NORTHBOUND HIKERS,** a sign here seems to indicate the Continental Divide Trail turns right (north) onto the Middle Ute Creek Trail. This is incorrect. Continue on the left fork east and south to climb to a nearby ridge instead of descending into Middle Ute Creek.

OTHER HIKES

WEST UTE CREEK LOOP

Approximate loop distance: Variable, but at least 24 miles
Difficulty: Moderate

West Ute Creek Trailhead: See *Access* for the next segment.

Several loops are possible from this one trailhead. All require at least one night out. Hike several miles up the trail through Alaska-size meadows to Black Lake. About 0.2 mile past the lake, the trail forks. You can take the right fork to West Ute Lake. The left fork leads to several more trail branches that give you a choice of continuing to Twin Lakes or Ute Lake. The Continental Divide Trail links all these lakes, which sit in an exquisite alpine basin.

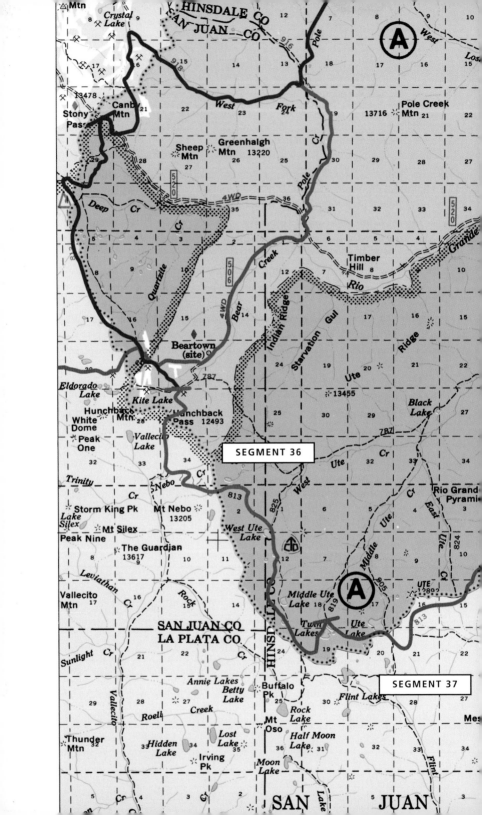

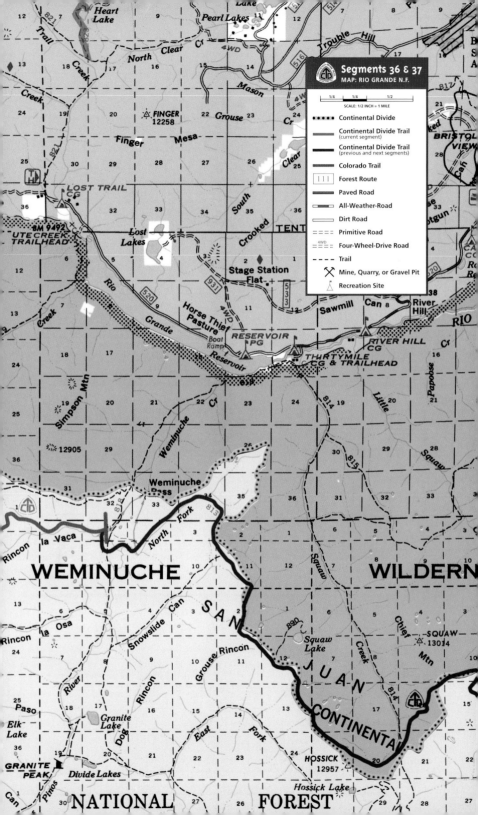

Segments 36 & 37
MAP: RIO GRANDE N.F.

SCALE: 1/2 INCH = 1 MILE

- **Continental Divide**
- **Continental Divide Trail** (current segment)
- **Continental Divide Trail** (previous and next segments)
- **Colorado Trail**
- **Forest Route**
- **Paved Road**
- **All-Weather-Road**
- **Dirt Road**
- **Primitive Road**
- 4WD **Four-Wheel-Drive Road**
- ✕ **Mine, Quarry, or Gravel Pit**
- ⌂ **Recreation Site**

Segment 37
Twin Lakes to Weminuche Pass

Evening light, Weminuche Wilderness

11.4 miles
Difficulty: Strenuous

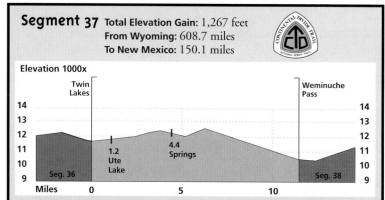

Segment 37 **Total Elevation Gain:** 1,267 feet
From Wyoming: 608.7 miles
To New Mexico: 150.1 miles

CONTINENTAL DIVIDE TRAIL
NATIONAL SCENIC TRAIL
CDT

Elevation 1000x

THIS
SEGMENT IS
OPEN TO:
FOOT AND
ANIMAL
TRAFFIC
ONLY

Twin Lakes

Weminuche Pass

14
13
12
11
10
9

14
13
12
11
10
9

1.2
Ute
Lake

4.4
Springs

Seg. 36

Seg. 38

Miles   0   5   10

THE CDT continues its traverse of the vast Weminuche Wilderness here, passing through a remote section of this pristine land where it is rare to see other people. Please review the rules governing wilderness travel on page 269. Once you pass Ute Lake at mile 1.2, there are no good places to camp until you pass under The Window 6.0 miles distant. There is water on the south slope of Ute Peak at mile 4.4.

About 85 percent of this segment is well above timberline, so the prudent hiker will plan to be done as early in the day as possible. The area around the Divide crossing at mile 6.2, near The Window, seems to act as a lightning rod when Rio Grande Pyramid grows grumpy and whips up a sudden storm. As with many other mountains in the world, this one creates its own weather, so good wilderness camping karma—and perhaps a gesture of deference to the power of the pyramid—may help see you safely over the pass.

Note that the trail depiction on the 1991 revision of Trails Illustrated map #140 and the 1976 USGS Rio Grande Pyramid quadrangle are not accurate here.

 MOUNTAIN BIKE NOTES: This segment lies entirely within the Weminuche Wilderness, where mountain bikes are prohibited.

MAPS

TRAILS ILLUSTRATED: 140
USGS QUADRANGLES: Rio Grande Pyramid, Weminuche Pass
USFS: Rio Grande National Forest, San Juan National Forest, page 274–275

ACCESS

 Smooth road to trailhead **UTE CREEK TRAILHEAD:** 20 miles north of Creede on Colorado Highway 149 (toward Lake City), turn left (west) onto the Rio Grande Reservoir Road, bear left at a fork 0.5 mile from the highway, and continue 16.8 miles to a left turn at a sign for Ute Creek Trailhead. Continue 0.2 mile to a large parking area. The trail, which starts at a kiosk, sets off through some willows and then disappears into the bridgeless Rio Grande River. Spring runoff can make the crossing quite challenging, but it's usually manageable after June. Pick up the clear trail on the other side and follow it about 6.5 miles to Black Lake. In 0.25 mile, the trail forks on the edge of a broad valley of peaceful meadows and winding streams. Take the left (south) fork across some of the streams. Bear right at another fork at the

These indians

[Shoshones]

believe also

that God pulled out

the upper teeth

of the elk

because the elk

were meant

to be eaten

by the indians,

and not

the indians

by the elk.

—Gracy Hebard

RANGER DISTRICTS:
Columbine
Divide

southwest end of the valley and ascend along Middle Ute Creek. Continue 2.5 miles to another junction and bear right again. In about 1.0 mile, you'll hit one last fork. Bear left (south), cross two forks of the creek, and climb 0.75 mile to the intersection with the Continental Divide Trail near Twin Lakes.

 WEMINUCHE CREEK TRAILHEAD: See the next segment.

(Distance from graded road: 6.5 miles)

SUPPLIES, SERVICES, AND ACCOMMODATIONS

There are no towns close to this segment of the trail.

TRAIL DESCRIPTION From the intersection of the CDT and the trail that descends to Middle Ute Creek, climb away from Twin Lakes to the southeast. The CDT levels at mile 0.9 above a large wet meadow and passes a short distance above scenic Ute Lake at mile 1.2 (11,980). Campsites in this area are not as easy to find as the map seems to indicate. The trail swings to the southeast and passes an etched post at mile 1.8. After a brief climb, you will meet the Flint Lakes Trail at another post. Bear left (southeast) and climb above the Flint Lakes valley. Continue past a trail branching to the left at mile 2.4 (12,010) and ascend the ridge via obvious switchbacks to the east. Views to the west of the aptly named Needle Mountains are astounding.

You will reach the top of the ridge at mile 3.2 (12,380). Follow the trail along a mostly even contour to the north-northwest and avoid a trail that descends rapidly due east into the Rincon La Osa drainage. The trail rejoins the Continental Divide at mile 3.8 (12,470) on the edge of an extension of Ute Peak's abrupt south ridge. This gives you one last spacious view of the sublime Ute Creek drainage.

As the Divide follows the steep, rocky ridge to the summit of Ute Peak, the CDT veers to the right (northeast) to traverse across the peak's southeast flank. Springs in this area provide the last water until you pass a pond at mile 7.5. Follow the trail's gradual descent to a saddle at mile 5.2 (12,043), where it rejoins the Divide near the intersection with the East Ute Creek Trail. Switchback along the Divide up the ridge to the east and use cairns where the trail fades. At a plateau area at mile 5.6, the trail turns left (north) and leaves the Divide to traverse up to a saddle at mile 6.2 (12,620). Posts guide you northeast across the saddle to where the trail descends on the other side. You may have to cross a snowfield here.

The CDT descends to the northeast as the vast meadows of Weminuche Pass come into view far down the valley. A short distance later, you will pass under the magnificent Window high on the Divide ridge. A steep descent into Rincon La Vaca starting at mile 8.3 follows a cascading stream into a cool, refreshing forest. You will reach a trail intersection on the edge of the great expanse of Weminuche Pass at mile 11.4 (10,575 feet; N37° 40.18', W107° 20.00'). This is the end of this segment. To continue on the next segment, walk across an irrigation ditch to the right (southeast) and make an immediate left onto a trail descending into the meadow.

OTHER HIKES

UTE CREEK TO WEMINUCHE CREEK LOOP
Approximate loop distance: 28.0 miles or variable
Difficulty: Strenuous

Ute Creek Trailhead: See *Access* for this segment.
Weminuche Creek Trailhead: See *Access* for the next segment.

If you don't have time to hike the entire Weminuche Wilderness, this loop gives you a good taste of the varied terrain and scenery along the route. As with most of the wilderness area, it is a long, full-day hike just to get to the Divide from the trailheads, so you should plan at least two nights. Begin at one trailhead and arrange for a shuttle vehicle or a pick-up at the other one. Several loops are possible. The one that passes by Ute Lake via Middle Ute Creek and then follows the CDT east to Weminuche Pass offers views of the stunning Needle Mountains in the far western reaches of the wilderness. It also gives you 10.2 miles of hiking on the CDT. To slice about 5.0 miles off the route, use the East Ute Creek drainage instead of Middle Ute Creek.

Segment 38
Weminuche Pass to Squaw Pass

On the way to Squaw Pass, Weminuche Wilderness

14.8 miles
Difficulty: Strenuous

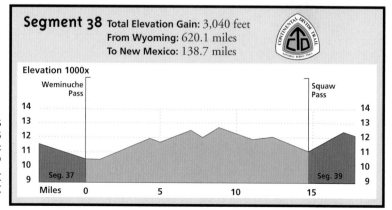

Segment 38 Total Elevation Gain: 3,040 feet
From Wyoming: 620.1 miles
To New Mexico: 138.7 miles

Elevation 1000x

Weminuche
Pass

Squaw
Pass

Seg. 37

Seg. 39

Miles   0   5   10   15

THIS
SEGMENT IS
OPEN TO:
FOOT AND
ANIMAL
TRAFFIC
ONLY

WEMINUCHE PASS is an interesting feature along the Continental Divide. The meadow on the pass is so broad and flat that it is impossible to determine the route of the Divide just by looking. The water in the area gives few clues as it flows lazily through numerous streams or rests in a few ponds. To confuse matters, two ditches, one on each side of the meadow, carry water from the Pacific watershed to the Rio Grande Reservoir on the Atlantic side. The Divide actually crosses the north end of the meadow more than a mile away from the trail.

Because of the friendly lay of the land, this area was a favorite Divide crossing of the Weminuche Indians, a subtribe of the Utes. There were well-established Ute trails here and elsewhere in the Weminuche area when Europeans arrived en masse in the 19th century. Although someone had the idea of laying rails through this area at the turn of the century, it was never used as a major crossing by whites. By the 1870s, the Indians were being squeezed out by the steady flow of pioneers from the East. In the wake of mineral discoveries near here in 1873, they had no choice but to give up most of their land and move to reservations to the west and south under the terms of an agreement called the Brunot Treaty. By 1881, the Utes had been pushed even farther west, into Utah.

Local legend has it that a captain in the U.S. Cavalry riding through this area with a few of his men in 1852 found a stream that was full of gold. The captain had business in California, so he continued on his way but returned to Colorado to rediscover the treasure. He was never able to find it, and locals say his ghost still wanders the area on a pale horse, particularly around Squaw Pass and Hossick Lake, in an eternal search for the elusive gold.

This segment lies entirely within the Weminuche Wilderness. Please review the rules governing wilderness travel in Segment 35, page 269.

Water is plentiful on this segment, but you should use the map to plan your refills. Lightning is a serious hazard here, and the broad ridges of the Divide provide little opportunity for escape.

> In Wildness
>
> is the preservation
>
> of the world.
>
> —Henry David
> Thoreau,
> "Walking"

MOUNTAIN BIKE NOTES: Mountain bikes are prohibited on this segment due to its passage through the Weminuche Wilderness.

MAPS

TRAILS ILLUSTRATED: 140
USGS QUADRANGLES: Weminuche Pass, Little Squaw Creek, Granite Lake, Cimarrona Peak
USFS: Rio Grande National Forest, San Juan National Forest, pages 284–285

RANGER DISTRICTS:
Columbine
Divide
Pagosa

Distance from graded road 6.5 miles

WEMINUCHE CREEK TRAILHEAD: Twenty miles north of Creede on Colorado Highway 149 (toward Lake City), turn left (west) onto the Rio Grande Reservoir Road, bear left at a fork 0.5 mile from the highway, continue 10.5 miles, and turn left into Thirtymile Campground. Cross the river and take an immediate right turn at a three-way fork. Go right at another fork, and turn right 0.3 mile from the main road into the "Backpacker/Fisherman Parking Only" lot.

Now walk 0.1 mile to the trailhead by following the sign toward Squaw and Weminuche Creek Trails. Turn right at a three-way fork and take an immediate left onto the trail. Walk 50 yards up the trail to a kiosk and follow the right fork onto Weminuche Creek Trail. The left fork follows Squaw Creek, forming an excellent loop hike to the Divide.

Hike up Weminuche Creek 5.0 miles to a sign for Weminuche Pass where the trail breaks out into a vast park. Continue past this sign into the park and stay on the right (west) side of an irrigation ditch (Raber Lohr Ditch) at a trail fork in 1.0 mile. Follow the trail west through some trees and continue about 0.4 mile to an intersection with the CDT at a post that reads "CDNST." Southbound hikers should turn left here.

Distance from graded road 9.0 miles

SQUAW CREEK TRAILHEAD: See the next segment.

There are no towns close to this segment.

TRAIL DESCRIPTION   From a CDNST marker on the Raber Lohr Ditch, follow a trail descending to the south into the meadow and cross the Rincon La Vaca stream in 0.1 mile. Continue straight into the meadow to a trail intersection at mile 0.3 that is marked by three posts.

Turn left, pass the third post, and head a little north of east toward more posts in the meadow. There is no visible tread now. Cross the stream where possible near a post at mile 0.4. There is a second, trickier crossing in another 0.2 mile where deep water is hidden by innocent-looking grass. It may be easier to cross a short distance upstream to the north (left). Continue across the meadow in the same direction to a narrow post at the first of two more water crossings. From this post, head for a post hiding on the edge of the trees at compass bearing 110° (mile 0.9; 10,560).

Continue past the post and into the trees on a clear path that crosses the Fuchs Ditch at mile 1.0 before climbing steadily into an enchanting, mossy forest. After opening onto a large, pristine meadow near timberline, the CDT crosses to the south side of the Piños River North Fork at mile 3.3 (11,475). The trail leaves the trees at mile 4.1 and reaches the indistinct ridge of the Continental Divide at a post at mile 4.3 (11,940). Walk straight past this post on its left side onto a fainter trail to the southeast. Ignore a post 20 yards to the right (southwest). Head for another post just to the right (west) of a pond at mile 4.4. The trail follows the ambiguous path of the Divide through some more ponds at mile 5.0 (11,730).

Now the CDT stays very near the Continental Divide. Follow its climb toward the top of the ridge where it fades somewhat at mile 6.3 (12,200). From here a series of well-placed cairns guides the trail south (right) to an unobtrusive high point amid a garden of alpine grass and large rocks at mile 7.1 (12,450). Among the awesome views, look for the distinctive Window and the Rio Grande Pyramid to the west-northwest.

Descend on an unexpectedly steep, rocky path to a saddle between Grouse Rincon and the Squaw Creek drainage at mile 7.7 (12,060). At a fork shortly thereafter, follow large cairns to ascend the ridge. Starting at mile 8.3, follow some posts 0.1 mile to the crest of the ridge. Then turn right and continue to climb to the south, leaving the trail of posts, which turns left and descends. One last burst of energy will propel you to this segment's high point at mile 8.8 (12,780).

Now the CDT descends gradually to the east to a point at mile 9.5 (12,470), where it bends left (northeast) to drop into a stunning series of bowls, or cirques, that cradle numerous lakes and ponds right at timberline. Follow several wide switchbacks into this paradise, cut across the floor of the first cirque, and, where the tread disappears, climb via cairns into the next cirque. Pick up the trail again as it makes a 90-degree turn to the right (south) toward a large pond at mile 10.9. Cross the pond's outlet stream at mile 11.1 (11,860) and continue 0.1 mile to a second pond where the trail again fades. Walk around this pond's left (north) side, turn 90 degrees to the right (south), and walk to the steep terrain behind the pond. Pick up an intermittent trail that cuts a traverse across the hillside through some willows.

Follow a clearer trail into a third cirque with several ponds in it and cross a small rise into cirque #4. At mile 12.4 (12,080), the trail tops out one last time above yet another set of ponds and descends to cross a stream at mile 13.7 (11,540). Follow a sharp turn to the left (east) and drop to a large meadow at Squaw Pass. Walk through the meadow to the end of the segment at a trail intersection at mile 14.8 (11,210 feet; N37° 36.17', W107° 12.91'). You can turn left (north) here to hike back to Thirtymile Campground, or you can continue straight ahead onto the next segment of the CDT.

OTHER HIKES

WEMINUCHE CREEK/SQUAW CREEK LOOP
Approximate loop distance: 30.0 miles
Difficulty: Strenuous

Squaw Creek Trailhead: See *Access* for the next segment.
Weminuche Creek Trailhead: See *Access* for this segment.
  This is an ideal loop hike because it uses only one trailhead. Walk up either creek and follow the CDT 14.4 miles to the other creek. The terrain here is not as rugged as it is farther west in the wilderness, but this may be a blessing because the trail can stay on the Divide ridge for most of its path, providing non-stop views in all directions. The cirques on the CDT between miles 9.5 and 12.4 combine with numerous ponds to offer a unique alpine camping experience. Watch for lightning here, and remember that you are in designated wilderness.

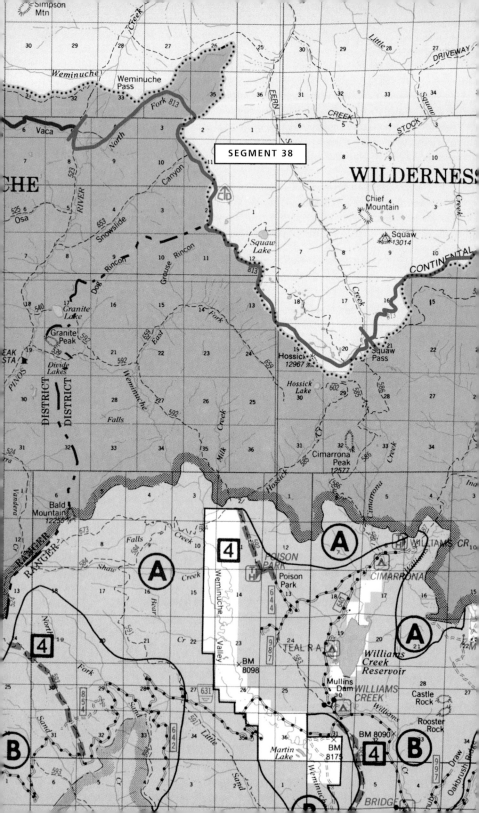

SEGMENT 38

WILDERNESS

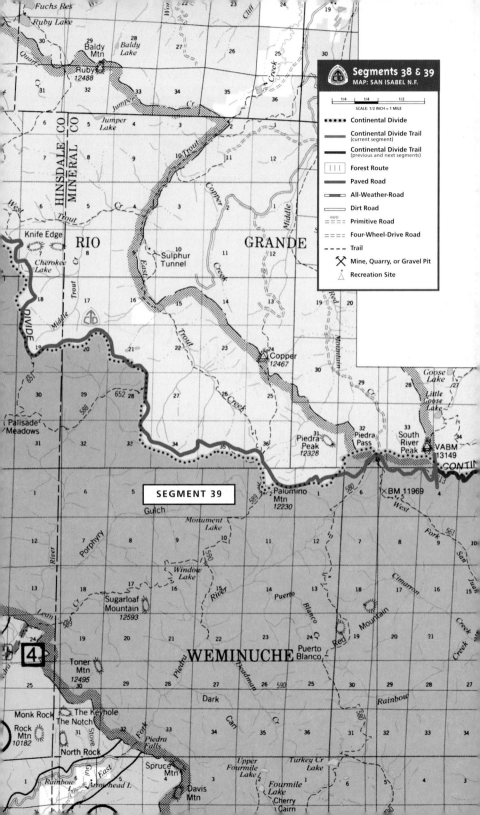

SCALE: 1/2 INCH = 1 MILE

1/4   1/4   1/2

Continental Divide
Continental Divide Trail
(current segment)
Continental Divide Trail
(previous and next segments)
Forest Route
Paved Road
All-Weather-Road
Dirt Road
Primitive Road
Four-Wheel-Drive Road
Trail
Mine, Quarry, or Gravel Pit
Recreation Site

Fuchs Res
Ruby Lake
Baldy
Mtn
Baldy
Lake
Ruby
12488
Jumper
Lake
Knife Edge
Cherokee
Lake
Sulphur
Tunnel
RIO
GRANDE
HINSDALE CO
MINERAL CO
DIVIDE
Copper
12467
Goose
Lake
Little
Goose
Lake
Palisade
Meadows
Piedra Peak
12328
Piedra
Pass
South
River
Peak
VABM
13149
CONTIN
SEGMENT 39
Palomino
Mtn
12230
BM 11969
Gulch
Monument
Lake
West
Fork
Porphyry
Window
Lake
Sugarloaf
Mountain
12593
Puerto
Cimarron
Mountain
San Juan Creek
Leon Cr
4
Toner
Mtn
12495
WEMINUCHE
Puerto
Blanco
Red
Mountain
Dark
Can
Rainbow
Monk Rock
The Keyhole
The Notch
Rock
Mtn
10182
Piedra
Falls
North Rock
Spruce
Mtn
Davis
Mtn
Rainbow
Arrowhead L.
Upper
Fourmile
Lake
Turkey Cr
Lake
Fourmile
Lake
Cherry
Cairn

Segment 39
Squaw Pass to South River Peak

Clearing storm above Piedra Pass, Weminuche Wilderness

26.5 miles
Difficulty: Strenuous

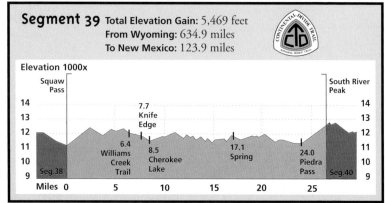

Segment 39 Total Elevation Gain: 5,469 feet
From Wyoming: 634.9 miles
To New Mexico: 123.9 miles

CONTINENTAL DIVIDE TRAIL · CDT · NATIONAL SCENIC TRAIL

Elevation 1000x

Squaw Pass

South River Peak

THIS
SEGMENT IS
OPEN TO:
FOOT AND
ANIMAL
TRAFFIC
ONLY

14							14
13		7.7 Knife Edge					13
12							12
11	6.4 Williams Creek Trail			17.1 Spring			11
10		8.5 Cherokee Lake			24.0 Piedra Pass		10
9	Seg.38					Seg.40	9

Miles 0   5   10   15   20   25

THIS IS THE LAST SEGMENT whose entire length lies within the bounds of the Weminuche Wilderness. The terrain is varied and breathtaking, and there are some airy—even hair-raising—traverses across steep slopes that fall away into secluded valleys far below. Please review the rules governing travel in the Weminuche in Segment 35, page 269.

This segment includes a jaunt across Piedra Pass, which is archaeologically significant. Researchers recently discovered the remains of an Anasazi settlement in this area with artifacts that may date back to 5900 B.C. This is remarkable when you consider that the oldest known cities in Mesopotamia have been dated from 5000 B.C., and the era of the Egyptian Pharaohs began a mere 2,500 years before the time of Christ.

Water is a little more scarce on this segment than other parts of the CDT in the Weminuche. You won't find good water between miles 8.5 and 17.1, and it is infrequent after that until mile 23.5, where water flows plentifully in the Piedra Pass area.

The actual end of the segment is on an exposed ridge at an elevation of 12,710 feet. Look for a more hospitable campsite in the area around Piedra Pass 2.3 miles west of the segment break. The end of this segment is not the best access point for a food drop because it requires 14.0 miles of hiking just to get to the CDT at South River Peak.

 MOUNTAIN BIKE NOTES: Mountain bikes are prohibited in the Weminuche Wilderness.

MAPS

TRAILS ILLUSTRATED: 140
USGS QUADRANGLES: Cimarrona Peak, Little Squaw Creek, Palomino Mountain, South River Peak
USFS: Rio Grande National Forest, San Juan National Forest, pages 284–285

ACCESS

Distance from graded road — 9.0 miles

SQUAW CREEK TRAILHEAD: 20 miles north of Creede on Colorado Highway 149 (toward Lake City), turn left (west) onto the Rio Grande Reservoir Road, bear left at a fork 0.5 mile from the highway, continue 10.5 miles, and turn left into Thirtymile Campground. Cross the river and take an immediate right turn at a three-way fork. Turn right at a second fork and turn right one more time at mile 0.3 from the main road at a sign for the "Backpacker/ Fisherman Parking Only" lot.

The mountains

lie in curves

so tender

I want to lay

my arm about them

as God does.

—Olive Dargan,

Twilight

RANGER DISTRICTS:
Pagosa
Divide

Now walk 0.1 mile to the trailhead by following the sign toward Squaw and Weminuche Creek Trails. Turn right at a three-way fork in the road and make an immediate left onto the trail. Walk 50 yards up the trail to a kiosk and take the left fork onto Squaw Creek Trail. (The right fork follows Weminuche Creek and provides an excellent loop hike to the Divide.) Follow the trail 9.0 miles up Squaw Creek to Squaw Pass where the trail intersects the CDT in a broad, flat meadow on the Divide. Avoid side trails on the way up and follow posts where the trail is obscure as you near the pass.

Distance from graded road	🚶 14.0 miles

IVY CREEK TRAILHEAD TO SOUTH RIVER PEAK: See the next segment.

SUPPLIES, SERVICES, AND ACCOMMODATIONS

There are no towns near this segment.

TRAIL DESCRIPTION From the CDT's intersection with the Squaw Creek Trail, follow the CDT out of the north end of the meadow. After an easy climb through the trees, the trail crosses a good stream at mile 0.7, turns right (east), and climbs steadily to a shallow saddle on the Divide at mile 2.4 (12,400). A whole new world opens before you every time you cross the Divide, and this crossing is no exception.

Descend to another saddle east of Point 12,531 at mile 3.7 (11,900). Some ponds at this point are part of a last refuge before you climb high across the Divide ridge. Follow the trail as it curves around the north side of Point 12,615 and climbs back to the Divide at mile 4.6 (12,330). Look straight ahead (east) at the monstrous south face of Point 12,740 where you can see the CDT as a tiny line etched diagonally across the mountain. You'll reach one more saddle before setting out across that face at mile 5.1 (12,130). Acrophobes beware! This slope plunges 1,000 feet into the Williams Creek valley with slope angles well over 45 degrees (a 100-percent grade). Although the danger of a serious fall is minimal, all that space on your right side gives the impression of creeping precariously over a great chasm. You can easily see New Mexico far to the south on a clear day, and you'll feel you are very near the top of the world when you crest the ridge at mile 5.8 (12,360).

Follow the trail's sharp turn back to the left (north) to descend in the direction of Trout Lake. On the flat, grassy land above the lake, the CDT intersects the Williams Creek Trail at mile 6.4 (12,010). Continue straight ahead (northeast). At mile 6.7, the trail curves around the ridge to the right (east) as the next vertiginous proposition on this segment comes into view. This is the Knife Edge, whose steep slopes have claimed the lives of several horses. Horse parties would be wise to descend from mile 6.4 on the trail to Trout Lake, turn north toward the West Trout Creek drainage, and finally take the trail that climbs south to the more benign east end of the Knife Edge.

The Trout Creek Trail, which is the horse bypass described above, joins the CDT at mile 7.5 at a post marking the CDT. Continue a short distance to the point of the Knife Edge and turn sharply to the right (south and west) to descend its south side. The trail veers left (east) into a wide, grassy bowl at mile 8.1 (11,720). As the trail fades here, continue due east across a meadow toward a large, rocky point. Pick up a clear tread just shy of that point at mile 8.3 and follow a bend to the right (southeast). Pass above Cherokee Lake at mile 8.5 (11,650). This is the last reliable water for 8.6 miles.

The trail climbs to a ridge at mile 9.1 (11,750), veers sharply to the right (west-southwest), and ambles up to the rolling Divide ridge. You may surprise some elk as you come around this corner. The CDT traces the Divide precisely now as it crosses above a wall of cliffs and passes the turnoff to Palisade Meadows at mile 11.0. Stay left and continue east to a high point at mile 11.1 (12,063). There are numerous ups and downs now as the trail stays on the ridge and trends generally east. There are no easy escape routes off the ridge for the next mile.

The CDT reenters the trees and descends to a quiet saddle at mile 12.6 (11,780). Climb a short distance to Point 11,842 and turn 90 degrees to the right (southeast) to descend into another saddle that precedes a climb to Point 11,846. The CDT breaks out of the trees at mile 13.8 and continues across a meadow to the east. You will see a pond in a clearing below the trail on the left (north). Don't plan this as a water stop; the pond looks stagnant, and it is 300 vertical feet below the trail.

Now the CDT rolls in and out of trees and meadows as it bends to the right to track south at mile 14.5. Follow it around the left (east) side of a high, sharp, bald knob where it maintains an even contour before dropping off the Divide to the north at mile 16.1 (11,720) to avoid a rugged section. The trail climbs east-southeast to a reliable spring and some pools at mile 17.1 (11,840).

Follow the trail around the north end of a side ridge jutting out from the main Divide ridge. Climb to another ridge at mile 18.5 (11,900) where the trail bends southeast (right) and fades in a broad meadow. Climb toward some small clumps of trees, pick up the tread again, and continue to a trail fork at mile 19.2 (11,940) in an eerie white landscape of eons-old volcanic ash. The right fork, which is the Middle Fork Trail, trends south along the Divide toward Palomino Mountain. Take the left fork, climb to a small saddle on the next ridge at mile 19.7, and turn right (southeast) at another trail junction.

 NORTHBOUND HIKERS: This intersection may be obscure for northbound hikers. Follow the faint, higher tread to the left (west).

There is a reliable stream at mile 20.2 (11,965). Shortly after this, you will pass near some interesting geologic features, including deep gullies eroded into the ash. When you reach the east ridge of Palomino Mountain, which is also the Continental Divide, at mile 20.6 (11,930), continue to the left (east) and follow the ridge's descent toward Piedra Pass. A badly eroded trail leads you into the trees and to a saddle at mile 21.3 (11,490). At mile 21.9, follow the long "Walk of a Billion Stones" across the gauntlet of jumbled rock on the north side of Point 12,067. The broad west face of Piedra Peak dominates the view to the east. Continue east into the trees. You will cross a good stream in a small ravine at mile 23.5 and reach the broad meadow of Piedra Pass a short distance later. At mile 23.8, turn left onto the Turkey Creek Trail and follow its bend to the right (east). Continue past an intersection with an old jeep road at mile 24.0 and follow a single-track trail 0.2 mile north past a post with a CDT symbol on it. The water in this area is the last for 12.3 miles.

The trail passes briefly through a stand of trees and sets out toward South River Peak, the high, flat hump to the northwest. Climb to the top of the southwest bowl of the peak in one giant traverse to a single switchback at mile 26.2 (12,515). Continue climbing to a trail intersection at mile 26.5 (12,710 feet; N37° 33.98', W106° 58.54'). This is the end of the segment. The left fork heads north 14.0 miles to the Ivy Creek Trailhead. The right (southeast) fork is the beginning of the next segment of the CDT. Pause here to enjoy expansive views of the wilderness area to the west.

OTHER HIKES

TROUT LAKE
Approximate one-way distance: 8.0 miles
Difficulty: Moderate

Trout Creek Trailhead: From Creede, follow Colorado Highway 149 north (toward Lake City) 6.2 miles to a turnoff on the left for Middle Creek Road. Continue about 8.5 miles to where the road begins to climb. The trailhead is just off the first switchback on the right (south).

This trail is an excellent access point for an array of hikes through some of the most interesting terrain in the Weminuche Wilderness. Follow the trail up the creek. Several crossings here may be high early in the season. After about 5 miles, take a fork to the right (west) toward Trout Lake. Soon you will pass under the impressive Knife Edge, a volcanic extension of the Continental Divide ridge that rises more than 1,000 feet above the valley. Just after a brisk climb lifts you over the Trout Creek headwall, a trail takes off to the south to climb to the CDT on the Knife Edge.

You may also continue a short distance to an intersection with the Texas Creek Trail. Turn left (south) to reach Trout Lake and, a short distance beyond, the CDT. If you turn right, you will climb over expansive tundra 2.5 miles to a group of alpine ponds called Red Lakes. From there you can continue north about 7 miles to the Fern Creek Trailhead, which is about 19 miles from Creede and a short distance off Colorado Highway 149.

Squaw Creek, Weminuche Wilderness

Segment 40
South River Peak to Wolf Creek Pass

Indian paintbrush below Mount Hope, Weminuche Wilderness

21.1 miles
Difficulty: Moderate

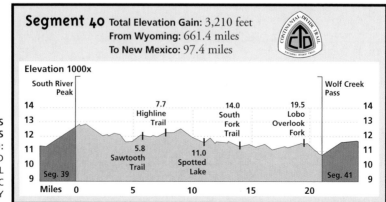

Segment 40 **Total Elevation Gain:** 3,210 feet
From Wyoming: 661.4 miles
To New Mexico: 97.4 miles

THIS
SEGMENT IS
OPEN TO:
FOOT AND
ANIMAL
TRAFFIC
ONLY

Elevation 1000x

South River Peak — Wolf Creek Pass

7.7 Highline Trail

14.0 South Fork Trail

19.5 Lobo Overlook Fork

5.8 Sawtooth Trail

11.0 Spotted Lake

Seg. 39 — Seg. 41

Miles 0 — 5 — 10 — 15 — 20

THIS SEGMENT COMPLETES the CDT's traverse of the Weminuche Wilderness and delivers the through-hiker to the first paved road in 146.3 miles. This makes the stretch between the highways over Spring Creek Pass and Wolf Creek Pass the longest such section on Colorado's CDT.

As in the rest of the Weminuche, the trail hugs the Divide for most of its course here. Dips below 12,000 feet are rare over the first 10 miles, and lightning is a significant hazard. Start early and keep an ear out for that ominous sound of distant thunder.

Water is scarce until mile 9.9, so it is best to load up near the end of the previous segment. Quiet hikers have a good chance of seeing elk here.

MOUNTAIN BIKE NOTES: Mountain bikes are prohibited on this segment because of its passage through the Weminuche Wilderness.

MAPS

TRAILS ILLUSTRATED: 140
USGS QUADRANGLES: South River Peak, Mount Hope, Wolf Creek Pass
USFS: Rio Grande National Forest, San Juan National Forest, page 297

ACCESS

Distance from graded road	14.0 miles

IVY CREEK TRAILHEAD TO SOUTH RIVER PEAK: From Creede, follow Colorado Highway 149 north (toward Lake City) 6.2 miles to a turnoff on the left for Middle Creek Road. After about 4 miles, turn left onto Forest Road 528 (Lime Creek Road). Drive 3.5 miles to Forest Road 526 (Red Mountain Creek Road), turn right, and proceed about 2 miles to the Ivy Creek Trailhead.

Follow the clear trail as it climbs steadily along Ivy Creek through meadows and beautiful, healthy stands of timber. After the trail climbs sharply to the east out of the Ivy Creek drainage, bear right (south) at an intersection and continue past Goose Lake, which sits at timberline at approximately mile 10.0. This is a nice place to camp if you want to take two days to reach the CDT. Climb approximately 2.0 miles south to Little Goose Lake. Then climb past the summit of South River Peak (13,148) in about 1.5 miles and descend 0.5 mile to the intersection with the CDT.

Smooth road to trailhead	

WOLF CREEK PASS: See the next segment.

The substance

of the winds

is too thin

for human eyes,

their written

language is

too difficult

for human minds,

and their spoken

language mostly

too faint

for the ears.

—John Muir

RANGER DISTRICTS:
Divide
Pagosa

SUPPLIES, SERVICES, AND ACCOMMODATIONS

PAGOSA SPRINGS: From Wolf Creek Pass, you may descend east on US-160 19.5 miles to South Fork or west on the same highway 23 miles to Pagosa Springs. I recommend the latter, where there is slightly more going on and you can soak in the wonderful hot springs at the Spring Inn. Hitching in either direction should not be too difficult. It helps to walk to the popular Continental Divide kiosk on the summit and strike up some conversations.

DISTANCE FROM TRAIL: 23 miles

ZIP CODE: 81147

Bank	Citizens Bank, 703 San Juan St.	(970) 264-2235
Bus	None	
Camping	Pagosa Riverside (KOA) Campground, 1.5 miles east of town on Hwy. 160	264-5874
Dining	Amore's House of Pasta, 121 Pagosa St.	264-2822
Gear	Pagosa Sports, 432 Pagosa St.	264-5811
Groceries	City Market, 755 San Juan St.	264-2217
Information	Chamber of Commerce, 402 San Juan St.	264-2360
Laundry	Mary's Laundromat, 358 Pagosa St.	264-2938
Lodging	Spring Inn, 165 Hot Springs Blvd.	264-4168
Medical	Pagosa Springs Family Medicine Center, 75 S. Pagosa Blvd.	264-4131
Post Office	250 Hot Springs Rd.	264-5440
Showers	Spring Inn, 165 Hot Springs Blvd.	264-4168

SPECIAL NOTES: The hot springs at the Spring Inn are the main attraction in this town. A therapeutic soak is available anytime, 24 hours a day.

TRAIL DESCRIPTION From the trail intersection, continue southeast along the CDT and curve around the south side of Point 12,925. Look south into the deep valley of the San Juan River West Fork. At the mouth of the canyon, you can see a large green meadow that is familiar to anyone who has ever driven west over Wolf Creek Pass. The meadow is part of a view from the top of the pass that looks like something out of a fairy tale.

The trail peaks out on a flat ridge at mile 0.3, descends to a saddle, and then climbs as it traverses across the steep southwest face of an unnamed, flat-topped peak. When the trail switchbacks to the left (north) on top of the peak, you are in for what may be the most breathtaking experience on the entire CDT. Enough said! If you've been through-hiking the Weminuche Wilderness, this is a good place to turn back to the west and wave one last goodbye.

Just in case your breath has not yet been taken completely away, the next switchback goes so close to a sheer cliff in 0.1 mile that you have the sensation of being led on some rickety old platform right into the void. Pause and enjoy the airy vista over the Goose Creek drainage—but make sure your footing is solid! Follow several switchbacks down the steep east side of this fantastic feature of the Continental Divide and bottom out in a saddle at mile 2.6 (12,035).

Now the CDT rolls along the quiet, grassy ridges and saddles of the Divide on an obvious trail. After the trail passes through some trees, it reaches a saddle at mile 4.9 (11,740) and starts a brisk 0.7-mile climb. Then it descends slightly to an intersection with the Sawtooth Trail at mile 5.8 (12,060), which descends sharply to the north. Continue east to the intersection with the Beaver Creek Trail at mile 7.0 (11,980). The CDT follows a heavenly route to 12,550 feet over the next 2.0 miles, and the Beaver Creek Trail is the last good escape route off the ridge for the next 2.9 miles. Now the CDT bends to the right (south) and climbs to a saddle at mile 7.7 (12,240). At the intersection with the Highline Trail here, continue to the south (right). In 0.6 mile, the trail begins yet another journey into the sky, reaching its ethereal destination at mile 9.0 (12,550). Needless to say, the views are fantastic.

Follow many switchbacks into the Archuleta Lake bowl and continue south as the trail flattens near the lake at mile 9.9 (11,920). This is the first reliable water since the end of the last segment. Pass by the Archuleta Trail on the left at mile 10.4 and continue 0.5 mile to the delightful meadows around Spotted Lake. You'll find nice springs and secluded campsites above the lake to the north.

Cross Spotted Lake's outlet stream (11,650) and start an immediate climb to the top of a ridge, which you will reach at mile 11.5 (11,900). Descend slightly to a pleasant walk through a tranquil forest. A more pronounced descent starts at mile 13.0 and ends just before an intersection with the South Fork Trail, which is at mile 14.0 (11,315). The CDT continues east (straight) and then south from here, but it soon begins a general trend to the east with a mellow climb. Follow a clear tread through many ups and downs along the Divide ridge. At mile 15.2 (11,305), you will reach Rock Lake, which is really a stagnant pond. As the trail climbs across a steep slope on the south side of the Divide ridge at mile 18.7, it begins to veer to the south (right). After you top out in a meadow at mile 19.3 (11,650), descend slightly 0.2 mile to a trail junction. Turn right (south) and mount one final climb to mile 19.8 (11,620). (The fork continuing straight ahead leads to Lobo Overlook, a vehicle-accessible trailhead near the radio tower.)

 NORTHBOUND HIKERS will enter the Weminuche Wilderness at this point. Please review the rules governing hiking here in Segment 35, page 269.

At mile 20.8 (10,880), about 0.1 mile from the highway over Wolf Creek Pass, the trail disappears. Turn right (just west of south) onto the trace of a trail that becomes more obvious after a few paces. This trail reaches highway level at mile 20.9 and turns right (west) to parallel the highway for a few hundred yards before turning left (south) to meet the highway at a round post. Cross the highway to a large kiosk—and the end of the segment—on the summit of the pass at mile 21.1 (10,830 feet; N37° 28.96', W106° 47.97').

OTHER HIKES

WEST FORK LOOP

Approximate loop distance: 36 miles
Difficulty: Strenuous

Borns Lake Trailhead: Nine miles west of the summit of Wolf Creek Pass on US-160, turn north onto Forest Route 648. Drive approximately 3.5 miles to a parking lot at an elaborate gate.

Obey signs and follow the obvious trail as you traverse private property. The trail takes you into the deep, breathtaking gorge of the San Juan River West Fork, crosses the river, and continues upstream through the gorge. After 4.2 miles, you will pass the Beaver Creek Trail, which climbs very steeply to the right (east). You will descend on this trail if you plan to hike the loop. Continue up the West Fork Trail (also called the Rainbow Trail) to the CDT and turn east. After 11.9 miles, turn right onto the Beaver Creek Trail, which descends south into the Elk Creek drainage. For a description of the CDT part of this hike, start at mile 24.2 of Segment 39 and continue to mile 7.0 of Segment 40.

MOUNT HOPE

Approximate one-way distance: 12.1 miles
Difficulty: Strenuous

Wolf Creek Pass Trailhead: See *Access* for the next segment.

This pleasant hike along the Divide follows the CDT to the crossing of 12,550-foot Mount Hope, offering stunning views in all directions. To make this hike shorter and cut off the demanding climb at the end, consider stopping at Spotted Lake (10.2 miles) for a peaceful stay in the shadow of the Divide. Follow Segment 40's directions in reverse for this hike.

Tom Jones and Staci Haines at Wolf Creek Pass

Segment 41
Wolf Creek Pass to Elwood Pass

Montezuma Peak, Rio Grande National Forest

19.1 miles
Difficulty: Moderate

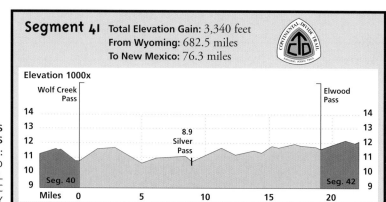

Segment 41 **Total Elevation Gain:** 3,340 feet
From Wyoming: 682.5 miles
To New Mexico: 76.3 miles

CONTINENTAL DIVIDE TRAIL
NATIONAL SCENIC TRAIL

THIS SEGMENT IS OPEN TO:
FOOT AND ANIMAL TRAFFIC ONLY

Elevation 1000x

Wolf Creek Pass

Elwood Pass

14
13
12
11
10
9

14
13
12
11
10
9

8.9
Silver
Pass

Seg. 40

Seg. 42

Miles   0   5   10   15   20

THIS SEGMENT BEGINS THE FINAL STRETCH of the Continental Divide Trail in Colorado. You will undoubtedly encounter a lot of tourists near Wolf Creek Pass, but their numbers decrease rapidly the further you go from the highway. The trail plays hide-and-seek with the Wolf Creek Ski Area for the first couple of miles. Skiing here is usually excellent, and annual snowfall ranks among the highest in the state.

This area has a lot of treasures: Treasure Mountain, Treasure Pass, Treasure Falls, Treasure Creek, etc. This is no coincidence. A plausible story tells of a French expedition that mined (in today's dollars) between $10 million and $30 million worth of gold in this area in the 1790s. They buried it near Treasure Mountain before their numbers were decimated—from 300 down to 17—by disease, malnutrition, and Indian attacks. Only two of the 17 survived the flight east, and they never returned to seek the treasure. Others have come and gone, digging holes and pouring money into the effort, but none have found a trace of the gold. Perhaps it is still protected by the ghosts of the men who hid it more than 200 years ago.

This segment may cross more named passes than any other on the CDT. Along with Wolf Creek and Elwood, you'll cross Treasure, Railroad, Silver, Bonito, and Summit passes. None has a very rich history.

Water on the trail is rare on this segment. The most reliable place to fill up is near Bonito Pass at mile 12.4. In a pinch, you can descend 450 vertical feet below the trail to Alberta Park Reservoir at mile 5.0. You'll find water at the end of the segment, 6.7 miles beyond Bonito Pass, but you should definitely use a filter or iodine tablets because this is a popular grazing area. Water is plentiful beginning at mile 2.5 of the next segment.

MOUNTAIN BIKE NOTES: Most of this segment is unrideable for a variety of reasons, including rock slides, marshy areas, steep terrain, and lack of a tread.

MAPS

TRAILS ILLUSTRATED: 142
USGS QUADRANGLES: Wolf Creek Pass, Elwood Pass
USFS: Rio Grande National Forest, San Juan National Forest, pages 302–303

ACCESS

Smooth road to trailhead

WOLF CREEK PASS: Follow US-160 23 miles east from Pagosa Springs or 19.5 miles west from South Fork to the summit of Wolf Creek Pass. The trail reaches the highway at a post on the north side and departs near the kiosk on the south side.

The first fall of snow

is not only an event,

it is a magical event.

You go to bed

in one kind of world

and wake up

in another

quite different,

and if this

is not enchantment,

then where

is it to be found?

—J.B. Priestley,

Apes and Angels

RANGER DISTRICTS:
Pagosa
Divide
Conejos Peak

ELWOOD PASS: See the next segment.

From the summit of Wolf Creek Pass, South Fork is 19.5 miles east on US-160 and Pagosa Springs is 23 miles west. I recommend Pagosa Springs. Hitching is usually fruitful here. See Segment 40, page 294.

TRAIL DESCRIPTION Start on a developed trail that is 20 yards left (east) of the kiosk at the top of Wolf Creek Pass. Walk 0.1 mile south to where the trail ends at the edge of the trees and turn left (east) onto a wide tread in the forest that soon bends right (south). There are no signs to identify this as the Continental Divide Trail. The trail climbs immediately up a ridge and reaches an open area (actually, a ski run) at mile 0.4. Where the trail forks, turn 120 degrees to the right (west) and continue up the trail. After climbing through several switchbacks, the trail passes by the top of a lift tower at mile 1.0 and starts to follow the Divide ridge near its crest. At mile 1.5 (11,660), after climbing along a huge rockslide and less than 0.1 mile short of another ski lift, look for a trail breaking off to the right to contour along the west side of the Divide ridge. After passing through a healthy stand of trees, the CDT breaks out on the flat top of a steep ridge. Enjoy beautiful views of the Lane Creek drainage as you parallel the course of the Divide to the south-southeast. You will soon rejoin the Divide and head more to the left (east). Continue to follow posts and a faint trail across the top of the bare ridge. At mile 2.9 (11,630), the trail cuts a traverse along the steep south side of Alberta Peak, whose north side lures double-diamond skiers to Wolf Creek Ski Area.

At mile 3.5, after passing under some cliffs, the trail comes to the top of the ridge at a bare, sandy area. Follow cairns to the east across the top of the ridge and pick up a faint trail on the other side that disappears again in 0.2 mile. Follow cairns and wooden posts along the top of the ridge. When the trail veers into the trees on the left (northwest) a short distance later, watch for a post in the trees and continue in that direction. A clear single-track trail develops as the CDT descends off the ridge into more trees on the left. Follow a clear tread on a steady descent to mile 4.8 where the first CDT post in about a mile marks a road going to the right and a single-track trail descending to the left (north). Follow the single-track, which is obscure but easy to follow if you pay attention, along a winding, slight descent toward Alberta Park Reservoir. Just after the reservoir comes into view below the trail to the left (north) at mile 5.0 (10,620), the trail ascends away from the lake to the east on a good tread with a gradual climb. As the trail makes a hairpin turn to the right (southeast) at mile 7.8, avoid the barricaded trail to the north. You will reach an intersection at Silver Pass at mile 8.9 (10,790). Continue straight ahead to the southeast. Just after it traverses across some steep south and west-facing slopes, the trail disappears in a high meadow at a post but continues on the other side of the meadow to the southeast. Follow a clear tread above more steep slopes that fall away to the Silver Creek drainage. The trail reaches a high point at a post in a saddle at mile 11.3 (11,760).

Now the route is a little tricky. Turn slightly to the left (compass bearing 140°) and walk toward some scruffy trees about 40 yards away. There you will find a faint trail that bends a little more to the left (compass bearing 120°) before it switchbacks down the south-southeast side of Point 11,810. Occasional tree blazes are helpful here. The 1966 USGS Elwood Pass quadrangle incorrectly shows the trail passing south of Point 11,810. It actually goes north of it.

Four switchbacks lead to a meadowed area on gentler terrain (mile 11.7). A clear trail descends a little east of north through a nice spruce forest to Bonito Pass at mile 12.4 (11,250 feet; N37° 26.68', W106° 42.50'). You'll see two posts on the other side of a meadow here. Head a little to your right (north of east) to the one on the right (east), which identifies the CDT. The trail continues to the southeast and reaches a developed walkway across a small meadow at mile 13.1. Cross an intersecting trail and continue straight (north) over a second walkway.

After the trail traverses east across a high ridge with sweeping views to the south at mile 13.8 (11,500), it crosses over the ridge to the left (north). At this point, you will see another trail parallel to the CDT about 20 yards to the left. The new trail is much clearer, but ignore it and follow cairns, posts, and tree blazes through the trees. At mile 14.3 (11,390), the CDT joins a clear trail.

NORTHBOUND HIKERS should leave the clear trail here and follow posts to the northwest.

You'll encounter multiple trails at mile 14.4. The CDT is the clear trail that follows tree blazes. At mile 15.5 (11,840), after traversing steadily up a steep ridge, you will reach a prominent cairn at the top of the ridge. Turn left (northwest) and follow an even contour past two posts in a grassy field. From a gigantic cairn at the other end at mile 15.7, the CDT turns southwest and follows the rolling Divide ridge. At mile 16.4 (11,860), as the trail fades near the top of a mostly treeless ridge, follow a line of cairns running along the crest of the Divide to your left.

At mile 16.8, as the cairns run out, the ridge takes a brief dip into a shallow saddle. Look 45 degrees down to the right for another post. Proceed to that post and look up ahead to where two trails trend off to the southeast; head for the one on the right. At mile 17.5, the trail makes a 90-degree turn to the right (south) and then seems to disappear along with any other markers into a wide, grassy meadow frequented by cows. Continue straight into the meadow, and you will soon spot more posts. Follow a better tread to Elwood Pass Road at mile 19.0 and turn left (south). Follow an immediate curve to the right (southwest). Walk 80 yards down the road to mile 19.1 (11,615 feet; N37° 24.28', W106° 38.65') where a post marks the trail's continuation off to the right (west). This is the end of this segment.

OTHER HIKES AND RIDES

There are no other well-established hiking or biking trails available in this segment.

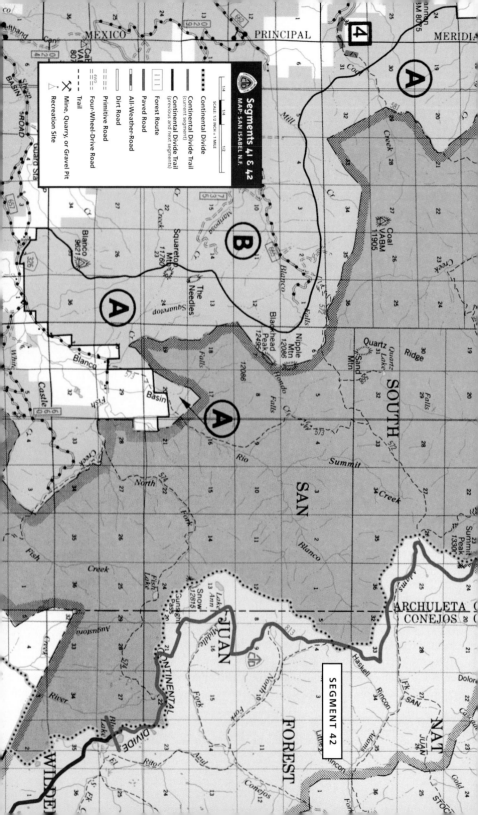

Segments 41 & 42
MAP: SAN ISABEL N.F.

SCALE 1/2 INCH = 1 MILE

████			Continental Divide
••••			Continental Divide Trail (current segment)
— —			Continental Divide Trail (previous and next segments)
▓▓▓			Forest Route
▓▓▓			Paved Road
═══			All-Weather-Road
═ ═ ═			Dirt Road
= = =			Primitive Road
═══ 4WD			Four-Wheel-Drive Road
- - - -			Trail
✕			Mine, Quarry, or Gravel Pit
△			Recreation Site

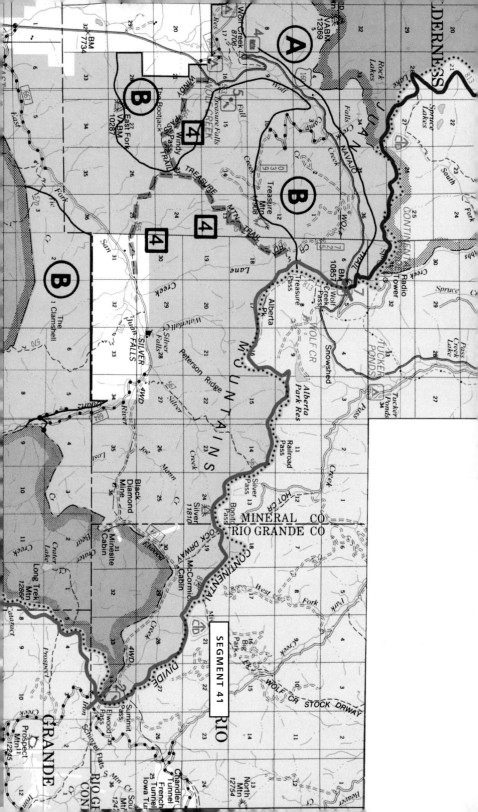

SEGMENT 41

Segment 42
Elwood Pass to Blue Lake

Peaks of the South San Juan Wilderness

27.1 miles
Difficulty: Strenuous

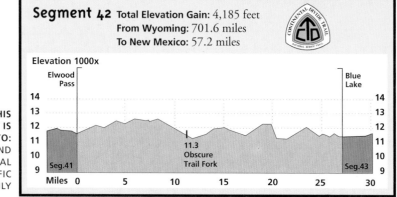

Segment 42 **Total Elevation Gain:** 4,185 feet
From Wyoming: 701.6 miles
To New Mexico: 57.2 miles

CONTINENTAL DIVIDE TRAIL · CDT · NATIONAL SCENIC TRAIL

Elevation 1000x

Elwood Pass

Blue Lake

14
13
12
11
10
9

11.3
Obscure
Trail Fork

Seg.41

Seg.43

Miles   0   5   10   15   20   25   30

THIS
SEGMENT IS
OPEN TO:
FOOT AND
ANIMAL
TRAFFIC
ONLY

ELWOOD PASS served for a while as the only route over the Divide for settlers in the San Luis Valley traveling west. It was built in 1876 and became a toll road the next year. U.S. soldiers worked on the road in the late 1870s to transport supplies to Fort Lewis, a prison built in Pagosa Springs to contain the Ute Indians in this area. Long before any whites, the Indians probably used the pass to travel from the San Luis Valley to the hot springs at what is now Pagosa Springs. The pass was considered twice as a route for a state highway, but the 25-percent grades on its west side have prevented it from becoming anything more than a jeep road. It takes its name from a settler named T. L. Woodvale, who combined his initial "L" with the first part of his last name to come up with the moniker.

This segment takes you near what is considered to be the last best hope for grizzly bear habitat in Colorado. A rancher on the west side of the Divide saw three huge bears in 1979 that he swears were too big to be black bear, which still roam the state in healthy numbers. A grizzly bear was killed near Blue Lake in 1951. Researchers and wildlife advocates are making a concerted effort to find conclusive evidence proving the continued existence of the grizzly in Colorado. Don't be too concerned—any remaining Colorado grizzlies would be very shy of humans. Besides, your chances of getting hit by lightning are much greater than those of even seeing a great bear.

Water is frequent on this segment in the form of springs, ponds, and small streams. Most of the trail is above timberline and exposed to inclement weather.

Nature,

to be commanded,

must be obeyed.

—Francis Bacon,

Novum Organum

MOUNTAIN BIKE NOTES: This segment lies almost entirely within the South San Juan Wilderness where mountain bikes are prohibited.

MAPS

TRAILS ILLUSTRATED: 142
USGS QUADRANGLES: Elwood Pass, Summit Peak, Elephant Head Rock
USFS: Rio Grande National Forest, San Juan National Forest, pages 302–303

BEGINNING ACCESS POINT

Distance from graded road 19.0 miles

ELWOOD PASS FROM THE WEST: Drive 10.5 miles east of Pagosa Springs or 12.5 miles west of the summit of Wolf Creek Pass on US-160 to East Fork Road on the east side of the highway. Follow signs east for 19 miles to the summit of Elwood Pass.

RANGER DISTRICTS:
Conejos Peak
Pagosa

ELWOOD PASS FROM THE EAST: Drive 7 miles west from South Fork or 12 miles east from the summit of Wolf Creek Pass on US-160 to Park Creek Road (Forest Route 380) on the south side of the highway. **NOTE:** This road is only open from 8 a.m. to 4:30 p.m. due to restricted access to the EPA Superfund cleanup at the Summitville Mine. Avoid the left fork to Summitville 15 miles from the highway. Continue 3.5 miles beyond this point and turn right at a sign for the CDT and Elwood Pass. The CDT crosses the road in about 150 yards. It is marked by signs.

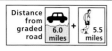

BLUE LAKE: See the next segment.

There are no towns near this segment.

The trail leaves the road at a post that says "Cont Div Tr" and crosses a meadow to the west. If there is no water here, check farther down the slope to the south. Note that this area is heavily grazed. At mile 0.1, the trail enters the trees and makes a brief swing to the left (southwest) and soon starts a gradual climb. The trail steepens at mile 0.8 and follows switchbacks to the northwest. You will pass above timberline at mile 1.1 as the trail briefly arcs back to the southeast. It then continues west to meet the Divide ridge, which it follows south to an intersection with Trail #707 at mile 2.0. Ignore this and continue along the Divide to the west and south.

Expansive views open to the south of the Prospect Creek drainage, and the crags of Summit Peak loom farther away, over the horizon. As the trail makes a wide swing to the left (south), there is a small pond on the right at mile 2.5 (12,120). A sign announces "National Forest Wilderness" 0.2 mile beyond this, even though you will not enter the South San Juan Wilderness for a few more miles.

A clear tread continues behind the sign to the southwest, but the CDT follows Trail #813 past posts just east of south (left) across a shallow saddle. At a cairn at mile 2.8, follow a very faint trail south to where the trace of a trail contours up a hill. The trail bends back to the right (southwest) at mile 3.1 (12,200). Climb on a gentle slope almost due southwest toward Point 12,866, the high, green-sloped peak just ahead. As the trail flattens at mile 3.4, look for a post to the west-southwest and continue in that direction via cairns and posts. As you near the steeper slopes of Point 12,866 at mile 3.7, the trail breaks to the left (south) to climb south-southeast along the lower tier of those slopes and tops out at mile 4.1 (12,480). Turn south-southwest and descend along the point's south side. If you look just west of south, you can see the imposing gray mass of Montezuma Peak. In the foreground between you and the peak is something that looks like a gigantic sand bunker on a golf course. As the trail disappears here, strike a course for the high ground on the other side of this feature. Follow some dilapidated cairns, cross a stream at mile 4.3, and follow the trail's turn to the left (south) around the back of the bunker at mile 4.6. Climb toward a cairn and crest the ridge at mile 4.7 (12,445). As the trail once again disappears, descend due south on a gentle slope via cairns to a post where a faint tread leads to the bottom of a shallow valley (mile 4.9, 12,290). Walk to the right (west) edge of a saddle here for a rare view of a massive expanse of talus above scenic Crater Lake.

Follow more cairns uphill, just west of south, to where the trail vanishes at mile 5.1. Turn more to the right (southwest), toward the rocky summit of Montezuma Peak, and continue in that direction until you meet a very faint tread marked by frequent cairns and posts. Turn left (just east of south) and follow the trail up a hill. It crests a ridge at mile 5.4 (12,660) and then turns right (southwest) to run along the right (north) side of a shallow gully. Obscure cairns lead 0.2 mile to an easy trail over gentle tundra south of Montezuma Peak. From here, you will follow the CDT all the way around the edge of the massive cirque before you and pass under Summit Peak, which now dominates the southern horizon. But first, as you near a low saddle on Montezuma Peak's southwest side, you will reach a trail fork at mile 6.2. Take the high fork toward the saddle.

N **NORTHBOUND HIKERS:** A similar fork in the trail near the saddle may confuse northbound hikers. Take the lower fork toward the narrow band of talus coming down off Montezuma Peak.

The trail brushes the saddle at mile 6.4 (12,600) and turns left to track southward toward magnificent Summit Peak. In 0.1 mile an inconspicuous sign announces your entry into the South San Juan Wilderness.

WILDERNESS ALERT:

The South San Juan Wilderness was designated in 1980 by federal law to be "an area where the earth and its community of life are untrammeled by man, where man himself is a visitor who does not remain." It contains 158,790 acres of what may be the wildest land in the state. Please remember these rules governing wilderness areas:

1. Camp out of sight, at least 200 feet from lakes and streams, on dry, durable surfaces.

2. Use a stove instead of building a fire; use existing fire rings if you must have a fire.

3. Keep water sources pure by washing at least 200 feet from them. 4. Bury human waste six inches deep and 200 feet from lakes and streams. Pack out toilet paper.

5. Hobble or picket livestock at least 200 feet from lakes and streams, and use only treated, weed-free feed and grain. 6. All dogs must be on a leash. 7. No mountain biking. 8. Pack out all trash. Don't attempt to burn it.

A saddle at mile 7.1 (12,540) offers fantastic views in all directions, including the crags in the western end of the Weminuche Wilderness, far off to the northwest. You may think a drop of pure blue sky has fallen to earth at mile 7.4, but that's just a pond situated squarely on the Divide. Just after the pond, there are several treads traversing up the small hill in front of you; stay high as you come around the corner and you will spot the clear trail curving to the left (east) above and behind a small lake. The trail traverses the very rocky north flank of Summit Peak and reaches the east side of the mountain at mile 8.2 (12,600), where it bends to the right (south) and fades in the grass. Continue by climbing slightly up the side of the ridge past cairns to where a prominent trail approaches from the left (northeast). Ignore this trail and continue south along the CDT 0.2 mile to where the two trails intersect on a flat bench southeast of Summit Peak.

You may notice large cairns a short distance away on both sides of the trail. Ignore them and continue south-southwest (compass bearing approximately 200°) along a faint tread toward the lone, craggy chunk of rock peeking over the horizon. There are a number of places to camp here if you don't mind a little exposure to the elements. At mile 9.1, a barely discernible tread bends left (east) to skirt a low ridge, curves back to the right at mile 9.3, and disappears between two hills. Continue to the southwest on a faint tread as the deep valley of the Adams Fork River comes into view to the left (southeast). The trail improves as it descends gradually to the head of the valley and reaches some willows at mile 10.0 (12,100). When you exit the willows in 80 yards, there are two immediate 180-degree switchbacks that drop you into the Adams Fork valley, which you will follow to the east for the next 2.0 miles.

You can see the volcanic history of this area in the banks of the river and the walls of the valley, where the slow work of erosion has exposed the ancient lava.

Cross a stream at mile 11.3 (11,500) to a post that says 813. Forty-five yards past this post, look for a cairn on the right (south) side of the trail that indicates an obscure turnoff onto an invisible trail. If you miss this turn, you will continue to descend gradually toward Platoro Reservoir along the north side of the Adams Fork River.

From the cairn, look southeast (compass bearing 150°) for a clear trail cut on the bank of the main stream. Descend to that point by following cairns, cross to the south side of the stream, and walk east on the trail through willows and sparse spruce trees. There are some nice camp spots here. The trail is occasionally obscure; watch for it to break away from the water in a short distance and traverse up through the trees to reach a saddle at mile 12.1 (11,309).

The CDT climbs slightly from the saddle and enters a massive avalanche slide path at mile 12.5. Note the evidence of the fury of an avalanche: sparse, immature trees; branches completely stripped from the uphill sides of the trees; and the remnants of larger trees decapitated by the rushing snow. The trail is gentle until mile 13.2 (11,620), where a series of switchbacks leads up a very steep slope. You will reach the top of the steep part at mile 13.9 (11,930). Follow the flat top of the ridge east for a short distance until the CDT makes an important switchback 180 degrees to the right (southwest). A gradual climb over numerous springs and streams ensues and culminates in a saddle on the Divide at mile 15.1 (12,010). The views of the Rio Blanco valley to the west are astounding. Note the rounded bottom of the valley, evidence of the glaciers that sculpted this land more than 10,000 years ago.

Traverse to another Divide crossing through a saddle at mile 15.5 (11,860). Now the CDT tracks south high above the valley of the Conejos River North Fork. At mile 16.2, begin a gradual descent. As the trail curves right (southwest) into the main cirque of this drainage, look across the valley to the broad, rocky north slopes of Point 12,641. The CDT switchbacks up along the dark water mark in the middle of the face and passes over the shoulder to the left (east) of the summit.

The trail crosses a stream at mile 17.3 (11,520) and disappears in a grassy meadow. Continue east of south to where the trail resumes in about 100 yards. Cross the main stream in this cirque at mile 17.5 on several precarious stepping stones, climb out of the streambed, and make a right turn to continue the southerly trend. A sign at mile 17.8 lets you know you are still on Trail #813 while several other signs indicate a trail intersection. Continue on the CDT as it begins a brisk climb to the east, then south. A cairn at mile 18.8 (12,140) marks the end of the climb.

Now the trail rolls over a high, broad plateau to the southeast. At mile 18.9, follow cairns around the left (east) side of a marshy area. A short distance ahead, a prominent trail forks off to the left while the fainter CDT, marked by a cairn, continues to the right (south). Just after some ponds at mile 19.3, large cairns guide you through an obscure section. Follow the trail over the southeast ridge of Point 12,641 at mile 19.6 (12,200) and into a sharp turn to the right (south). Now you can see Gunsight Pass to the southwest, an obvious low point in the toothy range of unnamed peaks that ring the broad drainage of the Conejos River Middle Fork.

In another 0.2 mile, the trail completes its swing to the right and descends to the head of the valley far to the west. It bends to the left (south) at mile 20.5 (11,360) and disappears in a grassy area but is well-marked by cairns and posts. Cross a stream, exit the other side of the grassy valley, and pick up a faint tread that leads to the east. You'll see a pretty waterfall at mile 20.8. The trail hovers at about the same elevation until mile 21.5 (11,320) where it veers right (south), enters the trees, and climbs slightly. At mile 21.9, the trail crosses a deep streambed and curves back to the northeast. From here, cairns lead you through a seemingly relentless climb.

At mile 23.4 (12,090), the trail tops out next to a large depression that holds snow well into late season. It exits the depression trending north of east, crosses over a small ridge, and descends east along the ridge. Be alert for cairns when the tread occasionally disappears in meadows. At mile 24.4, the trail comes out above an idyllic lake at the head of the Navajo River and swings left (north) to traverse a very steep slope.

The terrain flattens at mile 24.6 (11,540) as you turn right (east) to follow the Divide across a narrow ridge with expansive views on both sides. After passing an exquisite pond at mile 24.8, the trail reaches a very large, flat meadow at mile 25.6 (11,580) and turns right (south) to follow cairns. After the intersection with the trail to Fish Lake at mile 25.7, a very clear trail meanders south and southeast. A little climb starts at mile 25.9 and tops out in a flat area at mile 26.3 (11,700). The trail turns left (east) for 0.1 mile and then bends back to the right (south) as scenic Blue Lake comes into view. You will reach the lake at mile 26.7 (11,480). Turn right and follow the trail around the lake's west side to a trail fork and an old kiln at the south end of the lake (mile 27.1; 11,480 feet; N37° 14.30', W106° 37.70'). This is the end of the segment. You'll find a developed camping area between the two forks.

    To continue on the CDT, take the right (west) fork. When the trail disappears in a meadow, continue straight across to the south 80 yards to an intersecting trail. Turn right (southwest) and continue on a clear tread.

OTHER HIKES AND RIDES

BLUE LAKE LOOP

Approximate loop distance: 31 miles
Mode of Travel: Hiking
Difficulty: Moderate

Three Forks Trailhead: See *Access* for the next segment.
Adams Fork Trailhead: Follow the directions to the Conejos River Trailhead, but instead of turning left at the 4-mile point on Forest Route 247, turn right and continue 1.0 mile to where the trail departs to the southwest on the outside of a broad, 180-degree turn to the right.

    This hike will give you some incredible views of the Divide country here, some of which is so remote it may still conceal grizzly bears. Not to worry—they are so shy, there have been no confirmed sightings since 1979, and that was very deep in the wilderness. Be sure to look down into the awesome Navajo River valley from just above Blue Lake.

    The stretch of CDT you will be hiking here runs from mile 11.3 to 27.1 (southbound). It is about 7 miles from the CDT to the trailhead along the Adams Fork River stretch, and 5.5 miles from Blue Lake to the trailhead on the Conejos River. The two trailheads are 3 miles apart, so you can use one car and make this a loop without adding much extra walking.

    The CDT section is almost entirely above timberline, so great views—and lightning danger—are everywhere. Water is plentiful. Don't forget this is in the South San Juan Wilderness, where special restrictions apply (see this segment, page 309).

ELWOOD PASS MOUNTAIN BIKING
Approximate distance: Variable
Mode of Travel: Biking
Difficulty: Moderate

To ride among the quiet meadows of the Divide, take your bike and follow the directions for either route to Elwood Pass described in *Access* for this segment. Make it into a shuttle or a loop by riding all the way over the pass and using scenic US-160 over Wolf Creek Pass as a connector between the two routes. This is all open to motorized vehicles as well.

There is plenty of room for improvisation and exploration as well. You might try Forest Trail #571 up Quartz Creek, south of East Fork Road; or take Forest Route 380 through rolling alpine tundra beneath the Divide south of Elwood Pass.

DO GRIZZLY BEARS STILL ROAM SOUTHERN COLORADO?

Late in 1952, just as the colorful activity of a Colorado summer was giving way to the deadly chill of the approaching winter, a large predator killed 35 sheep near the Continental Divide in what is now the Weminuche Wilderness. The supposed culprit, a female grizzly bear, was promptly trapped, pursued over five miles of rough mountain terrain (while dragging a leg-hold trap attached to a solid eight-foot by one-foot-diameter spruce log), and shot. After a tragic history that began in 1821 with the first grizzly killed by a white man, and after thousands more met a similar fate, the last grizzly bear in Colorado was gone, according to the Division of Wildlife.

Or was it? In 1979, a guide named Ed Wiseman was out with a client hunting elk with bow and arrow in the remote country near the headwaters of the Navajo River, near what is now the South San Juan Wilderness. Wiseman was attacked by a grizzly bear after his client, exploring nearby, spooked the animal, sending it loping off in Wiseman's direction. In the course of suffering a shattered leg, serious injuries to his other three limbs, a crushed shoulder, and 77 separate wounds requiring numerous stitches, the man was lucky enough to reach one of his arrows and jab it into the chest of the great animal, which died a short time later. And so it was, in an inauspicious wrestling match with an elk hunter, that the last grizzly disappeared from the Colorado landscape.

Or did it? In the years since the Wiseman incident, more and more evidence supports the theory of many naturalists and bear experts that the grizzly still roams the remote wilds of the South San Juan Wilderness. Large samples of dung, chunks of soil scraped in massive, solid pieces from the ground, the discovery of telltale hair, and some very credible sightings all hearten wilderness advocates who would love to prove conclusively that grizzlies are still hiding out in the dark secret places of the Colorado wilds.

As David Petersen points out in a well-reasoned argument in his book, *Ghost Grizzlies*, the chances of a human dying at the claws of a Colorado grizzly are statistically almost nil. Any bear that came into contact with humans during the last 175 years was likely to be killed, so natural selection has favored those whose instinct it was to avoid humans. Any remaining Colorado grizzlies are of a gene pool propagated by a population of creatures that run the other way when they hear, smell, or see *Homo sapiens*.

So, while hiking in bear country, it's still a good idea to hang your food and avoid taking anything into your tent that might attract a hungry critter, not only because of the possible presence of grizzlies, but also because of the widespread presence of black bear, Colorado's other ursine inhabitant. And, of course, be sure to keep a camera handy. You could be the person to settle the grizzly bear mystery once and for all.

Blue Lake, South San Juan Wilderness

Segment 43
Blue Lake to Cumbres Pass

Conejos Peak, South San Juan Wilderness

30.1 miles
Difficulty: Moderate

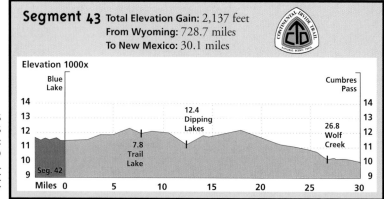

Segment 43 Total Elevation Gain: 2,137 feet
From Wyoming: 728.7 miles
To New Mexico: 30.1 miles

THIS
SEGMENT IS
OPEN TO:
FOOT AND
ANIMAL
TRAFFIC
ONLY

Elevation 1000x

Blue Lake — Cumbres Pass

12.4 Dipping Lakes

26.8 Wolf Creek

7.8 Trail Lake

Seg. 42

Miles 0   5   10   15   20   25   30

THROUGH-HIKERS might experience mixed emotions when they hike this segment of Colorado's Continental Divide Trail. For scenery, this area does not disappoint. The views are frequent and sublime, and the South San Juan Wilderness is quiet and remote. But it is the last segment in the state, and any enthusiasm for the scenery may be tempered by the reality that this journey is almost over.

The land here is different from anywhere else on Colorado's CDT. Much of the trail is on expansive, flat ridges, yet stunning canyons open up from the forested lands below. Huge rocks and boulders strewn over the high ridges are reminders of a more violent epoch, but now they stand like silent sentinels watching over dozens of still lakes and ponds sparkling along the Divide. The land is a blend of Colorado's mountains and New Mexico's mesas and canyons, a gentle transition to the next distinct section of this National Scenic Trail.

This stretch of the CDT passes through the heart of the South San Juan Wilderness, widely regarded as Colorado's wildest corner. If grizzly bears still live in Colorado, this is the place they call home. Evidence suggests that the great bears do still roam the remote reaches of these thick forests, but they are shy and avoid humans. None have been seen near what is now the CDT since one was killed along El Rito Azul, near Blue Lake, in 1951. (A grizzly was killed by a hunter in this wilderness area in 1979, but that was deep in the wilderness, far from the trail.)

Water on this segment is plentiful except from mile 14.8 to 26.8. You can still find water some distance off the trail; consult the maps, which accurately depict the ponds and streams here.

MOUNTAIN BIKE NOTES: This segment lies almost entirely within the South San Juan Wilderness where mountain bikes are prohibited.

MAPS

TRAILS ILLUSTRATED: 142
USGS QUADRANGLES: Elephant Head Rock, Victoria Lake, Archuleta Creek, Cumbres Pass
USFS: Rio Grande National Forest, San Juan National Forest, pages 322–323

ACCESS

Distance from graded road	🚗 6.0 miles	+	🚶 5.5 miles

THREE FORKS TRAILHEAD TO BLUE LAKE: From the town of Monte Vista on US-285, drive south on Colorado Highway 15 approximately 16 miles to a turnoff on the right (west) that is marked by a sign for Platoro. Follow this winding

Here I am,

safely returned

over those peaks

from a journey

far more beautiful

and strange

than anything

I had hoped for

or imagined—

how is it that

this safe return

brings such regret?

—Peter Matthiessen

RANGER DISTRICT:
Conejos Peak

road (Forest Route 250) 32 miles to a right (west) turn onto Forest Route 247. Continue another 4 miles to a fork and bear left, staying near Platoro Reservoir on Forest Route 247. The road dead ends in the parking lot in 2 miles. The trailhead is at the south end of the lot.

Follow an easy trail up the Conejos River. After about 2.0 miles, don't miss a left (south) turn onto a side trail that climbs along El Rito Azul an additional 3.5 miles to Blue Lake. The trail forks near Blue Lake; a left turn will have you heading southbound on the CDT, and a right turn will start you northbound. The camping area mentioned in the trail description for the last segment is a short distance ahead, between the two forks. The trailhead and the first part of this access hike appear on the USGS Platoro quadrangle.

CUMBRES PASS: The pass is about 8 miles northeast of Chama, New Mexico, on Colorado Highway 17. From the town of Antonito, Colorado, on US-285, drive west on Colorado Highway 17. You'll find a parking area about 0.1 mile west of the pass summit on the south side of the highway. The trail starts inconspicuously across the highway, on the north side. There is a sign about 20 yards up the trail that says "813."

Smooth road to trailhead

SUPPLIES, SERVICES, AND ACCOMMODATIONS

CHAMA, NEW MEXICO, is about 8 miles southwest on Colorado Highway 17. Most services are available there.

ZIP CODE: 87520

DISTANCE FROM TRAIL: 8 miles

Bank	Sunwest Bank, 541 Terrace Ave.	(505) 756-2111
Bus	None	
Camping	Twin Rivers Campground (near supermarket)	756-2218
Dining	Viva Vera's Mexican Kitchen, 2202 Hwy. 17 at the "Y"	756-2557
	Branding Iron Restaurant, 1511 W. Main St.	756-9195
Gear	Dark Timber, 2242 Main St.	756-2300
Groceries	Chama Valley Supermarket, Hwy. 84 and Hwy. 17, at the "Y"	756-2545
Information	Chama Valley Chamber of Commerce, 499 Main St.	756-2306
Laundry	Speed Queen Laundry, Pine St.	756-2479
Lodging	Branding Iron Motel, 1511 W. Main St.	756-2162
	River Bend Lodge, Rt. 1	756-2264
Medical	Dunham Clinic, 211 Pine St.	756-2143
Post Office	5th and Maple	756-2240
Showers	Twin Rivers Campground (near supermarket)	756-2218

SPECIAL NOTES: To celebrate your arrival in New Mexico, treat yourself to a massage at InnerGlow Bodywork in the Jones Carriage House, 311½ Terrace Avenue, 756-2908. Or enjoy a breathtaking train ride back across the Divide at Cumbres Pass on the Cumbres & Toltec Scenic Railroad, the country's longest and highest narrow gauge steam railroad. Call 756-2151.

TRAIL DESCRIPTION From the trail sign near the kiln, take the right fork. After only 40 yards, the trail disappears in a meadow. Continue across it to the south 80 yards until you intersect a very clear trail and turn right (southwest). The CDT now trends west and south to bypass some marshes and ponds and then turns east-southeast at mile 0.3. Cross El Rito Azul at mile 0.7. At mile 1.0, you will come out above the impressive valley of the Conejos River South Fork on the left (east). A clear, flat trail trends southeast.

After the deep forest canyon of the Conejos River South Fork fades from view, a grassy, marshy, and nearly flat valley appears near the trail on the left at mile 1.7 (11,580). This valley runs north-south, roughly parallel to your path, as it rises inconspicuously just ahead of you to cross the Continental Divide, which crosses the valley at right angles. If you look hard, you can see a faint trail cutting across the valley from west to east and climbing into the trees on the opposing slope. That trail is the CDT.

 About 0.1 mile after the valley comes into view, be on the lookout for a faint trail branching off to the left (southeast) and descending toward the valley. This side trail is very obscure and almost invisible for the first 50 yards. If you make the correct turn, the tread becomes very clear, and you will soon see a cairn with a post sticking out of it a few hundred yards ahead to the southeast. It is counterintuitive to leave the very clear tread of the original trail, especially since it is also marked by cairns. Should you stay on it and miss the turnoff, don't be alarmed—you still have several opportunities to regain the CDT. The first of these is at a small stream crossing 100 to 150 yards past the original turnoff. Look down the hill along the stream (northeast) and spot a faint tread and the cairns of the CDT.

If you miss this one as well, you will soon see cairns down the slopes to your left (east). Make your way back to an established tread and head for those cairns.

Finally, if you still haven't made it, the trail you are on will soon disappear after a short, steep climb. From there, turn left (east) and look for a trail on the slopes of the opposite ridge. Walk to that trail and you will be back on the CDT.

A short, gentle climb into the middle of the meadow ends at mile 2.3 (11,560 feet; N37° 13.26', W106° 36.60'). After a 20-yard dip in the terrain, the trail resumes climbing to the southeast up the east ridge of the valley. At mile 2.5, the trail passes a sign for Blue and Green Lakes. It tops out at mile 3.7 (11,880) and levels off on top of the ridge near several ponds.

At mile 4.8, the CDT begins a moderate, short climb toward the top of the mesa-like hump straight ahead (south), which is Point 12,244. At mile 5.0, on one last flat spot before the climb, you will reach a sign for Cañon Verde and South Fork Conejos to the southeast. Although a clear tread continues in that direction, ignore it, walk south (right) to two signs nailed to a tree about 30 yards distant, and follow the sign for Trail Lake. A line of inconspicuous cairns lead west of south to the west side (right) of the base of a steeper slope. At mile 5.2, find a faint trail that climbs through krummholz and past the steep and rocky west side of Point 12,244. Cairns mark the way to a very large depression that holds snow through the summer in normal snow years. The CDT exits this depression at mile 5.7 and continues a gradual climb south toward Point 12,371. After passing a small pond that is not on the maps, the trail swings left (east of south) and tops out in a shallow low point on the horizon (mile 6.7; 12,300 feet).

A slight descent leads toward Trail Lake, which comes into view at mile 7.5. You will reach the lake 0.3 mile later (11,980) on its northwest side and then immediately climb away to the southeast. The rolling, green tundra and long, narrow lake are reminiscent of Scotland. You will reach a triangular intersection very near the lake. Walk about 100 yards just north of east past a small pond to a sign for Dipping Lakes and Laguna Venada at mile 8.0. Turn right (south) toward Dipping Lakes and follow cairns over the indistinct terrain.

Around mile 9.0, you will see two high ridges separated by a long saddle on the right (west) side of the trail. This is the last view of the Continental Divide in Colorado. It runs along the tops of the two ridges to the summit of the second one, which is distinguished by a band of cliffs, and then it veers straight away from the CDT to the west.

The trail begins a barely perceptible descent here. Ignore the line of large cairns off to the left (east). At mile 10.0, you can see steeper terrain on the left side of the trail and the long, wooded valley of Elk Creek. The trail curves around the top of the cliffs and heads for a more moderate slope before a sustained descent starts around mile 10.9 (11,900). Soon you will see Dipping Lakes in the forest below. The trail reaches the first of these lakes at mile 12.4 (11,220) and soon passes a heavily used campsite. The trail is a little obscure here, but just continue over the barren ground to the continuation of the trail on the other side. After it passes the second lake, the CDT begins a climb to the east.

At mile 13.3, the trail virtually disappears as it emerges from the trees. Follow a very faint tread across a large meadow to the northeast. At the far side of the meadow, a small cairn marks the trail's continuation through some trees on a tread that is easy to see. Continue 0.1 mile into another meadow, where the trail makes a sudden 90-degree turn to the right (south). Walk 20 yards to the edge of the trees and make another 90-degree turn to the left. Continue uphill to the east and pick up a clear trail switchbacking up through the trees and into a large area of boulders. After some steep climbing, the CDT tops out on a wide, flat plateau at mile 13.9 (11,800). Cairns and a faint tread lead southeast.

At mile 14.8, the trail passes to the right (west) of a small rise in the land and reaches a meadow a short distance later. The trail vanishes here, but you can continue straight into the meadow and follow sparse cairns south-southeast toward the left end of a gently sloping ridge that constitutes the southern horizon in front of you. Follow cairns into krummholz on the left (east). A trail materializes here at mile 16.4 bearing due south and disappearing again in 0.2 mile as it climbs a short, rocky ridge. Turn right (south) at the top of the ridge and follow some cairns that soon vanish. Continue a gentle climb up the hill tracking just east of south (approximate compass bearing 170°). You're heading for the highest point in this area, so as long as you keep climbing until you can't climb anymore, you will be on-track. Cairns and a faint tread reappear at mile 17.6 and guide you to a cairn and a post at mile 17.9 (12,187) that mark the summit of Flat Peak.

Follow a much steeper descent off the other side of the point on a clear tread. The trail remains atop this ridge for most of the next 4.5 miles. At mile 21.0, there is a post with "Cont Div Tr" etched into it, followed by a fork in the trail a short distance later. Take the right (west) fork and climb on a clear trail to a saddle at mile 21.5 (11,360). Turn right (west) and follow a clear tread contouring across a steep slope.

This trail is not shown on the 1984 USGS Archuleta Creek quadrangle. The trail follows switchbacks down the hill and then strikes an even contour to the south. As you make a bend to the right (southeast) at mile 22.3, you can see Chama to the south, along with what seems like most of New Mexico.

At a sign for the CDT at mile 23.4 (11,090 feet; N37° 01.99', W106° 30.27'), the trail bends left (southeast, then northeast) for a short distance, enters some trees, and winds to a post in a meadow at mile 23.8 where it promptly disappears. Walk to another post across the meadow just east of south and pick up a clear tread again.

The CDT passes onto the 1967 USGS Cumbres quadrangle in this area. The trail is incorrectly depicted and labeled on this map. For a more accurate representation, see Trails Illustrated map #142 or the Rio Grande National Forest map put out by the Forest Service.

Follow the trail into the trees to the southeast and avoid another trail that heads off to the northeast (left). At mile 24.8, the CDT leaves a fenced-in private property boundary that it has been paralleling and turns left (east) to descend along a ridge. A switchback to the southwest at mile 25.6 begins a meandering descent that generally trends to the east. You will cross Wolf Creek at mile 26.8 (10,220). A very clear tread continues toward Cumbres Pass. A nice view of the pass and the idyllic green valley to its west open before you at mile 29.2 (10,070). The trail descends to and flattens in a meadow at mile 29.6, passes through some trees to the southeast, and turns left (northeast) at some railroad tracks at mile 29.9. You will reach the road a few paces later at a post that proclaims "Cont Div Tr 813."

N **NORTHBOUND HIKERS** Just after passing under a railroad trestle at this point, northbound hikers will see a faded sign on the right side of the road that says "CDNST" pointing to the trail turnoff on the left (southwest).

Turn right (southeast) onto the road, pass under a railroad trestle, and reach a cul-de-sac in less than 0.1 mile. Follow a footpath toward the highway to the left (east). You will descend to reach the highway a few yards later.

N **NORTHBOUND HIKERS:** can confirm they are on the right path here when they pass a post that says "813" about 20 yards from the highway.

Cross the highway to a pullout on its southeast side. This is the end of the segment (mile 30.1; 10,002 feet; N37° 01.31', W106° 26.90'). A trail continues south from here about 1.5 miles to the New Mexico border where it promptly disappears. The actual CDT follows the course of the highway to Chama, New Mexico.

OTHER HIKES

SOUTH FORK – CAÑON VERDE LOOP
Approximate loop distance: 30 miles
Difficulty: Moderate

Three Forks Trailhead: See *Access* for this segment.

This trailhead presents many possibilities for exploring the rugged land of the South San Juan Wilderness and the Continental Divide Trail. Follow the directions to Blue Lake in *Access* for this segment, but turn east just before the lake and follow the trail down the unique forest canyon of the Conejos River South Fork. At the confluence with Cañon Verde, turn south and hike up a rugged canyon featuring waterfalls along the way. You can camp at Green Lake. Continue to the CDT, follow it north to Blue Lake, and hike back to the trailhead.

You'll spot an impressive waterfall along the Conejos River Middle Fork. Hike up this trail by avoiding the left turn at mile 2.0. Continue to the CDT, turn south, and head for Blue Lake. The views into the valley of the Navajo River from above Blue Lake are some of the best in the state. Hike back to the car from Blue Lake, or use the many other trails here for an extended stay in the backcountry.

Note that hiking in the South San Juan Wilderness is governed by special rules. Please see Segment 42, page 309, for a review.

CONEJOS PEAK
Approximate one-way distance: 9 miles
Difficulty: Strenuous

South Fork Conejos River Trailhead: Follow the directions in *Access* for this segment toward the Three Forks Trailhead, but continue south on Forest Route 250 instead of turning onto Forest Route 247. Continue roughly 15 miles to the trailhead, which is on the west side of the road.

Conejos Peak climbs to an elevation of 13,172 feet and offers a spectacular overview of a large portion of the wilderness area. Much of the hike is well above timberline on a seriously exposed ridge, so plan your hiking around the weather. You can tie this hike into the one for Cañon Verde (above) and create a long, multi-day experience.

Tom Jones at Cumbres Pass

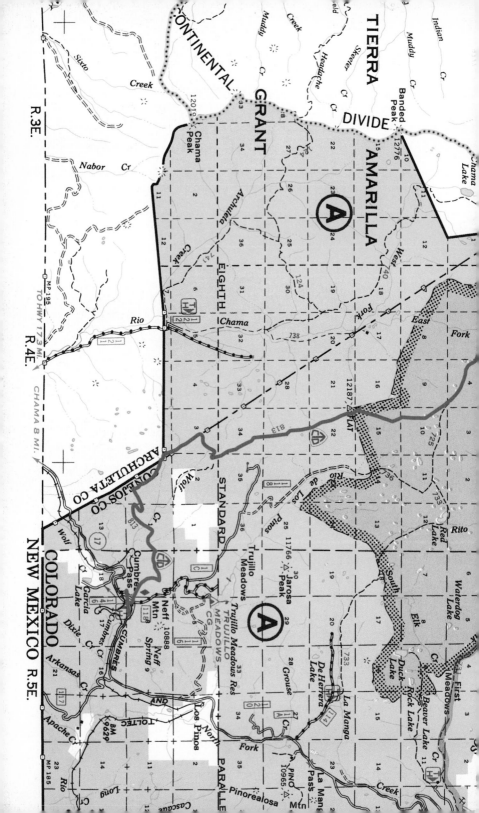

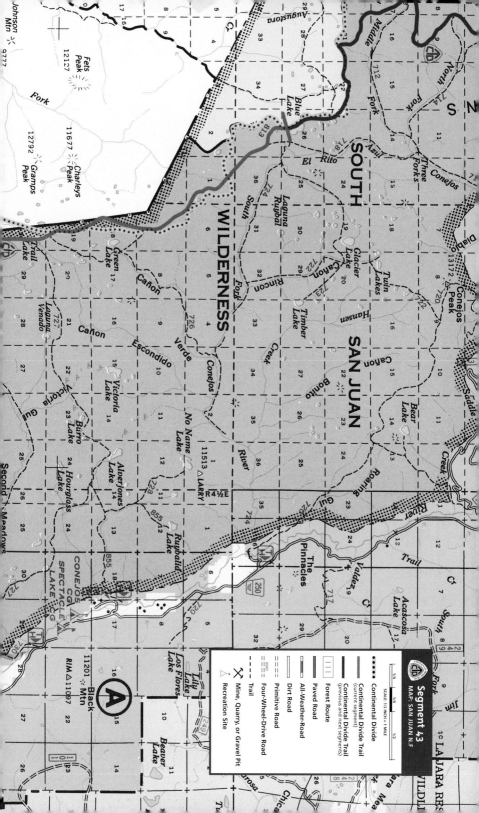

SCALE 1/2 INCH = 1 MILE

1/4		1/4	1/2

Continental Divide
Continental Divide Trail
(current segment)
Continental Divide Trail
(previous and next segments)
Forest Route
Continental Divide
Paved Road
All-Weather-Road
Dirt Road
Primitive Road
Four-Wheel-Drive Road
Trail
Mine, Quarry, or Gravel Pit
Recreation Site

Appendix A: U.S. Forest Service Ranger Districts

MEDICINE BOW NATIONAL FOREST (WY)
Hayden Ranger District
204 West 9th Street
P.O. Box 187
Encampment, WY 82325
(307) 327-5481

ROUTT NATIONAL FOREST
Hahns Peak Ranger District
57 10th Street
P.O. Box 1212
Steamboat Springs, CO 80477
(970) 879-1870

Parks Ranger District
2095 6th Street
P.O. Box 1210
Kremmling, CO 80459
(970) 724-9004

ARAPAHO NATIONAL FOREST
Sulphur Ranger District
62429 Highway 40
P.O. Box 10
Granby, CO 80446
(970) 887-3904

Clear Creek Ranger District
101 Chicago Creek
P.O. Box 3307
Idaho Springs, CO 80452
(303) 567-2273

PIKE NATIONAL FOREST
South Platte Ranger District
19316 Goddard Ranch Court
Morrison, CO 80465
(303) 697-0414

WHITE RIVER NATIONAL FOREST
Dillon Ranger District
135 Highway 9 (Blue River Center)
P.O. Box 620
Silverthorne, CO 80498
(970) 468-5400

Holy Cross Ranger District
401 Main Street
P.O. Box 190
Minturn, CO 81645
(970) 827-5715

SAN ISABEL NATIONAL FOREST
Leadville Ranger District
2015 North Poplar
Leadville, CO 80461
(719) 486-0749

Salida Ranger District
325 W. Rainbow Blvd.
Salida, CO 81201
(719) 539-3591

GUNNISON NATIONAL FOREST
Taylor River – Cebolla Ranger District
216 North Colorado
Gunnison, CO 81230
(970) 641-0471

RIO GRANDE NATIONAL FOREST
Divide Ranger District
13308 West Highway 160
Del Norte, CO 81132
(719) 657-3321

Saguache Ranger District
P.O. Box 67
Saguache, CO 81149
(719) 655-2547

Conejos Peak Ranger District
P.O. Box 420
La Jara, CO 81140
(719) 274-5193

SAN JUAN NATIONAL FOREST
Columbine Ranger District
367 S. Pearl Street
P.O. Box 439
Bayfield, CO 81122
(970) 884-2512

Pagosa Ranger District
2nd and Pagosa
P.O. Box 310
Pagosa Springs, CO 81147
(970) 264-2268

Vestal and Arrow Peaks loom above the Divide, Weminuche Wilderness

Appendix B: Equipment Checklist

ALWAYS CARRY THE TEN ESSENTIALS
matches and lighter
knife
emergency shelter
(tarp or ground cloth)
food and water
mirror or whistle for signaling
extra clothes
headlamp or flashlight
with extra batteries
compass and maps
first aid kit
sunglasses and sunscreen

**CONSIDER ADDING THESE ITEMS
FOR DAY HIKES**
daypack
moleskin
insect repellent
cord or rope
trowel for catholes
lightweight hat and gloves
extra socks
insulating layer top and bottom
(fleece, wool, etc.)
rain gear
camera and film

FOR OVERNIGHT OR THROUGH-HIKES
sleeping bag
insulating ground pad
pillow
tent or shelter
groundcloth
stove, fuel, and eating/cooking utensils
extra bags for garbage,
leftover food, etc.
food bags (for hanging)
extra clothing
long underwear
light shoes for around camp
water filter or iodine tablets
toiletries and personal hygiene kit
sewing kit
repair kits for tent, stove,
water filter, etc.
pack cover

OPTIONAL
water bag
chair
journal
reading material
watch
fishing gear
binoculars
candle lantern
walking stick
radio
kitchen sink

Appendix C: Map Sources

TRAILS ILLUSTRATED
P.O. Box 3610
Evergreen, CO 80439
(800) 962-1643

UNITED STATES GEOLOGICAL SURVEY
Denver Federal Center
P.O. Box 25286
Lakewood, CO 80225
(303) 202-4700

DELORME MAPPING
Colorado Atlas and Gazetteer
P.O. Box 298
Freeport, ME 04032
(207) 865-4171

SHEARER PUBLISHERS
The Roads of Colorado
406 Post Oak Road
Fredericksburg, TX 78624
(800) 458-3808

Forest Service maps are available at the district offices throughout Colorado. Contact one of the districts listed in Appendix A, page 325, for more information.

Appendix D: Conservation and Trail Advocacy Groups

COLORADO
ENVIRONMENTAL COALITION
777 Grant Street, Suite 606
Denver, CO 80203
(303) 837-8701

COLORADO MOUNTAIN CLUB
710 10th Street, #200
Golden, CO 80401
(303) 279-9690

COLORADO WILDLIFE FEDERATION
7475 Dakin Street
Westminster, CO 80210
(303) 429-4500

CONTINENTAL DIVIDE
TRAIL ALLIANCE
P.O. Box 628
Pine, CO 80470
(303) 838-3760

CONTINENTAL DIVIDE TRAIL SOCIETY
3704 N. Charles St. #601
Baltimore, MD 21218
(410) 235-9610

NATIONAL FOREST FOUNDATION
1099 14th Street NW, Suite #5600W
Washington, DC 20005-3402
(202) 501-2473

SIERRA CLUB
Regional Office
2037 10th Street
Boulder, CO 80302
(303) 449-5595

TROUT UNLIMITED
655 Broadway Street #475
Denver, CO 80203
(303) 595-0620

THE WILDERNESS SOCIETY
7475 Dakin Street
Westminster, CO 80210
(303) 650-5818

Appendix E: Map Lists

TRAILS ILLUSTRATED MAPS
needed to through-hike Colorado's CDT
102
103
104
108
109
110
115
116
117
118
126
127
129
130
139
140
141
142
200

USGS MAPS
required for through-hikers

Wyoming Maps
Dudley Creek
Solomon Creek

Colorado Maps
Archuleta Creek
Baldy Cinco
Berthoud Pass
Bonanza
Boreas Pass
Bowen Mountain
Breckenridge
Buffalo Pass
Byers Peak
Chester
Cimarrona Peak
Cochetopa Park
Copper Mountain
Cumberland Pass
Cumbres
East Portal
Elephant Head Rock
Elk Park
Elwood Pass
Empire
Farwell Mtn.

Finger Mesa
Frisco
Garfield
Grand Lake
Granite
Granite Lake
Grays Peak
Halfmoon Pass
Homestake Reservoir
Howardsville
Hyannis Peak
Jack Creek Ranch
Jefferson
Keystone
Leadville North
Little Squaw Creek
Loveland Pass
Monarch Lake
Montezuma
Mount Elbert
Mount Ethel
Mount Evans
Mount Hope
Mount Massive
Mount Ouray
Mount Richthofen
Mount Werner
Mount Zirkel
North Pass

Pahlone Peak
Palomino Mountain
Pando
Parkview Mountain
Pole Creek Mountain
Rabbit Ears Peak
Radial Mountain
Rio Grande Pyramid
Saguache Park
San Luis Peak
Sargents Mesa
Shadow Mountain
Slumgullion Pass
South River Peak
Spicer Peak
St. Elmo
Storm King Peak
Strawberry Lake
Summit Peak
Tincup
Vail Pass
Victoria Lake
Weminuche Pass
West Baldy
West Fork Lake
Whiteley Peak
Winfield
Wolf Creek Pass

Appendix F: Other Reading and Bibliography

Abbott, Carl, et. al. *Colorado: A History of the Centennial State*. University Press of Colorado, Niwot, Colorado, 1994.

Anderson, Lenore and Litz, Brian. *Wilderness Ways*. Colorado Outward Bound School, Denver, Colorado, 1993.

Benedict, Audrey DeLella. *A Sierra Club Naturalist's Guide: The Southern Rockies: The Rocky Mountain Regions of Southern Wyoming, Colorado, and Northern New Mexico*. Sierra Club Books, San Francisco, 1991.

Berger, Karen and Smith, Daniel R. *Where the Waters Divide*. Harmony Books, New York, New York, 1993.

Borneman, Walter R., and Lampert, Lyndon J. *A Climbing Guide to Colorado's Fourteeners*. Pruett Press, Inc., Boulder, Colorado, 1994.

Bruce, Robert Keady. "History of the Medicine Bow National Forest, 1902–1910." Master's thesis, University of Wyoming, 1959.

Chronic, Halka. *Roadside Geology of Colorado*. Mountain Press Publishing Co., Missoula, Montana, 1980.

Donadio, Stephen, et. al., eds. *The New York Public Library Book of 20th-Century American Quotations*. Warner Books, New York, 1992.

Eberhart, Perry. *Guide to the Colorado Ghost Towns and Mining Camps*. Sage Books, Chicago, 1970.

Gebhardt, Dennis. *A Backpacking Guide to the Weminuche Wilderness*. Basin Reproduction and Printing Company, Durango, Colorado, 1976.

Gilliland, Mary Ellen. *Summit! A Goldrush History of Summit County, Colorado*. Alpenrose Press, Silverthorne, Colorado, 1980.

Gilliland, Mary Ellen. *The New Summit Hiker*. Alpenrose Press, Silverthorne, Colorado, 1995.

Helmuth, Ed and Helmuth, Gloria. *The Passes of Colorado: An Encyclopedia of Watershed Divides*. Pruett Press, Inc., Boulder, Colorado, 1994.

Jacobs, Randy. *The Colorado Trail: The Official Guidebook*. Westcliffe Publishers, Englewood, Colorado, 1994.

Jocknick, Sidney. *Early Days on the Western Slope of Colorado*. The Rio Grande Press, Inc., Glorieta, New Mexico, 1968.

Partnow, Elaine, ed. *The Quotable Woman*. Corwin Books, Los Angeles, 1977.

Paul, Rodman W. *The Far West and the Great Plains in Transition, 1859–1900*. Harper & Row, New York, 1988.

Pearson, Mark. *The Complete Guide to Colorado's Wilderness Areas*. Westcliffe Publishers, Englewood, Colorado, 1994.

Petersen, David. *Ghost Grizzlies*. Henry Holt and Company, New York, 1995.

Roach, Gerry. *Colorado's Fourteeners: From Hikes to Climbs*. Fulcrum Publishing, Golden, Colorado, 1996.

Roeder, Penny L. and Tillerson, Bob. *Weminuche Wilderness Primer*. Pagosa Chapter, San Juan National Forest Association, Pagosa Springs, Colorado, no copyright date given.

Rossetter, Laura. *The Mountain Bike Guide to Summit County, Colorado*. Sage Creek Press, Silverthorne, Colorado, 1989.

Ruhoff, Ron. *Colorado's Continental Divide: A Hiking and Backpacking Guide*. Cordillera Press, Inc., Evergreen, Colorado, 1989.

Sprague, Marshall. *The Great Gates: The Story of the Rocky Mountain Passes*. Little, Brown & Company, Toronto, 1964.

Tighe, Ronald. *Journey to the Top of the Divide*. Golden Bell Press, Denver, 1979. (Available at Bud Werner Memorial Library, 1289 Lincoln Ave., Steamboat Springs, Box 774568, 80477. 303-879-0240).

Tilton, Buck. *America's Wilderness: The Complete guide to More Than 600 National Wilderness Areas*. Foghorn Press, San Francisco, California, 1996.

Ubbelohde, Carl, et. al., eds. *A Colorado Reader*. Pruett Press, Inc., Boulder, Colorado, 1982.

Walker, Bryce S. *The Great Divide*. Time-Life Books, New York, New York, 1973.

The Merriam-Webster Dictionary of Quotations. Merriam-Webster, Inc., Springfield, Massachusetts, 1992.

The Continental Divide Trail Alliance
Protecting a Vital National Resource

How can you help?

By becoming a member of the Continental Divide Trail Alliance (CDTA). Your willingness to join thousands of concerned citizens across the country will make the difference. Together, we can provide the financial resources needed to complete the Trail.

CDTA is a non-profit membership organization formed to help protect, build, maintain, and manage the CDT. CDTA serves a broad-based constituency and includes people who enjoy recreating on public lands, as
well as those concerned about over-development.

As a CDTA member, you will:

- Protect a vital and precious natural resource
- Ensure Trail maintenance and completion
- Improve Trail access
- Support informational and educational programs
- Champion volunteer projects
- Advocate for policy issues that support the CDT

What does It Take to Help Us? Just One Cent A Mile

We realize there are a lot of demands on your time and budget. That's why we're only asking you to give a little—just one cent a mile to support the Trail. For a modest membership fee of $31, you will help us go so very far, and finish what was courageously started so long ago.

For more information
or to send your contribution, write to:
Continental Divide Trail Alliance
P.O. Box 628
Pine, CO 80470
Please make checks payable to CDTA.

Index

NOTE: Bold citations denote trail descriptions; citations followed by the letter "p" denote photos; citations followed by the letter "m" denote maps.

Acknowledgements

Special thanks to Loretta McGrath, whose support through the peaks and valleys has gone far beyond friendship.

Thanks to M. John Fayhee for his help and to John Fielder for his support and trust. Harlene Finn, Rebecca Finkel, Pat Shea, and Bonnie Beach made this book a reality in spite of numerous deadlines missed by the author.

I greatly appreciate the encouragement the following people have given me with respect to my writing: Mary Ellen Gilliland, Susan Metzger, Anthony Effinger, Peggy Hammes, Suzanne Noyes, Basia Kaczkowski, Donna Taylor, and Jane Stebbins.

Thanks to Currie Craven, Robert Ray, and Mark Minter for rides and re-supply. For great hiking companions, I highly recommend Staci Haines, Steve Burgess, Mike and Baloo, Ted Olsen, Holly Gayley, and Tundra.

This trail would not be possible without the efforts of countless Forest Service employees all across the state. I would especially like to thank Loretta McIlhenny and Sandy Thompson for their time and expertise.

Many other people contributed in some way to the production of this book. Thanks to T. Alex Miller, Bill and Mary Kay Stoehr of Trails Illustrated, Jacqueline Leonard, Bruce and Paula Ward, Lou Tyler, Lenore Anderson, and Dennis Haddow.

Thank you to Drs. Janes, Oberheide, and Nieters, who showed sincere concern in getting me ready for the trail.

The following companies generously supplied most of the gear for my hike: Fabiano (Waxed Hide boots); PUR (Hiker water filter); Trails Illustrated (maps); Traveling Light (Outback Oven); Leki (Makalu hiking poles); Sierra Designs (Clip Flashlight tent; Liten Up sleeping bag); Cascade Designs (Therma-Rest mattress; Quantum sleeping bag); and the Magellan Corporation (GPS navigator).

Special thanks to Wilderness Sports in Silverthorne, who supplied everything else, including the author.

About the Author

TOM LORANG JONES

missed being a Colorado native by just a few years, something for which he
will never forgive his parents. Still, he has had ample time since his family
moved here, when he was six years old, to explore the natural backways of
Colorado and to immerse himself in his favorite environment—the hidden
pockets of pure wilderness this state still conceals in abundance.

An avid telemark skier and rock climber, Tom lives in the shadow
of the Eagles Nest Wilderness in Summit County, Colorado. He works in his
family's outdoor store, writes about the natural environment and the things
humans do there, and pursues an eternal quest to improve his chess game.